HANDBOOK OF
Primary
Geography

Safe in Our Houses

HANDBOOK OF
Primary
Geography

Edited by Roger Carter

THE GEOGRAPHICAL ASSOCIATION

Acknowledgements

This book results from a team effort on the part of both members and staff of the Geographical Association.

Much pioneering work on the book was carried out by Margaret Smeaton and Stuart May, and I would like first of all to acknowledge their substantial contribution. Next I should acknowledge the contribution of the many colleagues who offered ideas and material, or made constructive comments and suggestions, in the formative stages. My involvement in the book was at the invitation of the GA's Publications and Merchandise Standing Committee, and the Publications Officer at the time, Professor Bill Marsden; my thanks to them for enabling me to assume the role of Editor and take the book through to publication.

At a time when professionals in education are under increasing pressure at their places of work, I am particularly indebted to all the contributors listed on page 8 who have given freely of their talent, time and effort to the development of the book. To them my gratitude, along with special thanks to Fran Royle, Diane Wright and Anna Gunby at the Geographical Association, who gave their full support to me and the book throughout its development. I would also like to thank Rose Pipes for her meticulous editorial work, which has been of enormous help in seeing the book through to its final stages, and Andrea Hill at Armitage Typo/Graphics, who laid out the pages so attractively.

One of the features of this book is the quantity and quality of the children's work which we have used to illustrate the text. For this, and many of the photographs, we are specially indebted to Colin Bridge (formerly Headteacher, Whitstable Endowed School), Kent Dewer (Headteacher Ainthorpe Primary School, Hull), Chris Garnett (formerly an Advisory teacher for Geography) and Steve Watts (University of Sunderland), who searched out suitable pieces of children's work or photographed particular subjects. A high proportion of the children's work was supplied by the pupils of Whitstable Endowed School, Kent; unless otherwise acknowledged, the illustrations are their work. Some pieces of work were unlabelled, but wherever possible, we have included with each piece of work the name of the child who produced it.

Roger Carter
June 1998

ISBN 1 899085 52 1
First published 1998
Impression number 10 9 8 7 6 5 4 3 2
Year 2001 2000

Published by the Geographical Association, 160 Solly Street, Sheffield S1 4BF.
The Geographical Association is a registered charity: no 313129.

The Publications Officer of the GA would be happy to hear from other potential authors who have ideas for geography books. You may contact the Officer via the GA at the address above. The views expressed in this publication are those of the authors and do not necessarily represent those of the Geographical Association.

Edited by Rose Pipes
Illustrations by Paul Coles and Linzi Henry
Index by Margaret Binns
Design and typesetting by ATG Design, Leeds
Printed and bound in Hong Kong by Colorcraft Limited

Foreword

Geography is a dynamic and exciting subject with great appeal for young children. It takes them out of the classroom into the local and other environments and in imagination into the wider world. It offers stimulating enquiries, provides settings for topical events and makes sense of fleeting media images.

Through geography pupils can begin to understand places from an early age, enhancing their own self-image and sense of belonging. By means of a widening range of case studies they will have opportunities not only to explore their own home and school locality, but also to make meaningful comparisons with other places in this country and overseas. Geography introduces children to natural and human processes, the development of rivers and the structure of towns and villages. It introduces them to the patterns of landforms and settlements and to ways of viewing these, such as aerial photographs, satellite images and maps.

Photo: Chris Garnett.

The subject develops skills in thinking and reasoning and it offers opportunities for discussion and group collaboration. Geographical texts introduce new vocabulary and stimulating reading matter, while the subject gives wide scope for a variety of forms of writing, as well as a valid context for mathematics and Information and Communications Technology. Most importantly, geography makes a vital contribution to the development of environmental awareness and understanding; it prepares children for their role as world citizens at the start of a new millennium.

In recent years geography has become an established feature of the primary curriculum. Through fieldwork, pupils have experienced their own neighbourhood in new ways, seeing familiar sights with heightened awareness. It has also taken them to contrasting localities, on day visits or residential courses, sometimes including localities overseas. By means of stimulating resources they have been carried to faraway places – a village in rural India, a South American rainforest or to meet a family on a Caribbean island.

Geography is rich in subject matter and varied in approaches: such abundance can be daunting. This book has been designed to enthuse and guide primary teachers so they can approach the subject with confidence, explore its potential with their pupils and celebrate the diversity of people and places they meet along the way. Good luck on your journey!

Wendy Morgan
April 1998

Contents

The contributors

The *Handbook of Primary Geography* could not have come into existence without the generosity of the following people, who freely gave their time, talent and experience to their contributions and to this book:

Rachel Bowles is Lecturer in Education and Environmental Studies at the University of Greenwich, Avery Hill Campus

Steve Brace is Head of Development Education, ActionAid, London

Roger Carter is Adviser for Geography, Jersey Education

Simon Catling is Deputy Director of the School of Education, Oxford Brookes University, and a past President of the Geographical Association

Geoff Dinkele is a Consultant for Geography in Education

Liz Essex-Cater is Senior Lecturer in Geography and Environmental Education at the University of Northumbria at Newcastle

Marcia Foley is Advisor for Geography, Kent LEA

Wendy Garner is Lecturer in Primary Geography at Liverpool Hope University College

Taahra Ghazi is Development Education Manager, ActionAid, London

John Halocha is Lecturer in Humanities Education in the School of Education, University of Durham

David Hicks is Professor in the Faculty of Education and Human Sciences at Bath Spa University College

Mike Hillary is Senior Adviser for Geography, Dorset LEA, and OFSTED Inspector

Jo Hughes is Associate Director of the Geography Inset Primary Project and tutor for geography and history on the Primary PGCE course in the Department of Education at the University of Liverpool

Jeremy Krause is Senior Advisor in Geography at Cheshire County Council, and Honorary Secretary of the Geographical Association

Liz Lewis was formerly Senior Lecturer in Primary Geography Education at the University of Sunderland and is now course leader in Primary PGCE at the University College of St Martin, Carlisle Campus

Margaret Mackintosh is Senior Lecturer at the Rolle School of Education, University of Plymouth, and Honorary Editor of *Primary Geographer*

Karen Mansfield is Deputy Head of Howden Junior School, East Yorkshire

Bill Marsden is Director of the Geography Inset Primary Project and Emeritus Professor of Education and Honorary Research Fellow in the Department of Education at the University of Liverpool

Angela Milner is Head of Primary Education, Edge Hill University College, Ormskirk

Wendy Morgan is Consultant in Primary Geography and President of the Geographical Association 1997-98

Steve Rawlinson is Senior Lecturer in Geography and Environmental Education at the University of Northumbria at Newcastle

Paula Richardson is Advisor for Geography

Alison Rudd is Education Officer for ActionAid, London

Kate Russell is Teacher Adviser for Geography with Staffordshire LEA and a member of the Geographical Association IT Working Group

Stephen Scoffham is Senior Lecturer in Primary Geography at Canterbury Christ Church College

Margaret Smeaton was Head of the Geography Department and co-ordinator of Professional Studies at Herfordshire College of Higher Education/Hatfield Polytechnic and for some years was Chair of Professional Studies.

Greg Walker is Senior Lecturer in Primary Geography Education, Roehampton Institute, London.

Alan Waters is Inspector for Geography, Cumbria LEA

Maureen Weldon is Deputy Head at Longthorpe CP School in Peterborough and a former Advisory Teacher for Geography in Lincolnshire

Introduction

Children in schools today will have an adult life which may stretch well beyond the middle of the next century. What kind of education will prepare them for this future world? The past decade has seen heightened interest in this question on the part of parents, politicians, teachers and the media – coupled with a growing urgency to define and raise standards.

The outcome has been a marked quickening of pace in curriculum development and change, reflected in Geographical Association publications. Geographical Work in Primary and Middle Schools (GA, 1981) needed thorough revision for its second edition only seven years later (GA, 1988). Since then and throughout the 1990s teachers have grappled with a new language of programmes of study, key stages, level descriptions and OFSTED. The new Handbook needed to respond to these developments.

The contributors to this Handbook were writing against this background of change and anticipation. They have sought through their contributions to identify the best possible provision for geography, and then encourage individual teachers and schools to assess the extent to which this might be mediated in local circumstances. Consequently the book is concerned not simply to address current requirements, be they statutory or discretionary, but to look beyond them to what might be worthwhile experiences for today's children – tomorrow's adults. Curriculum 2000 provides an opportunity to reflect on the future needs of children who are now in school, and how geography may make a distinctive contribution to these needs. We need to identify worthwhile geography and celebrate it; specifically the aim is that geography should contribute to an educational vision for the future.

Learning about the local area: a worthwhile geographical experience. Photo: Chris Garnett.

The Primary and Middle Schools Section Committee of the Geographical Association has set out an agenda for geography in the twenty first century (see below), and much of this Handbook develops these themes. Curriculum 2000, whilst reducing some statutory content at key stage 1 and key stage 2, gives greater prominence to four elements in the revised Order for geography: sustainable development, global citizenship, values and attitudes and locational knowledge. Each of these elements is identified in the table, and developed in the chapters which follow.

The aim of the Handbook is therefore twofold: to help teachers respond effectively to current legislation and requirements for teaching geography, and to encourage forward thinking about the needs of children beyond the current National Curriculum, into the millennium, and how these needs may be addressed through good geographical experiences.

The book is organised into two parts. The focus for Part 1 is the nature of geography, the capacity of children to engage with it, and the many and varied contributions the subject can make to the wider curriculum within and beyond what is prescribed. Guidance is offered on planning and assessing a differentiated geography programme which connects with the whole primary curriculum. Co-ordinators are offered advice on how to lead the subject in school, how to resource it, and how to present geography for external inspection.

The emphasis of Part 2 is on teaching and learning geography. In turn attention shifts from developing geographical skills (Section 4), to teaching and learning about places (Section 5), and studying geographical themes (Section 6). There is widespread consensus that these elements of the subject are best taught together rather than in isolation. Thematic

Primary geography into the twenty-first century

- **Using mapwork – wayfinding** Children should be able to locate themselves in their surroundings and find their way with increasing confidence from one place to another

- **Graphicacy – the fourth ace in the pack** The ability to interpret and represent spatial relationships is a key skill in the modern world

- **Travel and communication** Personal mobility and confidence with information and communications technology are new life skills

- **Knowing your locality** Children need to develop attachments to their surroundings to promote their educational and psychological development

- **Global understanding** As well as learning about their local area, children need to be introduced to a global perspective and put the interests of the UK and Europe into a world context

- **Citizenship in an interconnected world** Children need to be introduced to appropriate knowledge and experience at school if they are to participate in the democratic process as adults

- **Respecting the diversity of cultures** Unless schools challenge biased images and negative stereotypes, children may develop unbalanced perceptions of different peoples and places

- **A sustainable world – caring for the environment** There is an urgent need to adopt policies which will genuinely serve to protect environments

- **Participation and responsibility – taking an active role in society** The human community faces an unprecedented range of problems; everybody needs to be involved in helping to find solutions

- **Future vision – living with change** Far too much time is spent educating young people for yesterday and today, and far too little on educating them for tomorrow. Geography concerns itself with the processes that produce the context of tomorrow's world

- **Fieldwork and enquiry** Fieldwork is geographical enquiry. Geographical enquiry reveals the nature of the world in which we live

- **Imagery and curiosity** Our attitudes to places are based on the depth of our feelings and the quality of our personal interpretation

- **Patterns and processes – learning to learn** The distinctive nature of geographical concepts and the interpretations they inspire provide the language for explanation and prediction about the world and its future

- **Forming attitudes and opinions** Through exploring issues, geography is ideally placed to develop children's attitudes and opinions

- **Sharpening language and thinking skills – raising attainment** Geography is about the world in which our children live and grow. It provides a distinctive mode of language and analysis which is vital to coherent, independent thinking

work is best investigated in the context of real places and at various scales; places used to draw out patterns and processes of physical, human or environmental importance. Skills in geography should be learned and applied to actual places or themes investigated. These relationships have been summarised in the form of a cube. Figure 1, which is repeated at the start of Part 2, suggests through an example how such a cube may be used as a planning device to ensure the integration of skills during work on places and themes.

Separation of places, themes and skills in Part 2 is therefore for clarity; inevitably, it gives rise to some overlap and repetition. For example, Geoff Dinkele's chapter on geographical questions and enquiry finds echoes in many other contributions. This is understandable, since enquiry routes of sequenced questions permeate much good work in geography, whatever the focus.

The book is for teachers who have not specialised in the subject, as well as those who have. It is also for Headteachers with an overarching responsibility for the curriculum, for geography co-ordinators and for teachers in training. Readers will find their own best route

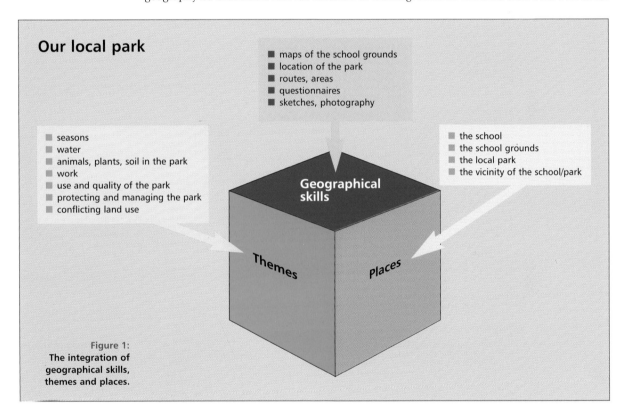

Our local park

- maps of the school grounds
- location of the park
- routes, areas
- questionnaires
- sketches, photography

- seasons
- water
- animals, plants, soil in the park
- work
- use and quality of the park
- protecting and managing the park
- conflicting land use

- the school
- the school grounds
- the local park
- the vicinity of the school/park

Geographical skills

Themes

Places

Figure 1:
The integration of geographical skills, themes and places.

through the various sections in ways which most closely reflect their particular needs. Boxes at the end of each chapter give cross references to related content elsewhere in the book. In this way it is hoped that the book will provide valuable support and guidance for the wide and varied readership for whom it is intended.

Roger Carter

Photo: Chris Garnett.

Children, geography and the National Curriculum

1

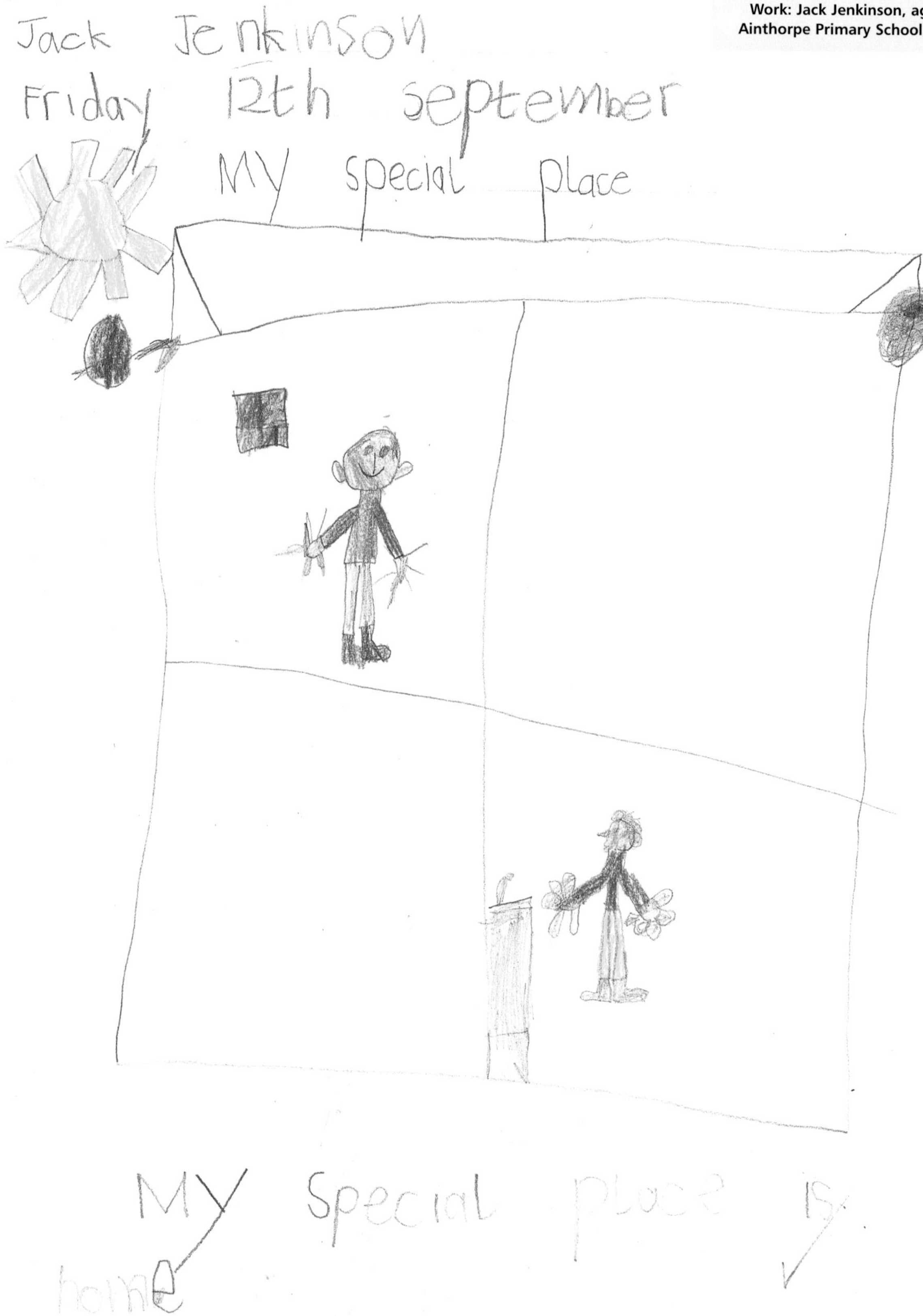
Jack Jenkinson
Friday 12th september
MY special place
MY Special place is
home

Work: Jack Jenkinson, aged 6, Ainthorpe Primary School, Hull.

Questioning geography

Children are natural geographers. From the moment of birth they start to learn about their surroundings. First they become familiar with their own environment, then, through a variety of stimuli, they begin to form perceptions of other places beyond their direct experience. These perceptions may be fragmentary or distorted, but they will be taking shape before any formal education. They are part of the process whereby children begin to place themselves in the world.

> *'A sense of place describes a particular kind of relationship between individuals and localities. For individuals different places are imbued with different meanings'* (Matthews, 1992).

So it is that by the time they go to school most children have acquired some awareness of the world around them and have begun to form a notion of their own identity within it. In short they are young geographers with a world inside their heads.

What is the geography that they will come to meet in a more formal sense in school? The central purpose of geographical education is to give children a fuller, more rounded, structured opportunity to view, perceive, understand and respond to the world in which they live. Geography describes our world and geographers seek to understand and explain the interaction of human beings with their environment. In order to describe, understand and explain geographers ask questions about places – where are they, what are they like, what life is like in them, how and why they are changing, and ways in which they are linked. With the ability to read, write and calculate, children can develop the capacity to examine and interpret not only environments they can study at first hand, but also those which are described through the written and spoken word, illustrated in pictures or represented on maps. They can do this over the range of scales from local to global.

Photo: Jacky Chapman/ Format Photography.

Questions such as those set out in Figure 1 are important to geography since they indicate the aspects of places with which the subject is concerned. The importance of such questions in developing geographical enquiries is explored in different ways throughout this book. They form an enquiry route through which to study geography, and an organisational framework through which teachers may teach and pupils may learn about places near and far.

Questions to ask in geography	Examples of consequent activities
What do I already know about this place?	**Speculating**
What will I expect to find?	Drawing upon the child's previous experience
What will it be like?	Perceptions culled from direct and indirect experiences
What do I think about it?	Imaginative work
Where is it?	**Describing**
Are there many or few people?	Locating, describing, collecting and sorting information
What is it like to live there?	Classifying, using books, maps, atlases, globes, artefacts, people
What is the weather like?	Fieldwork
Are there many visitors?	
What is distinctive about it?	
Why is it like this?	**Explaining**
Why is it where it is?	Connections between factors (e.g. climate and farming)
How did it get like this?	Relationship between people and environments
Why did it happen?	Connections between places
How can we explain it?	Factors which explain
How is life affected by the place – or its location?	Bringing together evidence from a variety of sources to seek explanations
How have people used or modified the place?	Making comparisons
How does it link with other places?	Reasoning
Why is it similar to/different from where we live?	
How is it changing?	**Predicting**
How might things change?	Using newspapers, magazines, television programmes and videos to identify change or possible change
With what impact?	Looking at current issues, questions or conflicts
What decisions will be made?	Simulation games
Who will decide?	Computer prediction models
Who will gain or lose?	
Will the changes bring improvement? For whom?	
What would it feel like to be here?	**Responding**
What are the views of the people who live here?	Imaginative work
What do others think and feel about it?	Curiosity – empathy
What do I think and feel about it?	Use of literature and television
What can I do?	Account of journeys
	Diaries
	Photographs
	Letters from distant places
	Making pictures
	Role play

Figure 1:
Enquiry: Questions to ask about places.
Source: Channel 4, 1995.

What do I already know about the place?

Since children will bring their own private geographies to the classroom, it is worth drawing on their previous experiences and existing perceptions as a starting point to build upon. It is likely that what they bring to the investigation will be partial and distorted, as is the case with all of us, but children's initial perceptions of a place will give a teacher something to work on. Anticipating what a place will be like also adds to the excitement at the start of an investigation.

Where is it?

There is a public perception that geography is about locating places and that geographical education should teach children where places are. Certainly knowledge of places is a very important aspect of the subject. It calls upon the skills to use maps, atlases and globes not only to locate places in absolute terms, but also to understand their relative location over space and time given the rapid changes and reductions in space through technology. Further questions relate to describing, classifying and sorting information. These take the study beyond locating a place to identifying the physical and human characteristics which give it its character. Such activity inevitably generates further questions about the place.

Constructing a place can start in the sandpit!.
Photo: Steve Watts.

Why is it like this?

If geography is about the interaction of people with their environment, the subject must go beyond identifying and describing the location and components of a place to seeking explanations for what is observed. This moves us into the pursuit of connections, relationships and inter-actions between the features we describe. Generally this calls upon higher level thinking skills, but even the youngest pupils are capable of seeing more straightforward relationships.

How is it changing?

An essential characteristic of any place is change. Human beings' interaction with their environment has always changed. Change is taking place around us all the time, and we can anticipate future change to places we study. Yet we can also recognise the extent to which places show continuity over time. These two ideas of continuity and change help us to understand the dynamism of place and the relevance of geography to the present and future. Pupils need to understand that people, including themselves, can make a difference in and to places for good or ill.

What would it feel like to be here?

Geographers do not study places simply as neutral observers. Implicit in our study of the world is our commitment to it, along with what is often a very personal response to the places we live in or experience vicariously. We should acknowledge this when working with children, by providing space for them to explore and articulate their feelings about the places they study.

These are among the questions geography asks. In combination they can bring us nearer to understanding the complex relationship of people and places at a variety of scales from local to global. They can lead children into a wide range of learning activities, and provide structure to what might otherwise be a random process of finding out. You should not feel bound by them, systematically working through each one in turn: that could lead to formulaic teaching. Any investigation is likely to generate its own questions, and the pupils are sure to come up with more. We need to develop curiosity, encouraging children to raise whatever questions occur to them. In time they will come to recognise the questions geographers ask, and begin to frame geographical questions themselves. These ideas will be explored further throughout the book.

References

Channel 4 (1995) *Geography: Whose Place Teachers' Guide.* London: Channel 4 Learning Ltd.
Matthews, M. H. (1992) *Making Sense of Place.* Hemel Hempstead: Harvester Wheatsheaf.

Chapter 1: What is geography?

Ideas introduced in this chapter are developed elsewhere in the book. Themes and places identified in Figure 1 form much of the focus of Part 2. The key questions discussed here are applied to a case study by Geoff Dinkele in Chapter 12. Stephen Scoffham explores further the idea of 'children as geographers' in Chapter 2.

Young geographers

Chapter 2

Stephen Scoffham

> *'Radiating from that house, with its crumbling walls, its thumps and shadows, its fancied foxes under the floor, I moved along paths that lengthened inch by inch with my mounting strength of days'* (Lee, 1959, p. 14).

The way in which children learn about places is complex and researchers are only slowly piecing together the story. Part of the problem is that there is no entirely logical or inevitable sequence of events. Learning is for many people a surprisingly idiosyncratic process in which ideas are acquired in an apparently random manner. Most people do not become systematic thinkers until they reach adolescence or even later.

It is also remarkably difficult to discover what is actually going on inside a child's head. We were all young once but it is impossible to recapture the sense of awe and wonder which children experience on doing something for the first time. Adults can often only observe and deduce what seems to be happening from the outside.

Despite these complexities there is, however, one clear message. The skills and competencies of young children appear to have been consistently under-estimated. In part this is due to an uncritical acceptance of Piaget's theories. Few people nowadays would contest Piaget's central thesis that children pass through developmental stages as they grow older. However, the age at which this happens and children's ability to operate at different levels of understanding is much more variable than first thought. The more we find out about different aspects of geographical learning the further the roots go back into childhood.

Photo: Joan Crookes.

Spatial awareness

Children first begin to discover the location of objects as they play with toys in their cots. Initially taste and touch provide the main clues, but after about three months their vision improves and they become capable of focusing more sharply on objects. From about ten months onwards children begin actively to explore their environment. As they develop the ability to crawl, and then walk, the scope and range of the places they can visit expands enormously, though parents usually restrict these early forays for fear of dangers. However, as youngsters grow in ability and

Photo: Chris Garnett.

confidence, so they are allowed to go further afield. This introduces them to the environment beyond the front door and the wider world.

Maps are essential tools in the discovery process, but how do young children learn to use maps and find their way from place to place? Wiegand (1992) describes an investigation by Bluestein and Acredolo which provides some interesting insights. Sixty 3-5 year-olds were asked to find a toy elephant hidden in a room. They were given a map that showed the layout of the furniture with the position of the toy marked with a cross. The results were impressive. Half the three-year-olds, three-quarters of the four-year-olds and all the five-year-olds were able to find the toy. Generally the children had little difficulty interpreting the map and appeared to understand that the room, furniture and toy were shown symbolically. Subsequent investigations showed the importance of aligning the map. When the map was rotated by 180 degrees only the oldest children were able to use it correctly and even they had difficulty.

Blades and Spencer (1986) went a stage further and studied children's ability to follow a route. In one experiment they positioned a number of coloured buckets in a nursery playground and asked the children to follow the route shown on a map. The youngest children (four-year-olds) seemed unable to understand the task, but the older ones (five-year-olds) generally completed it with few mistakes. A further test involved using a map to find the way through a maze in the playground. Again, the results were similar with the children aged over about four-and-a-half achieving considerable success.

One issue which has occupied many researchers is whether there is a difference in spatial ability between boys and girls. Simple experiments in which children draw free-hand maps of a familiar journey, such as the route from home to school, have tended to show a clear distinction. Boys are more likely to use plan views and show a larger area than girls who prefer to be precise and include small details. Generally, too, boys appear better at arranging the different elements of a map in their correct relationship and mastering abstract conventions.

These results are interesting because they reveal something about the way children perceive the spaces around them. How the differences arise is a matter for debate but Matthews (1992) argues that parents allow boys considerable freedom to explore the local

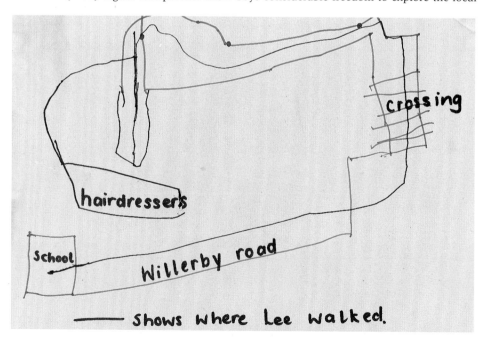

A walk to the shops.
Work: Lee Jagger, age 4,
Ainthorpe Primary
School, Hull.

surroundings. Girls, by contrast, are expected to help around the house, are allowed out less often and not permitted to go so far. These restrictions seem likely to impair their spatial development.

Whether or not this is still true nowadays, schools can certainly help to rectify any imbalance in environmental experience. This was acknowledged by the working party which wrote the first version of the Geography National Curriculum when it declared:

> *'It will be important for teachers to select methodologies and topics which are "girl-friendly" in the sense that they will compensate for any difference in experience – for instance, by encouraging both sexes to explore a range of environments under supervision'* (DES, 1990, p. 79).

In addition the research provides compelling reasons for introducing children to mapwork from an early age. Many infant school teachers already take this opportunity and create 'pictures' to show journeys associated with stories and fairy tales. The route taken by the wolf in 'The Three Little Pigs' is a typical example. However, the fact that many children seem to draw maps spontaneously long before they learn to read or write suggests that spatial awareness is a fundamental skill which should be developed in nurseries and other pre-school groups as a basic educational entitlement.

Exploring the local environment

Most of us remember the place where we were brought up in some considerable detail and often recall it with fondness. These first impressions of the outside world stay with us throughout our lives and provide a rich source of experience. Authors such as Laurie Lee, Virginia Woolf, George Orwell and Marcell Proust recall their early memories with great sensitivity in their novels. Our sense of identity, it seems, derives in some part from the social and physical environment in which we spend our childhood.

The way children interact with their immediate surroundings is important not only for their psychological well-being, it also promotes their educational development. Many play activities involve rehearsing or re-enacting previous events and situations. Through imitation children are able to give full reign to invention and fantasy. Piaget argues that make-believe play allows children to assimilate knowledge and forms the basis of a child's thought even before it can speak. Certainly the opportunity to model and manipulate experiences seems to be an essential part of the learning process.

Several researchers have attempted to find out more about children's private geographies. One of the key studies was undertaken by Hart (1979) (Figure 1) who made a detailed investigation of a New England township over a two-year period. Hart discovered that the children put a particularly high value on water features such as rivers, lakes and ponds. They also favoured woods and trees for climbing and hiding games. The places they feared matched the archetypal scary places of children's literature – attics, cellars and abandoned buildings and bedrooms and garages at night. Very few of the children selected places for their aesthetic qualities alone.

Hart comments on the way children treasure informal routes and pathways which they often use as 'short-cuts' even when they are actually longer. Other researchers, too, remark on children's affinity for secret routes and alleyways. As they explore their surroundings children construct private geographies which meet their physical and emotional needs (see Figure 2).

Further insight into children's thinking is provided by the names they invent for their favourite places. Matthews (1992) reports how, when drawing maps of suburban Coventry, children labelled a variety of local features. Examples included the 'Moth-hawk tree', the 'dump', 'Charlie's field' and the 'back alley'. Sometimes these personal names denote the activities that can be done in a place rather than its appearance, e.g. 'Roller-coaster place'.

It is worth remembering in this context that the most intensively used play areas are often small patches of dirt. Children need places where they simply loiter or day-dream. Edmund Gosse, the Victorian naturalist, is one of many authors who have left us with a description of his childhood pleasures:

Photo: Steve Watts.

Age	Physical growth and play activities	Place knowledge and perception	Social and emotional development
First twelve months	Able to sit (7 months) Moves on hands and knees (10 months)	Can visually follow an object (4 months) Distinguishes mother's face from others (8 months)	Attachment to adults at first unselective Special attachment to parents (7 months)
One year old	Stands momentarily alone (12 months) Walks and seldom falls (18 months) Runs without falling (2 years)	Can differentiate and identify a wide range of sounds Displays perceptual preferences – tastes, sounds, colours	Still largely pre-social Play is solitary or parallel to the play of others
Two years old	Throws ball without losing balance Area of free movement increases gradually By 3 years can ride a tricycle	Begins to form mental representations of the environment, e.g. can recall familiar routes Knows the geography of household furniture in minute detail Develops spatial knowledge only of those areas experienced through locomotion	May be frightened by almost any new situation Tends to play in 'parallel' Truly co-operative play is rare
Three years old	Spends much time 'going places' with tricycle Makes roads, bridges and tunnels in sand tray Sedentary play for longer periods	More aware of spatial relations such as inside-outside, top-bottom, front-back	Much better able to accept parent's temporary absence Able to fit words to actions Increasingly able to handle co-operative play
Four years old	Very active and expansive Enjoys balancing activities Makes more complicated structures	Perception much more rapid than in pre-school years Only half children able to master concepts of left and right	Preference for play in small groups but not yet well-adapted socially
Five years old	Climbs with sureness Likes to help around the house Active, vigorous games preferred more by boys than girls		More socially adaptive Enjoys group projects, e.g. constructing houses, garages, city planning
Six years old	Almost constantly active Returns to earlier interest in earth and water Ball games and pretend play popular with both sexes Demands common rules in play	Recognises that the same landscape may appear different to people in different positions	Surrenders much of previous dependence on parents and home Peer group develops May fear high places and unfamiliar impressions – cellars and attics, ghosts and creatures
Seven years old	Repeats performance to master skills More capacity for play alone	Onset of period of 'concrete operations' Develops ability to orientate using co-ordinated system of reference	Calm periods and longer periods of self absorption Developing sense of ethical conduct
Eight years old	More graceful with fluid body movements Capable of organising simple games such as hide and seek	Increasing maturity in judging road traffic	'Gang age' Boys and girls segregate Fears of frightening places reduce
Nine years old	Works and plays hard Tries to improve skills purposefully Interested in competitive sports		More integrated social behaviour Demands independence in the home

Figure 1:
Children's experience of place – the first ten years. After: Hart, 1979.

'By the side of the road, between the school and my home, there was a large horse pond. Here I created a maritime empire – islands, a seaboard with harbours, lighthouses, fortifications. My geographical inventiveness had its full swing. Sometimes, while I was creating, a cart would be driven roughly into the pond, shattering my ports with what was worse than a typhoon. But I immediately set to work, as soon as the cart was gone and the mud had settled, to tidy up my coastline again and scoop out anew my harbours' (Gosse, 1965, p. 136).

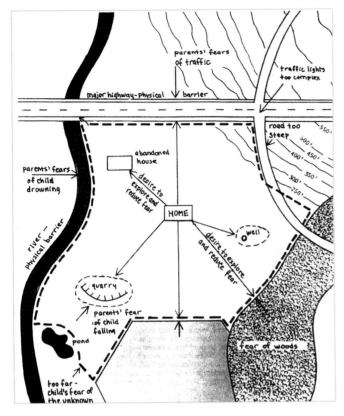

It is through transactions of this kind that children come to invest their environment with meaning. The attachment to places which we develop as adults is derived from these childhood interactions. We identify with our home area in lots of different ways. Some people support their local football team, others become involved with local history or trace their family tree. Historically people used to believe they belonged to the soil of a particular place in an organic and religious relationship. The Romans recognised the spirit or essence of a locality (its *genius loci*) by setting up shrines to local deities. Anthropologists have recorded similar beliefs among the original inhabitants of Australia and North and South America.

These studies remind us that the quality of an environment is a very complex issue. As well as quantifying physical and human processes, geographers seek to take account of subjective and personal responses. What a place is like is not simply a matter of fact. It depends equally on how we perceive it and what we feel about it.

Today, concerns over personal security and the relentless growth of road traffic are serving to erode children's personal freedom and their links with the environment. In an authoritative and far-reaching study Hillman (1993) found that the number of unaccompanied activities undertaken by junior school children at weekends had halved between 1971 and 1990. He comments on how this may affect their emotional and social development. When children explore the environment they have opportunities to take initiatives, learn survival skills, develop a sense of adventure, gain self-esteem and accept responsibility for their actions. The physical activity also helps to keep them fit and healthy.

Figure 2:
Forces influencing eight year olds as they explore their environment.
After: Hart, 1979.

Exploring the environment helps children to develop a sense of adventure.
Photo: Chris Garnett.

Restoring this richness to children's lives is a challenge which schools cannot expect to meet on their own. However, they can at least promote children's awareness and provide some form of environmental experience. Geography fieldwork has a unique contribution to make to this process. On one level fieldwork can consist of environmental walks and simple data collection activities in and around the school buildings. It can also involve work in local streets and journeys to nearby places. In addition many schools organise some form of residential experience or school journeys.

Investigating the quality and character of different places is an essential component of any worthwhile geography curriculum. Children are uniquely equipped to undertake these studies as they have a freshness of vision and a strong natural desire to explore their surroundings. We need to encourage them in this endeavour from the earliest age.

Distant places

Children's ideas about distant places develop alongside their knowledge of the local area. Fairytales and picture books often provide settings which are way beyond a child's immediate experience. Some stories involve journeys to the other side of the world. Others describe adventures in mountains, forests or deserts. Birds and animals provide much of the interest in young children's literature. Pictures of lions, tigers and other creatures frequently decorate the walls of toddlers' bedrooms and many children first learn about Africa and Australia through their wildlife.

At the same time images of the wider world filter into our homes through the media. Satellite images and scenes from foreign lands are beamed to us by television. Soap operas, with their focus on people and strong storylines, are a particularly powerful influence. Advertisements and magazines are another source of information which amplifies the message. Children's natural curiosity about distant places feeds off these stimuli. At first they may not be too sure about the difference between real and fictitious places. They will probably also be very confused about distances. However, as they grow older they gradually begin to sort out their ideas more logically.

As well as being exotic and exciting, some psychologists have postulated a deeper reason for children's interest in faraway lands. Egan (1990) suggests infants try to cut loose

Young children in
Mochudi, Botswana,
use bricks and stones
to create a plan of
their school.
Photo:
Margaret Mackintosh.

from the restrictions of family and neighbourhoods by thinking about imaginary or distant locations. In this way they begin to acquire detailed information about specific places such as villages, harbours and small islands. As well as being reassuring, a knowledge of the boundaries of the world builds up children's self confidence and helps to develop their sense of individuality.

What then are the images of the Earth which young children carry around in their heads? Wiegand (1992) began at a fundamental level by asking 222 children from different Yorkshire primary schools to write down the names of all the countries that they knew. The seven-year-olds typically named about five countries focusing especially on the larger land masses such as America, Africa, India and Australia. By age eleven the children's knowledge had expanded and they were on average able to name 15 countries. Generally they appeared to have a good knowledge of Western Europe but the countries of Africa and many other parts of the developing world still did not feature significantly on their mental maps.

What children think about a country is of course more important than the ability to name it. In recent years numerous activities have sought to reveal their images and ideas. Generally it appears that infants and lower juniors tend to associate countries with food and animals but are likely to be confused. Older children exhibit a wider range of responses but also include an increasing number of negative images such as war, famine and poverty.

A detailed study of children's perceptions undertaken by Graham and Lynn (1989) carried these investigations further. Working with top infant and top junior classes they interviewed children in groups of six to eight. Each group was shown photographs portraying scenes in the developing world and invited to discuss them using an open-ended schedule of questions. They reported that:

> '... a large proportion of infants and many less mature upper juniors associated the scenes in Bengal and Bangladesh with a hunter-gatherer lifestyle. One infant group, in no way an exception, thought there would be no roads and people would rub sticks to make fire, "cos there's no matches"' (Graham and Lynn, 1989, pp. 29-30).

Another junior group discussing daily life in Bangladesh declared, 'They sleep on skins from the bears they've killed with spears'.

Speculating on their findings Graham and Lynn suggest that a child's development stage affects their ideas. Young children appear to relish stories about prehistoric life and the simple hunting life which pictures of the developing world can easily reinforce.

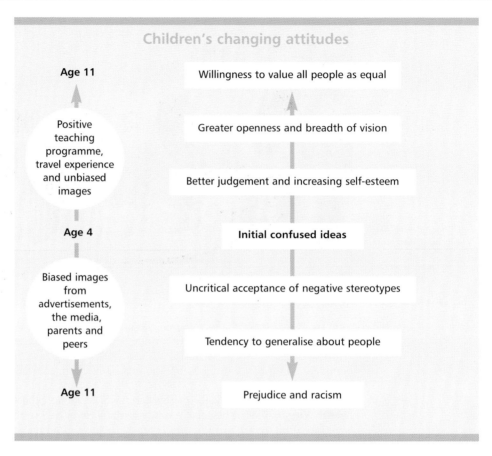

Figure 3:
How schools can promote global citizenship and international understanding. Source: after Scoffham, 1989.

Teachers need to be aware of these predispositions so that they can provide classroom activities which will broaden children's thinking. If left unchallenged, crude stereotypes can easily harden into prejudices, especially when reinforced by peer or group pressure. Infants, it appears, learn attitudes in the same way that they learn facts. Stereotypes are thus fairly easy to dislodge at this age. By the time children reach secondary school their attitudes are much more entrenched and difficult to modify (see Figure 3).

Implications for teachers

The fact that children develop their geographical understanding from the earliest age has significant implications for teachers. To begin with it is important to discover what children already know before teaching them something new. Not only does this serve to eliminate repetition, it also helps with lesson planning. New knowledge, as Bruner has pointed out, is much more secure if it is keyed into existing patterns of understanding. Conversely, misconceptions can obstruct even the best planned lesson, confusing children as they seek to grasp new ideas.

Regarding curriculum content, there are strong reasons for introducing children to geography from the earliest ages upwards (see Figure 3). Children have within them a powerful desire to explore the world, to model it and recreate it in their minds. Teachers are uniquely placed to harness this energy. We need to be careful not to underestimate young children, many of whom (if given the opportunity) can make sense of abstract ideas, whilst contributing to children's personal, social, intellectual and emotional development (Figure 4).

Personal Development
Lifeskills
Practical skills (including ICT)
Locational knowledge
Mapwork and wayfinding
Graphicacy
Environmental literacy

Emotional development
Attachment and belonging
Sense of identity
Sense of place
Caring for the environment
Valuing other people
and cultures

Intellectual development
Learning skills, e.g. describing,
explaining and predicting
Key concepts, e.g. change,
pattern and process
Metacognition: transferring
concepts from one context to
another

Social Development
Using the resources of places and communities
Responding to current issues
Development education
Trends and lifestyles
Citizenship

Figure 4:
What geography can contribute to children's learning.
Source: Bridge, 1998.

References and further reading

Blades, M. and Spencer, C. (1986) 'Map use by young children', *Geography*, 71, 1, pp. 47-52.

Blyth, A. and Krause, J. (1995) *Primary Geography*. London: Hodder & Stoughton.

Bridge, C. (1998) 'The way ahead' in Scoffham, S. (ed) *Primary Sources*. Sheffield: Geographical Association, pp. 52-53.

Bruner, J. (1969) *The Process of Education*. London: Harvard.

DES (1990) *Geography for Ages 5-16*. London, Cardiff: DES/WO.

Egan, K. (1990) *Romantic Understanding: The Development of Rationality and Imagination, Ages 8-15*. London: Routledge.

Gosse, E. (1965) *Father and Son*. London: Heinemann.

Graham, L. and Lynn, S. (1989) 'Mud huts and flints: children's images of the Third World', *Education 3-13*, 17, 2, pp. 29-32.

Hart, R. (1979) *Children's Experience of Place*. New York: Irvington Press.

Hillman, M. (1993) *Children, Transport and the Quality of Life*. London: Policy Studies Institute.

Lee, L. (1959) *Cider With Rosie*. Harmondsworth: Penguin.

Scoffham, S. (1998) 'Young children's perceptions of the world' in David, T. (ed) *Changing Minds 1*. London: Paul Chapman.

Matthews, M. H. (1992) *Making Sense of Place*. Hemel Hempstead: Harvester Wheatsheaf.

Wiegand, P. (1992) *Places in the Primary School*. London: Falmer.

Chapter 2: Children as geographers

The way children interact with their immediate surroundings should inform plans for local area work (Chapter 16). Children's ideas about distant places near and far also have implications for the teacher (see Chapters 17 and 18). The relationship between developmental stages and syllabus design are explored by Alan Waters in Chapter 5 on progression and differentiation.

Introduction

Habitats And life cycles - Animals in Danger

A sense of environmental stewardship can start from work on habitats and the lifecycles of animals. Work: Chloe Guariglia.

This term we are going to lean about habitats and how animales lean to survie in thier different habitats. We will find out about how plants and animales grow and how the young are protected from danger. we will observe the school pond and grow a plant.

We Will also discover about Why some animals are in danger of becoming estinct and Why some are already are.

Geography in the National Curriculum and beyond

Chapter 3

Simon Catling

Background

Geography is a key part of the school curriculum because caring about the environment is essential to our survival. We must know how to make best use, responsibly, of our resources and opportunities. Additionally, geography channels the natural human desire to understand how the world works – the processes and patterns that shape our lives, actions, places and environment.

Geography has been a required subject in primary schools since the establishment of the 1902 Education Act, but it was already established in the elementary curriculum, supported by several series of 'Geography Readers' dating back to the mid-1800s. The 1932 Hadow Report, as also the Plowden Report in 1967, identified the role, value and content of geography in the education of primary children. The 1988 Education Reform Act, which introduced the National Curriculum, confirmed geography's vital role as a contributor to young children's knowledge, understanding, skills and values.

KEY ISSUES FACING PRIMARY GEOGRAPHY

At the start of the 1970s, evidence suggested that geography was generally soundly taught in primary schools. However, by the end of the 1970s, and increasingly during the 1980s, considerable concern had developed about the quality of geography teaching and geography's continued existence in the curriculum (DES, 1989). Five major concerns stood out.

The need to:

- clarify the key ideas, content and skills of geography;
- teach geography-focused topics and to make teaching and learning geography explicit in topics that covered more than one curriculum subject;
- develop coherent geography policies and curriculum plans which support progression in children's learning and which enables teachers to plan, teach and assess children's learning effectively;
- improve the quality of geographical activities and tasks for children and use a wider variety of resources and teaching techniques;
- ensure explicit and effective curriculum leadership in geography in the school.

Where good practice did exist in primary geography, it was generally based around well-planned investigation of the local area of a school, building on children's own knowledge and experience to develop their understanding and skills and using a variety of resources including large-scale maps.

TOWARDS THE GEOGRAPHY NATIONAL CURRICULUM

Recognising this situation, in the mid-1980s HMI identified explicit objectives for primary

Photo: Chris Garnett.

geography within the context of overall aims for geographical education (DES, 1986). These became the basis for the aims and objectives of the Geography National Curriculum (DES/WO, 1990). HMI also argued for the need to plan the geography curriculum throughout the primary school. This gave rise to a number of publications on the subject (e.g. Palmer, 1994; Blyth and Krause, 1995; Martin, 1995; Chambers and Donert, 1996; Foley and Janikoun, 1996; Milner, 1996).

The introduction of National Curriculum geography for key stages 1 and 2, followed by a strong push to initiate geographical understanding through the nursery curriculum (SCAA, 1996), aimed to tackle the issues identified by HMI and to support the development of teacher's geographical knowledge and teaching skills.

In 2000, the content of the National Curriculum may change, following a period of review of current provisions. Already, following the Secretary of State's proposals which took effect in September 1998, the requirement to follow the programmes of study for geography and other foundation subjects has been lifted. However, schools are still under statutory obligation to teach a broad and balanced curriculum and so must continue to have regard for the programmes of study in all foundation subjects.

The role of primary geography

In many cultures around the world it is a key social principle that 'the Earth is loaned by children to their parents for safe keeping'. This sense of **environmental stewardship** lies at the heart of geographical education. Equally, there is widespread recognition that **a sense of place** is important both to personal wellbeing and to environmental stewardship. To understand, sustain and improve the quality of the world in which we live, we need to know **where** features, environments and places are, the **processes** that create and change them and the **patterns** that exist and help to explain their development and impact.

THE AIMS OF PRIMARY GEOGRAPHY

Primary geographical education focuses on the development of **attitudes and values** and **knowledge, concepts and methods.** The Geography Working Group (DES, 1990) made it clear in their aims and proposals for National Curriculum geography that geography not only has a clear role in developing positive environmental values but is **the** subject, *par excellence*, to do so in the school curriculum. The first three aims in Figure 1 set out their explicit intention that geography teaching must develop positive and informed attitudes to places and the environment, locally and globally. The final three aims identify broadly the areas of geographical knowledge, concepts and methods which children need to

Attitudes and values

1 stimulate and develop children's interest in their own surroundings and the variety of human and physical environments and conditions over the Earth

2 engage children's sense of wonder at the beauty and variety of the world

3 develop in children informed concern about human impact on the quality of the environment and places in order to enhance their sense of responsibility for the care of the Earth and its peoples in the future

Knowledge, concepts and methods

4 enable children to extend their knowledge about the features, nature and character of their immediate surroundings and more distant environments and places, to support a sense of what it means to live in one place rather than another and as the basis for a framework in which to place information appropriately in a local and global context

5 develop children's appreciation of geographical location and links and their understanding of human and physical processes in creating and changing geographical patterns and relationships in different landscapes and human activities

6 build children's competence in using the methods of and skills in undertaking geographical enquiry and in analysing and communicating geographical information

Figure 1:
The aims of National Curriculum geography. Sources: adapted from DES, 1986; DES/WO, 1990.

understand, appreciate and apply if the Earth is to be 'returned' to the next generation in as good as or better shape than it was 'inherited'. These six aims for geographical education identify the role and purpose of primary geography.

The structure of primary geography

THE CORE DIMENSIONS

Primary geography is structured around three key geographical dimensions: **natural and human environments, place** and **geographical space.** Figure 2 identifies some of the key aspects of environment, place and space and some of the appropriate geographical questions which should form the basis for the study of geography in the primary curriculum (see also Chapter 1).

Figure 2:
The three dimensions of primary geography.

Natural and human environment

The study of natural and human environments helps children to:
1. identify the features and types of different environments and landscapes, and knowledge of their distribution over the surface of the Earth
2. understand the inter-relationships between people and environments, in particular human activity in and human use of the environment and its resources
3. identify processes at work in the environment that create and change features, landscapes and human activities
4. develop knowledge about human impact on the environment
5. recognise and understand their own and others' perceptions of and views about the environment
6. develop understanding of the need to manage and sustain the human and physical environment
7. become aware of issues involved in human activities in and use of the environment and its resources
8. value the environment
9. appreciate the interdependence of people and environments over the Earth
10. develop a sense of global diversity

Some appropriate geographical questions
A Where are these features, resources, environments?
B What are these features, resources, environments like?
C What is the impact of natural processes and human activities on the environment?
D What are the emerging issues about the use and treatment of the environment?
E What are alternative and appropriate ways to manage, sustain and improve environments?
F What are the perceptions and views of different people about the use and treatment of and change to environments?
G How can decision makers be influenced to adopt positive strategies to environmental use and change?

Place

The study of **place** helps children to:
1. understand and appreciate places as the localities and areas (regions) in which people live
2. identify their features and the human activities that occur in places
3. describe the character of places in terms of what they are like and what type of places they are
4. describe how people perceive and feel about places
5. develop a sense of place and community
6. develop a sense of their common experiences and of the diversity of experience among people in places across the world
7. develop awareness of the regional/national/global contexts of localities

Some appropriate geographical questions
A Where is this place?
B What is this place like?
C How has this place become like this?
D How is this place changing?
E What is it like to live in this place?
F What do you feel about this place?
G How does it compare/contrast with other places?

Geographical space

The study of **spatial location, patterns and processes** locally and over the Earth enables children to:

geographical location
1. observe and identify the location of places and features and activities in the environment
2. describe and explain the location of places and features and activities in the environment
3. appreciate the significance of geographical location for places and the environment

geographical patterns
4. recognise and identify links and relationships between places and features and activities in the environment
5. describe and explain patterns that can be observed and identified in places and in the environment
6. appreciate the significance of geographical patterns in understanding places and the environment

environmental processes
7. recognise and identify changes that create, modify and develop places and natural and human environments
8. describe and explain the way in which changes and developments occur in, and the impacts they have on, places and natural and human environments
9. appreciate the significance of the **natural and human processes** at work which shape the environment and places

Some appropriate geographical questions
A Where do these features, events, places occur?
B What are the connections between particular features, places or events?
C Can a pattern be discerned between them, and what is that pattern?
D How can these patterns be explained?
E Which processes occur that cause or create change in places and the environment?
F What is the impact of these processes on people, places and the environment?
G Can changes be predicted and/or planned?

These three dimensions are not to be studied separately; they are inextricably intertwined (see Figure 3). In studying particular places, consideration is given to:

- the local environment and its features;
- people's perceptions and local issues;
- the location of features and activities;
- the patterns of features such as building and land use;
- the changes and developments in the locality;

Similarly, in exploring a specific environment, the following are considered:

- its location;
- the processes that shape it;
- patterns that can be discerned in it and in other similar and contrasting environments.

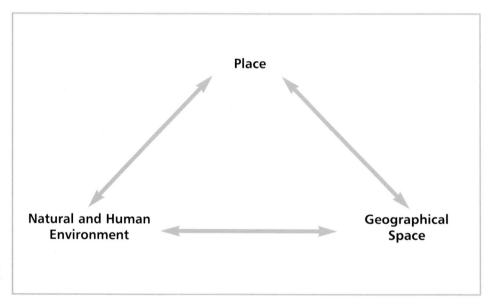

Figure 3:
The relationship of the three dimensions of geographical study.

THE STUDY OF PLACES AND ENVIRONMENTS

For primary geography, the National Curriculum emphasises development of children's understanding of places through the study of localities, and of environments through the study of geographical themes. The geographical concepts of location, pattern and process are developed in these contexts. While the environment and character of localities are to be studied in national and global contexts, geographical themes must be studied through real examples and, in effect, have a place-based context, whether local or continental in scale (see Figure 4). The 1995 Geography Order (DFE, 1995) required the study of the local area of the school and another locality at key stage 1, while at key stage 2 it required the study of the school's locality, another UK locality and a locality in Africa, Asia (excluding Japan) or South and Central America including the Caribbean. In Curriculum 2000, the Order has increased the choice of localities at key stage 2: a UK locality, rather than the school locality *and* a contrasting UK locality.

Places

1 Investigation of three localities
   - the local area of the school
   - another locality in the UK
   - a locality in another part of the world

2 Focus of locality studies
   - physical/human features and environmental issues
   - building/land use and changes in use
   - how features influence nature/location of activities
   - nature and impact of change within the locality
   - the character of the locality

3 The context of each locality
   - regional and national setting
   - links with other places

4 Comparing localities
   - similarities and differences between localities
   - commonality and diversity around the world

5 Locational knowledge
   - the shape and key features of the Earth
   - where places are around the world

Geographical themes
Investigation of the environment through human and physical geography and of environmental values and issues

1 Settlements (human geography)
   - use of buildings
   - land use, function, change, issues
   - location of activities
   - sizes and types of settlements
   - character and location of settlements reflect economic activities

2 Landscapes, rivers and weather (physical geography)
   - landscape features
   - weather/climate
   - rivers, landforms and physical processes

3 Environmental quality and change (environmental geography)
   - environmental preferences
   - human impact on environments
   - changes to environments
   - managing, sustaining and improving environments

Figure 4:
Place and thematic studies in primary geography.

Geographical enquiry
The use of geographical enquiry enables children to:

- use questions provided for them to investigate places and aspects of the environment
- develop the knowledge and understanding to construct questions to investigate places and aspects of the environment
- suggest and use key geographical questions to study places and features in and a variety of aspects of the environment:

  e.g. – Where is it?
       – What is it like?
       – How has it become like this?
       – How is it changing?
       – How does it compare/contrast with other places/features?

- develop competence in their investigation, analysis and communication of geographical information and understanding

Geographical skills
The development of geographical skills enables children to:

- develop experience and competence in their observation and use of fieldwork skills in the environment
- develop their mapping skills in the environment and in gathering and presenting information from and on maps at a range of scales
- develop their photograph reading and interpretation skills
- select and use a range of written, numerical and graphical secondary sources in their investigations
- use a variety of equipment, technologies and techniques appropriately and effectively

Figure 5:
Methods of geographical study.

USING GEOGRAPHICAL METHODS OF STUDY

In undertaking geographical investigations children will call on a variety of **geographical methods of study** (see Figure 5). The 1995 Geography Order requires children to learn to read aerial photographs and to use large-scale Ordnance Survey maps and atlas maps.

DEVELOPING GEOGRAPHICAL UNDERSTANDING THROUGH THE CURRICULUM

Figure 6 shows the core aspects of geography that are introduced, developed and extended as children progress through key stages 1 and 2. Figure 6 also includes aspects of geography that are broadened and introduced during key stage 2.

It is important to consider sequencing the development of the dimensions, methods and aspects in primary geography and this is done in Figures 7 and 8 which provide an overview for the structure outlined in Figures 1-6 (see also Blyth and Krause, 1995; Foley and Janikoun, 1996; SCAA, 1997).

Aspects of geography to introduce, develop and extend across key stages 1 and 2

1 Place
- local area, including school grounds
- other localities
- land and building use
- the character of localities
- comparing places: commonalities and diversity
- sense of the wider world: local and global

2 Natural and human environment
- features of the environment
- features of settlements
- change in environments
- weather
- personal and people's views on the environment
- environmental sustainability and improvement

3 Geographical methods
- use of enquiry/investigative process
- fieldwork
- mapping skills, large scale to globes/atlases
- use of secondary sources on places and environment, including photos and ICT programs

Aspects of geography to broaden in key stage 2

1 Place
- changes in localities
- connections and links between places
- locational knowledge

2 Natural and human environment
- weather and seasons
- topical local and global awareness
- environmental issues
- land use variety and issues

3 Geographical methods
- use of 'geographical' instruments and techniques

Aspects of geography to introduce in key stage 2

1 Place
- change in places

2 Natural and human environment
- settlement size
- economic activity in settlements
- rivers
- explaining patterns in the environment

Figure 6:
The geography to study in key stages 1 and 2.

PRE-SCHOOL
Nursery and Reception

Focus: Provision of practical and active experience through stories and toys, role and open-ended play; observation in the immediate and nearby environments; discussion of the observations and experiences in places; development of appropriate language to name and talk about observations and experiences; recording comments and views; care for the immediate environment.

Geographical activities should help children:

1 observe and name a variety of natural and human features seen in the immediate area and in photographs of that and other places
2 talk about experience of places, both their own area and places other than those in the immediate locality to foster awareness of the wider world
3 develop awareness of the purpose of some local features
4 express personal views about the environment
5 look after the nursery environment and living things
6 use language of relative direction and proximity
7 develop awareness that events occur in the environment
8 use experience, observations and resources to respond to and ask questions about places and the environment
9 use a variety of resources, particularly the nursery environment, toys and artifacts for play and photographs of features and places

KEY STAGE 1
Years 1 and 2

Focus: Provision of practical activities and of fieldwork experience to observe and investigate places and the environment; use of appropriate vocabulary to identify and describe features and activities; use of stories and imaginative contexts about places; development of local knowledge; building a sense of place; develop concern for the environment; become increasingly aware of the wider world.

Geographical studies should help children:

1 recognise, identify and describe natural and human features, including buildings and land use, locally and in another locality
2 identify the key characteristics of a locality from its features
3 become aware of where one lives and of the world beyond the local area, nationally and globally
4 identify and describe natural and human processes, such as weather conditions and their impact on people or the jobs people do and the journeys they make
5 express personal views about features in an environment
6 consider how environments, perhaps locally, can be improved and sustained
7 identify the location of features, referring to proximity and direction
8 notice layouts of and connections between features
9 recognise similarities and differences between features in different localities and environments and identify characteristics that help identify these
10 realise that changes occur to features in environments
11 select and use information provided to respond to and ask questions and to suggest ways to undertake investigations
12 use observation, data collection, vocabulary, maps and photographs appropriately in investigations of places and environments in and outside the classroom

Figure 7:
A framework for the structure of the geography curriculum from nursery through to key stage 1.

Years 3 and 4

Focus: Provision of practical activities and of fieldwork experience to develop investigations of places and the environment; development of appropriate geographical vocabulary to describe and explain observations; use of imagination and appropriate stories to explore geographical ideas and experiences; development of knowledge about local and other places; become aware of processes that affect places and the environment; develop concern for the environment.

Geographical studies should help children:

1 describe, sort and compare natural and human features in localities, using appropriate geographical vocabulary

2 describe and give some reasons for the distinctive character of localities, based on features and human activities

3 develop a personal sense of place

4 recognise that localities are set within a broader geographical context, nationally and globally

5 describe natural and human processes, such as how site conditions influence local weather, the changes to seasonal weather patterns or how land is used in different ways

6 offer reasons for personal views about environmental matters and appreciate that other people may have different points of view

7 describe ways in which people affect the environment and consider how people can manage and improve environments

8 describe and give reasons for the location of features and places

9 identify patterns made by natural and human features and consider reasons for these

10 identify and offer reasons for changes that occur to features and localities

11 describe and offer reasons for similarities and differences between localities and environments

12 show awareness of the common nature of and diversity in human experience around the world

13 respond to and ask some suitable geographical questions when undertaking investigations into localities and the environment, drawing on information selected to support the enquiry

14 use maps, photographs, observations, relevant vocabulary, and a variety of basic equipment to gather data appropriately in investigations of places and environments in and outside the classroom

Years 5 and 6

Focus: Provision of practical activities and of fieldwork experience to extend enquiries and investigations into places and the environment; extension of appropriate geographical terminology to describe and explain findings from research; use of creative skills and appropriate stories to examine geographical ideas, content and issues; extension of knowledge about local and other places; further development of a sense of place; developing increased understanding of processes that affect places and the environment; justify views held about environmental matters and issues.

Geographical studies should help children:

1 describe and classify natural and human features and activities in localities, using appropriate geographical terminology

2 explain how natural and human features and activities create the distinctive character of localities

3 describe a personal idea of place

4 describe how localities are set within a broader geographical context, regionally, nationally and globally

5 describe and explain how natural and human processes create and shape places and the environment, such as: that weather conditions vary over the Earth; how river processes work and create landscapes; that settlements vary in size and that their character reflects their economic activities; how goods and services are provided for a community; and that issues can arise over the use of land

6 explain and justify personal views and identify and explain different views held by other people about environmental matters and issues

7 describe and explain ways in which human activities have an impact on the environment and describe approaches people can take to managing, sustaining and improving environments

8 describe and appreciate how the location of activities can be affected by natural and human features and that economic activities can influence their own location and the character of places

9 describe and understand the links between places

10 explain and appreciate the importance of patterns made by natural and human features and activities

11 explain and appreciate the significance of changes and their impact on places and environments

12 compare and contrast aspects within and between localities and environments

13 appreciate and value what is common to, and the diversity of, human experience, places and environments around the world

14 identify relevant geographical questions and appropriate approaches to investigation when planning enquiries into localities and the environment, selecting information appropriately and offering plausible conclusions

15 use a range of appropriate equipment accurately to obtain data and use a variety of secondary sources, including maps, photographs and graphic and written information, and appropriate geographical vocabulary in enquiries into places and environments in and outside the classroom

Figure 8:
A framework for the structure of the geography curriculum at key stage 2.

Challenges for primary geography teaching

Since the introduction of the Geography National Curriculum for key stages 1 and 2, there has been a consistent improvement in the planning and teaching of primary geography. There are, however, a number of challenges that continue to face primary schools and teachers if children's geographical learning is to maintain its progress and continue to develop from year to year. These are challenges that must be addressed not just at national and local education authority levels but by schools and individual teachers. They are as much to do with attitudes as they are with the content and resources of geographical education. Three challenges stand out.

1 VALUING GEOGRAPHY IN PRIMARY EDUCATION

Teaching is most effective when the teacher values what is being taught. Teachers are encouraged, and geography will be seen as valued by pupils, when it is held in high esteem by the leadership of the school – the headteacher, the subject leader and the governing body. The basic challenge for class teachers and headteachers is to understand and value, both personally and as educators, the role and importance of geographical education. This means taking on board the *aims* of geographical education.

2 FOSTERING ENVIRONMENTAL AND GLOBAL/LOCAL UNDERSTANDING

The outcome of primary geographical education must be children's developing knowledge, understanding and values in relation to environment and place. This requires that teaching and children's learning take place in a supportive and caring environment in which values, such as care for the environment and for people in the local community, are part of the ethos of the classroom and school. The challenge for primary schools is to put these values into practice.

Understanding the local area and its community, and other localities and their communities, requires carefully planned teaching if pupils are to appreciate fully the diversity that exists between places and environments, lifestyles and activities. It requires an active approach to fostering children's knowledge and their sense of belonging, however challenging that might be in local circumstances.

3 IMPROVING TEACHERS' GEOGRAPHY SUBJECT KNOWLEDGE

For the teaching of geography to be done well, it is vital for teachers to continue to develop and maintain personal subject knowledge. This means setting time aside, on a regular basis and in a planned way, to reflect upon and enhance their own geographical knowledge and understanding. Maintaining up-to-date awareness of developments in primary geography requires support which has to be underpinned by the school's planned teacher development budget, and, therefore, funding by the governing body.

The development of teachers' geographical knowledge and understanding will involve attendance at INSET geography programmes, whether run in or out of school. INSET opportunities must therefore be consistently and properly planned for to support and develop teachers' confidence in their understanding of geographical education. It is this growing confidence that enables teachers to develop and maintain high expectations of their pupils.

Developing geography teaching in primary schools

The inspection and evaluation of primary geography highlights the variety of opportunities that exist and need to be taken to maintain and improve quality and standards. Seven are identified and discussed below.

INTEGRATION IN GEOGRAPHY

No aspect of geography can be taught in isolation. The study of a locality will include aspects of its environment; a study of rivers will involve examples from a variety of places at different scales and should aim to develop geographical concepts, perhaps ideas to do with location or natural environmental processes. When planning for integration, consideration should be given to methods at the same time, covering, for example, the demands of the enquiry process to be used, the level of map skills to be used and developed, the types of maps to be worked with and the vocabulary to be extended.

As well as integration *within* geography, aspects of geography appear in and are supported by other subjects in the primary curriculum. For example, work in art helps children to develop their visual skills and so to appreciate not just the features of environments but their textures and feel. The study of water, soils and rocks in science is integral to an appreciation of landscape and an understanding of river action, which clearly involves solution and forces. Scientific observation and investigation and the application of mathematical processes clearly support the development of geographical understanding. Identifying the content of geographical studies should therefore involve the study of a range of subjects.

Producing work in art helps children to develop their observational skills. Work: James Howard, age 11, Ainthorpe Primary School, Hull.

PROVIDING EXPLANATIONS

Fundamental to geographical understanding is the analysis of what is happening in the places and environments around us. In studying places and exploring environmental features, areas and issues, children must be involved not just in describing what they observe but also in offering explanations and reasons for what is happening.

At the heart of planning geographical topics will be the development of children's understanding of the core geographical concepts: geographical location, geographical pattern and environmental process. The best learning occurs when children are encouraged and challenged to offer their own explanations for phenomena they have observed or identified. In these situations children begin to develop their ability to use geographical ideas and principles to understand the places and environments they study. This must be planned into geography topics. Promoting explanation in geography develops children's higher-order thinking skills.

AWARENESS OF THE WIDER WORLD

Studying the children's home and school locality is a vital part of geographical study, grounding their experience in personal knowledge. However, geography is not just about the local area but about the whole Earth, and children must begin in the primary years to develop their sense of the wider world. This implies providing experience through examples of places and environments which open their eyes to the diversity across the planet. It means beginning to develop a global view of the Earth through the use of globes and atlas maps. It also means encountering a variety of examples of places at different scales to give context to their locality and thematic studies. This should be planned for, selecting examples carefully. Opportunities should be taken to use incidental and topical news, whether personal to the children or in the national television and press news coverage, to maintain their developing sense of the world about them.

If you look at a globe or a map of the world, you will see that there is much more water than land. Nearly three-quarters of the world is covered by sea. There are five great oceans and a number of smaller seas.

Chantelle Williams

Working with globes and atlases help children develop a global view of the Earth. Photo: Chris Garnett. Work: Chantelle Williams.

EXPLICIT CURRICULUM PLANNING

Primary geography needs to be planned at three levels: whole school, units within year schemes and day-to-day teaching (SCAA, 1995). This provides an essential context for the development of geographical learning and for enabling progression in children's geographical understanding (see Chapters 4 and 5). The key points are:

- A well-planned **subject framework** for the development of geographical knowledge, ideas, values and skills for the whole school, where the aims of geography in the school are succinctly stated and the long-term planning explicitly reflects these. This should be broad-based and provide the structure and focus of geographical work throughout the school.

- Clearly stated overall objectives and geographical content in medium-term **units of work** which reflect the long-term planning. The particular areas of the topic to be covered, the outcomes expected from it, the main teaching activities to be used and the key resources needed should all be included.

- Day-to-day, or short-term, **session plans** that have sharp foci to enable the achievement of the objectives of the geographical units of work. These should state the specific content to be taught, the particular activities and tasks to be undertaken and the resources to be used (see Chapter 4).

ASSESSING GEOGRAPHICAL LEARNING

Clear curriculum planning supports teachers when assessing children's geographical learning. The aims indicate the direction in which geographical content and teaching is taking the child's learning. The unit and day-to-day learning objectives and expected outcomes provide a basis for identifying what a particular child has begun to appreciate or extend understanding in. For example, a particular unit might involve the use of specified map skills and ideas to do with patterns in the local area. Specific sessions may use grid referencing tasks to develop use of this skill and to identify the location of types of land use. Day-to-day observation and marking of children's work on such tasks can lead to identifying the extent to which the child has understood and used the particular skills and ideas throughout the topic unit, resulting in a clear end-of-unit record of achievement (see Chapter 6).

Photo: Wendy Morgan.

PROVIDING STIMULATING ACTIVITIES

Children are enthused by tasks which provide challenge, use their experience, draw on their understanding, have practical dimensions and involve them actively. Such activities should involve reinforcement as well as extension of experience and understanding, perhaps through new contexts or examples as much as through new ideas and content. There should be variety in the tasks used and they should test children's thinking, however incrementally.

The planning of geography units and sessions must offer children a variety of tasks and contexts. For example, a topic on local weather might include:

- discussion of weather types,
- recording weather through observation and the use of equipment,
- analysing weather data to see if patterns emerge,
- predicting weather day-to-day,
- describing weather extremes around the world using secondary sources
- identifying some causes of weather activity.

The range of activities is likely to include:

- fieldwork investigations;
- making charts and graphs using paper and pencil and a data recording programme;
- responding to questions, perhaps using a worksheet or from the board;
- identifying, sifting and writing up information from books, posters, television programmes, a CD-ROM, atlases and other resources;
- presenting information, ideas and analysis orally and on paper.

Presenting information orally.
Photo: Chris Garnett.

RESOURCING GEOGRAPHY TEACHING

Geographical resources need to be continually up-dated because geography is about the world as it is today. The local area does not stand still: traffic levels increase; a building or land area changes use, people move in and out; services develop and goods in shops change; streams are fuller or lower and carry more or less silt; weather changes day-to-day. This is true elsewhere too. Environmental change and issues are ever present but new ones continually emerge. Commercial publications provide examples of the geography of other places but they date very quickly, indeed they begin to date the moment they appear.

In the local area and in places they visit for day or residential fieldwork, children can be involved in the gathering of information and resources and logging this onto a database for future use in making comparisons over time. Photographs can be taken, and new data on traffic or building and land use can be recorded. From the local authority planning department, teachers can collect copies of new maps showing planning applications for local developments; they can set up contacts with other sources such as estate agents, travel agents, local shopkeepers and local environmental groups. Teachers can also take photographs of places visited and collect leaflets and other free resources which are available to tourists in the UK and many other parts of the world. In other words, there are many good geographical resources that can be readily and cheaply obtained.

Although children can create some resources themselves, and many can be obtained very cheaply, or for nothing, some resources must be purchased. It is essential, therefore that proper financial budgeting takes place in school. Ordnance Survey maps, a set of atlas maps, a variety of reference books on an area or topic and CD-ROMs can be expensive. They need to be carefully selected in relation to the topics to be covered, the children who will use them, and their lifespan. It must be realised that they will need replacing at regular intervals to maintain an up-to-date view of the world. The valuing of geography as a 'current' subject, about the world as it is now and as it is changing, is fundamental to making the decisions that ensure children can use honest, accurate and recent resources to explore the world they are growing up in (see Chapter 9, Resources and Bibliography).

Conclusion

The essence of geographical learning is to encourage us all to stop and think about what the world is like, what is happening to it and what can be done to hand it back to our children in an improved state. None of us wants a future in which a poem like this one comes true.

Work: Sophie Clark, age 6, Ainthorpe Primary School, Hull.

I spy on the road

Red metal road sign,
Concrete bridge, building sites,
Rows of lorries, cars, coaches,
Stop, go, traffic lights,

Roundabout, factories,
No entry, shopping stores,
Traffic wardens, car park,
Office block (20 floors).

Mummy, what's that?
Over there – can you see?
That thing coloured green.
That, my dear, is a tree.
(Charles Thomson, in Nicholls, 1993)

Primary geography is a subject which helps us to understand the world around us, to get to know it, to begin to understand how it works, to see what people do and the impact of what is done by natural forces and human activities. It is also fundamentally an ethical subject (Sack, 1997). The aims, ideas and content of primary geography have a clear outcome in mind: the informed, concerned and responsible member of the community, whose sense of wonder, interest and fascination with the world around her/him leads to active involvement in the sustaining and improvement of local life and the wider world. That is what makes geography such an essential subject for primary children.

References

Blyth, A. and Krause, J. (1995) *Primary Geography: A Developmental Approach.* London: Hodder & Stoughton.

Chambers, W. and Donert, K. (1996) *Teaching Geography in Key Stage 2.* Cambridge: Chris Kington Publishing.

Department for Education and Science (DES) (1986) *Geography from 5 to 16: Curriculum Matters 7.* London: HMSO.

DES (1989) *Aspects of Primary Education: The Teaching and Learning of History and Geography.* London: HMSO.

DES/WO (1990) *Geography for Ages 5-16.* London/Cardiff: DES/WO.

DES (1991) *Geography in the National Curriculum (England).* London: DES/HMSO.

Department for Education (DFE) (1995) *Geography in the National Curriculum (England).* London: HMSO.

Foley, M. and Janikoun, J. (1996) *The Really Practical Guide to Primary Geography* (second edition). Cheltenham: Stanley Thornes.

Martin, F. (1995) *Teaching Early Years Geography.* Cambridge: Chris Kington Publishing.

Milner, A. (1996) *Geography Starts Here! Practical Approaches with Nursery and Reception Children.* Sheffield: Geographical Association.

Nicholls, J. (1993) *Earthways Earthwise: Poems on Conservation.* Oxford: Oxford University Press.

Palmer, J. (1994) *Geography in the Early Years.* London: Routledge.

Sack, R. (1997) *Homo Geographicus.* Baltimore: John Hopkins University Press.

School Curriculum and Assessment Authority (1995) *Planning the Curriculum at Key Stages 1 and 2.* London: SCAA.

SCAA (1996) *Nursery Education: Desirable Outcomes for Children's Learning.* London: SCAA.

SCAA (1997) *Expectations in Geography at Key Stages 1 and 2.* London: SCAA.

Welsh Office (WO) (1991) *Geography in the National Curriculum (Wales).* Cardiff: HMSO.

WO (1995) *Geography in the National Curriculum (Wales).* Cardiff: HMSO.

Chapter 3: Geography in the National Curriculum and beyond

This important overview of geography, within current curriculum requirements and beyond, provides an essential rationale for teachers, and especially co-ordinators responsible for writing policy documents (see Chapter 8). The material on developing geography teaching in primary schools introduces strands which are explored elsewhere: integrating the dimensions (Part 2); awareness of the wider world (Chapters 18 and 19); curriculum planning (Chapter 4); assessment (Chapter 6); resources (Chapter 9).

One teacher's explanation of how cross-curricular learning is planned.

Year 3 is the first year of junior school. At the age of 7/8 years old the children are still ego-centric with life centred around their immediate environment.

The first term in integrated studies has a history focus but it begins with an introduction into the year's theme - PROTECTION. The children study their own homes and look at their family and people who protect them before moving onto the history focus.

The second term has a geography focus with a local study element. The children are given the opportunity of going out - making a study of a local street and look at the houses there. From this there is a move into looking at the wider world. By looking at "Hot and Cold Lands" a comparison can be made with the children's own environment using the key theme of "Protection".

The third term gives the children an opportunity of a science focus taking the theme "Looking at Nature". The children study their own environment where living things, namely plants and animals, live and survive. The wider world theme of "Habitats in Hot and Cold Lands" is focussed upon using the key theme of "Protection". A visit to Howletts Zoo Park is an integral part of the term's work where consideration is not only given to those animals reared there whose natural habitats are in the wider world but also to the important topic of conservation of our world.

I.H. LOFT
Class
Teacher

The planning process

Chapter 4

Roger Carter
Karen Mansfield

The introduction of the National Curriculum highlighted the need for careful and detailed planning in primary geography: without such planning, children would be unlikely to receive their full entitlement to the programmes of study. This represented no small task for primary teachers as they juggled with what is essentially a secondary, subject-based curriculum model and attempted to marry it to more familiar primary approaches. Teachers in small schools, where classes are of mixed age and sometimes straddle key stages, have faced particular problems. The Dearing revisions went a long way towards slimming and simplifying overall requirements, offering an opportunity in our teaching, assessment and monitoring to do less, but to do it better. The decision to release teachers from fully implementing the geography Order, during the period leading up to the review in the year 2000, introduces a further set of considerations for planners. Schools must decide whether or not an increased focus on literacy and numeracy is justified for their pupils and, if so, what revisions are necessary to the foundation subjects to accommodate this. There are three considerations here:

1. Schools are still required to provide a broad and balanced curriculum. Within this they must still teach geography.
2. Great care needs to be taken when planning a reduction of the geography programme to ensure that the balance of places, themes and skills is retained and that children have a worthwhile and recurring experience of the subject.
3. Secure planning will remain an important factor when developing quality programmes in geography. The programmes of study will continue to provide a reliable context for such planning, even though the legislative requirement for them has been relaxed.

The planning process is best seen as an ongoing cycle. The subject co-ordinator may well take the lead in helping colleagues to agree policy for the subject, developing overall plans and units of work, and supporting teaching approaches. But it is important that all teachers in the school have a sense of ownership and shared understanding of this process. Equally important is that, as they are developed, these policies and plans are kept under review, evaluated from time to time, and revised as necessary to ensure that good practice is recognised and developed (see Figure 1).

There is no lack of guidance on planning for geography. The Geographical Association has produced several guidance books to support the process (Norris Nicholson, 1992; Sebba, 1991; Morgan, 1995). Useful support is also available in Chambers and Donert (1995). In 1997 the Schools Curriculum and Assessment Authority (SCAA) published a leaflet (SCAA, 1997) which develops the approach to planning previously explained in *Planning the Curriculum at Key Stages 1 and 2* (SCAA, 1995). All these guidance materials stress the importance of planning at several levels – whole school, long-term planning for each key stage, medium-term planning of units of work, and short-term planning of lessons. Planning at each level sits within the larger plans of the level above (see Figure 2 which refers to planning at key stage 2, but is clearly relevant to all key stages).

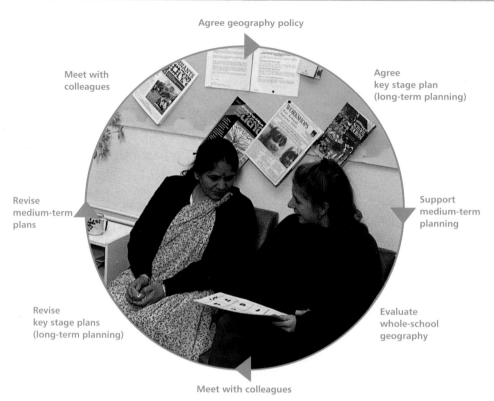

Agree geography policy

Meet with colleagues

Agree key stage plan (long-term planning)

Revise medium-term plans

Support medium-term planning

Revise key stage plans (long-term planning)

Evaluate whole-school geography

Meet with colleagues

Figure 1:
The planning process.
Photo: John Birdsall
Photography.

Figure 2 suggests that at each level of planning, important decisions are needed about how the geography programme will be developed in your school. Of course these decisions will be influenced by the overall shape of the curriculum and how geography is apportioned alongside all other curriculum areas. Some general considerations to bear in mind when deciding what to do are outlined in Figure 3.

Good planning will make possible a rich, balanced learning experience for children, but it cannot ensure that this will happen – that is in the hands of teachers working with their pupils. One way of judging if the plans have been successfully translated into practice is by checking against a set of criteria, such as those listed in Figure 4.

Developing plans

LONG-TERM PLANNING
As Figure 2 shows, long-term planning involves producing a key stage plan for geography which includes a description of the geography to be covered in each year.

Places, themes and skills
The units within the long-term plan in geography are (traditionally) generated from the National Curriculum programmes of study. However, unlike some subjects, such as history, there are no predetermined blocks of content which allow easy translation into units of work. What geography does have are three facets: **places**, **themes** and **skills** (which are specified within the programmes of study), and to ensure that 'good geography' is taught, all three need to be present within a unit of work. For example, in year 2 pupils may focus on the school as the place, and the environment as the theme, with skills such as fieldwork, map work and enquiry being developed and used in these contexts.

The long-term plan needs to describe the themes to be covered within a unit, and the scale of the place element. Thus, in year 4 a Rivers unit may use examples from places perhaps within a day-trip radius of the school, and in year 6 use examples from Europe, or focus on a European river.

Whole-school planning

Produce a policy statement for geography which addresses:

- the aims of geographical education and the distinctive contribution of the subject at key stage 2;
- geography's role in reinforcing literacy, numeracy and ICT (basic skills);
- geography's contribution to personal and social education and to elements of the whole curriculum, such as environmental education;
- opportunities for a wide range of teaching and learning experiences, including fieldwork, in geography;
- how much time will be devoted to geography in the key stage.

Long-term planning (key stage)

Produce a key stage plan for geography which outlines:

- how often and in what depth geographical work will feature during the key stage;
- whether geography will be taught separately or linked with other subjects;
- progression from geographical work undertaken in key stage 1;
- the enquiry focus and the broad sequence of content for each geography unit;
- how places, themes and skills will be integrated in each geography unit;
- development of the skills of geographical enquiry.

Medium-term planning (e.g. half a term)

Produce a plan for a unit of work which includes:

- a more detailed list of specific enquiry questions;
- a sequence of teaching and learning activities;
- learning objectives (knowledge/understanding/skills) and assessment opportunities;
- resource needs and fieldwork arrangements;
- the amount of time needed.

Short-term planning (e.g. lesson)

Produce a lesson plan which clarifies:

- the lesson focus or question and the learning objectives;
- the way in which skills are integrated with place studies and thematic work;
- learning activities and, if appropriate, assessment opportunities;
- how the children should be grouped, how resources are to be used, how other adults can be involved;
- additional strategies for teaching the most and least able children;
- opportunities for feedback to pupils.

Figure 2:
Planning geographical work at key stage 2. Source: SCAA, 1997.

1   Be sure that all pupils have a recurring experience of geography throughout the primary years. They should have some, if only brief contact with the subject every term.

2   In all years provide a mix of local and global material. For younger pupils 'local' means within their known world, and 'global' means any new experience which extends it.

3   Increase the proportion of distant place work as children progress through the years.

4   Help pupils to connect their work on familiar and unfamiliar places, and to bring together work on places, themes and skills.

5   Think about the order in which pupils study topics. Allow for pupils to return to key ideas and aspects several times through their primary years.

6   Build progression into your planning by introducing more demanding skills and widening the range, complexity and methods of study.

7   Adopt an enquiry approach by structuring your teaching units around a series of key questions. Share these with your pupils.

Figure 3:
Seven points to remember when planning your geography programme.

A good geography curriculum should be one which:

1   recognises that children *have their own experiences* and knowledge of the world;

2   gives children concrete experiences *outside the classroom*;

3   gives children access to a *wide range of visual materials*, including pictures, artefacts, maps and data, and accurate and up-to-date resources;

4   *uses maps* in the context of studies of *real places*, and helps children to develop and understand *scale*;

5   encourages children to look for *patterns in distribution* in space and to *ask questions* about these patterns;

6   encourages children to look for relationships between *people and places*.

7   enables children to learn to use a *range of ways to describe the world*, e.g. specialist vocabulary, maps, diagrams, models;

8   integrates *skills, themes and real places*;

9   includes a study of a *range of types of real places* across the world;

10 provides activities which are *enquiry based*, using the same approaches as in other subjects, and which encourage children to look for issues, ask questions, and formulate hypotheses and to test them against evidence.

Figure 4:
The features of a good geography curriculum.

Units of geography can be built by bringing together elements from 'places', 'themes' and 'skills' as outlined in the programmes of study. However, the process is more complex than it may seem. For example, only one theme is explicit at key stage 1, and at key stage 2 themes are specified *within* places. Some schools may therefore prefer to adopt predetermined units of work (see examples below for each key stage).

Key stage 1

The programme of study for key stage 1 is designed not only to provide children aged 5-7 with appropriate teaching experiences for their age, but also to lay foundations for future learning. Thus, although rivers, weather and settlement do not appear as specified themes until key stage 2, the key stage 1 programme is designed to allow for initial experiences in these areas, drawn from investigations in and around school.

Elements of the key stage 1 programme of study are identified in Figure 5. It is likely that many of these will be developed within a larger topic which draws on a wider curriculum. For example, a topic on 'Our School' could provide an opportunity to place the school in its locality and introduce geographical ideas; to explore some historical perspectives relating to changes in the school over time; and to make links with science by looking at the structure of the building and the materials it is made of.

Key stage 2

As Figure 6 shows, 11 units of geography are proposed for key stage 2. This allows for some flexibility in one term in year 5 or 6 which could include a residential visit. The following points should be considered at the long-term planning stage:

■ A mixture of place-led units and theme-led units will provide a clear basis for assessment.

■ There needs to be a balance of place and theme units, and human and physical aspects, each year.

■ To ensure a spiral curriculum, each theme needs two planned visits in key stage 2; one in year 3/4 (see Figure 6) and one in year 5/6 (see Figure 7).

■ The length of units will vary according to the content of the programmes of study to be covered, and the preferences of schools.

■ Units involving fieldwork need to be placed at an appropriate time of the year.

■ Geographical skills will be developed throughout all units.

Place and theme elements	Year	Notes
Classroom: variety of themes, mainly human	Reception	A large-scale floor plan could be used to show, e.g. areas of the classroom used for different purposes, routes to office, toilets.
School and grounds: variety of themes	1 or cycle A	Jobs people do around the school, and the rooms they use could be a theme here. Work could include tracing routes around the school and grounds, and grouping rooms according to their different uses.
The locality of the school: variety of themes, mainly human	2 or cycle B	The locality of the school is its immediate vicinity.
A contrasting locality (either within the UK or overseas): variety of themes	1 or cycle A	The concept of settlement will be developed within this unit. The choice of a contrasting locality within the UK, which the children could visit, is recommended. For urban schools this might be a rural village; for village schools it might be a market town.
An investigation into the **quality of the environment** in any locality. Introduces the environment theme	2 or cycle B	The school can be used as the place context for this unit, which looks at attractive and unattractive features and how things are changed, the reasons for this change and what needs to be done to maintain the quality of the environment.
Places within the UK		An opportunity to focus and extend the children's knowledge of places. Use their first-hand experiences, postcards, television places, stories, etc.
Places beyond the UK		There are many ways to build up locational knowledge of places beyond the UK, including through cross-curricular topics such as Journeys. Ensure that opportunities are planned in. These may well exist within other subject areas but must be managed throughout the key stage. Use can be made of stories, television programmes, news, and children's experiences outside school.
Physical features, Geographical terms: introduces the rivers theme		Opportunities to identify and name physical features (leading to rivers at key stage 2) must be planned in.
Weather: study effects on people and their surroundings. Introduces the weather theme		Observations and simple measurements of the weather can be collected in specific months (September, December, March and June) and patterns identified from them.
Stories		These can provide a focus for reception or nursery or/and 'free terms'.

Figure 5:
Key stage 1 geography.

Focus	Theme(s)	Place contexts
Physical landscape	Rivers	Examples from the 'home region'
How environments change	Environmental change	Locality of the school
Catchment area of the school	Various – mainly human	Locality of the school
Contrasting locality: e.g. village, town, part of seaside place or part of an urban area	Various – physical and human	Seaside, urban or village
How settlements differ	Settlement	Examples from the UK
How weather varies between places and over time	Weather	Locality of the school, studied localities, examples from around the world
Planned visit in year 3/4		

Figure 6:
Key stage 2 – year 3/4.

Focus	Theme(s)	Place contexts
Rivers and their effects on the landscape	Rivers	Examples from UK/Europe
Environmental geography – investigating how environments change	Environmental Change – can relate to physical and/or human geography	Examples from the home region
An urban area – how settlements differ and change	Settlement	Urban place which demonstrates patterns of land use
Village or part of a town in an Economically Developing Country	Various	Locality in Africa, Asia, Central or South America
Differences in weather – microclimates around the school	Weather	School grounds
Planned visit in year 5/6		

Figure 7:
Key stage 2 – year 5/6.

MEDIUM-TERM PLANNING

At this level of planning, the main concern is the details within each unit of geography. Central to medium-term plans are the broad learning objectives. These are the concepts, knowledge, skills and attitudes we expect and aim for the child to acquire during a unit. They also provide a focus for assessment.

In summary, medium-term planning should:

- focus on each unit of work;
- ensure equal access to the curriculum for all children;
- relate to programmes of study;
- specify broad learning objectives;
- pose key questions which reflect the enquiry methodology;
- detail learning experiences;
- list appropriate resources;
- include the contribution of ICT;
- be managed by the geography co-ordinator;

When drafting a medium-term plan, the following considerations need to be taken into account:

Content: The programme of study identifies a range of places, themes and skills to be taught. These should be integrated into teaching schemes so that real places are studied in relation to the themes, using appropriate skills in the process. In your planning, look out for opportunities to connect your content to the wider curriculum of other subjects and to make cross-curricular links.

Themes: At key stage 2 these are Rivers, Weather, Settlement and Environmental Change. Over the four years of this key stage these themes will need to be revisited to reflect children's growing capability to understand the ideas relating to them.

Places: Check the required locational knowledge expected of children at key stage 2, as indicated in Maps A, B and C in the Geography National Curriculum document.

- Decide which places will be included and at what scale.

- Consider which of the places you choose to study are the most appropriate to use as contexts for work on the themes.

Skills: The study of places and themes will provide opportunities to develop geographical skills. Careful planning will ensure that these are introduced in appropriate teaching contexts. In relation to your plan you might consider:

- which aspects will be enhanced by the use of ICT;

- what geographical vocabulary can be developed;

- where the best opportunities are to work outside the classroom;

- where the use of maps, atlases and globes can be developed most effectively;

- which key questions will develop enquiry skills and provide a direction for the work.

Figures 8 and 9 show examples of units of work for key stage 1 (Figure 8) and key stage 2 (Figure 9) geography. Other examples can be found in Morgan, 1995 and in guidelines produced by LEAs. *Primary Geographer* (number 25, April 1996) also contains a useful example of progression in a unit on Rivers for key stages 1 and 2.

For many pupils a small village forms the basis of their studies into a contrasting locality. Photo: Paula Richardson.

Unit of work: A village as a contrasting locality   Theme: various, especially settlement   Year group: 1 or 2

Programmes of study	Content focused key questions	Ideas for activities	Resources	Some learning outcomes
Introducing settlement theme	What is a village like?	Discussion, naming villages they know and fictional villages	Village stories 1, 2, 3 and Away	Can name the villages they know
5a about physical and human features that give the localities their character 3a use geographical terms in exploring their surroundings	What do the children expect to find in a village? What physical and human features can we identify?	Discussion about what a feature is. List features they might find in a village; this can be used as a checklist in the field. Using pictures to sort features into physical and human categories	Big books, pictures, aerial and other photographs	Can list features they think they will find in a village – telephone box, post box, shop selling variety of goods, fields, public house, different types of houses, bus stop, village hall, church, football/cricket pitch. Name and sort pictures of features into physical (natural) and man made (artificial).
5d how land and buildings are used 3f use secondary sources to obtain geographical information	What are the land and the buildings used for around our school?	List and find pictures of different types of building; sort into uses. Match photographs to the function of buildings. Sort into ones that would be found around the school and which in the village	Pictures of different types of buildings	Realise that our locality is mainly buildings. List the sort of buildings they would find around the school and the villages – houses, shops, factories, schools, churches, spare time activities.
3e use maps and globes	Where is the village?	Discuss how far away the village is, and how long it will take to get there	Maps	Can explain where the village is in relation to where they live.
5a about the main physical and human features that give the localities their character 3d make maps and plans of real and imaginary places, using pictures and symbols 3b undertake fieldwork activities 3a use geographical terms	What are the main features in the village? What are the land and buildings in the village used for? What can you see from the village?	Fieldwork in the village. Check off features including types of buildings they see. Put these on an outline map, devise symbols, take photographs which can be linked to the map. Draw a sketch map of the route of their walk round the village. Look out from different parts of the village and describe what can be seen; take photographs.	Outline map of the village	Can put features (see above list) onto a simple outline sketch map; list features (see above list) found in the village; draw a sketch map of the route they have taken; recognise that the village is surrounded by open farmland.
5b how the localities are similar and different	How does this village compare with our locality?	Compare photographs of the different localities; list features of both which show similarities and differences	Photographs of both localities, video	Can list similarities and differences in features, facilities and size.
5 A contrasting locality	What are villages like? What would it be like to live in a village? What could you do in the village?	Sum up in discussion, or pictures and writing, what the area is like. Compare with pictures of other villages.	During the study pupils will generate further resources by making their own maps, taking photographs and conducting interviews, etc. Photographs of the village and its surrounding area, photographs of other villages	Realise that there is more open space in a village, that most of the village buildings are houses, and the area around is farmland. Describe the area as rural. Realise that some of the facilities we use around our school are not in the village.

Figure 8: Year 1/2 unit of work on a contrasting locality.

Unit of work: Our school environment   Theme: Environment   Year group: 3/4

Programmes of study	Content focused key questions	Ideas for activities	Resources	Some learning outcomes
10 Investigating how environments change	What is the environment?	Brainstorm what the term means to the children	pictures	Understand that the environment is all around us.
10a how people affect the environment 3e use secondary sources of evidence – pictures, photographs (including aerial) – to inform their studies 3f use ICT to gain access to additional information sources	How have people changed various environments? Why have they done these things?	Use pictures (before and after) to label/identify people's large-scale influence on the environment Use images from CD-ROMs to explore changes made through quarrying, building reservoirs and motorways. Discussion – are all these changes necessary?	before and after aerial photographs/ other images of reservoirs/quarrying/ motorways	Realise that people can affect the environment in large-scale ways and that change is often necessary. Appreciate that change can be positive and negative. Identify human features which have changed the environment on aerial photographs and pictures.
5d about recent or proposed changes in the locality of the school Human activities affect the environment	Have we changed the environment where we live?	Discuss and list on a large piece of paper, the ways people have changed the environment in their local street, e.g. benches, flower beds, repaired/maintained gardens, houses, fences	photographs of local area, outline sketch map, street plans	Are aware that people can affect the environment. Can list features that are the result of change, either for better or worse.
10b how and why people seek to manage and sustain their environment 3f use ICT to assist in handling, classifying and presenting evidence 3a use appropriate geographical vocabulary to describe and interpret their surroundings 3b undertake fieldwork using appropriate techniques	Enquiry into the quality of the local environment. How are we going to find out? Fieldwork in the local area Extended enquiry: Is there a particular area which needs attention or one which is being sustained particularly well?	Design streetometer. Mark on maps ways people have managed the local environment. Use a spreadsheet for the results. Look at reasons for this change and the results Case study of this area identifying ways it can or has been improved. Survey appropriate groups and assess their needs	ideas from *Time and Place Geography Teacher's Book 1* (Simon and Schuster)	Realise that we can measure the quality of the environment by looking at our local street: play areas, car parking, traffic, etc. Appreciate that different people have different attitudes towards the environment. Demonstrate an understanding of why people seek to sustain or change their environment. We can all have an impact on the environment.

Figure 9: **Year 3/4 unit of work on the environment.**

SHORT-TERM PLANNING

Planning at this level is very detailed. Some features of short-term planning are that it:

- identifies how the content is to be taught;
- specifies differentiated learning experiences which are matched to the children's ability;
- details learning objectives – what the children will be able to do, know or understand at the end of a session – against which assessment takes place;
- focuses on classroom organisation;
- maximises the flair and individuality of the teacher.

Short-term planning includes, for example, identifying the route and stops on a year 6 field trip.
Photo: Chris Garnett.

The successful outcome of fieldwork is a direct result of good planning.

ASSESSMENT

Planning and assessment cannot be separated in geography since assessment informs curriculum planning. Level Descriptions can give us a general feeling of what to expect from an 'average' child in different age groups, and are therefore useful when generating broad learning objectives within the medium-term plan. They are also useful when making summative assessments; this involves matching several pieces of a child's work to the Level Descriptions.

Regular formative assessments will be made much more frequently by matching pupils' work against the specific learning objectives in the short-term plan and broad learning objectives in the medium-term plan. These are much more likely to inform our learning and teaching strategies (see Chapter 6 for a detailed discussion of assessment).

References and further reading

Chambers, B. and Donert, K. (1996) *Teaching Geography at Key Stage 2*. Cambridge: Chris Kington Publishing.

Mansfield, K. (1996) 'Progression within the rivers theme', *Primary Geographer*, 25, pp. 23-25.

Morgan, W. (1995) *Plans for Primary Geography*. Sheffield: Geographical Association.

Norris Nicholson, H. (1992) *Geography and History in the National Curriculum*. Sheffield: Geographical Association.

School Curriculum and Assessment Authority (SCAA) (1995) *Planning the Curriculum at Key Stages 1 and 2*. London: SCAA.

SCAA (1997) *Geography at Key Stage 2: Curriculum Planning Guidance for Teachers*. London: SCAA.

Sebba, J. (1991) *Planning for Geography for Pupils with Learning Difficulties*. Sheffield: Geographical Association.

Chapter 4: The planning process

Secure teaching plans should start not from statutory requirements but from children's capabilities, interests and development (Chapter 2). Examples of units of work included in this chapter can be set alongside those in other chapters. For example, the unit of work 'A village as a contrasting locality' (Figure 8) can be linked to the example described in Chapter 17, while environmental examples from the school's region (Figure 9) can be cross-referred to Chapter 21.

The 3 pigs.

Our maps.

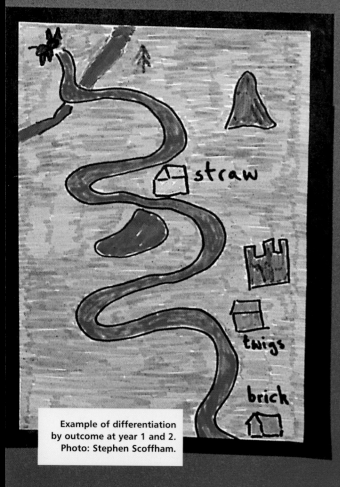

straw

twigs

brick

Example of differentiation by outcome at year 1 and 2. Photo: Stephen Scoffham.

wolfs valley

house

river

house

castle

pond

mountains

cave

wood

house

Progression and differentiation

Chapter 5

Alan Waters

Introduction

Progression and differentiation are features of the planned curriculum which help to ensure effective learning. In essence they are both aspects of planning which aim to match the provision for learning with pupils' needs. This chapter will explore the characteristics and contribution of each to effective planning for primary geography.

Progression

Planning for progression is principally concerned with the longer term sequencing of ideas, knowledge and skills in such a way as to present a logical route for learning. The central aim is to develop pupils' learning in an orderly and helpful way, so that previously acquired skills and abilities assist future progress. Bennetts (1996) has developed the notion of progression as a route for learning and makes the following comments in relation to the role of teachers and their plans:

*'When planning for progression, teachers have to design routes along which their pupils can acquire knowledge and develop understanding, skills, attitudes and values. Such planning requires a clear sense of direction, as well **as good knowledge of the terrain over which they will lead their pupils**' (Bennetts, 1996, p. 81).*

Implicit in this is a clear knowledge of subject content. The established position of geography as part of the statutory curriculum in the primary years has gone a significant way towards increasing both teachers' knowledge and confidence with the subject, to the extent that pointed questions are now frequently being asked by primary teachers about the nature of progression in the subject. This renewed focus on how pupils' learning advances in the study of people, places, processes and patterns, and consequently on how best to plan in such a way as to support their progress, has exposed the paucity of research findings upon which we might draw to underpin and guide future planning. Work on the progressive development of map skills provides a notable and easily understood exception to this general situation and provides some useful pointers.

Progression: some definitions

Attempts to define the essential components of progression in geographical learning are of greatest value when they relate clearly to the process of curriculum design and planning. One such attempt in the 1980s, and still of considerable value in guiding our understanding, was made by HMI in *Geography from 5 to 16 (Curriculum Matters 7)* (HMSO, 1980). Here, progression was seen as having the following elements:

- An increase in breadth of studies – the gradual extension of content, places, themes and environments to be considered.
- An increasing depth of study – the gradual development of general ideas and concepts and deeper understanding of increasingly complex and abstract processes, patterns and relationships.
- An increase in the spatial scale of study – the shift in emphasis from local, smaller scale studies to more distant, regional, national, continental and global scales.
- A continuing development of skills – to include the use of specific geographical skills such as map work and more general skills of enquiry matched to pupils' developing cognitive abilities.
- Increasing opportunity for pupils to examine social, economic, political and environmental issues – the chance to develop greater appreciation and understanding of the influence of people's beliefs, attitudes and values on alternative courses of action relating to people, places and environments.

The thinking was only to a limited extent embodied in the original programmes of study for National Curriculum geography (DES, 1991). However, in the supporting teacher guidance materials (NCC, 1993) the NCC drew heavily on *Curriculum Matters 7* and identified the components of progression shown in Figure 1.

a Jeep

Progression

National Curriculum geography expects teachers to offer their pupils a sequence of work which gradually increases:

- the level of difficulty of practical and intellectual tasks,
  e.g. **from** the use of letter/number co-ordinates **to** four-figure grid references **to** six-figure grid references;
- the breadth of study,
  e.g. **from** certain aspects of a local stream **to** making a similar analysis of a whole river network;
- the depth of study,
  e.g. **from** the local shop and a survey of its produce **to** explanation of its supply pattern, its changing clientele and sales pattern;
- the complexity of phenomena studied and tasks set,
  e.g. **from** a short, straightforward child's journey to school **to** the study of route networks and transport systems;
- the range of scales studied,
  e.g. **from** a solely local area focus **to** distinguishing between the local area, home region, global;
- the understanding of generalised and abstract matters as opposed to the concrete and specific,
  e.g. **from** rainfall in schools grounds **to** the rainfall pattern in the home region;
- the awareness of social, political and environmental issues,
  e.g. **from** personal preference in the locality **to** conflicting, well argued cases for action in the local environment;
- the range, accuracy and complexity of vocabulary used,
  e.g. **from** 'a valley' **to** 'a steep-sided V-shaped valley with a narrow flood plain'.

Not all of these would be present at any one time. Two or three will give a short series of lessons some reliable progression. However, a year's work or whole key stage plan needs to build on most of them.

Figure 1:
Progression in GNC.

During the revision of the earlier statutory Order, SCAA (1994) refined its thinking in terms of the gradual development of learning across both key stages. The programmes of study for each successive key stage prescribe a widening range of places and themes to be studied, through which progression should be planned.

During key stage 1 it is suggested that pupils will increasingly:

- broaden and deepen their knowledge and understanding of places and themes;
- recognise and describe what places are like, using appropriate geographical vocabulary;
- offer their own explanations for what they observe;
- make comparisons between places and between geographical features;
- develop and use appropriate geographical skills

Continuing into key stage 2, SCAA suggests that pupils will increasingly:

- broaden and deepen their knowledge and understanding of places and themes;
- recognise and describe what places are like with accuracy and coherence;
- offer explanations for the characteristics of places;
- identify physical and human processes and describe some of their effects;
- apply geographical ideas learnt in one context to other studies at the same scale;
- acquire information, from secondary sources as well as first-hand observation, to investigate aspects of local and more distant physical and human environments;
- develop and use appropriate geographical skills

(SCAA, 1994).

TOWNS

1) *What a Town Needs*

A town needs houses and flats or anything else which people can live in.Place where people can work,schools and colleges where people can learn.Emergency services,fire engines,police ambulance and if the town is by the sea, coastguard.Public transport and roads,stations etc. for us to use.A town also needs a power source and running water.Public toilets are useful for people travelling through as are car parks.

Our houses need running water,gas and electricity.We need a place to get our food and a service to collect our rubbish.We need the sewage system to keep our houses hygienic.

2) *Who Depends on Who?*

We depend on people who generate the power and they depend on us to keep on buying it,likewise with the water company.We depend on the bin men to get rid of our rubbish.The people who run the schools depend on children going to them and the children depend on the teachers to educate them.We depend on the police to keep the town in order,the fire engine if we have a fire and the ambulance if we are ill.

How might this work on towns progress from here? Work: Kieron O'Connell.

Progression and planning

These descriptions of progression present a view of the development of geographical capability on a broad front, along a gradual incline of difficulty. It is worth considering the implications of this view of progression at each stage in the planning process. Hopkins (1997) has usefully summarised these planning issues into a table as shown in Figure 2.

Three levels of planning	Learning objectives
Long-term (key stage)	Here learning objectives for the key stage are fairly general and should be closely related to the PoS, i.e. knowledge, understanding and skills.
	To promote progression in the development of these objectives over the key stage, decisions focus on how the PoS can be divided into topics or study units, and when these are planned. For example, a spiral approach to the key stage plan could be chosen; this helps pupils revisit, develop and extend their knowledge, concepts and skills.
Medium-term (topic)	Here progression is concerned with the development of knowledge, understanding and skills within a topic or unit, commonly over a term. The focus is on planning sequences of more specific learning objectives that will help ensure pupils make progress, for example by broadening and deepening their knowledge and understanding, and relating these objectives to assessment. Evaluation at the end of the unit helps focus on the progress pupils have made.
Short-term (lesson)	Progression in individual lessons is concerned with the (often small) steps pupils make in the development of knowledge, understanding and skills. Planning is focused on deciding specific objectives, activities and opportunities for assessment, and on differentiation. So at this level progression is an integral part of teaching and learning, related to deciding strategies for individuals and groups, assessing and monitoring progress and deciding future objectives.

Figure 2:
Levels of planning and learning objectives.
Source: Hopkins, 1997.

Clearly, progress for individual pupils is a more complex affair than the above might suggest. Daugherty (1996) refers to the personal and idiosyncratic nature of learning for individuals and the consequent difficulty of developing schemes which would provide such an overview of how learners typically progress. Similarly, all teachers will be aware of the uneven progress (or even regression!) made by some pupils in various aspects of the subject and at various stages in their education, and furthermore of the difficulties of making assumptions about progress based on constructs such as Piaget's stages of intellectual development (depth of geographical understanding!).

However, taking all aspects of current thinking into account, Figure 3 may help to provide an overview of how we might consider progression in our planning: it is set in the context of topic work as this is the planning framework in which geography is usually taught.

Progression in the National Curriculum programmes of study

The National Curriculum programmes of study now embody many of the elements of progression evident in the previous model. In terms of the breadth of places studied, the emphasis is clearly upon the local area in key stage 1 whereas the study of a wider range of distant and contrasting localities becomes more prominent in key stage 2. Similarly, the implied depth and complexity of ideas built in to the study of both the localities, and in the much wider range of themes to be covered during key stage 2, is further evidence of a progressive model of geographical learning in terms of its breadth and depth of knowledge and understanding. Though this is not made explicit, the localities selected for study should get progressively larger and geographically more varied as children mature. Pupils' increasing knowledge – about where places are, what they are like and how they differ; about physical and human features and processes; and about the changes that are occurring in different parts of the world – provides a necessary foundation for their development of geographical understanding.

Progression of understanding and vocabulary

Progression in pupils' geographical understanding has at least two main components:

1 development of the ability to describe geographical features, patterns, processes and changes, using increasingly specific vocabulary associated with the subject, and

2 an increasing ability to apply reason and explain geographical conditions and relationships; this being associated with a grasp of general geographical ideas (concepts, generalisations and models) and the ability to apply them to new situations.

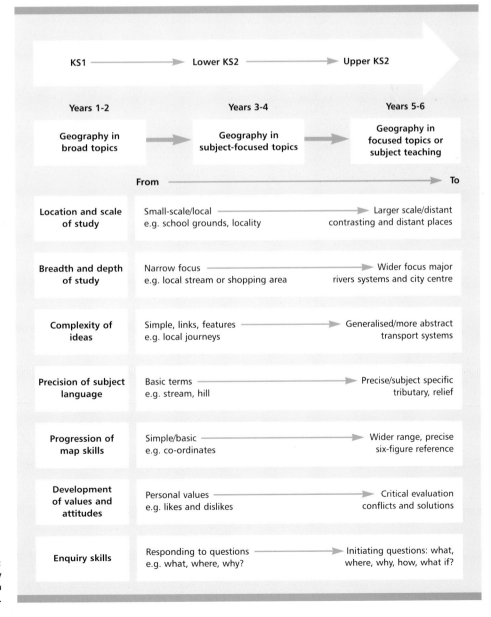

Figure 3:
Planning the geography programme through topic work.

Bennetts illustrates this thinking in the following way:

> 'While the understanding of young pupils is to a large extent limited to objects, actions and relationships which have concrete expression, they gradually develop the ability to think in more general terms. For example, from studying specific cases, pupils can be helped to understand the nature of different types of economic activity and different types of settlement; from studying weather conditions in different parts of the world, they can be helped to understand the meaning of climate. Their acquisition and correct use of geographical vocabulary is intimately linked to their grasp of corresponding concepts. As they mature intellectually, pupils acquire the capacity to appreciate more fully the complex relationships within and between places, and to apply general ideas to their interpretation of information, both from direct observations and from secondary sources such as maps, photographs and written accounts' (Bennetts, 1995, p.46).

To encourage this progression in our planning it may be helpful to follow this sequence:

1 identify the key geographical ideas to be included within a topic;

2 analyse these ideas in terms of the elements of knowledge and understanding required;

3 sequence the elements with regard to pupils' age, ability and previous experience, in a logical and helpful way;

4 identify and introduce the vocabulary necessary to aid progression in understanding;

5 prepare learning materials and tasks which assist pupils to develop their understanding progressively.

An example of one aspect of this planning sequence is shown in Figure 4 which relates to the theme of Rivers. Here the core vocabulary (shown in normal type) associated with particular key stages has been identified, together with the additional vocabulary (shown in italic type) which some pupils might be encouraged to develop. Given the close association between understanding and the active use of subject terminology, such a checklist could provide a guide to the progressive planning of the rivers theme in the primary years. Similar lists could be drawn up for other themes and places during planning.

KS1:	river, stream, hill, slope, steep *mountain, waterfall, valley, flow*
KS2 (lower):	river, stream, hill, slope, steep, mountain, waterfall, valley, flow *source, spring, channel, lake, mouth, erosion*
KS2 (upper):	river, stream, hill, slope, steep, mountain, waterfall, valley, flow, source, spring, channel, lake, mouth, erosion *tributary, reservoir, dam, weir, flood-plain, meander, gorge, rapids, estuary, delta, weathering, transportation, deposition*
Associated vocabulary:	landscape, feature, upper course, middle course, lower course, load, pollution, water cycle

Figure 4:
**River vocabulary:
progression.**

Progression in map skills

A feature common to both key stages is the importance attached to the development of a wide range of skills. Bennetts (1996) notes that the term 'skill' is frequently applied to a great variety of achievements, ranging from performing simple techniques to the use of highly developed intellectual and social competencies. He goes on to separate specific geographic techniques, such as those associated with fieldwork and map work, from general categories of cognitive activity and strategies for enquiry. However, all are important for geographical learning to be effective and all must be planned progressively as far as it is possible.

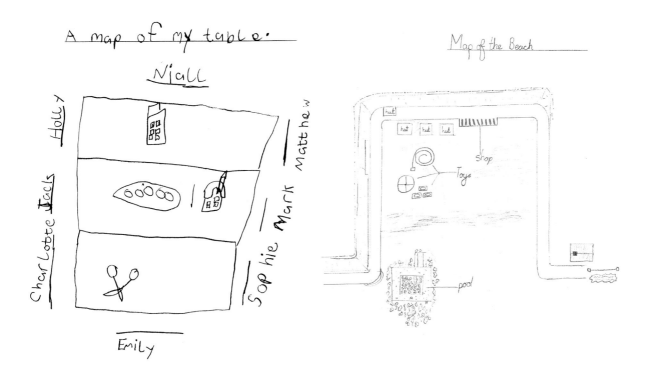

Examples of progression in map skills from key stage 1 to key stage 2. Work: Emily Horsfield, Ainthorpe Primary School, Hull and Carl Stedman, Whitstable Endowed School, Kent.

As Bennetts reminds us, progression in map skills is perhaps the easiest category to plan for within schemes of work. Foley and Janikoun (1996) provide us with a useful grid identifying the components of map skills expected at various age-related levels and this is shown in Figure 5.

The grid attempts to consider the progressive development of skills in terms of the prerequisites necessary to support the next steps in learning. Clearly in this and other aspects of skill development it is necessary to plan increasing complexity in the activities to which the skills relate and increasing precision in their use. In this sense it is clear that skill development is inextricably linked to the progressive development of the context for their application: that is progressively deeper knowledge and understanding of themes and places.

Progression in enquiry and fieldwork skills

As with map skills, the progressive development of fieldwork skills requires careful consideration. We might regard progression in their use as having the following components:

- increasing precision and detail in observation and recording;
- increasing sophistication in the analysis and interpretation of the data;
- increasing spatial scale in which the fieldwork techniques are applied, moving from the familiar to the increasingly unfamiliar;
- increasing complexity of the ideas developed and understanding achieved.

Year/Level	Location	Representation	Distance	Perspective	Style	Drawing	Map use	Map knowledge
Infants (R and Y1)	Follow directions: e.g. up and down, left and right, behind, in front of.	Use own symbols on imaginary maps.	Use relative vocabulary: bigger/smaller, like/dislike, etc.	Model layouts; draw round objects to make a plan.	Extract information and add to picture maps; use globes.	Draw picture maps of imaginary places and from stories.	Talk about own picture maps.	Constant reference to countries, seas and place names on the globe and large maps.
Infants (Level 1/2)	Follow directions: north, south, east and west.	Use class agreed symbols on simple maps.	Spatial matching: begin to match the same area, e.g. continent, country, on a larger or smaller scale map.	Look down on objects to make a plan; plan view needs teaching.	Land/sea on globes; teacher-drawn base maps and large-scale OS maps.	Make a representation of a real or imaginary place.	Follow a route; use a plan; use an infant atlas.	Locate and name on map of UK major features, e.g. seas, rivers, cities, home location.
Lower Junior (Level 3)	Use letter/number co-ordinates to locate features on a map; use four compass points.	Introduce need for a key and standard symbols.	Spatial matching, boundary matching: identify the same boundary, e.g. country boundary on a different scale map.	Draw sketch map from high viewpoint; add slope and height.	Identify features on oblique aerial photographs.	Make a map of a short route with features in the correct order; simple scale drawing.	Use larger scale map outside; use maps of other localities.	Progress towards …
Upper Junior (Level 4)	Use four-figure co-ordinates to locate features on a map; use eight compass points.	Draw a sketch map using symbols and a key; awareness of some OS symbols.	Measure straight-line distance on a plan.	Increasing use of plan view mapping.	Use index and contents page in atlases; medium-scale OS maps.	Draw a variety of thematic maps, based on own data.	Compare large-scale map and vertical air photo; select maps for a purpose.	Identify points of reference specified on Maps A (UK), B (Europe) and C (World) in the National Curriculum document.
Access to key stage 3 programme of study for Level 4 and beyond.	Use six-figure grid references to locate features on OS map; latitude and longitude on atlas maps.	Use OS standard symbols; develop use of atlas symbols.	Scale reading and drawing; comparison of map scale.	Use models to introduce idea of contours; submerge or slice; interpret relief maps; identify relief features.	Interpret distribution maps; concept of globe as flat map.	Draw scale plans of increasing complexity.	Follow route on small-scale OS map and describe features seen.	Begin work on identifying points on Maps D (UK), E (Europe) and F (World) in the National Curriculum document.

Figure 5: **The development of map skills including all National Curriculum requirements. Source: Foley and Janikoun, 1996.**

The requirement to use and develop skills such as these within the context of geographical enquiry is clearly stated in the Geography National Curriculum, in the opening paragraphs to each key stage. The suggested way of meeting this requirement is the application of 'key questions' in increasingly demanding contexts throughout the primary years. The key questions are shown in Figure 6 and the commentary indicates the progressive 'hierarchy' of demands posed by each type of question. For each type of question there are clearly levels at which the question can be addressed. For example, the notion of what a place is like and why places are like they are may well be applied to the simple layout of either classroom or school buildings in key stage 1, whereas both could be more appropriately applied in the context of a detailed land use investigation during key stage 2. Various writers including Rawling (1992) and Lewis and Watts (1995) encourage us to 'ensure that geographical work does not just describe and categorise things as they are'. As children mature, they should explore the more challenging questions which require them to engage in more complex reasoning, explanation and prediction. This point is further developed in the analysis of Level Descriptions later in this chapter.

(a)

Examples of progression in observation skills (a) the gasholder, and the children's interpretations at: (b) reception, (c) year 2, (d) year 4 and (e) year 6. Source; McCloud and Chambers, 1998.

(b)

(c)

(d)

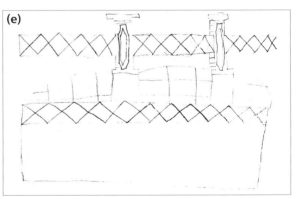

(e)

■ What is this?	Naming/identifying
■ Where is it?	Locating
■ What is it like?	Describing/comparing
■ Why is it like this?	Reasoning
■ What physical and/or human processes caused it to be like this?	Explaining
■ How might things change?	Predicting/hypothesising
■ What do I think and feel about this?	Evaluating/caring

Figure 6: Geographical enquiry: key questions.

Progression in the application of key questions has been built into the National Curriculum Level Descriptions and the increasing expectations are shown in Figure 7.

Level 1 Respond to questions using provided resources and their own observations.

Level 2 Ask and respond to questions using provided resources and their own observations.

Level 3 Use skills and sources of evidence to respond to a range of geographical questions.

Level 4 Suggest suitable geographical questions drawing on their knowledge and understanding.

Level 5 Identify relevant geographical questions drawing on their knowledge and understanding, select and use appropriate skills and evidence to carry out investigation.

Level 6 Identify relevant questions and suggest appropriate sequences of investigation. Select and make effective use of a wide range of skills and evidence to carry out investigation.

Figure 7:
Progression in expectations within Level Descriptions: key questions.

Progression in National Curriculum geography and Level Descriptions

While the purpose of Level Descriptions is principally for summative assessment, they are clearly designed to reflect the progression built into the programmes of study, and as such provide pointers to assist our planning. Though disaggregating each Level Description is certainly not advocated for assessment purposes, it is useful to be aware that they are built upon an understanding of progression in the four aspects of geography shown in Figure 8.

Aspect	Progressive development
Places	features and character contrasts and relationships
Enquiry and skills	geographical enquiry use of skills
Patterns and processes	geographical patterns geographical processes
Environmental relationships and issues	viewpoints and perspectives interactions and management

Figure 8:
Progression and the four aspects of geography.

Progressive expectations in each of these aspects can be traced at each Level (see Figure 9). So, for example, young children are expected to progress from holding their own views (Level 1) on environmental matters, to an appreciation that a variety of views (Level 2) may exist. The ability to compare and justify views is expected at Level 3, whereas the emphasis shifts towards the more abstract understanding of impacts and management at Levels 4 and 5. Following the appearance of Level Descriptions, further guidance was developed by SCAA (1997) to assist our understanding of progression in pupils' performance at ages 7, 9 and 11, adding to our overall appreciation of how we might recognise and monitor progress in learning.

Given the emphasis on manageability the Level Descriptions are by necessity limited in detail. Scoffham (1995) has developed the notion of 'year portraits' to reflect progress in pupils' achievement. Each portrait attempts to merge the requirements of the programme of study with the expectations within the Level Descriptions. As such these provide further guidance in the quest to understand how pupils' learning progresses (Figure 10).

Level	Geographical and enquiry skills	Knowledge and understanding		
		Places	Geographical patterns (physical and human processes)	Environmental issues
1	■ Make observations ■ Express their views ■ Use resources provided and own observations to respond to questions	■ Recognise and make observations about features of places, physical and human	■ Recognise and make observations about physical and human features	■ Express their views on features of the environment of a locality that they find attractive or unattractive
2	■ Describe features ■ Express views ■ Select information from sources provided ■ Use information to ask and respond to questions ■ Begin to use appropriate vocabulary	■ Describe physical and human features of places ■ Recognise features that give places their character ■ Show awareness of places beyond their own locality	■ Describe physical and human features ■ Begin to use the appropriate vocabulary	■ Express views on attractive and unattractive features of the environment or locality
3	■ Describe and make comparisons ■ Use skills and sources of evidence to respond to a range of geographical questions	■ Show awareness that different places may have both similar and different characteristics ■ Offer reasons for some of their observations and judgements about places	■ Describe and make comparisons between physical and human features of different localities ■ Offer explanations for the locations of some of these features	■ Make comparisons between physical and human features of different localities ■ Offer reasons for some of their observations and judgements about places
4	■ Describe patterns ■ Suggest suitable questions for geographical study ■ Use a range of geographical skills and evidence to investigate places and themes ■ Communicate findings using appropriate vocabulary	■ Appreciate the importance of location in understanding places ■ Show understanding of how physical and human processes can change features of a place, and how changes can affect lives and activities of people living there	■ Begin to describe geographical patterns and to appreciate the importance of location ■ Recognise and describe physical and human processes ■ Show understanding of how processes can change the features of places	■ Describe how people can both improve and damage the environment ■ Show understanding of how processes can change the features of places
5	■ Describe patterns and processes (range of physical and human) ■ Identify relevant geographical questions ■ Select and use appropriate skills and evidence to investigate places and themes ■ Present findings both graphically and in writing	■ Describe how processes can lead to similarities and differences between places ■ Describe ways in which places are linked through movement of goods and people ■ Investigate places and reach plausible conclusions	■ Describe and begin to offer explanations for geographical patterns and for a range of physical and human processes ■ Draw on knowledge and understanding to investigate themes and to reach plausible conclusions	■ Offer explanations for ways in which human activities affect the environment and recognise that people attempt to manage and improve environments

Figure 9: **Progression in National Curriculum geography through programmes of study and Level Descriptions.**

Year 1
Much of the work with children of this age will involve *naming and using vocabulary*.

Geographical skills
The children should be able to follow directions round the classroom and school building. They should know that objects look different when viewed from different angles, and be able to draw simple plan views. They will be able to recognise the shape of the British Isles on a map.

Places and themes
The children will begin to recognise that there are different types of shops and houses in the local area. They will be able to talk about changes in the school building and local area. They will know that there are other places and environments around the world which provide a habitat for plants and creatures.

Year 2
Much of the work with children of this age will involve *grouping and sorting*.

Geographical skills
The children should be able to draw a pictorial map to show their route from home to school, marking the landmarks in the correct order. They will have used large-scale maps and aerial photographs of the local area. They will be able to name the continents and oceans on an atlas or globe.

Places and themes
The children will be able to make simple comparisons between their own area and a contrasting locality. They will know that places change and that pollution affects the environment in a number of ways. They will be able to talk about attractive and unattractive places, discuss how places can be improved and obtain information from books and other secondary sources with guidance.

Year 3
Much of the work with children of this age will involve *making simple descriptions*.

Geographical skills
The children should be able to make a pictorial map of a familiar place or draw a picture to show the events in a story. They should show the features in the correct order but their maps will probably not be drawn to scale or show plan views.

Places and themes
The children should be able to follow a simple route in or around their school. They should be able to name selected places and talk about their characteristics using words like noisy, quiet, attractive and ugly. They will also be able to name the continents and be aware of different environments and weather conditions around the world.

Year 4
Much of the work with children of this age will involve *making comparisons*.

Geographical skills
The children should be able to make a simple map using symbols and a key. Their maps are likely to show personal details such as friends' houses, and mix pictures and plan views. They should be able to obtain information from photographs and other secondary sources to support their work and have an increasing knowledge of the world map.

Places and themes
The children will have studied the local area and a contrasting locality either in the UK or overseas. They will be able to describe some of the main characteristics such as the weather, houses, shops and jobs. They should be able to make simple comparisons with their own area, identifying similarities and differences and giving reasons for their opinions.

Year 5
Much of the work with children of this age will involve *giving explanations*.

Geographical skills
The children should be able to draw maps using plan views, follow routes and give simple grid references. They should also be able to use an atlas and be able to identify the UK, Europe and places in the wider world.

Places and themes
The children should be aware how people interact with their surroundings. They will have studied some of the main themes in physical and human geography such as rivers, settlement and environment. Through this work they will begin to offer simple explanations for the links and patterns that they have discovered.

Year 6
Much of the work with children of this age will involve *generalising and drawing conclusions*.

Geographical skills
Children of this age should be able to measure distance and direction on maps. They will be able to obtain information from atlases, reference books and ICT packages to answer geographical questions. They will also be able to plan simple fieldwork investigations in the local area and be familiar with the world map.

Places and themes
The children should be able to explain why the places they have studied are different from each other. They will be aware of issues and conflicts at a variety of scales and recognise that there are often no simple solutions to problems. They will be able to compare different places offering both explanations and generalised conclusions.

Figure 10: Progression in pupil performance in National Curriculum geography: Year portraits. Source: Scoffham, 1995a, b.

Differentiation: issues of context

Photo: Paula Solloway/ Format Photography.

Differentiation refers to the extent to which learning activities and experiences are matched to learning needs for pupils of differing ability. As such, its focus is clearly upon the quality of planned learning activities and their effectiveness in contributing to pupils progress. Equally it relates to the 'process of teaching and learning' and the degree to which the curriculum is made accessible to pupils of all ability.

Traditionally, differentiation has been considered to have a number of key aspects relating to both planning and classroom provision. The NCC (1993), in its guidance for the teaching of primary geography, offered five main approaches to differentiation, noting that no method or strategy should be expected to operate on its own. They are listed and illustrated below to help develop our understanding.

What differentiation involves

i. *Common tasks, sufficiently open-ended for all children to use*
    Differentiation is then seen in terms of outcome, that is the responses of each child.

ii. *Stepped tasks within a lesson or over a unit of work*
    Tasks with many parts where successive parts are more demanding and some children cover only the early parts.

iii. *Pupil grouping*
    Children with distinctive abilities and needs work in a group with similar children on tasks designed for that group; other groups have different tasks.

iv. *Different resources for individuals or groups*
    Some resources give more help to children while other resources demand more and give more scope for initiative.

v. *Teacher support tailored to individual or group needs*
    The form and amount of teacher support differs according to the ability or motivational needs or the specific physical, emotional, social or sensory needs of children.

The emphasis here would appear to be on planning and this is clearly a very important consideration. As Bennetts reminds us:

> *'The greatest scope for constructive differentiation in provision is in planning the curriculum. Teachers can decide how far it is appropriate, and practical, to have different specific objectives, content, teaching methods, learning activities, learning materials and assessment for different pupils' (Bennetts, 1995).*

To be fully effective, however, differentiation also relies on a wide range of professional considerations beyond planning. The challenge of effective differentiation is essentially the challenge of effective teaching in its widest sense. So how do teachers differentiate? What are the principles which underpin successful classroom practice and subsequent geographical learning? The following thoughts are based on observations of strategies at work in the classroom and as such they make the point that differentiation has always been with us. They are listed in the belief that effective differentiation is based upon a wide range of considerations, and not simply upon the design of tasks. Together they cover aspects of planning, classroom practice, response to outcomes and evaluation of provision. Their frequency of use and emphasis vary depending on the nature of the assignment, with 'fitness for purpose' ever present as a guiding principle. In Figure 11 a similar range of considerations is presented as a checklist of performance indicators for differentiation.

Enabling indicators	Process indicators	Outcome indicators
■ Variety of types of resources available	■ Pupils working independently – autonomy	■ Variety of outcomes to tasks set
■ Variety of reading levels within text	■ Pupils making own decisions	■ Personal progress for each pupil
■ Variety of tasks set	■ Pupils working in a variety of ways	■ Different outcomes for each pupil
■ Clear communication – teacher to pupils	■ Classroom organisation appropriate to task	■ Improved achievement
■ Teacher language accessible to all pupils	■ Pupils working on a variety of tasks	■ Improved behaviour – motivation
■ Attitudes to pupils – accepting and valuing	■ All pupils involved – motivated – on task	■ Improved school results – test results
■ Appropriate grouping of children	■ Variety of resources in use	■ Increased understanding by pupils of subject
■ Flexible timetabling and class sizes	■ Teacher accessible throughout lesson	■ A variety of completed tasks visible
■ Materials and tools readily available	■ Positive pupil-teacher interaction	■ Pupils able to plan for next stage of learning
■ Arrangement – organisation of classroom	■ Positive pupil interaction	■ Reduced truancy rates – monitored
■ Non-text resources available, e.g. visual	■ Pupils involved in negotiating their work	■ Less teacher stress – absence
■ Non-teaching assistant support available and used	■ Outcomes presented in a variety of ways	■ Improved awareness of pupils' needs
■ Teacher aware of pupils' prior learning	■ Variety of assessment techniques in use	■ Improved awareness of abilities
■ Clear presentation of task or lesson	■ Variety of teacher roles evident	■ Pupil awareness of purpose and objectives
■ Flexible deadlines for completion of work	■ Co-operative learning taking place	■ Improved whole-school ethos
■ Availability of training for staff	■ Appropriate worksheets and guides in use	■ Enjoyment in learning

Figure 11:
Monitoring and evaluation – performance indicators for differentiation.

When addressing differentiation the following issues might be considered:

Getting started: tasks must be presented so that all children know how to begin. This means careful consideration of language level, complexity of tasks, number of stages, degree of structure, and pace and manner of introducing the task. Generally, less able pupils need more structure and sequence, whereas higher attainers can frequently succeed with more open-ended enquiries.

Targets and objectives: we need to be clear in our planning and documentation about the learning objectives and anticipated outcomes for each activity, in terms of knowledge, skills and understanding. The identification of core objectives together with reinforcement and extension targets is a useful model to pursue at this stage.

Shared objectives: there is value in making clear to pupils at the outset the direction and intentions for the lesson, to enable them to:

- be clear about teacher expectations;
- take greater control of their learning;
- measure their own progress and achievement.

Variety of approach: since children vary in their learning needs, so should the strategies employed to attempt to differentiate the learning experience vary. Geography is fortunate in its potential for adopting a wide range of learning approaches to increase the possibility of matching learning needs. A variety of teaching and learning situations can both motivate and differentiate at the same time.

Selection of resources: here the potential range is enormous and the resources used should reflect a process of careful selection and evaluation. Pupils are usually capable of addressing the same overall question or task as long as they have material that is suitable for their needs. Bright pupils need to work at the edge of their understanding using appropriately demanding resources. Lower attaining pupils need to have barriers to learning removed. Textbook tasks rarely span the full ability range, and their use frequently requires us to provide supplementary materials and worksheets. Here issues of clarity, format, language and ease of access need to be at the forefront.

Open-ended tasks:
differentiation can be promoted through either open-ended or highly structured tasks, both approaches having their benefits. Given a suitable common task pupils can engage with a challenge and demonstrate their understanding in a variety of ways and at levels appropriate to their ability. However, such a response cannot be guaranteed and we need to be wary of regarding differentiation by outcome alone as a 'comfortable' solution to a complex situation. The transmission of teacher expectations plays a major role in this context.

Structured tasks: some pupils require a more structured approach to give their best. The use of a series of questions with an incline of difficulty is frequently used to good effect. Here again we need to be aware of the obvious pitfall of requiring all pupils, especially the more able, to perform a succession of low level tasks which offer little challenge before proceeding to more demanding activities.

Pace of learning: setting time targets at the outset or during lessons can be an effective technique. When sympathetically employed such targets can allow individuals and groups of pupils of varied abilities to control the pace and depth of their learning.

Teacher direction: this is a component of most classroom activity and we need to reflect on its impact on the pace of learning for the range

Structured tasks can include teacher participation.
Photo: Steve Watts.

London and the River Thames

Photo: Lisa Wollett/ Format Photography.

of abilities present in any teaching group. Excessive didactic teaching, frequently pitched at the middle ability band and with its associated uniformity of pace, can be beyond the needs of the least able while failing to stretch the brightest. Ideally, in order to make its contribution to differentiation, exposition should be carefully balanced against the time when pupils are working independently or collaboratively, at a variety of speeds and at a range of depths.

Consolidating learning: the techniques of breaking lessons down into a sequence of activities and consolidation points can be a useful approach. Periodic whole-class discussion to identify and bring together the key teaching points, to reinforce and record by use of a black/white board, and to relate this to the next activity can be of significant help to the learner. This is particularly so for those whose short-term retention is a barrier to progress.

Questioning: given the amount of time devoted to whole-class questioning, the quality of this form of teaching is of crucial importance. In terms of its impact on differentiation there are a number of relevant issues, including:

- the balance of closed and open-ended questions employed;
- the sequencing of questions towards the learning objective;
- the use of searching supplementary questions;
- the recognition of the value of pupils' responses (rather than the answer we are looking for);
- the atmosphere, positive or negative, in which questioning is employed.

Eyre reminds us of the importance of questioning as a means of stretching the more able, offering the following thoughts:

'*Teachers who do this well seem to be consistently asking pupils for their views and ideas, and encouraging them to spot discrepancies, inconsistencies and patterns. In short, as Bloom would term it, to analyse, synthesise and evaluate, therefore making sense of their learning. This enables the most able to become confident, articulate learners who can move forward independently' (Eyre, 1997).*

These postage stamp designs offer a useful assessment exercise, as they show whether pupils have identified the features that give St Lucia its character. Photo: Stephen Scoffham.

Teacher intervention: this is frequently regarded as the 'craft of the classroom' and concerns the capacity to know the needs of individuals, to make rapid judgement about levels of understanding, to diagnose difficulties, and to make positive responses at a variety of levels in order to move the learning forward. Set within a context of positive, consistent feedback this can be a powerful component of differentiated provision.

Assessment and feedback: the quality of feedback, both written and oral, provides a further opportunity to differentiate. To be effective in terms of progressing learning, it needs to be consistent, positive and provided during or as soon as possible after the learning experience. The hallmark is surely one of quality not quantity. The more we know about individual pupils the more we are able to differentiate their learning.

Pupil grouping and oracy: the extent to which a variety of learning situations are employed, and the emphasis and value placed on oral work, require careful planning in terms of differentiated provision. When set against lessons which are over-directed, pairwork and group discussion can provide opportunities to vary both the pace and depth of progress, to share knowledge and understanding, and to clarify values and attitudes in an accessible context. Discussion can enable pupils of all abilities to articulate and broaden their geographical understanding, and the organisation of groups and the value attached to discussion are key issues for consideration when planning schemes of work.

Learning environment: the creation of a lively, interesting classroom, and the degree to which resources and display are an aspect of planned and incidental learning, can provide a further dimension to differentiated provision.

The above collection of observations is certainly not exhaustive. However, what emerges is a recognition that differentiation is in large part simply effective teaching in its broadest sense and not merely the setting of open-ended or more targeted tasks for various ability groups. It is the planned process of opening out the curriculum to enable access for all pupils. It is a set of principles upon which classroom provision is based. Diversity of approach and flexibility are essential, as is the ethos and attitude of a school towards equal opportunity and entitlement. Figure 12 goes some way towards capturing the full range of strategies implicit in the previous discussion.

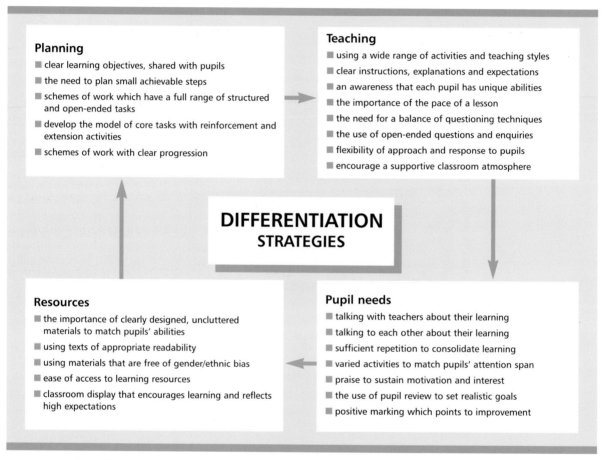

Planning
- clear learning objectives, shared with pupils
- the need to plan small achievable steps
- schemes of work which have a full range of structured and open-ended tasks
- develop the model of core tasks with reinforcement and extension activities
- schemes of work with clear progression

Teaching
- using a wide range of activities and teaching styles
- clear instructions, explanations and expectations
- an awareness that each pupil has unique abilities
- the importance of the pace of a lesson
- the need for a balance of questioning techniques
- the use of open-ended questions and enquiries
- flexibility of approach and response to pupils
- encourage a supportive classroom atmosphere

DIFFERENTIATION STRATEGIES

Resources
- the importance of clearly designed, uncluttered materials to match pupils' abilities
- using texts of appropriate readability
- using materials that are free of gender/ethnic bias
- ease of access to learning resources
- classroom display that encourages learning and reflects high expectations

Pupil needs
- talking with teachers about their learning
- talking to each other about their learning
- sufficient repetition to consolidate learning
- varied activities to match pupils' attention span
- praise to sustain motivation and interest
- the use of pupil review to set realistic goals
- positive marking which points to improvement

Figure 12:
Differentiation strategies.

References and further reading

Bennetts, T. (1995) 'Continuity and progression', *Primary Geographer*, 21, pp. 44-46.

Bennetts, T. (1996) 'Progression and differentiation' in Bailey, P. and Fox, P. (eds) *Geography Teachers' Handbook*. Sheffield: Geographical Association, pp. 81-93.

Daugherty, R. (1996) 'Defining and measuring progression in geography' in Rawling, E. and Daugherty, R. (eds) *Geography into the Twenty-first Century*. Chichester: John Wiley, pp. 195-215.

Department of Education and Science (DES) (1991) *Geography in the National Curriculum (England)*. London: DES/HMSO.

Department for Education (DFE) (1995) *Geography in the National Curriculum: England*. London: HMSO.

Eyre, D. (1997) 'Able children in ordinary schools', *Special Children Magazine*, March, pp. 17-19.

Foley, M. and Janikoun, J. (1996) *The Really Practical Guide to Primary Geography* (second edition). Cheltenham: Stanley Thornes.

HMSO (1980) *Geography from 5 to 16 (Curriculum Matters 7)*. London: HMSO

Hopkins, J. (1997) 'Planning for progression and continuity: the role of assessment' unpublished GA Examination and Assessment Working Group paper.

Lewis, E. and Watts, S. (1995) 'A world of words', *Primary Geographer*, 21, pp. 33-5.

McCloud, K. and Chambers, B. (1998) Student research project: changing perceptions of a local view', *Primary Geographer*, 33, pp. 26-7.

National Curriculum Council (NCC) (1993) *Teaching Geography at Key Stages 1 and 2: An Inset Guide*. York: NCC.

Primary Geographer, number 28, January 1997. *Focus on Differentiation*.

Primary Geographer, number 33, April 1998. *Focus on Progression*.

Rawling, E. (1992) *Programmes of Study: Try This Approach*. Sheffield: Geographical Association.

School Curriculum and Assessment Authority (SCAA) (1994) *Geography in the National Curriculum: Draft Proposals*. London: SCAA.

SCAA (1997) *Expectations in Geography at Key Stages 1 and 2*. London: SCAA.

Scoffham, S., *et al*. (1995a) *Geography Key Stage 1 Teacher's Resource Book*. Cheltenham: Stanley Thornes.

Scoffham, S., *et al*. (1995b) *Geography Key Stage 2 Teacher's Resource Book*. Cheltenham: Stanley Thornes.

Sebba, J. (1991) *Planning for Primary Geography for Pupils with Learning Difficulties*. Sheffield: Geographical Association.

Chapter 5: Progression and differentiation

It is vital that the planning process (Chapter 4) takes full account of children's different but developing capabilities. Examples used in this chapter link to other parts of the book (e.g. Figure 2: River vocabulary connects to Chapter 24; progression in map skills is identified in Chapter 11, and progression in enquiry and field skills in Chapters 12 and 14 respectively). The relationship between children's progress and how it may be rated using Level Descriptions is the focus of the next chapter.

COAL, OIL, GAS

BY

Charlotte Kennedy
+
Genesta Gunn

This house shows how we use coal, oil and gas in the homes.

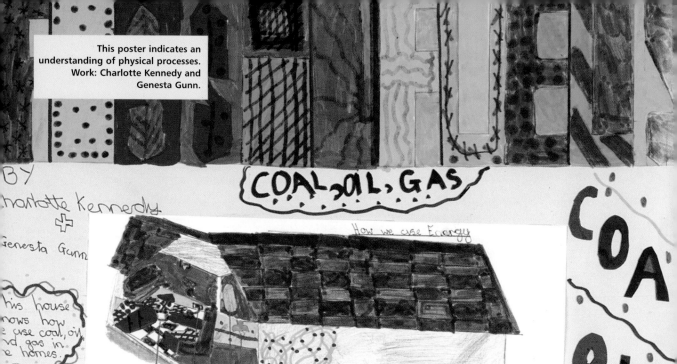

How we use Energy

Gas Cooker

Electric mains

lighting

Gas or electricity heated water

water pipe

Gas pipe

electricity pipe

COAL OIL GAS

How Oil Was Formed

...historic seas and lagoons teemed with plant and animal life. After they died, they become part of concentrated organic materials which built in the area were they had been carried by river or ocean currents.

...millions of years passed, the earth changed its form many times and this, organic material was covered by mud, silt and sand of passing ...s.

Coal to Gas

Coal reserved that are difficult to reach may be exploited by converting the coal to gas while still underground. Shafts are dug down to the coal seam and coal set alight. Carefully controlled amounts of oxygen or ... are pumped in so the coal only partly burns.

Assessment, recording and reporting

Chapter 6

Mike Hillary

Why assess geography?

Whether or not you decide to continue teaching the full Geography National Curriculum for key stages 1 and 2, it is important that the work children do should be accompanied by arrangements to assess it, record it, and report on their progress.

Any such arrangements need to be simple, straightforward and manageable. Experience has taught us that overcomplicated systems do not last for long and fall down under the day-to-day pressures of teaching in key stages 1 and 2. Assessment should be part of the normal planning, teaching and learning cycle (Figure 1).

Figure 1:
The interconnections between planning, teaching, learning and assessment.
Photo: Steve Watts.

Good assessment, recording and reporting systems will:
- allow you to assess the standard that pupils are reaching at any one point in time;
- help pupils to know how well they are doing and what they need to do to get better;
- provide information to help you plan more appropriate teaching and learning activities;
- provide information on pupils' progress for parents, colleagues in the school and for any transfer documentation to other schools.

For both assessing and reporting pupils progress, the Level Descriptions in the Geography National Curriculum provide a useful reference point. Also useful is the SCAA guidance document (SCAA, 1997a) which gives some examples of what children are expected to know, understand and be able to do by the end of year 2, year 4 and year 6. Assessing and recording pupils' attainment will help you plan for progression in pupils' learning and for continuity in children's experience across key stages 1 and 2.

The programmes of study and Level Descriptions can be broken down into four main areas:

> 1. knowledge and understanding of places;
> 2. knowledge and understanding of patterns and processes;
> 3. knowledge and understanding of environmental relationships and issues;
> 4. the ability to undertake enquiry and to use geographical skills
> (SCAA, 1997a).

Assessment does not have to relate to only one of these. Pupils carrying out an enquiry into their local river, for example, will be using a range of geographical skills and studying a range of physical or human processes. Similarly, pupils learning about a particular place and using photographs to help them may be developing their understanding of environmental relationships and issues, as well as developing geographical skills of photograph interpretation. Other examples can be found in Figure 2.

How to assess in geography

Assessment will be both formal and informal, formative and summative. We often underestimate the amount of informal assessment that goes on in the classroom through observation and discussion with children during day-to-day teaching and learning activities. This professional judgement is often an important component in, and starting point for, more formal assessments which might include written work, mapwork, oral presentations, group work, posters, role play and fieldwork. A range of assessment techniques is necessary to assess a pupil's full range of ability; some pupils are better at mapwork, others may find oral presentations easier. Also, some types of assessment lend themselves to a particular topic: role play and simulations are often a good way to explore the range of views connected to an environmental issue such as a local bypass; posters are effective in allowing pupils to 'express their own views on attractive and unattractive features of the environment' (Level 2); completing a table will allow pupils to compare two localities showing 'an awareness that different places may have both similar and different characteristics (Level 3) (see Figure 3); and using a large-scale map of the local area will allow pupils to 'begin to describe geographical patterns' (Level 4), e.g. street patterns. Assessing enquiries is particularly useful where pupils have had the opportunity to 'suggest suitable geographical questions for study', can 'use a range of geographical skills' and can 'communicate their findings using appropriate vocabulary' (Level 4). Fieldwork may allow more able pupils to 'describe and begin to offer explanations for a range of physical and human processes' (Level 5).

Assessment tasks should be integral to a unit of work, not bolt on additions at the end of the unit. This is *not* to suggest that Level Descriptions are used for detailed assessment of individual pieces of work but that pupils have a range of opportunities, in different contexts, to show what they are capable of. Level Descriptions are designed for end-of-key stage summative judgements, as a 'best fit' description of a child's ability in geography.

How can assessment help me in my planning?

Assessment of pupils' attainment can be used to inform any stage of the learning process (Figure 1). You might have information regarding the children's experience and ability which you can use in your initial planning. For example, looking at local area 1:5000 maps to explore street patterns (Level 4) will be difficult if children have not already understood similarities and differences in types of housing (Level 3). Day-to-day assessment of children's progress should inform short-term lesson planning if, for example, the children have clearly misunderstood something they have studied recently. Continuing with the

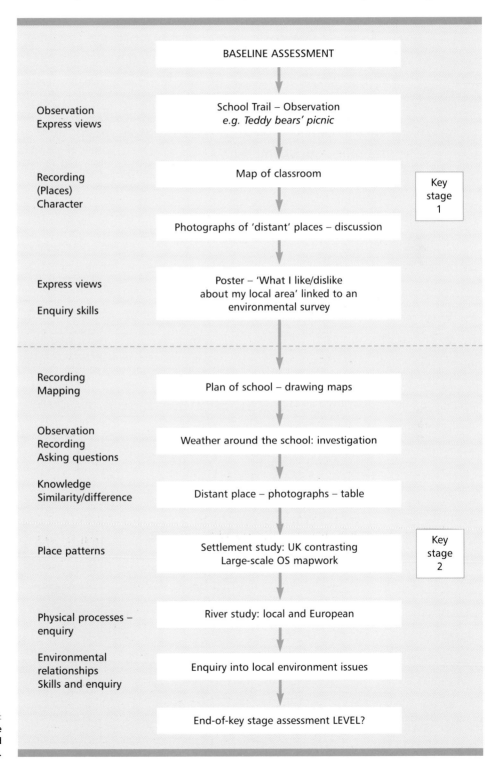

Figure 2:
A model of possible assessment and recording opportunities.

planned work may not be possible or desirable if children have failed to grasp the ideas involved, or to develop the skills necessary to complete the task. Short-term changes to teaching methods are also necessary if things are clearly not developing within the lesson as planned. More visual information is often required to help children understand physical processes, for example a video of flowing water or photographs to illustrate similarities and differences. Summative end-of-key stage assessment may make you reconsider the progress that certain types of children are making. Have more able year 6 pupils made sufficient progress based upon their key stage 1 assessment and evidence from year 4? Have less able pupils made appropriate progress related to their previous experience?

Assessment used in this way becomes a valuable tool for constantly monitoring planning, teaching and learning.

> It is a very small village very quiet much different than Bletchley. We found a net under a bridge in the water (River Marigold) Ms Grimble said that it was a net to slow the water down under the bridge.

	Furzton	Ilam
Surroundings:-	It is busy with lots of parks and not many fields.	It has lots of fields and animals. Trees and rivers.
Noises./Level.	You can hear lots of cars and lorrys. buses.	Animals, birds, rivers, flowing. Children shouting
Busy?	It is very crowded. busy and	It is quiet not at all busy not at all crowded.
Buildings.	They are quite new they are mostly made out of brick. They look	They are oldish the are mostly made of stone they look very could colourful. old fasioned
Population	There are lots 105 people in Furton It is very busy.	There arn't so many people it is very quiet.

what we are comparing in....	Furzton	Ilam
Jobs	There are lots of jobs to get because we have the city.	There arn't so many jobs because there arn't so many shops.
communications	There are lots of roads and it isn't very far from the air port.	There are twisty roads and not very many car of buses were used.

Figure 3: Examples of pupils' work on contrasting localities. What does it show the pupils can do? Source: SCAA, 1997b, p.16. Reproduced with permission.

When and what to assess in geography

If assessment is part of the normal planning, teaching and learning cycle then assessment opportunities should occur naturally throughout key stages 1 and 2. In Figure 2 we can see a model of possible opportunities for assessment. The number of assessment opportunities will vary according to the number and frequency of geographical activities. Baseline assessment will give some early indications of pupils awareness of the world around them. **Reception** pupils often differ widely in their perception of the world, as the briefest of conversations will soon reveal. In **year 1** pupils will often be asked to complete a school trail of some sort to visit different sites in the school or school grounds. This is an opportunity to assess their ability to observe and possibly record by drawing pictures of objects in the playground, etc. Even the youngest children might also be able to express their views about the environment, i.e. what they like and dislike about the playground/school grounds. This might be done as part of a 'Teddy bears' picnic' when children can be asked to select the best site for their afternoon picnic using their senses to assess characteristics such as surface, texture, shade, view, smell, etc.

Photo: Chris Garnett.

Maps of the classroom drawn by the children will help you to assess their early mapping skills and their ability to adopt a 'birds eye view'. In **year 2** the pupils' ability to describe and comment on attractive and unattractive features (Level 2) might be assessed through group discussions of photographs or posters that they make to illustrate a local environmental survey in the vicinity of the school. Discussion about distant localities will allow you to assess pupils' development of geographical skills and geographical vocabulary.

In **key stage 2** pupils often draw a plan of the school and this will allow you to assess the development of their mapping skills from key stage 1. Similarly an investigation of the microclimates around the school allows you to assess pupils' ability to carry out a geographical enquiry. The children can be asked to pose questions, many of which will be 'geographical' in nature. The children's ability to measure, record, present data and draw conclusions can also be assessed depending on the amount of teacher support. The amount of support could vary according to the age or ability of pupils. This will clearly need to be taken into account when deciding on the level of pupils' attainment in these areas.

A weather enquiry around the school will also provide an opportunity to assess the children's ability to carry out a scientific investigation and incorporate ICT skills such as storing, retrieving and presenting data. With older and more able pupils in key stage 2 you will want to assess their ability to make comparisons (Level 3), observe and record similarities and differences, and begin to identify patterns and processes (Level 4). Comparing your local area to a UK contrasting locality and a distant locality will allow you to do this (see Figure 4).

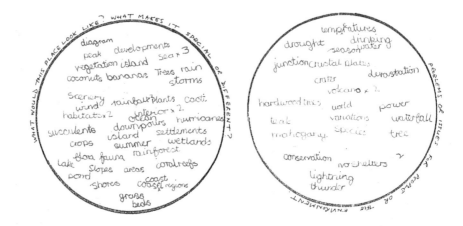

Figure 4:
An example of a pupil's work on a distant locality.
Source: SCAA, 1997b. p. 21. Reproduced with permission.

Developing map skills can be assessed in **years 3 and 4** by using large-scale (1:1250 or 1:2500) maps of your local area and elsewhere as part of your settlement studies. These maps together with smaller scale 1:25 000 and 1:50 000 maps can be used in **years 5 and 6** to assess the pupils' ability to describe patterns, for example street patterns, settlement patterns (village shapes) or river patterns in an area.

Globe and atlas skills can be assessed throughout the key stages by constantly referring to them and asking pupils to use them whenever possible to find places. In key stage 2 pupils can be asked to compare the characteristics of places, e.g. heights, temperatures, rainfall, and (for Level 4) to describe the patterns of temperature, rainfall, etc., across the UK, Europe and the world.

The development of enquiry skills can be assessed in **years 5 and 6** by allowing more independent investigations into themes such as environmental issues or river studies. The SCAA booklet (SCAA, 1997b, p. 24) illustrates the type of work you might expect by the end of year 6. These investigations will only be Level 4 however if pupils are allowed to 'generate their own geographical questions, select appropriate techniques and record their own conclusions'.

So from Figure 2 we can see that assessment may focus on one or two pieces of work per year to give a balanced view of pupils' abilities across geographical skills, places and themes by the end of the key stage.

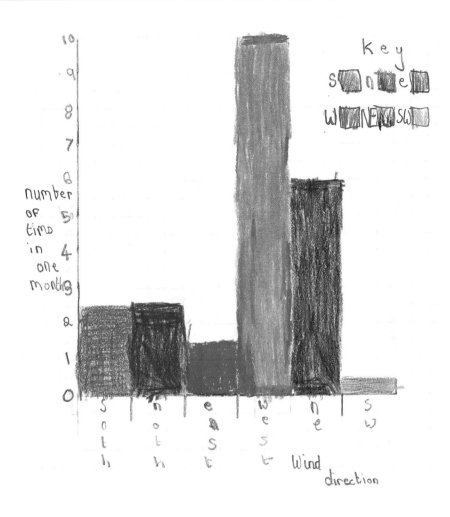

The ability to present data on weather studies can be assessed. Work: Helen, Newbottle Primary School, Sunderland.

River studies allow for independent investigations at years 5 and 6. Photo: Paula Richardson.

What to record

The assessment opportunities you choose will clearly depend on the school's own scheme of work. Similarly, the school's policy on assessment and recording may determine the amount of recording necessary. It is *not* necessary to record or keep evidence of individual pupil's work. The SCAA guidance makes it clear that it is up to the teacher and school how much evidence they want to keep in order to make their own professional judgement about a pupil's progress. Having said that it would seem sensible to record pupils' progress occasionally in the form of teachers' comments or records. If a scheme like the one suggested in Figure 2

Photo: Steve Watts.

was used it would be sufficient for you simply to indicate whether a child could or could not do certain things, like recognise the countries of the UK or be aware of places beyond their own locality, by the end of year 2. Class teachers together with the co-ordinator/subject leader could decide on a few basic skills that they agree to assess at some point during the year, e.g. related to map skills. In schools with more than one class per year class teachers might also agree to carry out the same activity and compare pupils' performance. A most valuable tool in helping to assess pupils' performance and progression is the subject portfolio.

Do I need to keep a portfolio of children's work?

You do not have to keep a portfolio of individual pupils work. However, developing a geography portfolio for the whole school is a good idea because it allows the co-ordinator/subject leader to:

- develop consistent judgements across year groups;
- come to a common understanding of Level Descriptions;
- help 'new' teachers to the school or year group develop appropriate expectations;
- show aspects of progression and continuity across the key stages/school;
- monitor the quality and standards of geography across the school.

A portfolio might include examples of pupils' work from different year groups, to show progression, or it might have pieces of work from different abilities within the same year group, to show differentiation. As well as pupils' work you could include photographs, teachers' notes, annotations to work, etc.

These annotations to pupils' work might include:

1 Context:
   - what instructions were given;
   - how much teacher support was provided;
   - resources used;
   - whether work was undertaken individually or in groups.

2 A brief commentary on the evidence the work offers of geographical knowledge, understanding, skills.

3 Other evidence of pupils' work – discussions, comments to the teacher, etc.

4 Comments relating to ways in which this work could be taken further, to constraints, e.g. resources, and to whether this work is in line with expectations.

Work from different abilities within the same year group show differentiation. Photo: Stephen Scoffham.

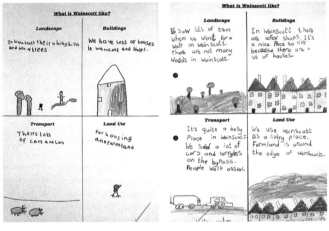

Such a portfolio of work would make an invaluable tool for INSET activities related to geography and an excellent record to show to parents, visitors and visiting OFSTED inspectors.

Subject leaders are playing an increasing role in monitoring their subject area and, for them, a good portfolio is an ideal alternative to visiting colleagues' classrooms to observe their teaching, particularly given the normal time constraints.

As part of school-based INSET teachers can be encouraged to complete a proforma for their children's work similar to 1-4 above then staff can discuss the relative merits of individual pupil's work and perhaps relate these to aspects of the Level Descriptions.

How should assessment help pupils?

Photo: Format Partners.

As well as feedback to teachers, assessment should also help provide feedback to pupils. Children and parents need to know how they are doing and how they can improve. They may want to know how they are doing in relation to the rest of the class and also in relation to national criteria, i.e. Level Descriptions. Teachers' comments on pupils' work tend to be limited to congratulatory statements, i.e. 'well done', 'you have tried hard', or comments related to the presentation of the work and while these are important and necessary it is useful to supplement them with more subject-specific comments.

Comments to pupils and subject reports to parents can also make reference to progress in the subject since last year and any target setting for individual pupils, for example:

- X has some interesting ideas about the local environment;
- X makes good use of geographical words;
- X gives good reasons for his/her observations about rivers;
- X is making good progress in developing his/her map skills.
- X has made good progress in geographical skills such as questioning and needs to develop his/her geographical knowledge of places.

A full report to the parents might read:

X has good knowledge of places. He/she is making good progress in his/her understanding of environmental issues. X needs to develop his/her observational skills further.

Conclusion

Assessment in geography in the short term needs to be part and parcel of everyday teaching to provide instant feedback to children. This helps to motivate pupils and helps the teacher to react quickly and deal with any misunderstandings or develop teaching points further than previously envisaged. Informal, everyday assessment of pupils' progress will help identify those needing support and revision and those who need an extra challenge and extension (i.e. differentiation). Assessment in the medium and long term will also help teachers and co-ordinators to monitor the progress that individuals and groups are making over a period of time: a term, a year, a key stage and so on.

Some further general observations about assessment are as follows:

- It should not be bolted on but form part of the planning, teaching and learning cycle.
- It can just as easily take place at the beginning of a topic as at the end, i.e. class discussions, topic webs/mental maps or generating a list of geographical questions for study (see Figure 5).
- It can take place as part of the normal teaching and learning activities in class time.
- An assessment focus or opportunity (Figure 2) may need to be identified in a particular term or topic.
- Using Level Descriptions in conjunction with the SCAA guidance may provide a useful starting point for assessing pupils' work in relation to the four key areas of geographical study.
- A range of assessment techniques should be used to assess the full range of abilities.
- Records of pupils' progress will help with the transfer of information and can also usefully inform medium-term planning.
- A school portfolio is invaluable for monitoring progress and staff training.
- Reports to parents should be subject specific, indicate progress made and set appropriate targets where possible.

Ultimately, assessment should help teachers to reflect on what and how they are teaching and help pupils to improve their performance in geography. It is not an end in itself!

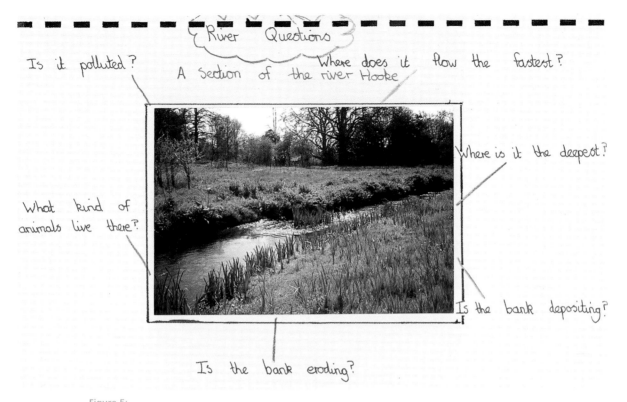

River Questions

Is it polluted?

A section of the river Hooke

Where does it flow the fastest?

Where is it the deepest?

What kind of animals live there?

Is the bank depositing?

Is the bank eroding?

Figure 5:
Using a photograph to generate geographical questions. Work: Year 6 pupil, Greenford School, Maiden Newton, Dorset.

References and further reading

Butt, G., Lambert, D. and Telfer, S. (1995) *Assessment Works: Approaches to Assessment in Geography at Key Stages 1, 2 and 3.* Sheffield: Geographical Association.

Janikoun, J. (1995) 'Working with Level Descriptions', *Primary Geographer*, 21, pp. 18-19.

Mee, K. (1996) 'Assessment: new opportunities', *Primary Geographer*, 24, pp. 16-17.

School Curriculum and Assessment Authority (SCAA) (1995) *Consistency in Teacher Assessment.* London: SCAA.

SCAA (1997a) *Geography at Key Stage 2: Curriculum Planning Guidance for Teachers.* London: SCAA.

SCAA (1997b) *Expectations in Geography at Key Stages 1 and 2.* London: SCAA.

Chapter 6: Assessment, recording and reporting

Assessment is integral to the planning process, not a bolt-on extra (see Chapter 4). It is therefore important to plan clear, measurable learning objectives appropriate to the age and ability of the pupils (see Chapter 5).

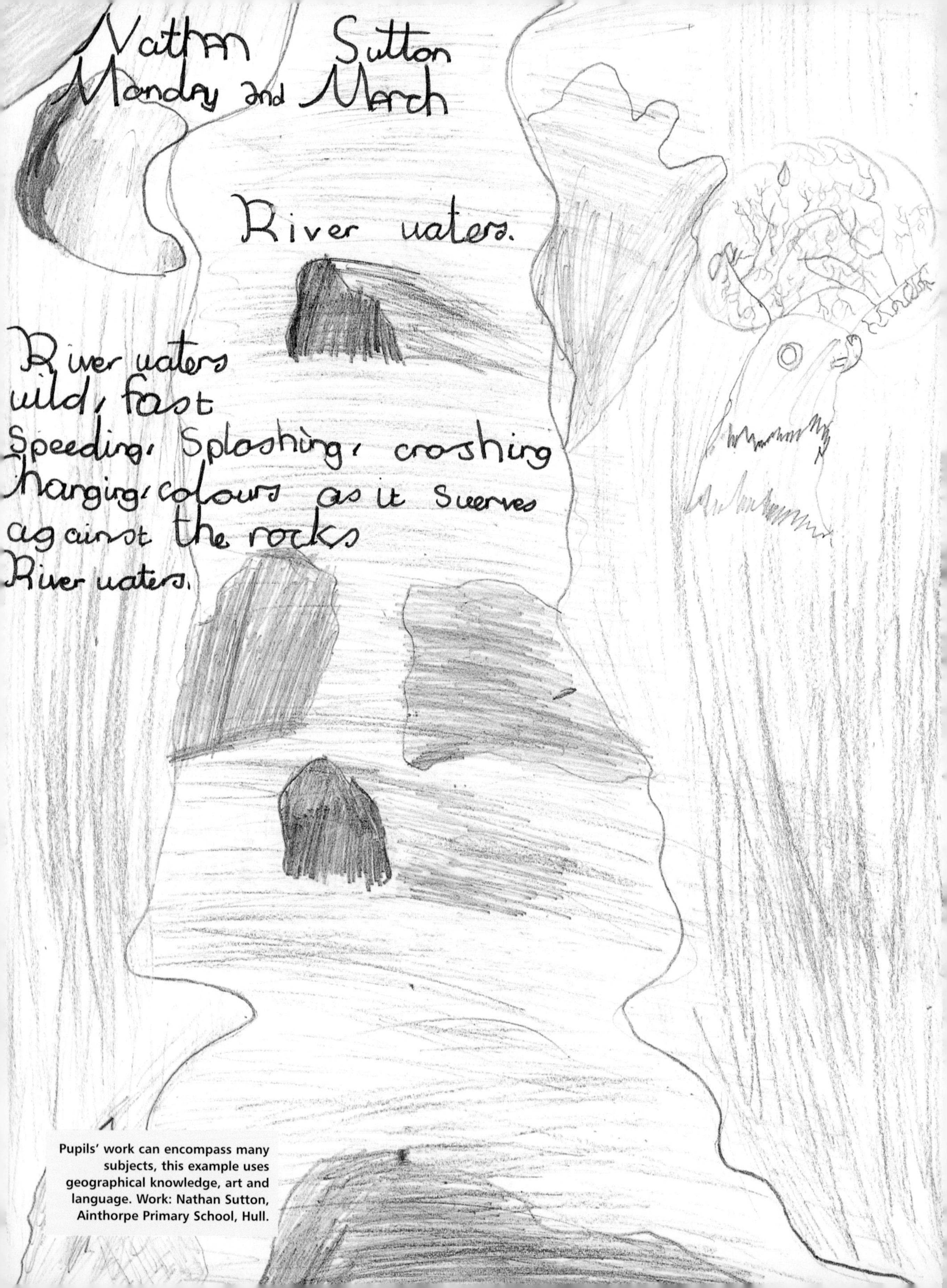

Nathan Sutton
Monday 2nd March
River waters.
River waters
wild, fast
Speeding, Splashing, crashing
changing colours as it swerves
against the rocks
River waters.

Pupils' work can encompass many subjects, this example uses geographical knowledge, art and language. Work: Nathan Sutton, Ainthorpe Primary School, Hull.

Geography in the whole curriculum

As children mature, they become increasingly aware of their surroundings, and of the character of the place where they live. Gradually, as a result of direct and indirect experience, their horizons expand and they begin to construct a picture of other places, some of which are very different from their own. This process will have started before they ever reach the school gates, and the mix of a child's natural curiosity about the world, and the widening freedoms associated with growing up, ensure that this personal geography will continue to grow with or without a formal education throughout the primary years. The central purpose of a geography programme is to provide for children a fuller, more rounded, structured opportunity to view, perceive, understand and respond to the world in which they live.

A balanced geography programme will take children into four areas of learning:

1 a growing knowledge and understanding of places
2 a growing knowledge and understanding of patterns and processes
3 a growing knowledge and understanding of people/environment relationships and issues
4 a growing ability to undertake geographical enquiry and to draw on a widening range of skills

These aspects are all identified in the National Curriculum and reflected in the Level Descriptions, designed to help assess pupils' progress in the subject. They are also developed elsewhere in this book. In total they represent a crucial contribution to children's education in helping them to understand the world in which they live.

Yet there is more. In addition to this important and distinctive contribution, geography can play a significant role in the broader education of young people through its contribution to larger aims. This chapter explores the relationship between geography and the core and other foundation subjects, and the cross-curricular themes.

Geography and the core curriculum

GEOGRAPHY AND LANGUAGE

It is self evident that children's learning fundamentally depends on their ability to read, write, speak and listen. It is right that the development of language skills is a major preoccupation in the early years curriculum. But language develops through its use in purposeful contexts, and the majority of these are likely to lie outside English lessons. Geography can provide rich contexts for language development (see Chapter 13).

Listening is as important a skill as reading, writing and speaking. Photo: Chris Garnett.

In geography pupils use spoken or written language to:

- *Engage:* relate new information to existing experience and knowledge
- *Explore:* investigate, hypothesise, speculate, question, negotiate
- *Transform/restructure:* argue, reason, justify, consider, compare, evaluate, confirm, reassure, clarify, select, modify, plan
- *Present/record:* demonstrate, convey understanding, narrate, describe
- *Reflect:* consider and evaluate new understanding

Geography work is developed using an enquiry approach which focuses upon key geographical questions such as 'What/where is it?', 'What is it like?', 'How did it get like this?', 'How and why is it changing?' This approach may begin with teacher-framed questions but should encourage children to pose their own questions, however simple, from an early stage. Such questions will take them into a wide range of activities – describing, explaining, predicting, responding – each of which will make some specific demands on the use of language.

If you develop geography topics through a series of organising questions, you will make possible a wide range of language activity in writing, reading, speaking and listening (see Chapters 12 and 13). Such an approach illustrates that it is not possible to teach geography without using language, that language development is a natural outcome of the topic, and that when teachers develop children's language use in geography they both contribute to general capabilities and strengthen subject understanding.

It is likely that the emphasis in early years will be upon establishing and developing a geographical vocabulary, and that progression through the primary years will involve increasing complexity and maturity in the use of language. Language is essential to concept formation. In planning geography it is useful to consider a list of starter vocabulary which may be introduced to the child, perhaps for the first time, or possibly to widen or deepen the meaning of a word already known. It is also worth considering how children's deepening understanding is reflected in the extended language they use. For example, Figure 1 shows how work on scales and sequences can help develop children's understanding, and enable them to make sense of higher order concepts, such as relief and weather systems, in later years.

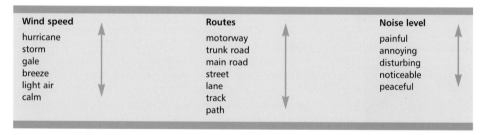

Wind speed	Routes	Noise level
hurricane	motorway	painful
storm	trunk road	annoying
gale	main road	disturbing
breeze	street	noticeable
light air	lane	peaceful
calm	track	
	path	

Figure 1:
Some environmental
word scales.
Source: Ward, 1998.

Many teachers have come to see the value of well chosen stories (and indeed nursery rhymes, fairy tales and poems) to develop children's ideas about the world. This is particularly, but not only, appropriate at key stage 1, where story time is a well established and popular part of the classroom day. Stories allow children to visit people, places and situations which they could not have direct experience of. They can introduce a breadth of place, giving a different perspective of a situation, and making space for the child to respond. A well illustrated story book can both stimulate and motivate, sometimes providing a secondary source to link to the child's own experience. You need to remember that very few children's stories have been written specifically to meet the needs of the geography curriculum, and that care is needed, as always, to avoid stereotyping and distortion. Given that, there is a growing range of beautifully written and illustrated story books which, when used to complement other resources, can support the programmes for both geography and English in an imaginative and stimulating way.

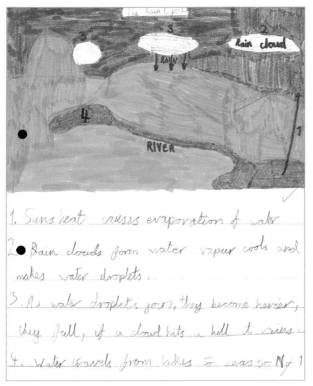

The Rain Cycle

rain cloud

RIVER

1. Suns heat causes evaporation of water

2. ● Rain clouds form water vapour cools and makes water droplets.

3. As water droplets join, they become heavier, they fall, if a cloud hits a hill it rains.

4. Water travels from lakes to seas or No 1

Making sense of weather systems.

GEOGRAPHY AND MATHEMATICS

The relationship between geography and maths is equally strong, and mutually reinforcing. Go to any maths scheme and you are likely to find activities which draw on local investigations of traffic or houses, shops or the weather. Children need to use and apply mathematics in real contexts which are meaningful to them. It makes sense to co-ordinate the teaching programme so that some number activity can be developed through geographical investigations, the mathematical skills being identified and introduced for the first time or used as reinforcement. This will give a double benefit. It will make more efficient use of time, and will reduce the proportion of isolated, second-hand exercises which characterise some maths schemes.

There is no shortage of contexts in geography for the development of mathematical skills. Geography needs to use number in relation to a wide range of spatial concepts – area, location, direction, scale, distance, size, and so on – which it shares with mathematics. OFSTED reports sometimes criticise geography work in primary schools when mapping skills are taught separately from place or theme contexts. Children need to use these skills in pursuit of their investigations if they are to understand their value and application. If this is the case within the subject, how much more is it so that mathematics needs to be brought to life by its use when applied to real situations?

Skills relating to large-scale plans and maps, such as using grid references, compass points or scale, can extend to the mathematical aspects of the globe and of atlas maps. Exploration of lines of latitude and longitude and the special parallels of Equator, Tropics and Arctic/Antarctic circles, can be compared on globes and world maps in order to understand how a rounded surface may be represented on a flat surface. Without familiarity with lines of latitude and longitude, children will have difficulty locating places in an atlas using the index. Time zones, day and night, the seasons, all depend on an understanding of the Earth as a sphere and its movements around the sun.

When children collect records of weather observation over a period of time, display them on a chart and draw conclusions about patterns and trends, they are using number in ways essential to geographical enquiry.

There are four stages which are characteristic of most field activities:

1 Collecting data (amount of rainfall, proportion of cloud cover, temperature).

2 Recording data (using tables, tally sheets or charts to cumulate scores).

3 Presenting data (producing tables, block and line graphs, pie diagrams).

4 Interpreting data (converting to percentages, summary tables, before comparing patterns, making linkages or drawing conclusions).

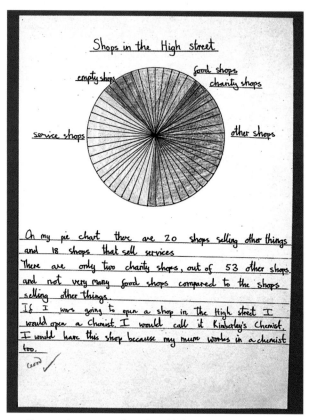

Using mathematics in geography investigations. Photo: Stephen Scoffham.

In investigations such as a weather study, a shopping survey, or a river study, the use of measurement and number gives precision and focus. It moves children beyond qualitative judgements, giving sharpness to their investigation. Similarly, there are many activities relating to sorting, ordering and classifying features, which benefit from mathematical approaches. Collections of leaves, beach pebbles, plants in a quadrat, vehicles in a traffic survey, may all be sub-divided, grouped or sorted for their distinctive or overlapping characteristics – an important set work activity in mathematics.

Arguably it is easier to track progression in a subject such as mathematics, which is essentially linear in structure, than it is geography. The maths which pupils use in geography should be commensurate with their number ability, and this implies a need to cross-check regularly. One aspect of progression which is common to both subjects, and indeed others, relates to increasing precision. Pupils towards the end of key stage 2 should be using equipment (compass, clinometer, rain gauge) to measure accurately. They should be able to use figures (e.g. for temperatures or rainfall) rather than just describing places as hot or wet.

The use of number is important in describing and analysing geographical patterns and processes, so just as we should ensure that geography provides contexts to develop mathematical applications, so equally should we look for numerical approaches to bring precision and rigour to our work in geography.

GEOGRAPHY AND SCIENCE

The Dearing revisions to the National Curriculum went some way towards clarifying the previous overlapping content in science and geography. Subsequent relaxation of the Orders for foundation subjects has made it more important still to consider where the content of the science Order (which remains statutory) can support work in geography. Current primary practice, in which content is often integrated, means that remaining areas of overlap or contact may be seen more as helpful than problematic to geography.

Aspects relating to rocks, plants and soils are largely to be found in science programmes, although it is inevitable that many outside investigations of local environments will bring science and geography content together. We find other contact points in relation to the built environment and materials and their properties, and indeed in the science relating to the Earth and beyond, which considers the relative position of the Earth and sun and effects upon seasonal changes. Since some content overlap or connection remains strong, we need to consider the best curriculum sequence to ensure coherent learning and the most efficient use of time. Successful learning in one area often requires prior learning in another. For example, the Rivers theme at key stage 2 geography

Photo: Cory Bevington/
Photofusion.

includes studying the main components of the water cycle. In the same key stage pupils should be taught in science the part that evaporation and condensation play in the water cycle. Should these two aspects be taught together? ... or one before the other? ... and if so, which one? Introduction of new material, and subsequent reinforcement, depends upon careful curriculum mapping. Whatever aspects of both programmes may be brought together in a teaching scheme, we should remember that the specific focus of geography is people in their physical environments.

Much process work in the two subjects is similar. In geography the enquiry approach is advocated in all key stages and this closely matches the scientific investigation requirements. For example, the importance of 'fair testing' could well emerge when pupils investigate the speed of flow of a river section by timing floats across a measured distance. Testing, experimenting, hypothesising, collecting evidence systematically and using graphical skills to display it, are all parts of a scientific approach which is common to both areas. Common ground is most apparent when working in the field, but the scientific approach permeates much classroom work as well.

GEOGRAPHY AND TECHNOLOGY

Children need to see the relevance and application of information and communications technology to their geographical enquiries. The availability of high quality subject-specific software has until recently been a limiting factor, although this situation is fast improving, and perhaps outstripping the ability of schools to pay for it! Meanwhile there is much generic software relating to word processing, graphing and mapping, and desk-top publishing which is more widely available for use in geography contexts. The potential contribution of geography to ICT is more fully discussed in Chapter 15.

Some content in geography links well to the technology Order. For example, many processes which might be studied in a geographical investigation (how a farm works, making cars, how river basins are formed) can be represented and explained through a systems approach which sets out inputs, processes and outputs. This is essentially the same methodology as in design technology. There are opportunities to construct materials in support of geographical investigations, for example:

- A scale model of the playground to develop an environmental improvement scheme.
  – Where would be the best place for ... a new bench? ... a bird table?
- A sand tray model to demonstrate the effect of running water on slopes, or to illustrate how contour lines are used to describe slopes.
- Making a range of equipment to use when measuring in the field (a quadrat, a clinometer, home made measuring tapes).
- Designing experiments to show how hot air rises, air pressure can change, water evaporates or condenses.
- Designing and constructing home made weather recording instruments, possibly to be used in conjunction with commercial instruments (weather vane, rain gauge, sundial).

Using home-made
recording
instruments.
Photo: Kate Russell.

In each case the design, construction and usage of technology is tested against, and used to develop, ideas in geography.

In summary, a confident case can be made that geography can bear directly on children's progress in the core subjects. Although it is important to cross refer with core subject programmes, it is evident that it would be difficult to do geography at all without using language, or number, or scientific methods and practical applications. This is less a matter of planning in these cross elements than of being aware of wider learning opportunities when devising work in geography. Other planning issues emerge in relation to geography and other foundation subjects.

Geography and the other foundation subjects

Children do not see the world in self-contained chunks called history or science. The National Curriculum in primary years is presented using what is essentially a secondary subject-based model. Yet it remains the case that most primary schools for most of the time organise children's learning though topics or themes which straddle several curriculum areas. Teachers, especially at key stage 1, have worked wonders to retain broad, child-centred topics as a vehicle through which to develop much of the prescribed curriculum in meaningful ways. A discernible trend in junior years has been some movement towards reducing the range of topics, and perhaps grouping them around fewer subjects, possibly giving a clear lead to one subject at a time. Teachers have also found that some subject-specific content is best taught 'straight', possibly outside the topic framework, and in some instances schools have moved towards a subject-based timetable, particularly in years 5 and 6, as a way of meeting new demands.

Figure 2 represents an attempt to plan out a geography programme in this way, by gradually moving the emphasis from broad to more focused, and then quite specific topics. The proposition is that geography at key stage 1 can well develop alongside much else through a range of familiar, child- centred topics, while topics in key stage 2 become narrower.

At its best, topic work can be outstandingly good and should be defended, provided that note is taken of recent OFSTED criticism so that:

- pupils keep some contact with geography between topics which fully include it;
- pupils do not go too long without meeting the subject;
- pupils know when studying geography that that is what they are doing;
- some topics have a clear geography focus.

Links are well established with history, although the way in which the history programme of study is set out in history study units does not match the geography presentation. Local area work is common to both, and given the shared interest in ideas of continuity and change it would be almost perverse to not seek to bring the programmes together. In Figure 3, Foley and Janikoun (1996) bring together nicely an enquiry sequence to combine place and time dimensions in a local investigation. Where history study units on distant places are developed (e.g. Egypt, Greece, Benin) there is scope to extend the time dimensions

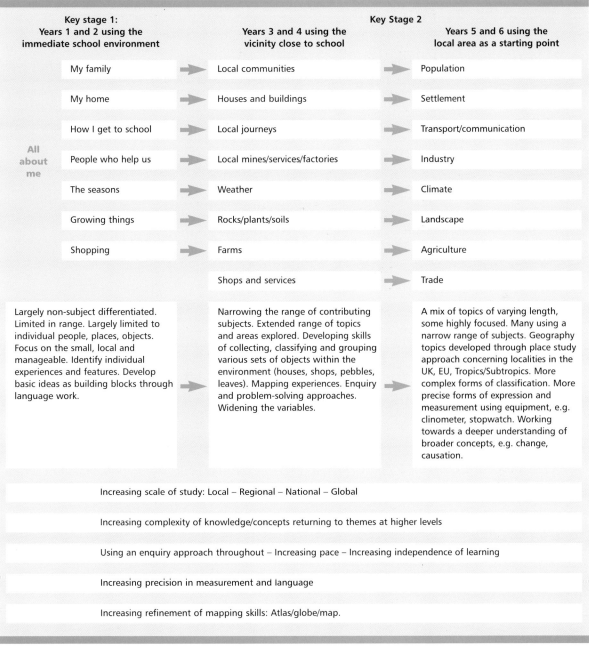

Key stage 1: Years 1 and 2 using the immediate school environment	Key Stage 2 Years 3 and 4 using the vicinity close to school	Years 5 and 6 using the local area as a starting point
My family	Local communities	Population
My home	Houses and buildings	Settlement
How I get to school	Local journeys	Transport/communication
People who help us	Local mines/services/factories	Industry
The seasons	Weather	Climate
Growing things	Rocks/plants/soils	Landscape
Shopping	Farms	Agriculture
	Shops and services	Trade

All about me

Largely non-subject differentiated. Limited in range. Largely limited to individual people, places, objects. Focus on the small, local and manageable. Identify individual experiences and features. Develop basic ideas as building blocks through language work.	Narrowing the range of contributing subjects. Extended range of topics and areas explored. Developing skills of collecting, classifying and grouping various sets of objects within the environment (houses, shops, pebbles, leaves). Mapping experiences. Enquiry and problem-solving approaches. Widening the variables.	A mix of topics of varying length, some highly focused. Many using a narrow range of subjects. Geography topics developed through place study approach concerning localities in the UK, EU, Tropics/Subtropics. More complex forms of classification. More precise forms of expression and measurement using equipment, e.g. clinometer, stopwatch. Working towards a deeper understanding of broader concepts, e.g. change, causation.

Increasing scale of study: Local – Regional – National – Global

Increasing complexity of knowledge/concepts returning to themes at higher levels

Using an enquiry approach throughout – Increasing pace – Increasing independence of learning

Increasing precision in measurement and language

Increasing refinement of mapping skills: Atlas/globe/map.

Figure 2:
Planning a geography programme through topic work.

Geography (now)	History (then)
Where is this place?	Where is/was this place?
What is it like now?	What was it like in ...?
Why is it like this?	Why was it like this?
How is it changing?	Why did it change?
How can we find out about it now?	How can we find out what it was like then?
What is it like to live there now?	What would it have been like to live there then?

Figure 3:
Key questions for geography local area/ history supplementary study. Source: Foley and Janikoun, 1996.

from past to present to future through combining the two subjects. In both local and distant studies at key stage 2, the predominant scale is smaller in geography than history even if the revised geography Order requires work at a range of scales.

Less often developed, though potentially of great value, are the connections that may be made with art. This is particularly the case in relation to environmental education, where studies of both built and natural environments may be enhanced through aesthetic/emotional aspects and indeed the analytical, observational approaches which an art perspective can bring. Art has much to offer in raising sensitivity to places both through skills application and sensory response. In *Primary School Geography*, Marsden and Hughes (1994) usefully identify contact points between geography, art and history (Figure 4) in both skills and concepts.

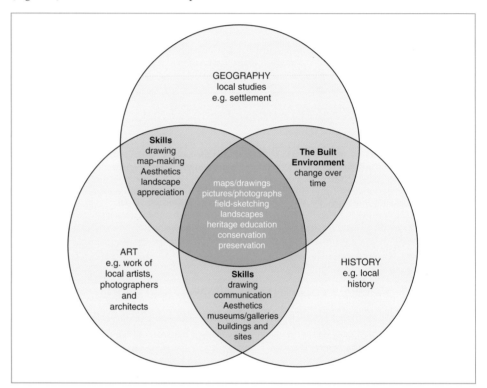

GEOGRAPHY
local studies
e.g. settlement

Skills
drawing
map-making
Aesthetics
landscape
appreciation

The Built Environment
change over time

maps/drawings
pictures/photographs
field-sketching
landscapes
heritage education
conservation
preservation

ART
e.g. work of local artists, photographers and architects

Skills
drawing
communication
Aesthetics
museums/galleries
buildings and sites

HISTORY
e.g. local history

Figure 4:
Cross-curricular contact points.
Source: Marsden and Hughes, 1994, p.113.

Geography and art combine in the urban and rural environments.

Looking at the types of work people do at Reception (Jarrod Beauchamp, Ainthorpe Primary School, Hull) and year 2 (Peter Adcock, Sharrow N&I School, Sheffield).

Geography and the cross-curricular themes and dimensions

The whole curriculum is more than the sum total of its subjects. The NCC (1989) identified a range of cross-curricular dimensions, skills and themes designed to permeate all our work in schools. The dimensions concerned all aspects of equal opportunity; and much in geography – particularly where it brings children into contact with cultures and ethnic groups different from their own – offers important opportunities to contribute to multicultural education. Whole-curriculum learning skills such as oracy, numeracy and graphicacy can all find expression and development in geography, and many have been referred to above.

Cross-curricular themes first appeared in the context of the original National Curriculum. These are economic and industrial understanding, health education, careers education, environmental education, and citizenship. Guidance booklets were issued relating to each theme at a time when teachers were trying to come to terms with the subject Orders and appeared to represent substantial additional content to an already overloaded curriculum (NCC, 1990a-e). The subsequent Dearing revisions related only to subject reductions, and very little has since been said or written about the cross-curricular themes. Nevertheless, they should not be neglected; neither should they be thought of as yet more content to be squeezed into the curriculum. More productive is to see them as a way to make geography more meaningful and relevant to children's lives and learning. If through a geography programme children emerge without a concern for their environment and some understanding of how they can be involved in protecting it, then something has gone badly wrong. Looking at the different types of work that people do in the school locality is not only addressing part of the geography programme, but also presenting children with role models and contributing to their economic understanding. Similarly, any work which focuses on people–place issues is likely to generate questions about who decides, how, and what can be done to influence decision making. All this is the beginnings of an understanding of citizenship (Figure 5).

Above all we need to be aware that today's pupils are tomorrow's citizens. They will not only function in local and national contexts within which they will carry rights and responsibilities; increasingly their lives as European citizens will become important:

> 'Whatever Britain's future role in the EU, whatever the degree of political unification, integration with mainland Europe is unavoidable; understanding our European neighbours and avoiding xenophobia are not just lofty aspirations, they will be survival skills. Anglicised package holidays; glamorous brochures and advertisements; stereotyped images in films and television programmes; they all play a part in distorting the reality of life in other European countries. By carrying out a balanced study of an EU locality in the classroom we can avoid the stereotypes and present our children with more realistic images, fostering tolerance and appreciation of the language, culture and ways of life of other European peoples' (Krause et al., 1994, p. 6).

Finally, and perhaps most importantly, young people are global citizens who should be entitled to have access to, and the skills and understanding to handle knowledge about global as well as local events – along with the ability to see how these are connected. Such abilities include:

> ■ 'being open minded and having a questioning approach to the world around them;
>
> ■ having confidence in themselves and standing up for justice and equality;
>
> ■ a willingness to develop their own identities, language and culture;
>
> ■ a willingness to learn from the perspectives and viewpoints of others.'
> (DEC(Birmingham), 1997).

Figure 5:
Geography as a basis for citizenship.

Geography deals with:
- **everyday people** in
- **everyday places** in the
- **everyday world,**

and so it is an ideal vehicle to develop many aspects of:
- economic and industrial understanding
- health education
- careers education
- environmental education
- education for citizenship

at a level appropriate to the primary school.

Figure 6:
Geography within the whole primary curriculum.

Whole-curriculum characteristics	Supported by geography Orders	Extended/enriched by optional activities
■ mastery of basic skills; reading, writing, number	reinforce basic skills through use of television, radio, photos, stories, maps, information books related to the geography programme	The Order carries examples of appropriate activities to deliver the statutory core. Teachers may build on this to provide extension/ enrichment opportunities.
■ some familiarity with basic ICT skills	use software to develop geographical skills, knowledge and understanding through place and theme investigations	
■ development of new language to establish basic concepts across core and foundation subjects	widen vocabulary relating to exploration of their own and other places, and geographical themes identified in the programme	Examples of extension opportunities might be designed to meet one of the following:
■ an identified knowledge base	Places: see NC revised Orders and maps. Themes: see NC revised Orders	
■ foundation experiences in science/technology	identify current overlap/contact with each subject. Use of scientific/practical approaches in geography programmes	■ differentiate individual learning needs by extending or reinforcing the concept or skill
■ development of aesthetic sensibilities	foster in children a sense of wonder at the beauty of the world around them	
■ establishment of learning skills – listening, speaking, thinking, interacting	reinforcement of general learning skills through geography. Specific geographical skills – handle a globe, make own simple sketch maps, use models and large-scale plans, present information in a variety of ways which include writing, speaking, drawing pictures and simple graphs	■ provide pupil or group guided choice/opportunity to develop a topic further ■ introduce new concept or content to reinforce
■ establishment of social skills – co-operating, sharing, respect for others and property	develop an interest in/concern for the school, the local environment and community, as well as more distant people and places. Learn to work together on geographical investigations	■ contribute a geography element to a cross-/whole-curriculum initiative
■ development of physical skills, including fine motor skills	handle geographical resources and equipment both in and out of the classroom	■ connect the geography programme to a school-based initiative
■ development of self-knowledge, self-confidence and self-esteem	placing the child in his or her world. Knowing home address, aspects of people and places locally, connecting with other localities, as part of one world	
■ development of curiosity	through identifying and pursuing geographical questions	■ capitalise upon pupil, group or teacher enthusiasm or a topical event
■ experience of learning opportunities which are: first-hand, pupil centred, practical/experiential, interactive, investigative	contribute to/enhance through geographical work the range of learning opportunities appropriate to children in primary schools	

Cross-curricular themes can be made explicit through geography work when teachers are aware of them and seek to link learning in geography to children's wider experiences. Helping children to make connections within geography, between geography and other learning, and between geography and their lives outside school, is something only partly to do with planning and forethought. As much, it concerns the age-old capacity of good teachers to maximise learning opportunities as and when they occur.

Some of the connections identified in this chapter are listed in Figure 6. You might consider the extent to which your geography plans already support whole-curriculum aims, and the extent to which they could be made to do so further.

References and further reading

Carter, R. (1990) 'Planning the geography programme through topic work', *Primary Geographer*, 5, pp. 12-13.

Development Education Centre (DEC)(Birmingham)/Birmingham City Council (1997) *Forward Thinking* (leaflet), Birmingham: DEC/Birmingham CC.

Foley, M. and Janikoun, J. (1996) *The Really Practical Guide to Primary Geography* (second edition). Cheltenham: Stanley Thornes.

Krause, J., Pulle, F., Janaway, S. and Jones, S. (1994) 'Don't jump the European ship', *Primary Geographer*, 19, pp. 4-6.

Marsden, W. and Hughes, J. (1994) *Primary School Geography*. London: David Fulton.

National Curriculum Council (NCC) (1989) *The National Curriculum and Whole Curriculum Planning*. York: NCC.

NCC (1990a) *Education for Economic and Industrial Understanding: Curriculum Guidance 4*. York: NCC.

NCC (1990b) *Health Education: Curriculum Guidance 5*. York: NCC.

NCC (1990c) *Careers Education and Guidance: Curriculum Guidance 6*. York: NCC.

NCC (1990d) *Environmental Education: Curriculum Guidance 7*. York: NCC.

NCC (1990e) *Education for Citizenship: Curriculum Guidance 8*. York: NCC.

Ward, H. (1998) 'Geographical vocabulary' in Scoffham, S. (ed) *Primary Sources*. Sheffield: Geographical Association, pp. 20-21.

Chapter 7: Geography in the whole curriculum

In Chapter 13 Liz Lewis explores further the interdependence of language development and geographical understanding. The wider contribution of geography to the whole primary curriculum is also referred to in Chapter 3.

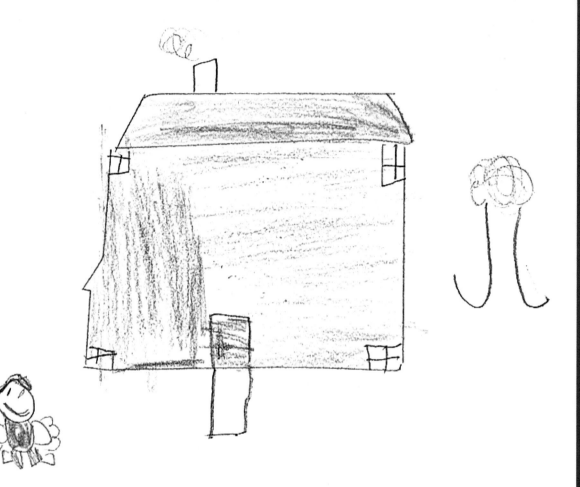

a SPecial Place a scAhool be causWe

Learn.

The geography co-ordinator

Introduction

As most primary teachers teach the full range of subjects, the advent of the National Curriculum, with its requirement for specialist subject knowledge in both core and foundation subjects, called for a new mechanism to help schools deliver the new requirement. Most schools have now appointed a teacher to co-ordinate each subject, including geography.

Geography is included as a foundation subject in the National Curriculum because it offers so much to our children as young citizens. The role of the co-ordinator is crucial to the success of the geography teaching in a primary school. As a co-ordinator you will need to be able to demonstrate to children its wide ranging contribution to the knowledge of places near and far, the ability to explain features of their world and the skills with which to investigate as well as to exist.

However, superior subject knowledge is not necessarily a criterion for the choice of a co-ordinator. In some cases, particularly in small schools, geography is co-ordinated by the Headteacher or Deputy headteacher in addition to a multitude of other responsibilities. And, although in an average-sized school most teachers have responsibility for co-ordinating only one subject, geography is frequently linked with history, often additionally with RE, and one co-ordinator is responsible for both or all subjects. Typically, senior teachers co-ordinate the core subjects and receive responsibility allowances; geography is often co-ordinated by the least experienced newcomer who receives no responsibility allowance.

The descriptions in Figure 1 derive from conversations with teachers in Cheshire, and give a sense of the diversity of background of geography co-ordinators.

Which of these descriptions best matches with the position you find yourself in?

- You were appointed this year as a newly-qualified teacher and were asked whether you would co-ordinate geography.
- You are in a small school where everybody has to carry a wide range of curriculum responsibilities and there was no one else to take responsibility for geography.
- You are the Headteacher and no one else felt able to do the co-ordinator job so it fell to you.
- You last studied geography when you were 14, but you are interested in outdoor education so it seemed natural to give the co-ordinator job to you.
- You are already the history co-ordinator and geography and history are seen as being very similar.
- You are a geography graduate and it was assumed that made you an ideal co-ordinator.
- You have attended INSET or further study linked to the work of geography co-ordinator and feel quite confident about the role.

Figure 1:
Descriptions of different geography co-ordinators.

So it is that teachers with a wide range of background and experience find themselves co-ordinating geography. This chapter sets out the responsibilities of the geography co-ordinator and helps you to match up your background and experience with your responsibilities, your school's agreed agenda for action and your own professional needs.

The 'person specification' of a subject co-ordinator

As demonstrated above, the teaching experience and subject expertise of geography co-ordinators may vary considerably. You are likely to teach most or all of the curriculum, although you may combine a generalist role with advice and support for geography; you may be a semi-specialist; you may teach geography full time. Whatever your background, however, to be a successful curriculum co-ordinator you need the elements shown in Figure 2.

- the professional skills to work with colleagues collaboratively, sharing curriculum expertise;
- a clearly defined role backed up by a job description which is linked to the school management structure;
- a sound working knowledge of the geography curriculum and access to appropriate INSET for professional development;
- a perspective of the geography curriculum in the context of a whole curriculum framework;
- the ability to produce a key stage plan or plans which meet statutory and school requirements;
- the ability to produce detailed topic or unit plans;
- the support of the Headteacher and governing body and full recognition of the role in the school development plan;
- clearly identified budgetary provision.

Figure 2:
Elements of a good geography co-ordinator.
Source: Cheshire CC, 1996.

What are the responsibilities of the geography co-ordinator?

The main responsibilities of the geography co-ordinator are shown in Figure 3, and each element is expanded in the paragraphs that follow. The order in which they appear is not intended to indicate a rank order. The first thing to do if you are appointed to this post is take stock of your situation: your priorities are likely to emerge from that process.

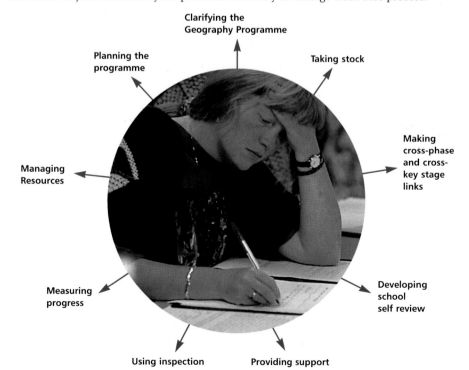

Clarifying the Geography Programme

Planning the programme

Taking stock

Making cross-phase and cross-key stage links

Managing Resources

Developing school self review

Measuring progress

Using inspection

Providing support

Figure 3:
The responsibilities of the geography co-ordinator.
Photo: Chris Garnett.

Taking stock

Discover what is expected of the geography co-ordinator in your school. There should be a 'job description'; if not, ask the Headteacher for one. Find out what geography is already being done, and what is going well; talk to colleagues to find out what they expect of you, and what confidence/expertise in geography they already possess, so you can identify areas where they would welcome support.

Check the place of geography in the school development plan; it should include costed development targets. Children should have a recurring experience of geography throughout the primary years; identify any gaps and make plans to fill them. Think about what geography you want the school to be doing next year – and in five years' time.

Clarifying the geography programme

Children should have the opportunity to study a variety of places, near and far (see Chapters 1, 2 and 3 for the nature of geography in early years, key stage 1 and key stage 2). Make sure that colleagues are using the enquiry approach (see Chapter 12), and integrating the study of places, themes and skills.

Given that schools are released from the requirement to cover the full National Curriculum programme of study at key stages 1 and 2 between September 1998 and September 2000, it is vital to ensure that your geography programme retains a good experience of the subject and fulfils the requirement to offer a broad and balanced curriculum; check that enough time is allocated for this.

Planning the programme

The programme for geography should be clearly set out, and each unit should be supported by a clear teaching scheme (see Chapter 4 for how it should be organised across the key stages and the main components of a scheme of work). Check that your colleagues are aware of the whole geography programme, not just the parts they teach; preferably, they should have been involved in its development.

Links with other curriculum areas must be clear, and opportunities planned in to reinforce literacy, numeracy and ICT through work in geography. Children should be able to enjoy geography in a variety of ways (fieldwork, visits, visitors, ICT, videos) and these will have to be planned into appropriate points in the programme. It should also be possible to take opportunities for 'incidental geography' (e.g. current events, school assemblies, displays).

You must ensure that the programme sets out clearly how continuity and progression in geography are to be achieved (see Chapter 5), both across and within the key stages.

Managing resources

Your school should possess enough teaching resources to deliver the geography programme to children of different abilities through a range of varied learning experiences. The first thing to do is check which resources you already have and identify any gaps; have regard to the need for a good balance of books, maps, photos, videos and software when you decide how they should be filled, prioritising expenditure sensibly by concentrating first on the main teaching units. The school library may contain resources which will support geographical work; include these in your survey; both fiction and non-fiction geography resources should support the literacy programme.

Ensure that your resources support active, investigative learning. Don't forget local resources – people, buildings, environments – which may support work in the field. Make sure that your resources are easily accessible and that all your colleagues know what and where they are.

**Choosing resources.
Photo: John Halocha.**

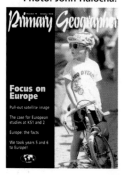

Keep your resources up-to-date; ensure that you receive a good range of product catalogues and resource lists. Joining the Geographical Association will give you access to up-to-date ideas via *Primary Geographer* as well as member's discount off a range of teaching resources.

Measuring progress

The assessment of children's geographical work is covered in Chapter 6. The co-ordinator's job is to ensure that colleagues are clear about how to assess geography, and that their assessment in geography is in line with the whole-school policy and practice.

Teaching plans should identify clear learning targets; work across classes should be compared, and work recorded and reported to parents. Achievement should inform the planning of future work. Feedback to children is important; they should know their strengths and weaknesses, and have the opportunity to assess their own work.

Using inspection

In preparing for an inspection, the geography co-ordinator is best placed to make sure that the presence of geography in the school is clear (plenty of geographical work on display) and well integrated into the whole curriculum. Make sure that colleagues are clear about the distinctive contribution of geography (world knowledge, sense of place, pattern and process, environment, skills) and understand how geography contributes to basic skills and wider aims.

Inspectors will also be looking to see that teachers are working to clear plans and have proper resources, that the children are challenged and motivated, and that any adverse comments made on previous inspections have been addressed.

Providing support

One of the most important roles of the co-ordinator is to facilitate INSET for colleagues. INSET sessions can range from 'one-to-one' advice and support; to the staff meeting after school; to a half day or whole day involving all your colleagues and sometimes including the support staff.

Here are some thoughts about an activity which can be quite traumatic and make you feel quite uneasy as someone who will be expected to have 'all the answers'!

- Good research and preparation are essential – you may not be the expert, but you should be able to refer colleagues to an appropriate source of help. The Geographical Association's publications, especially *Primary Geographer*, can be very useful here.

- One-to-one support is time consuming, but can be well targeted to need. It is particularly successful when it is combined with 'team teaching'; for instance, when you visit an outdoor centre for the day or overnight.

- Staff meetings after school tend to be time-pressured: get a crisp start and try to make sure you get the business done before colleagues have to leave. The golden rule is don't try and cover too much in the time available.

- Half and whole days are undoubtedly best. They work particularly well when you can involve your colleagues in devising curriculum materials themselves. Try and show your colleagues that the geography curriculum is within their grasp; for instance, their lives have a major geographical component simply in their journey to work.

- Inviting in an adviser or someone from a college can be very effective, but they need careful briefing ... make sure they address your agenda!

Developing school self review

Most schools have some system for reviewing whole school issues, in particular the effectiveness of curriculum management and teaching. However, evidence from the first round of inspections indicates that school self review is one of the weakest parts of a school's planning cycle. OFSTED reports indicate that monitoring is a very powerful tool for improving the learning environment and for raising standards of pupil achievement, but that most co-ordinators are not able to monitor directly or even indirectly the quality of geography in their schools.

> Was there a reference to geography in the main findings in your school's inspection report? Was this an area for which your school prepared an action plan?

Curriculum review using the OFSTED framework will identify areas which could be better structured and organised and could help to prepare the school for 'OFSTED 2', which will focus on 'school improvement'. The inspectors will assess the progress the school has made since its last inspection or over the last six years, whichever is the longer period. It will report on the school's response to the previous inspection and will include an evaluative summary of steps taken.

> Some of the areas a self review should investigate are:
> - the children's achievements;
> - the children's response to particular activities such as fieldwork visits;
> - geography's contribution to pupils' spiritual, moral, social and cultural development;
> - leadership and management, staffing, accommodation and resources;
> - health and safety issues, particularly risk assessment of fieldwork sites;
> - action research in the classroom.

Schools must identify specific areas for review in order to avoid superficial involvement with important issues and, as important, to make the review manageable.

Evidence for the review will come from a variety of sources depending on the item being covered. It must be qualitative and professional, not solely quantitative, and sources might include: discussion with teaching and non-teaching staff, Headteacher and Deputy

INSET sessions often include practical work inside and outside the classroom. Photos: Chris Garnett.

headteacher, children past and present, parents; monitoring and evaluation of resources, including the library, industry visits and fieldwork; and the efficiency of financial planning. The outputs of review will help in the production of a curriculum area development plan. Given the right climate it will provide an opportunity to celebrate success, something which can often be overlooked in these times of constant change.

Self review is intended to help schools to create a balance between consolidation and innovation. It is essential to build it into curriculum management to ensure the effective delivery of a stimulating and challenging curriculum.

Making cross-phase and cross-key stage links

An important aspect of the role of the geography co-ordinator is the need to ensure the coherence of children's geographical education as they move through their education. Prior learning must be acknowledged and assessed at the start of children's formal education, and at all points of transfer throughout their school life.

 'Young children become geographers before they become pupils, because they begin to think and feel about people and places they know, and also about unfamiliar and distant places, from an early age' (Blyth and Krause, 1995, p. 11).

> ## My Land Survey
> ### Report.
>
> Sunday the 30th June 1996 was cold, windy and rainy.
> It was also the day my family and I chose to survey our area of Staining for Mrs. Hetherington. We set off in wellingtons and raincoats because our area consisted of fields and country lanes.
> When walking round the boundaries on our map we were very careful not to trespass on private property. My mum and dad were suprised to find that there had been no new developments in our area. We also discovered that all the boundaries remained in their original locations.
> Mrs. Hetherington told us that the data had not been updated since about the 1960's. She also told us that it was important to record our data properly because it would eventually be used to produce a new map of the area.
> I'm glad my family volunteered and were chosen to help because we had a very enjoyable and interesting day, despite the weather.

Responses to fieldwork can form part of self review for co-ordinators. Work: Rachel Slack, age 8, Staining Primary School, near Blackpool.

Both pastoral and curriculum-related information must be exchanged, especially when there is a change of school. This is most important at the key stage 2/3 boundary, which often marks a significant change in the style and organisation of the geography curriculum.

> The following suggestions will help ensure a smooth transition between key stages 2 and 3:
> - sharing resources between your partner High School(s) to enable you to begin a curriculum dialogue;
> - forwarding information about the localities, in addition to the local area, which your children have studied;
> - acknowledging that High Schools tend to use themes rather than places (localities) as the main curriculum building block. Note: there are four key stage 2 themes which carry into key stage 3;
> - the High School acknowledging that your children will have a good working knowledge of their local area which can be shared with children from other schools in year 7.

What are my own professional development needs?

Continuous professional development (CPD) is now identified as essential to effective curriculum leadership, and your professional development needs should have been agreed as part of your appraisal and/or part of the school's development plan.

The key elements of a geography co-ordinator's CPD are externally provided INSET and the help of a curriculum adviser. The former will offer broad brush advice, applicable to all schools, whereas the latter can be tailored to your individual needs. The problem is that the latter can be expensive. The Geographical Association Annual Conference, held in a different location each Easter, offers both broad advice and specific support at minimal cost.

Your professional development can be enhanced by action research: you and your colleagues focus on a particular aspect of teaching and analyse your respective skills. It also gives you an opportunity to assess the work of your colleagues in a supportive and non-threatening manner.

The Teacher Training Agency has recognised that curriculum leadership is a demanding role and has been developing recognised and certificated qualifications. New standards for Qualified Teacher Status were put in place in June, 1998 and larger requirements for all Initial Teacher Training (ITT) courses later that year. Further work is afoot not only to establish statutory requirements for ITT courses, but also to recognise and accredit the role of curriculum leaders.

Constructing a geography policy

A geography policy is a statutory requirement to inform parents, governors and other interested people about how geography is taught in the school and how it contributes to pupils' development. It should reflect a consensus of staff views on the place of geography within the whole-school ethos.

It must be a clear and simple statement about how the school teaches geography and how the subject contributes to pupils' general development; it should be brief and jargon-free, and supported by a scheme of work. The main elements of a geography policy are given in outline below, using the example of the Geography Policy for Gorsey Bank County Primary School, Wilmslow, Cheshire (pages 106-109). It is included as an example to illustrate good practice, but your school will respond in its own particular way to match its own needs. It is based on the Geography National Curriculum programme of study, and although the specific requirement to follow the programme of study has been relaxed this policy offers a valid and viable scheme of work for delivering the geographical element of a broad and balanced curriculum.

An example of a geography policy statement

INTRODUCTION

This policy outlines the purpose and management of the geography taught and learned in Gorsey Bank County Primary School, Wilmslow, Cheshire. The school policy for geography reflects the consensus of opinion of the entire teaching staff, brought about through discussion in staff meetings. A structured framework has been designed, allowing for progression and continuity across the primary sector.

The implementation of this policy is the responsibility of all the teaching staff.

Importance of full staff involvement

THE NATURE OF GEOGRAPHY

Geography is concerned with the study of places, the human and physical processes which shape them and the people who live in them. Children study their local area, and contrasting localities in the United Kingdom and other parts of the world.

Geography helps children to gain a greater understanding of the ways of life and cultures of people in other places. The study of the local area forms an important part of the geography taught at our school, particularly at key stage 1. Enjoyable geographical activities are planned to build upon the children's knowledge and understanding of the local area.

Statement about the nature of geography

Through our teaching of geography we aim to:
- stimulate the children's interest in and curiosity about their surroundings;
- create and foster a sense of wonder about the world;
- inspire a sense of responsibility for the environments and people of the world we live in;
- develop children's competence in specific geographical skills;
- increase the children's knowledge and awareness of the world;
- help children acquire and develop the skills and confidence to undertake investigation, problem solving and decision making.

Aims should be clearly stated

We hope that children will increase their knowledge and understanding of the changing world and will want to look after the earth and its resources. We hope that they will begin to develop respect and concern for, and an interest in, people throughout the world regardless of culture, race and religion.

ROLES AND RESPONSIBILITIES

Each member of the teaching staff will have responsibility for the teaching of geography and they will need to ensure that their own knowledge is continually updated. The school has a geography co-ordinator to assist this process, and take specific responsibility for geography issues in the school. The geography co-ordinator should be a member of the teaching staff who has been trained to lead the teaching of geography. It is his or her responsibility to:

- support colleagues in teaching the subject content;
- audit current practice;
- instigate and organise teaching programmes, planning documents and schemes of work where necessary;
- develop a school policy;

- resource the curriculum by:
  - keeping abreast of the latest teaching methods and materials by subscribing to the Geographical Association quarterly magazine, *Primary Geographer*, and storing up-to-date publishers' catalogues and information about new software and equipment in the Geography Curriculum file;
  - renewing, updating and complementing resources where necessary, and drawing up action plans accordingly;
  - building up a collection of video and audio recordings;
  - ensuring that colleagues are made aware of the resources available in school and their location;
- facilitate the standardised assessment of children's work at moderation meetings;
- be a consultant to colleagues, and to plan the geography content of their teaching on a termly basis across the four management teams – Reception, Years 1/2, Years 3/4 and Years 5/6. Copies of the medium-term plan are located in the geography curriculum file.
- keep people informed of possible visits, exhibitions and courses.

ENTITLEMENT

Geography is one of the foundation subjects established by the National Curriculum and children are required to follow designated programmes of study in order to achieve particular levels of attainment. The time spent on geography in key stage 1 is 36 hours per year and at key stage 2 is 45 hours per year.

Description of content programme

At key stage 1 and 2 the programme of study is divided into three main areas:

- geographical skills
- the study of places
- thematic studies

At key stage 1 the theme is the quality of the environment in a locality either in the UK or overseas. At key stage 2 four geographical themes will be studied. These are Rivers, Weather, Settlement and Environmental Change.

All children are entitled to access the geography programme at a level appropriate to their individual needs. Those children who work below the levels defined by the National Curriculum Geography for their key stage will be given additional assistance by the class teacher. Progress will be carefully monitored; if necessary, and with full parental understanding and support, internal special needs help will be made available.

IMPLEMENTATION PROCEDURES

The National Curriculum programmes of study define the content of the school curriculum for geography, and activities undertaken by the children are planned from these.

PLACES

Detail of places to be studied

At key stage 1 children will be introduced to one local and one contrasting place study. All children at key stage 2 will be introduced to an in-depth study of the locality of the school (larger than the immediate vicinity) and two contrasting localities, one in the UK, and another in a country in Africa, Asia (excluding Japan), South America, or Central America (including the Caribbean). The locational knowledge on maps A, B and C in the Geography National Curriculum document is linked with place studies wherever possible.

In our locality studies equal emphasis is given to the roles of men and women at all levels of society. We focus on the lives of real people and families in order to avoid stereotyping.

SKILLS

The geographical skills outlined in the programme of study at both key stages are integrated with work associated with places and themes.

THEMES

The study of geographic themes will be built into the study of places at both key stages. However, to allow in-depth study and to fulfil the requirements that the studies should involve work at a range of scales from local to national, and that contexts should include the UK and EU, some studies will be discrete.

An investigative approach to geography involving children's active participation in enquiry, fieldwork, mapwork and the use of Information and Communications Technology is promoted.

Children are given opportunities to use a wide range of maps. Emphasis is given to the children developing skills of location, symbols, scale, perspective, and map use.

Geography is the main focus for teaching for one term each year. However, wherever possible, some geographical skills or place knowledge will be included in studies with other foci. Opportunities for learning provided by naturally occurring events, e.g. earthquakes, flooding and droughts, will be utilised sensitively and appropriately.

WHERE DOES GEOGRAPHY OCCUR IN THE CURRICULUM?

Location of geography within and beyond the formal teaching programme

- as a major focus for a topic
- as a smaller element within a topic
- as a discrete lesson/talk
- as part of an assembly
- in discussion (who saw the news last night?)
- during story time
- in displays both in the classroom and in other areas of the school

CLASSROOM ORGANISATION AND TEACHING METHODS

Classroom organisation will depend on the needs and abilities of the children and also on the aims of the lesson. However, a variety of approaches such as whole-class lessons, group, paired and individual work should be experienced by children in their geographical work. Use of relevant resources will be a determining factor in classroom organisation.

How the subject will be developed

During their reception year, children are helped to develop a sense of place by activities which encourage the use of appropriate geographical language and a study of their immediate surroundings in school. Planned activities within the classroom and further afield encourage full and active participation by all children, irrespective of ability. An enquiry approach is required by the programme of study at all key stages.

Fieldwork is also an important element of National Curriculum geography and helps promote learning in all aspects of the subject. To be effective, fieldwork should be purposeful and an integral part of the curriculum plan for geography. When engaged in fieldwork children are expected to behave in a considerate and responsible manner, showing respect for other people and their environment.

All children have opportunities to use ICT as part of their geographical work.

Children will have opportunities to use the following resources: globes, maps, atlases, pictures, aerial photographs, compasses, measuring equipment, cameras, books and games. Most of these items are kept in the resource area and are readily accessible to staff, who will select resources appropriate to the needs of the children.

Arrangements for assessment, recording and reporting

ASSESSMENT AND RECORDING

Children's progress will be assessed and monitored during the year through normal teacher planning and observation. Individual records, and portfolios of children's work, will chart progress. A class record of areas/topics will be kept to assist with future class teaching and planning for continuity and progression.

Meeting the needs of all pupils

SPECIAL NEEDS

Differentiation in terms of learning objectives, tasks, teaching methods and resources will be planned for children with special educational needs. All children should have access to materials and opportunities suitable to their specific needs. Exceptionally able pupils need to be challenged with open ended tasks which provide opportunities to tackle more complex issues and use a wider range of resources.

Review arrangements

REVIEW AND REVISION

This policy was drawn up in July 1997 by the Geography Co-ordinator of Gorsey Bank School and is based on the school's understanding of the Geography National Curriculum. It will be reviewed annually by the Geography Co-ordinator who will collect and collate the experiences and ideas of colleagues that arise during staff meetings and any designated INSET time.

BACKGROUND DOCUMENTATION

This document was informed by reference to the 1993 Order for geography, *Non-Statutory Guidance on the National Curriculum for Geography*, the 1995 Revised Programmes of Study and Attainment Targets for National Curriculum Geography, and guidance from Cheshire LEA.

Gorsey Bank County Primary School, Wilmslow, Cheshire
Headteacher: Maggie Swindells
Geography Co-ordinator: Fiona Pullé

References and further reading

Blyth, A. and Krause, J. (1995) *Primary Geography: A Developmental Approach.* London: Hodder & Stoughton.

Catling, S. (1993) 'Co-ordinating geography', *Primary Geographer*, 14, pp. 10-11.

Cheshire Advisory and Inspection Service (1996) *Planning the Curriculum in Cheshire Primary Schools.* Chester: Cheshire County Council.

Cheshire Advisory and Inspection Service (1997) *Putting it in the Right Place: Guidance for planning and organising the geography curriculum in your school.* Chester: Cheshire County Council.

Krause, J. and Garner, W. (1997) *Geography Co-ordinator's Pack.* London: BBC Education.

Marsden, B. and Hughes, J. (eds) (1994) *Primary School Geography.* London: David Fulton.

Rainey, D. and Krause, J. (1994) 'The geography co-ordinator in the primary school' in Harrison, M. (ed) *Beyond the Core Curriculum.* Plymouth: Northcote Press.

Chapter 8: The geography co-ordinator

The role of co-ordinator is likely to involve responsibility for planning appropriate schemes of work (Chapters 4 and 5), assessment and resources (Chapters 6 and 9), and presenting geography within and beyond your school (Chapter 7). These links are identified in Figure 3.

Evaluating resources

Chapter 9

Bill Marsden
Jo Hughes

Introduction

Geography is a strongly **resource-based** subject, and some resources are particularly distinctive to it. No other school subject is so reliant on maps and photographic materials, for example. Resource collection is an integral part of the curriculum planning process. In an ideal world, teachers and children might with advantage be the main resource collectors. But geography is a global study, and logistics dictate that the classroom users have neither the time, the opportunity, nor the financial clout to be able to obtain all their own materials. Geography is also resourced from the academic frontiers of the subject and, in the primary situation, non-specialist teachers may well not have the expertise to identify and produce the best possible resources, especially away from their local area.

There is much information and guidance on resources available to the teacher, whether from educational publishers, charitable bodies, media sources such as broadcasting companies, newspapers and the teachers' press, subject organisations such as the Geographical Association, local education authorities, libraries, record offices and museums, and various external agencies including environmental groups, planning departments, travel agents, and aerial and satellite photograph companies. The intention of this chapter is to try to hack a pathway through all the undergrowth to help subject co-ordinators and their colleagues, identifying different categories of resources, specifying where they can be obtained, making judgements on the pros and cons of different types, and finally offering a checklist for the evaluation of major resources such as study packs and textbook series.

Evaluating resources

While there is an embarrassment of riches on the resource supply side, funds are scarce on the demand side. In the light of this situation, we have attempted a 'good hotel guide' type of grading scheme. This provides a rough rank ordering of the likely value of different types of resources for primary geography. It is obviously subjective, but may help you to consider priorities. If you do not agree with our judgements, you could produce your own grading with your colleagues. A major influence on our judgement is the extent to which the resources are distinctive to geography and help to promote geographical skills, knowledge and understanding, though these are by no means the only considerations. In appraising resources, remember that in the end they are only as good as the way in which they are deployed. The potential of even the best resources can be undermined by passive, mechanical use. Our grading scheme is set out to the left, and is applied in the final column of Table 1.

Grading of resources

***** Indispensable

**** Very important

*** Good to have

** Useful support material

* Of lower priority

Resources	Pros/cons	Access	Rating
Cartographic School plans/picture maps	Key starting points at key stage 1: link plans with picture maps. Build in progression.	The school (see *Mapstart* series for ideas)	****
Large-scale OS maps 1:1250 (urban areas); 1:2500 (rural areas); 1:10 000	Indispensable for school locality, contrasting localities and wider school setting. Expensive.	Check LEA to see if it has a copyright licence. Also OS agents.	*****
Medium-scale OS maps 1:25 000 (Pathfinder); 1:50 000 (Landranger); OS leisure maps	More abstract, but important at key stage 2 for rural fieldwork and study of home region. Less expensive. Can be laminated.	Most good bookshops. Tourist offices.	****
Street and road maps	Important for developing the life skill of route finding.	Widely accessible.	****
Land use maps	*Goad Plans* for urban centre use. Updating forms a useful fieldwork exercise.	The publisher, who provides an educational pack for guidance.	****
Historical maps	Indispensable for British locality studies, especially large-scale old OS for nineteenth and early twentieth century.	Local library, record office, museum. Check with LEA.	***** or **** depending on locality
Tourist-type maps, e.g. route maps, town plans	Cover other nations. May be of varying quality and out-of-date.	In tourist guides from bookshops and travel agents.	**
Wall charts	Some excellent maps of continents and countries are available.	Map publishers	****
Satellite maps	Many of vivid quality at regional, national, continental and global scales. Check colour quality.	Specialist publishers	****
Atlas maps	Indispensable as a reference for global, locational knowledge. Check for up-to-date place names. Note problems of scale and abstractness. Avoid distorted projections, e.g. Mercator and Peters. Need for class sets matched to needs of the level. Also for range of atlases for reference in the school library.	Educational and other publishers	*****
Globes	Another indispensable geographical aid, showing 'roundness' and correct relative sizes and shapes. Helpful to have blank outline globe, a physical and political globe (showing countries). Note problems relating to small scale.	Educational and other publishers	*****
Plastic floor maps	Usefully sturdy outline maps, of large scale. Children can draw on them.	Eduational and other publishers	**

Table 1: (continued on next page)

Resources	Pros/cons	Access	Rating
Photographic Apart from maps, photographic and pictorial materials are the most distinctive resources for geography.			
Colour prints	For ground level shots of places you have visited, colour prints are very convenient. But they need to be more than holiday snapshots, and basic skills of how to photograph people and landscapes are needed. Readily available and economically gathered together in photopacks and textbooks.	Personal, photopacks, text and reference books	*****
Postcards	May be helpful in lieu of prints for places not visited. Check on colour and geographical validity. Very cheap.	Many shops	**
Transparencies	Less popular than prints in primary schools, but generally produce better images than prints, and can be projected into appropriately large size on screens, allowing whole class discussion. Require good blackout and screen.	Personal. Some educational publishers and photographic agencies	****
Oblique aerial	In terms of progression, use after ground level photographs. Very important in developing a sense of place, whether the locality or on a broader scale.	Photograph agencies/ photopacks/textbook series	*****
Vertical aerial/satellite	Less 'real' than oblique, and come next in terms of progression. Should be linked with maps at the appropriate scale.	As above	****
Television/video film	Excellent starting points. Unrivalled in terms of topicality and vividness. But content/format, etc., controlled by the producer (unless it is a school-based initiative).	School-based television companies. Commercial sources	****
Pictorial Pictograms and graphs (line, block, pie-charts)	An important means of processing geographical information. Link with cross-curricular skills. Important to use in fieldwork follow-up, e.g. traffic survey; and with weather study	In study packs/textbooks/ reference books. School-based	***
Flow diagrams	Again useful for processing, e.g. work on economic activity in settlements.	As above	**
Block diagrams	Useful for certain aspects of geography, e.g. water cycle.	As above	**
Landscape sketches	Basic landscape sketching a useful skill to develop – link wtih art. Good landscape sketches in text and study packs can eliminate some of the excess information on photographs. May be labelled to highlight key features.	As above, where not school-based	***
Talking heads/speech bubbles/cartoon strips	Popular in some textbook series and can be useful if tied to real localities and people. But too often offer pre-digested and over-simplified soundbites.	As above	*

Table 1: **(continued on next page)**

Resources	Pros/cons	Access	Rating
Historical materials Including: directories; census returns; local histories; old newspapers; old prints, photographs and postcards; old maps; old timetables; school and family records – including oral	All these are vitally important for linking with local study, whether the home or the contrasting locality, and for developing understanding of the growth of settlements.	Libraries, record offices, museums, local history books in bookshops	***** to *** depending on locality
Audio materials Audio tapes	Interviews can provide vivid materials on localities. Also good for nature sounds.	School-based	***
Radio broadcasts	Less used today than television but carry many of the same advantages.	Record from radio	**
Music	Can help create the atmosphere of particular places. An important cross-curricular link, e.g. with art, music and literature.	Record from radios, compact disks, etc.	**
Other materials Newspaper and magazine extracts	Provide up-to-date information and are vivid and topical. Link with internal schemes of work. Watch reading levels and check on accuracy and possible distortion. Good for sequence of weather forecasts – collect for the same place at different seasons.	Daily, weekly or monthly newspapers/journals, magazines. Note: *The European* and geographical magazines. Some available on Internet	***
Stamps	An under-used but very appropriate geographical resource. Excellent for developing classification skills. Can be collected by **themes** or **countries**. Can be used to build up world locational knowledge, and for cross-curricular links. Can be collected for charity.	Stamp shops. See stamp magazines for cheap kiloware. Educational stamp clubs nationally and local philatelic bodies	***
Travel brochures	Unused travel brochures can provide a cheap source of class sets for pictures and other information of geographical interest, but often communicate exotic stereotypes.	Travel agents (at end of season)	** to * depending on quality
Air, rail and bus timetables	Of real geographical interest in dealing with concepts of time and cost, as well as distance. Often complex and need processing by teachers.	Airports, rail and bus stations, travel agents, bookshops	***
Memorabilia from visits (especially overseas): air, bus and rail tickets; menus; guides/plans; local newspapers; package labels; adverts; poster/stickers; local postage stamps; local currency; local television details; travel brochures relating to Britain; t-shirts, etc.; flags; sport-linked materials; etc.	These can all be valuable support materials in evoking a sense of place. But beware of overuse of stereotyped souvenir-type material.	Personal collection. Friends or relatives overseas. School twinning	**
ICT software packages Concept keyboard; data handling; spreadsheet; word processing; graphing; desk-top publishing; games and simulations; CD-ROMs; geography specific	(see Chapter 15)	Commercial suppliers	****

Table 1: (continued on next page)

Resources	Pros/cons	Access	Rating
Measuring instruments Thermometers; rain gauges; wind vanes and socks; compasses; Silva compasses; metre rules; clinometers; quadrats; floats; stopwatches	These and other materials are vital for enquiry-based work in the field, for orienteering and for physical geography. Link with maths work.	Some can be home-made. Commercial suppliers	**** to ***
Physical geography resources Specimens of: soil; rock; mineral; fossil; plant	Very important outcome of fieldwork. Link with classification skills in science (see Chapters 14 and 23).	School collection where possible	**** to ***
Hardware models Relief	Associate with work on contours.	School produced	*** to **
Landscapes	Build up from above contour base, using balsa frames, papier mâché, plaster casts, cardboard, plastic, etc.	School produced	*** to **
Village or townscapes – streets, harbour areas, whole settlements, etc. **Photo: Bill Marsden**	Show land use well. Link with design and technology work.	School produced	*** to **
Games and simulations Simulation through drama	Can help to develop empathy towards other people. But bear in mind possibilities of bias and stereotyping.	School produced	*** to **
Geographical decision-making and problem-solving activities	These simplify more complex reality and can range from Treasure Island games to develop map skills, to more complex activities addressing environmental problems.	See 1996 issues of *Primary Geographer* and textbook series and DEC materials	*** to **
Quiz-type games and crosswords	Useful for assessing factual knowledge in a motivating way.		*** to **
ICT game packages	See *ICT software packages* above.	Commercial suppliers	*** to **
Photo-study packs (see page 357 and see 'Evaluation checklist' below) UK locality packs (note: also Europe packs to link themes, places and the European dimension)	Cover, in particular, contrasting locality studies in Britain. Contain usually excellent photographs and a range of maps and other materials, together with guidance for teachers. LEA packs usually focus on home locality.	GA/LEAs/educational publishers	**** to * depending on quality and need
Developing world locality packs	Emphasis on localities in developing countries. Usually very strong on human interest and the development of empathy. May be a smaller proportion of geographically distinctive material in aid organisation than in GA packs. In general study packs are useful for developing an in-depth sense of places and their peoples. They can be slotted well into internal schemes of work, but if used by themselves cannot give a balanced world coverage of places, even at primary level.	GA/overseas aid organisations/environmental groups/development education centres	***** to * depending on quality and need

Table 1: **(continued on next page)**

Resources	Pros/cons	Access	Rating
Textbook series (see Resources section) See 'Evaluation checklist' below	Bring together a wide range of resources, and are generally colourful, clearly structured and well-presented. Should provide materials teachers cannot reasonably be expected to collect themselves. Usually accompanied by teacher guidance and activity sheets. Potentially helpful in permeating themes and skills into real places, especially if a balanced world selection is offered. Can usefully be co-ordinated with photopack materials. The danger is if they are regarded mechanically as course books. Should offer flexibility, allowing integration into internal schemes and differentiation.	Educational publishers	**** to * depending on quality
Reference and library texts	Can be very valuable support material for individual or group projects on particular topics. Can include travel literature as support for place work. Ensure that children are helped to develop skills going beyond mere copying out.	Educational and other publishers. Bookshops	**** to * depending on quality
Children's literature	Nursery rhymes, fairy tales and stories can add atmosphere and interest to the study of places. Should help to promote empathy, and encourage creative writing and other skills. Not necessarily distinctively geographical. Help link geography with language, and can be used in time allotted for English.	Educational publishers. Bookshops	**** to * depending on geographical content

Table 1: The value of different types of resources for primary geography.

Evaluation checklists

Aerial photographs are useful progression material. Photo: Chris Garnett.

Whether or not resource materials are worth choosing will depend both on their particular value for geography (e.g. maps and oblique aerial photographs), and on their intrinsic quality. The grading scheme used in Table 1 emphasises geographical distinctiveness. But materials can be distinctive without being of high quality. To make judgements about quality it is first necessary to select criteria against which to match the materials. Our own criteria are set out below, and applied to the range of resources brought together in study packs, textbooks and other relevant books and sources of reference, rather than to individual materials, considered above.

In making an appraisal, things we need to evaluate include whether the materials reflect:

- good geographical practice
- good educational practice
- desired social purposes
- National Curriculum requirements
- high quality standards of presentation
- cost-effectiveness
- flexibility in terms of fitting in with internal schemes of work

Realistically, no materials can meet all of these demands, and it is not appropriate to apply all the criteria to all the materials. But a calculus of advantage and disadvantage offers essential information in making wise choices. Bear in mind that some criteria may be more critical in your own situation than they would in that of others, particularly if your school aims to strengthen numeracy and literacy through planned support from foundation subjects, or if you are planning some reduction to the Geography National Curriculum.

Photo: Elaine Jackson.

Geography offers many opportunities for cross-curricular activities. Photo: David Tothill/Photofusion.

Evaluation checklist

A. *Good practice*

1 Distinctive geographical content

- What types of material are provided? Are they geographically distinctive, with an appropriate range of maps and visual materials?
- Do the materials convey a sense of the places considered?
- Are geographical aims and objectives clearly stated and followed through?
- Do the materials go beyond a mere collection of geographical information and cover geographical concepts and principles?
- To what extent do they promote the development of geographical skills, e.g. of map and photograph interpretation?
- Are the materials as accurate and as up-to-date as can reasonably be expected?

2 Educational processes

- Are the materials well matched to the level targeted, e.g. in terms of language, complexity of sentences?
- Do the materials build in continuity and progression, e.g. do those intended for year 3 take account of the knowledge, understanding and skills likely to have been developed at key stage 1?
- Do they foster enquiry-based learning?
- Are the materials and associated activities learner-centred, e.g. do they serve to promote a range of thinking skills?
- Are they likely to be interesting to children, promoting positive attitudes to learning through, for example, offering a wide range of stimulating activities?
- Do the materials and associated activities encourage a range of styles of working, e.g. individual/pair/group?
- Do they offer flexibility of use, e.g. complementing other resources?
- Do they offer opportunities for cross-curricular skill development, e.g. with ICT?
- Do they cater for variations in ability through the inclusion of core, reinforcement and enrichment activities?
- Do they include a range of types of assessment, e.g. covering more than just written responses?
- Do the assessment activities encourage high but realistic levels of expectation of the children?
- Are the assessment activities well matched to the resources provided?

3 Social purposes

- Do the materials avoid, so far as possible, bias, e.g. do they cover major issues, whether local, national or global, in a well-balanced way or do you have the impression they are trying to impose a particular slant on the issues covered?
- Do they avoid stereotyping (bearing in mind that for younger children a degree of simplification is needed which might carry this danger)?

Floormaps are an excellent way to introduce the pupils to a range of scales. Photo: Wendy Morgan.

Understanding landforms. Photo: Dorothy Stevens.

- Are they more than merely parochial? Do they carry the potential for building towards a global dimension?
- Is the language inclusive, i.e. non-racist, non-sexist, non-classist, non-ageist?
- Do the materials offer the possibility of links with cross-curricular themes and dimensions, such as environmental and citizenship education, personal and social eduction, etc.?

B. *Programmes of study for geography*

Do the materials:

1 Cover the PoS at key stages 1 and 2 in terms of:
   - geographical skills
   - places
   - thematic studies

2 Cover also the statements found in the preambles introducing the detailed content of the PoS, e.g. in terms (as appropriate to key stage 1 or key stage 2) of:
   - focusing on geographical questions
   - recognising geographical patterns
   - investigating places across a widening range of scales
   - using geographical terms and including requisite locational knowledge
   - promoting fieldwork, and integrating with classwork
   - using secondary resources
   - setting themes within the context of actual places
   - involving work at a range of scales from local to national to global, including the UK and European Union contexts?

3 Creatively build on the opportunities suggested in the non-statutory illustrations (printed in italics in the Geography National Curriculum document)?

4 Help to build up a portfolio to form the basis for end-of year reports on progress in geography?

C. *Presentation*

1 Do the materials **support children's learning** in terms of:
   - spaciousness of layout, appropriate size of typeface, clear headings, good quality photographs of a size usable by younger children, etc.
   - quality and clarity of reproduction, especially of colour photographs
   - quality and geographical distinctiveness of artwork
   - balance between text, maps and other resources
   - inclusion of an index and/or a glossary
   - clearly identified links between resources and activities?

2 Do the materials **support the teacher** through, for example:
   - a teachers' guide, giving advice on good practice in assessment, etc.
   - additional pupil support materials, building in differentiation and progression, as specified above?

D. *Other*

1 Cost

- Are the materials cost-effective in comparison with alternative resources of similar quality?

- Do they offer opportunities for cross-curricular links which might result in some overall cost saving? (NOTE: Geographical-type material is now included in some reading, maths and science schemes, and might be acquired through the higher funding usually available for core subjects).

2 Flexibility and fit

- How well do the materials fit in with your own schemes of work?

- Do they help or hinder flexibility of use, e.g. in the case of a textbook series is it presented as a rigid course, or does it allow a selective extraction of materials to integrate with your own curriculum planning and/or with another type of resource?

Conclusion

Selecting resources for primary geography is a challenging and interesting task, though in a period of financial constraint it can be a frustrating one too. A wide range of high quality materials is available, and some detail about these is given in the Resources at the end of this book. Resources should be evaluated individually as regards quality and how they fit with the needs of the school. But once this is done, they should also be considered together. The particular strengths of each type of resource are enhanced when linked with others which offer complementary advantages. Thus maps, photographs, photopacks, textbooks, story books, ICT software and other materials can with advantage be brought together to provide flexible and stimulating approaches to teaching primary geography. Fitness for purpose is clearly an important criterion of choice, whether that purpose is to do with good practice in geography, pedagogy or social education. But a sensible choice of resources is only a start. It is how well they are applied thereafter that is a key to a high quality primary education in geography.

Reference

Catling, S. (1992) *Mapstart Books 1, 2, 3, OS (second edition)*. Harlow: Collins-Longman.

Chapter 9: Resourcing primary geography

Further resources and references are listed in relation to specific chapters (see, in particular, Chapter 16), and in the Resources and Bibliography. A catalogue of its publications is also available from the Geographical Association.

Geography-based displays are an obvious indication of good geography practice.
Photo: Rachel Bowles.
Work: Hope School, Derbyshire.

The inspection process

Chapter 10

Marcia Foley

The worth of pupils' learning in geography is at the heart of the inspection process. The 1990s have been a period of nationally organised school inspections, under the auspices of the Office for Standards in Education (OFSTED). Its purpose is to:

> *'identify strengths and weaknesses so that schools may improve the quality of education that they provide and raise educational standards achieved by their pupils'* *(OFSTED, 1995, p. 8).*

In January 1998, the Education and Employment Secretary took action to enable schools to use more time to develop the essential basic skills of numeracy and literacy by releasing them from the requirement to follow prescribed programmes of study in the foundation subjects. However, he confirmed that schools were required to continue to find a place for these subjects in the curriculum.

This action affects the inspection arrangements and, on 5 January 1998, Chris Woodhead (HMCI) set out the following revised provisions for inspecting primary schools:

- Primary inspections will focus on English, mathematics, science and ICT. Inspectors will follow the current inspection framework in these subjects.
- When inspectors observe lessons in other subjects they will evaluate the quality of teaching and learning. They will not comment on the extent to which teaching complies with the requirements of the existing programmes of study.
- Inspectors will comment on the contribution the quality of teaching in all subjects makes to standards in literacy and numeracy.
- No school will be criticised for failing to cover the existing programmes of study requirements in art, design and technology, geography, history, music and physical education.

Thus, while schools will not be criticised for failure to implement the Order for geography in full, they will be expected to provide a geography programme and, where this is observed during inspections, judgements will be made about the quality of teaching and learning. Inspectors are therefore likely to investigate the following questions:

- Is geography being taught in the school?
- What geography is being taught?
- To what extent is geography teaching contributing to pupils' standards of literacy and numeracy?
- What is the quality of teaching and learning in geography?

Ellie Colley   Water Poems

Water flows but no one knows just where it goes,
In the toilet,
Down the drain pipe,
To the sewers,
And out to sea.

Water sprinkling,
Out of the sparkling spring,
Down to the river,
And on to the sea.

Evaporating up to the clouds,
Falling as rain,
Down to the sea,
To start again.

At the seaside,
I see the sea,
Boats moored there,
Going up and down,
With the waves.

Using language in geography. Work: Ellie Colley.

For individual teachers, inspection can help by validating the geography they are doing with children or pointing out where weaknesses lie. Inspection is also useful for co-ordinators; the identification of strengths and weaknesses by an experienced and objective outsider can enhance the good co-ordinator's judgements, confirm his or her hunches and validate or stimulate ideas about the way to progress.

Inevitably, because the outcomes of an inspection are largely or partly unknown by those on the receiving end, there is an element of threat involved. Good preparation always helps, and should make the experience more tolerable and positive. Working on the premise that the more you understand about the inspection process and its purpose, the more effectively you will cope with it, this chapter highlights what geography inspectors are seeking to find out. It is addressed to the geography co-ordinator, and considers the three phases of inspection – before, during and after.

Before the inspection

As co-ordinator, you should know where you stand as regards both your paperwork – the policy, the schemes of work and resource listings – and the practice – the translation of the paperwork into real geography teaching and progress in learning in the classroom. The scheme of work (the long-term or key stage plan with its medium-term plan) is a key link as it helps interpret the policy in terms of practice.

It may be, for a variety of reasons, that your school has not prepared a policy and scheme of work. This is unfortunate, but it is important to remember that the bottom line is that the pupils' learning and progress should be good in practice. You can't do everything at once; if a lot needs to be done for geography in your school you can only prioritise, do a personal action plan to fit with the wider school development plan, then do your best in the time available. You will have to live with the judgement that there are some deficiencies – which should, ideally, have been identified in advance.

Before the inspection, you may find it useful to think through your answers to the questions below. They will help you to prepare for it by focusing on the practice of geography and you may be asked about them during the inspection.

- Do you as co-ordinator have a vision for the subject in your school?
- What is the place of geography within the school development plan?
- What are your expectations about standards in geography in your school?
- Have you acquired a view of what standards children reach in different years or key stages?
- Have you a notion of how much continuity and progression children have in their geography learning?
- In what ways does the school monitor and evaluate geography standards?
- How is pupils' progress in geography assessed?
- What are you doing with the information you have acquired?
- How do the staff and pupils feel about the subject – do they enjoy it?

Although it should not be necessary to make a special effort or put on a show for the inspector, most people, as when they have guests at home, like to smarten up and do their best to impress. The following checklist may help:

- Are the resources where they should be if they are not in use?
- Are they tidy?
- Do staff really know about them?
- Are there geography displays around the school?
- Can you give examples of how you support colleagues in their geography teaching?

Before the inspection, inspectors will begin the process of analysing relevant school documents. The geography inspector will be likely to take evidence from:

- the school development plan;
- the geography policy, which should be as personalised as possible in terms of the why? where? and when? of geography in *your* school;
- policies on whole-school matters which may be common to geography, e.g. assessment, health and safety, off-site visits;
- key stage or long-term planning for geography;
- medium-term planning which incorporates learning objectives and pupil activities;
- resource listings for geography if not appended to the policy;
- other general papers required for inspection which give details about staffing, in-service training received, finance related to geography;
- the job description for the geography co-ordinator.

An experienced specialist inspector will have a checklist of questions which he or she is using to analyse the paperwork in order to be as informed as possible about geography in the school when the inspection begins. The inspector will then refine the list of questions for the interview with the co-ordinator so that he/she can check out assumptions or explore issues emerging from the paperwork. Try out the questions in Figure 1 on yourself just to check that you are aware of current strengths and weaknesses.

- Is there a policy?
- Is it clear in its intentions?
- Will it be easily understood by staff?
- If some expected aspects are not dealt with in this policy, then is the reader referred to other school policies?
- Is geography part of the school development plan?
- Is there a co-ordinator?
- How much in-service training for geography have the co-ordinator and other teachers received?
- What budget is allocated to geography?
- Is the co-ordinator responsible for managing it?
- Are the resources adequate?
- To what extent do pupils use ICT in geography?
- Is adequate time allocated to geography?
- Is there evidence of the enquiry approach in planning and policy?
- Is there an indication of how geography supports speaking, listening, reading, writing and data handling?
- Is there any evidence of the subject's explicit contribution to social, moral, cultural and spiritual education?
- Is there a geography school portfolio or pointers to a methodology for staff becoming familiar with standards in the subject?
- Is there a balance of geography across years and, ideally, terms?
- Does the documentation provide information about the emphasis given to fieldwork, around and beyond the school?
- Are places, themes and skills integrated in planning?

Figure 1:
A typical list of questions for analysing geography paperwork.

TIMETABLE ISSUES

Just before the inspection teachers will be asked to provide class timetables for the inspection week. This is crucial to enable the inspector's team to plan the lesson observations effectively. Ideally the specialist inspector will plan to visit all geography lessons. In bigger schools it may be that two or more geography lessons are taking place at the same time in which case the geography inspector may delegate other inspectors to see these lessons or may decide to observe some part of all of the lessons. Be prepared for this. It is an inspector's responsibility to observe as many lessons as possible, especially in a subject like geography where less time is given to it than to some other subjects and therefore there may be fewer lessons anyway.

Teachers often ask 'Should we decide to put off fieldwork until after the inspection?' Remember fieldwork is a 'good practice' part of geographical education and is often particularly motivating for pupils so if fieldwork can naturally fall within the geography lessons of the inspection it makes sense to continue with it. It is up to the inspector to decide whether to accompany off-site visits or not, depending on how far away they are and the rest of his/her timetable.

Co-ordinators also ask 'What if no-one is teaching any geography during the inspection period?' The smaller the school, the more likely this is, especially if geography teaching is blocked into certain parts of terms. In a larger school, if no geography is found in a week, this does beg questions about the organisation of the subject throughout the year and the priorities given to it. Obviously it would be inappropriate to have geography on the timetable when it does not fit with the planned scheme of work. However, inspectors are likely to do a better job and provide more useful feedback if some geography teaching is going on. It is surprising how many inspection reports are obliged to state 'No geography teaching was observed'.

Finally, on the subject of timetabling issues, do ask teachers if they are teaching a topic to specify more than the topic title. This is specially pertinent to key stage 1 where a topic title may focus on an aspect of geography in that lesson. It is irritating for an inspector to think they are going to find out more about geography from a topic lesson only to find that the focus is on science or history. It is also irritating for the teacher to have an inspector arrive and then disappear suddenly!

During the inspection

So you have done your best to prepare yourself and your colleagues for the inspection – now what?

As co-ordinator you can expect to have a brief interview with the inspector (about 20 minutes) who will want to clarify points outstanding from the pre-inspection analysis and to gain a greater understanding of how you manage geography and aspects of its financing. These findings will contribute to those of the whole team on these aspects. The interview should also allow you to indicate your view of the subject in the school and to highlight where you would find the inspector's comments particularly useful.

Classroom teachers may also be asked informally about geography during lesson observations – for example, they may be asked what support they have had from the co-ordinator, and whether their resources are sufficient.

The inspection time is an intensive period for both staff and inspectors. Your geography inspector is trying to gather as much information as possible on quality in geography – through collecting data on:

- teaching
- expectations about standards
- pupils' progress and attitudes to geography
- its planning and management, including monitoring
- the staffing and researching of the subject
- its contribution to the whole-school curriculum

LESSON OBSERVATION

Lesson observation will be the major source of evidence. When inspectors visit classes to observe for all or part of a lesson, they will be collecting evidence which can be categorised under these headings:

- teaching
- response
- standards
- progress

The class teacher will see the inspector noting down evidence on a form and s/he will grade each aspect. Expect the inspector to sit alone, watch and listen. If it is possible to do so without interrupting the flow of the lesson, s/he may well sit next to a child or with a group and go through their work with them or ask them questions about what they are learning in geography. Inspectors often have the knack of sitting next to the child you would least like them to question on geography! A good inspector will soon sense this and seek a balance of evidence or redress the balance in the brief oral feedback due to you at the end of the lesson.

The inspector may take the opportunity to speak with the teacher sensitively during the lesson, having judged that doing so will not skew the course of the lesson. It is good practice for the inspector to give you a very brief feedback – possibly in the form of strengths and weaknesses on your lesson. Sometimes, because of a very intensive timetable, this can be very difficult for an inspector to fit in but you may always request feedback at the nearest possible time later in the day.

WHAT ARE THE FEATURES OF GOOD GEOGRAPHY TEACHING?

Good teaching is teaching that promotes effective progress and standards and can be identified in the case of geography as having the following features:

The inspector may ask a pupil to describe what they have learned using ICT in geography. Photo: Chris Garnett.

- a properly planned lesson with specific learning objectives related to geographical knowledge, understanding and/or skills, e.g. to relate the land use shown on the local area aerial photos to the land use patterns shown on the local area 1: 10 000 scale Ordnance Survey map;

- lesson plans which can be related back to the scheme of work;

- map work linked to real places;

- well prepared resources, ready at the beginning of the lesson;

- objectives of the lesson are shared with pupils at the start of the lesson;

- an appropriate range of resources which are stimulating and up-to-date is used, e.g. artefacts of distant or local places, photopacks, videos, maps, books, atlases, globes, CD-ROM and other ICT;

- occasional use is made of topical examples;

- there is development of an understanding of patterns, processes and application of skills;

- the 'technical' vocabulary of geography is used, e.g. 'hill' in year 1, and 'landscape' in year 6;

- resources are matched to the age and ability of pupils in the class, e.g. type and scale of map or photograph, text, worksheet, writing framework;

- an approach is adopted which promotes the skills of geographical enquiry through fieldwork and practical activities within the classroom, in addition to the use of second-hand resources;

- there is expectation that pupils will work through geographical questions for short or longer periods to collect, record, represent, communicate and analyse data, be it information collected during fieldwork or classwork;

- there is reasonable subject knowledge;

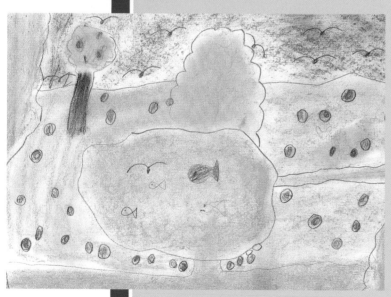

Using art in geography work. Work: Amy.

- opportunities are planned for pupils to discuss and recognise environmental, aesthetic and cultural attitudes and issues;

- there is a clear summary to the lesson, providing a quick resumé of pupils' overall learning;

- there is a good pace to the lesson – with pupils aware of timings.

WHAT CONSTITUTES A GOOD RESPONSE TO GEOGRAPHY TEACHING?

Inspectors are interested in how pupils behave and respond during lessons. Evidence of 'a good response' includes the following:

- good behaviour whatever the learning style – individual, paired or grouped;
- good co-operation with others when working together in fieldwork or classroom work to use or analyse resources;
- an inquisitive attitude and an enthusiasm for other places, people and cultures;
- the use of aspects of maths, English, art and other relevant subject areas as well as ICT skills in geography work;
- reasonable confidence in tackling tasks which are new, or already learned (e.g. atlas skills);
- an awareness of the points of view which may be held by others towards issues about the environment;
- a willingness to comment sensibly on the social, moral, cultural and environmental issues their geography raises.

HOW DO INSPECTORS JUDGE ATTAINMENT AND STANDARDS?

They will look for evidence which assesses the pupils' strengths and weaknesses relating to such aspects as:

- standards or Levels for pupils at the end of key stage 1 and key stage 2;
- knowledge of places, what they are like and how people adapt to living in them;
- how pupils are developing their geographical skills, including enquiry, through the use of maps, fieldwork and other visual and written resources, including ICT;
- pupils' understanding of the patterns and processes which affect people and landscapes and the environmental links between them;
- pupils' ability to apply aspects of geography already learned;
- pupils' ability to use suitable geographical vocabulary in oral and written form.

Assessing geographical skills may include work on directions. Work: Peter Adcock, Sharrow N&I School, Sheffield. Photo: Wendy Morgan.

Round th world in 7 days. peter.
munday I got in my plane and
I went south. and i Landid in
Spain. on Tusday I went to Brazil
in my plane. East.
on Wensday I went East again
to AUSTRALIA.
on Thursday I got in my Ship
and i went to AFrica East.
on Friday i went nouth to Europe.
on sat irday I went NOUTH to
NOR WAY.
on sunday i went sawTh to
The UNITed Kingdom

Geographical display
of fieldwork visits
assert the presence
of geography.
Photo: Steve Rawlinson.

WHAT PROVIDES EVIDENCE ABOUT SUITABLE PROGRESS?

An inspector will be looking to see if the pupils:

■ are making sound progress within the activities provided;

■ talk with reasonable confidence about current and previous work;

■ use previous knowledge and skills to progress, where possible;

■ use maps and atlases as ready tools to find places and talk about them;

■ give explanations about features, patterns or processes based on their research or work to-date;

■ demonstrate reasonable depth of knowledge about a range of real places, especially when they can refer to maps or their recorded work as a stimulus;

■ are able to talk clearly (at their ability level) about what they have as an individual learned in the lesson by reporting back to a group or the whole class – as the lesson organisation permits;

■ demonstrate progress in their geography learning over time as well as in a lesson, through what is recorded in their books as well as what they are able to talk about.

Clearly, even if evidence relating to all the above was available, an inspector will not be able to collect it all in every lesson: inspectors, like teachers, are not superhuman! However, most of this evidence will be available for some of the time in every lesson and it is an inspector's job to make an objective judgement about the quality of pupils' geographical learning in a lesson by focusing on as many of the criteria listed above as possible.

WHAT HAPPENS IF NO GEOGRAPHY LESSONS CAN BE SEEN?

If there are no geography lessons taking place at the time of the inspection inspectors will use the other evidence that they normally refer to during an inspection (see Figure 2) and which they collect in order to come to judgements. In addition they will need to have discussions about their geography work with individuals or groups of pupils representative of the age range of pupils in the school. This usually involves talking to pupils, and checking their books, in relation to work they have done, also using, say, a map, a photo or some pertinent geographical resource to focus the pupils in order to explore their current understanding and to assess how easily they can transfer this to new situations.

Sources of geography information	Inspector's focus
Samples of work from each year for an able, average and special needs pupil, with a major focus on years 2, 4 and 6. Geography portfolio, if one exists	What are standards like? Is there evidence of progression? Is there a range of work indicating varied teaching and learning styles? What is the quality of marking like?
Pupils' records and reports	Is pupils' progress assessed and recorded? How are records used? Do reports communicate the pupils' strengths and weaknesses? Are targets geographical?
Teacher's short-term planning and lesson notes (in addition to pre-inspection planning evidence)	Are there clear learning objectives? Is work differentiated?
Geography resources – equipment and paper resources	Are there enough? Are they accessible? Are they sufficiently up-to-date? Do resources offer equal opportunities?
The school library	Is there a geography section? How extensive is it? How up-to-date is it? Is there a variety of atlases?
Wall displays	Do they promote enquiry skills? Are they recent? Do they represent children's work?
Staff meeting minutes	Have all the staff discussed geography? Has the co-ordinator led in-service training in the school?

Figure 2:
Sources of geography
information.

FEEDBACK

Co-ordinators should receive oral feedback at the end of the inspection, and the feedback session should be scheduled for you. You may find you need to deal with it alone, but if you can be supported by another member of staff it is useful for them to take notes on the points the inspector makes which indicate strengths and weaknesses. Listening and taking key notes at the same time can be difficult in this situation. The inspector should indicate to you what his/her final judgements about the value of the geography in the school are likely to be. You will probably receive more feedback of direct use to you and the school at this session than you will in the written geography summary in the inspection report, the main purpose of which is to inform parents.

While you are not at liberty to disagree with the inspector, you may certainly have a professional dialogue and check facts which have been used to make judgements if you feel they are incorrect. A wise co-ordinator will also use the feedback session to pick up advice for the future which the inspector may be pleased to offer, by chance or design!

After the inspection

Currently OFSTED publishes a geography subject summary section in its inspection report on the school. Occasionally geography and history may be reported on together if little evidence was available for one or both. However inspection may change in the future, it is likely that the report will be made available for an audience beyond the school.

After the inspection it will be important for you to:

■ ensure you have written notes of the oral feedback and your response to it and that these are shared with your senior management;

■ read the published school inspection report to see what is said in the geography section but also to see where it is cross-referenced in other sections, such as resources, management, social, moral, cultural and spiritual education. For example, lack of monitoring may be referred to in geography but it may also be weak across the whole school and will therefore have to be highlighted in the post-inspection action plan.

The school has to address the key issues for action in the report. Geography could figure directly, in relation to the key issue of standards, for example. Alternatively there may be no key issues relating to aspects of geography but you may find smaller areas which are highlighted only in the geography subject section.

If geography has to appear in the main action plan, then the headteacher and governors oversee this initially, although you as the co-ordinator will need to extract the relevant parts for your own action. If geography does not appear on the main action plan, then it makes sense for you to look at your subject development plan if you have one, and to re-adjust it as necessary in the light of the inspection.

The first OFSTED annual reports identified the following as areas in geography lessons that were found to be weak:

- monitoring and evaluation
- assessment – to track progress and inform decisions about what pupils need to do next
- standards in lower junior classes
- properly developed schemes of work
- use of ICT.

Obviously, these change with curriculum development in geography, and there may be issues involved which are very particular to your school.

When you are drawing up a plan to develop your subject, you might find it useful to use the following list of headings to help you to focus in on priorities:

- the target
- evidence that shows that you have achieved the target
- people responsible for the target
- the date by which the target is to be achieved
- any known financial or other resource requirements

Action planning should be seen as the final positive phase of the inspection process. You have prepared for the inspection, survived the experience and now should be able to use it to help you plan a systematic way forward in the light of any weaknesses identified. Even if all the judgements were positive, you will still need a maintenance action plan for geography to ensure that it receives the attention it deserves, and does not become sidelined or overlooked.

Reference

Office for Standards in Education (OFSTED) (1995) *Guidance on the Inspection of Nursery and Primary Schools.* London: HMSO.

Chapter 10: The inspection process

Part 1 of this book identifies aspects of curriculum leadership that a geography co-ordinator is advised to consider before an external inspection takes place in their school. Good classroom practice in teaching and learning geography is described throughout Part 2 of the book.

Teaching and learning: linking skills, places and themes

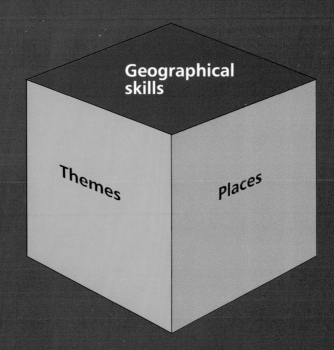

Using an Ordnance Survey Maps.

1) You look at the key to see what the symbol means.

2) ✝ is a church with a spire.

3) ∏ means a windmill (in use)

4) There are 11 chaples or churches in Whitstable.

5) The station S.E of Margate is Broad Stairs.

6) The name of the road from Whitstable to Canterbury is the A 290

7) The grid reference for Whitstable station is 115 665.

8) The grid reference for St. Nicholas at wade is 275 670

9) A castle is at 065 534.

10) An inn in Sutton is at 335 495.

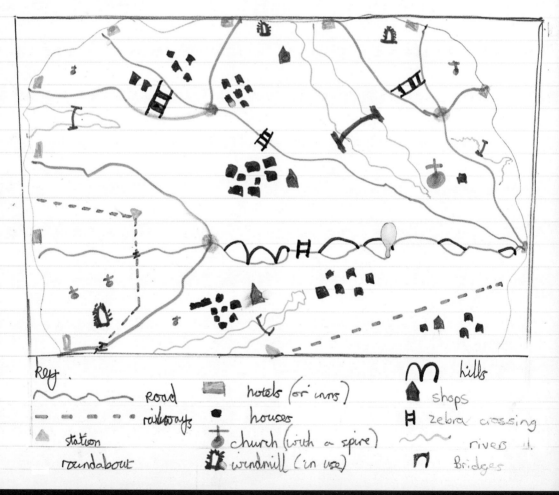

key.

〰〰〰 road   🛏 hotels (or inns)   M hills

– – – – railways   ▪ houses   🏠 shops

🔺 station   ✝ church (with a spire)   H zebra crossing

roundabout   ∏ windmill (in use)   ~ rivers   ∩ bridges

Photographs, diagrams and maps: understanding and using them

Chapter 11

Margaret Mackintosh

**Learning about plan views.
Photo: Kathy Alcock.**

What is graphicacy?

Children increasingly make sense of their world through visual images which, for young children, provide more information than text. The skill of interpreting pictorial forms of spatial information is known as graphicacy. It is an essential life skill which has been described as the 'fourth ace in the pack' alongside literacy, numeracy and oracy. Graphicacy is a form of visual literacy which can be compared with print literacy in that both employ similar processes: identifying, decoding and interpreting symbols. Prediction, observation, supposition and narrative are all needed to understand both print and images.

In developing their graphicacy skills children use signs, symbols, diagrams and photographs (including aerial photographs), as well as making and using maps and using atlases and globes. Generally, they will use these resources separately, but there will be times when they are using photographs to draw maps, comparing an atlas with a globe or using maps to locate photographs. Opportunities for using resources in combination are identified throughout this chapter, but for clarity, each type of resource is considered separately.

At key stage 1 you will be using photographs and introducing maps. Throughout key stage 1 and key stage 2 maps of different sorts will become increasingly important. You will be providing a wide range of activities (perhaps not all strictly geographical) to develop children's graphicacy skills so that, at key stage 3, where pupils will be mostly concerned with atlas and Ordnance Survey (OS) maps, they can handle these with confidence and competence.

Pictures and photographs

As adults we consciously or unconsciously interpret spatial information when we look at pictures in holiday brochures, cookery books, newspapers and estate agents' windows. We are gathering information about shape or form, scale, size and distance, as well as aesthetics. This is why illustrations are a powerful tool in geography teaching, and why they are essential for learning about localities.

We tend to assume that pictures are easy to understand, requiring little skill, and we often take it for granted that children see what they are asked to look at, and that they see what we see in pictures. But this is not so. The skill of looking at, understanding and interpreting pictures has to be taught through planned directed study. Research tells us that young children do not see a picture as a whole but as a series of apparently unconnected details selected at random. They also notice foreground and large background objects and tend to ignore the middle ground. Children need guidance in selection of detail, training in appreciation of size and in perception of the whole rather than the parts.

We know that, generally, the following responses occur:

Reception children focus first on big things, things they know, recognise and can name, then size and colour become important;

year 2 children pick on lots of detail, especially foreground detail, including things relatively unimportant to the understanding of the photograph, such as peripheral objects, but not necessarily the main essence of the picture;

year 4 children concentrate on the main essence and associated objects. Detail is less important than getting basic understanding of the picture;

year 6 children get a grasp of the picture and generalise.

HOW CAN YOU HELP YOUNG CHILDREN TO 'SEE' PHOTOGRAPHS?

Encourage and help young children to:

■ develop the specific vocabulary for identifying components, by labelling, describing, discussing photographs;

■ give the picture a title, to help generalise the 'whole';

■ see all of the picture: look at the foreground, the middle ground and the background, the right and the left, using appropriate positional language, e.g. *near to, next to, far from;*

■ place labels with specific vocabulary (which you have provided) around pictures as appropriate;

■ label or annotate a black & white photocopy, referring to the coloured picture;

■ label a 'field sketch' or line drawing of the photograph that you have provided.

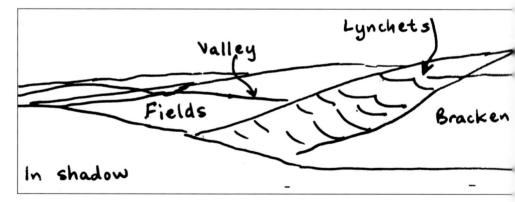

Looking west from Grimspound, Dartmoor. A panorama and accompanying field sketch which helps to highlight the human impact on the environment. Photo: Margaret Mackintosh.

HOW CAN YOU HELP CHILDREN 'READ' PHOTOGRAPHS?

Once you have helped children to 'see' photographs, they need to be helped to gather information from them, to 'read' them. This requires them to look closely, to focus on relevant detail, to categorise and compare.

Encourage and help children to:

■ sort geographical pictures: *e.g. river/not river; local/not local; like/don't like*, and explain their sorting;

■ sequence collections of photographs: *e.g. sequence pictures from a story, put a series of photos of local shops in order, sequence the landmarks seen on a recent walk, order photos of a river from source to mouth;*

■ join or overlap successive photographs (of townscape or landscape) into a panorama: *e.g. a set of photographs taken from the top of a tall building or hill* (to do this, take a series of photos with about 25% overlap, as you turn round on the spot);

■ match pictures: *e.g. same building taken from different perspectives or elevations; same view taken in different weather/season;* and explain. (This can often be resourced with postcards);

■ appreciate size, scale and distance, *e.g. talk about how big, how near or far the elements are;*

■ handle increasingly complex or unfamiliar photographs, encouraging both comparison and generalisation;

■ make a 'field sketch' or line drawing of a photograph, identifying key elements, buildings, landscape features: *e.g. by tracing (use a plastic pocket), freehand;*

■ label, annotate, colour elements of field sketch to indicate reading of photograph: *e.g. identify different types of land use such as agricultural, industrial, residential;*

■ take their own geographical photographs, to use for practical activities.

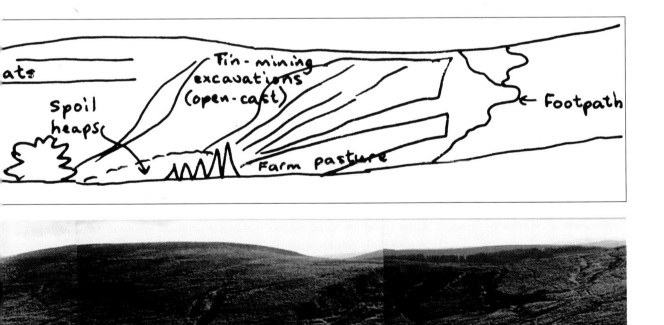

HOW CAN YOU HELP CHILDREN 'INTERPRET' PHOTOGRAPHS?

The information children gain from photographs is influenced by their past experience, geographical language, their imagination, preconceived ideas and stereotypes. These often need challenging. Use different types of questions to help children interpret photographs.

When interpreting photographs (see photograph of Mandinari) you might find it helpful to organise questions into categories:

- observation/description
  e.g. What can you see?
  What is it like here?

- *interpretation, explanation, classification – requiring children to locate learning in their own conceptual framework*
  e.g. Where do you think this is?   *What sort of place is it?*
  What is she doing?   *Why is she doing it outside?*

- comparison – requiring application of learning to a new situation
  e.g. Is the house like yours?

- evaluation – requiring children to make judgements, express opinions and evaluate information
  e.g. Would you like to live there?
  What do you think the bricks are for?

- extrapolation – requiring children to extend their understanding to determine implications or consequences of natural processes or human actions
  e.g. What would happen if ... they had electricity?

Ironing in Lamin Darboe's compound, Mandinari, The Gambia. Asking different types of questions can help children interpret photographs. Photo: Margaret Mackintosh.

Chambers (1996) gives a slightly different, but equally useful, sequence of open questions providing progression:

- concrete   *What can you see?*
- descriptive   *What is she doing?*
- speculative   *What are the bricks for?*
- reasoning   *Why is she working outside?*
- evaluative   *Would you like to live here?*
- problem solving   *How else could she do the ironing?*

Be creative in your use of photographs, use tried and tested activities and develop your own. Chambers (1996), McFarlane (1992) and the teacher's notes in most resource packs provide many ideas for appropriate activities. These include: labelling, titling, 'making friends', describing, sequencing, 'good' and 'bad' adjectives, speech bubbles, questioning, cropping/masking, 'outside the picture', freeze frame, matching sets, drawing photographs, alternative views, comparisons. Whichever you choose, think about the purpose of the activity – is it helping children to see, to read or to interpret the photographs, and what graphicacy skills and geography are they learning?

It is important for children to learn that, because geography involves attitudes and values, there is often no 'right' answer. Indeed, the photographer and the people being photographed will probably have different views of what is happening. Children will also discover that, because you may not know the answer, you will join in the enquiry or discussion with them. You might find it helpful to encourage children to work in pairs or small groups to explore and compare their own ideas, since each child's 'reading' or understanding of a picture is different, influenced by his or her own attitudes, perceptions and experiences.

WHAT DO YOU NEED TO DO?

1 Build up a range of pictorial resources:

■ 'big books' designed for key stage 1 – the younger the child, the larger the photographs should be;

■ collect large numbers of geographical photographs from simple and obvious to complex, more abstract, more generalised, for use throughout the school. Your collection could include:

Photo: Paula Richardson.

general views (urban and rural views, landscapes, townscapes, human and physical features) as well as *pictures relative to:* settlement *(homes, occupations, buildings, journeys, transport)*; environment *(aesthetics, issues, changes)*; land uses; weather *(types and effects)*; water in the environment *(rivers, sea, lakes, reservoirs, canals)*;

■ local photographs: from ground/above ground level, including human and physical features in different weather conditions, seasons, years, but also local issues and changes;

■ sequences of local photographs: a whole street, a panoramic view, each requiring several separate photographs;

■ photopacks focusing on UK, European and more distant localities.

2 Train children to use – to see, to read and to interpret – pictorial resources.

3 Develop strategies for progression and differentiation in the use of illustrations, including:

■ types of questions used to develop conceptual understanding;

■ using the familiar enquiry and issue-based questions with photographs.

Photo: Bill Marsden.

Aerial photographs

As adults we do not often use aerial photographs, although there has been renewed interest in them with the publication of several books of oblique aerial views of landscape, towns and coastline. Many of these images are available as commercial postcards. Satellite images also are now widely available.

Oblique and vertical aerial photographs have different characteristics. In oblique photographs features are easier to identify, but there is distortion because the foreground detail is larger than the background. In vertical photographs shapes, sizes and patterns are easier to identify, and since there is no distortion the photograph can be traced to make a map.

HOW CAN CHILDREN USE AERIAL PHOTOGRAPHS?

Aerial photographs make the link between the real world and maps. They are less abstract than maps, and show what is actually there, not what a map-maker has selected to include. Starting with the young child's experiences with toys and models, progress to real, familiar environments and then to the unfamiliar.

Photo: Chris Garnett.

Encourage and help children with:

- toys and models
  - take photographs of these from different perspectives and have multiple copies printed for the children to sort and match;
  - take oblique and vertical aerial photographs of different arrangements *(e.g. of train set, Lego models)* for the children to reconstruct, using the photograph as a pictorial map;
- real environments: school, school grounds, area around school
  - identify human and physical features including buildings (landmarks) and routeways, recognise plan shapes, colour, texture, tone and pattern;
  - label an outline drawing of a photograph;
  - make a sketch map of part of a photograph;
  - recognise different land uses;
  - trace a vertical photograph to make a map;
  - select and add detail to the map;
  - match a photograph to a real map, orientating appropriately;
  - identify relative and actual position, relative and compass direction, scale and distance;
  - identify the time of day or year when the photograph was taken;
- unfamiliar environments:
  - similar activities to above, extending learning to new situations, especially settlements, rivers, environmental changes and issues;
  - map patterns made by features (e.g. town buildings, road networks, rivers, fields), and patterns of land use;
  - compare with own area, identifying similarities and differences;
  - compare vertical and oblique views;
- satellite images:
  - identify features and patterns *e.g. settlement, transport, rivers, coastline, land use;*
  - link with vertical, oblique and ground level photographs;
  - describe routes;
  - link with maps and globes.

WHAT DO YOU NEED TO DO?

Build up a collection of:

■ vertical (plan) and oblique (side) aerial photographs *e.g. of classroom equipment (furniture, toys and models); the school (some taken from nearby tall buildings, if possible); the school grounds possibly taken from the school roof (close-up oblique); the local area; other localities;*

■ postcards and books showing oblique aerial views;

■ satellite images (available as posters and postcards) (Barnett *et al.,* 1994).

Signs, symbols, logos

In adult life we gather spatial information from road signs, locational and directional signs at airports and other public places and spaces, many of which include internationally accepted symbols. We also discover the location of significant buildings, including specific shops, railway stations, National Trust properties, by identifying logos, both in the real world and on maps (see 'Cityscape' maps). And, of course, we gather information from weather forecast maps by interpreting symbols.

HOW CAN CHILDREN MAKE AND USE SIGNS, SYMBOLS AND LOGOS IN SCHOOL?

Photo: Paula Richardson.

There will probably be some signs, symbols and logos in use in school already, for example, directions to the Head's office, and on the lavatories.

Encourage children to:

■ erect signposts around school, indicating direction and distance to, for example, the library;

■ erect a playground signpost, indicating direction and distance to nearby landmarks *(e.g. the town centre, the comprehensive school),* to nearby towns and villages, and to more distant localities *(e.g. London, Edinburgh, New York),* providing opportunities to incorporate compass and map work;

■ start in the nursery or reception class with symbols to indicate the location of equipment – link these with symbols for children to place on a model or plan of the classroom;

■ put appropriate symbols on various spaces and places in and around school;

■ place 'traffic' signs at key points to encourage safe movement in and around school: older children, identifying a movement problem in school, might like to study and 'solve' it with the use of signs and symbols;

■ create their own weather forecast symbols and charts, collect newspaper weather charts, and watch television weather forecasts.

Giving children opportunities to design and use their own symbols will help them to understand Ordnance Survey symbol conventions when they meet them.

Diagrams

In adult life we interpret the spatial information in diagrams when we use a car maintenance manual or a dress-making pattern, assemble flat-pack furniture, wire up electrical equipment, plan a new kitchen or use diagrams in textbooks or newspapers. These are two-dimensional representations of three-dimensional structures, requiring the ability to interpret perspective.

HOW CAN CHILDREN USE DIAGRAMS?

Much in the same way as children need to be taught to 'see' photographs, they also need to be taught to 'see' diagrams, for example, to see a perspective drawing of a cube, and the familiar water cycle or river system diagrams as three-dimensional.

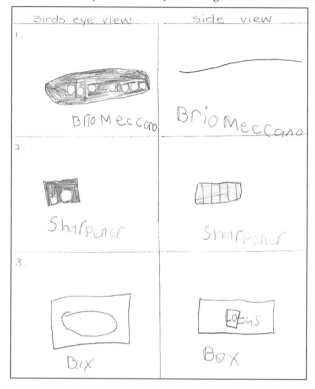

Developing the skill to understand two-dimensional representation of three-dimensional structures starts with toys. You should provide children with opportunities to:

- follow the assembly diagrams with construction toys, *e.g. Lego;*
- make models from diagrams *e.g. with boxes, wooden bricks, Unifix cubes;*
- assemble more advanced construction kits and models, *e.g. Meccano, Airfix vehicles;*
- use diagram/field sketches alongside geographical photographs.

Understanding different views. Work: Ainthorpe Primary School, Hull.

Many of these opportunities will be cross-curricular, relating especially to technology, maths and science.

HOW CAN CHILDREN MAKE DIAGRAMS?

Most of the early opportunities for making diagrams to communicate spatial information will occur when children record constructions they have made. Many of these opportunities will be cross-curricular, particularly in art, maths and technology.

Encourage children to:

- record constructions made with Unifix, Lego and other materials;
- use maths solid shapes to create simple structures and to record them in line drawings in both side and plan view;
- make drawings/diagrams of play situations *(e.g. the home corner set out as a cafe, a travel agents, a shop)*, recording the layout;
- make and annotate line drawings or field sketches from geographical photographs (see photograph of Mysore).

Field sketches are a particularly geographical form of diagram. They are hand drawn summaries of townscape, landscape or landform, to identify or generalise key features in an environment, *e.g. areas of different surface type or usage of the school playground, change of slope in a river valley landscape, distinct residential and industrial sectors in a view of a town.* Making field sketches is a skill to be acquired from landscape or human-interest photographs in the classroom and practised outside on fieldwork.

A tourist buying spices from a young street trader in Mysore, India. Making a diagram or 'field sketch' can enhance and, at the same time, assess understanding. Photo: Margaret Mackintosh.

INSET Activity 1 (see page 149) is a practical activity which illustrates opportunities to make maps and diagrams in the field, using a range of graphicacy skills. It is best carried out in woodland (where it can be used to introduce children to ecology or biogeography), but could be adapted for use indoors.

Maps

We all use many types of maps for different purposes, for example to locate and find the route to a tourist attraction, or to check where to change trains on the London Underground. Some of us may even look up rainfall and temperature maps of an overseas

River Humber

The Humber

Children's maps of a fourteenth century plan of Hull (British Museum).

holiday destination. It is important to remember what a wide range of maps we use, or make. As well as OS maps there are parish maps, road atlases, sketch maps in brochures, weather forecast maps (on television and in the newspaper), street maps, pictorial town and information maps.

Try to use maps with the children in the situations when adults would refer to maps, and do so throughout the curriculum, not just in geography lessons. There are, for instance, many opportunities to use maps in history. And map use should permeate the geography curriculum. Graphicacy skills are best learned in the context of place and thematic studies, supported as necessary by mapwork lessons focusing on specific skills.

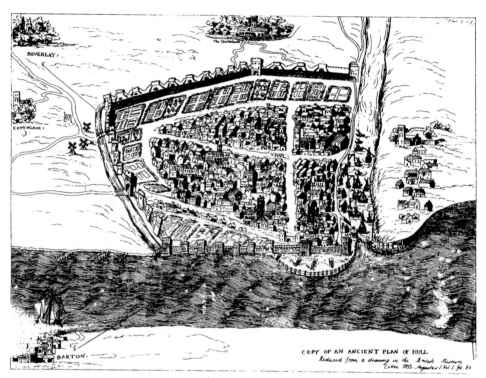

Before you ask children to draw or create a map, you need to be sure that they have had experience of real maps. They need to know what maps look like, and to begin to understand what they are for and what range of functions they can serve. At key stage 3 pupils will be focusing on OS and atlas maps, but at key stage 1 and key stage 2 it is important that you give children many opportunities to look at and use spatial representations in a wide range of styles and scales, especially pictorial maps. Your Geography Adviser will probably have information about the availability of Ordnance Survey Superplan (centred on your school if you wish) and other OS maps through the local authority. Many authorities are licensed to provide these to schools.

HOW CAN YOU HELP CHILDREN TO USE MAPS?

There are two complementary aspects to children using maps, and you should provide opportunities for each, preferably integrated into the study of real places or geographical themes:

1　in the real environment, in context, using the whole map to gather information and way-find;

2　for study, to find out how a map works, to be introduced to or to focus on a discrete element.

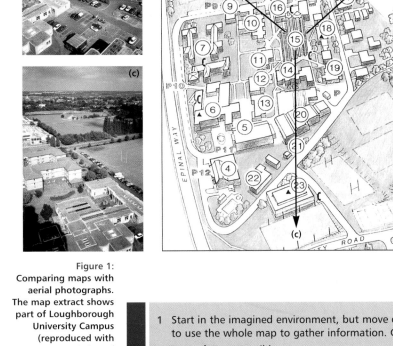

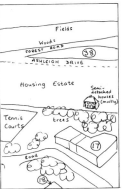

Figure 1:
Comparing maps with aerial photographs. The map extract shows part of Loughborough University Campus (reproduced with permission of Loughborough University). The accompanying photographs were taken from the top of Towers Hall (number 15 on the map) (a) looking east, (b) looking south, with accompanying field sketch, and (c) looking north-west. Teachers could ask: 'What is in the space between number 17 and 38 on the map?'
Photos: Margaret Mackintosh.

1 Start in the imagined environment, but move quickly to the real environment in context, to use the whole map to gather information. Children should be encouraged to use maps:

■ as often as possible;

■ with stories, e.g. the *Katie Morag* books by Mairi Hedderwick;

■ with toys: playmats, train set, farm layout, *e.g. provide simple layout maps for the children to follow*;

■ with models, *e.g. from imagination, of school, school grounds, local area, contrasting and distant locality*;

■ of their school and grounds (linked with aerial photographs); before and after making local and more distant journeys, asking *Where are we going? Which way will we go? How far is it? What's the route like? What shape was our journey?*;

■ of weather forecasts: local, national, European on television and in newspapers;

■ to locate places they are studying, asking *'Where is this place? How will/could we get there?* 'nesting' the place from its global to national to local position and the other way round;

■ to gather information about the places they are studying, from a range of current maps, and past maps to identify changes;

■ to sequence maps of different dates, to tell the 'story' of the place;

■ to link photographs to maps, *e.g. Where are these buildings (in the photographs) located? Where did the photographer stand to take this photograph? Which direction was s/he facing?*

■ to compare maps with aerial photographs (Figure 1);

■ to link maps with globes: here you might find *Atlas-wise: Ideas and Themes for Atlas Work* (Scoffham, 1997) useful.

2   For study – to find out how a map works and to be introduced to or focus on a discrete element – you could hardly do better than refer to a series like *Mapstart* (Catling, 1992). This series of four books provides a structured scheme for the development of map skills. You will find it particularly useful for reference, as a source of ideas to integrate into your place and thematic work. It would be well worth the time and effort to transfer the ideas from the localities used in the series to your own location and situation. Use your own local area, your chosen contrasting and distant localities as the context for the activities suggested by Catling, resourcing your school with the appropriate maps and photographs. These books are so readily available that there is no need to repeat the detail of activities here.

The four *Mapstart* books introduce children to, and revisit throughout the series:

1   The elements of maps:

i. plan-view:	perspective, aerial photographs;
ii. arrangement:	direction – from relative direction *(right, left, up)* to compass points; location – from relative location *(next to, near to)* to alpha-numeric co-ordinates (A3, C5) and grid references. It is worth checking with your maths co-ordinator that there is no confusion between the maths and geography usage of co-ordinates: do you both read them →E ↑N (or in the door and up the stairs?);
iii. map-language:	use of colour; point, line and area symbols; words;
iv. proportion:	scale, size, distance, relief;

2   selection of information shown on a map, and map purpose;

3   language of spatial movement and representation;

4   practical activities for the study of map elements and information gathering.

The series uses the full range of mapwork resources, as you should in your classroom:

■ oblique and vertical aerial photographs:	from toys and models and maps of these, to real environments and large-scale maps of these;
■ maps on a full range of scale:	from plans, through pictorial and conventional maps, to small-scale atlas maps;
■ globes:	from simple sea/land globes to political (showing countries) and physical (showing topography and indicating vegetation/climate).

HOW CAN YOU HELP CHILDREN TO MAKE MAPS?

Many transferable and graphicacy skills are used to draw a map. This is illustrated by INSET Activity 2 (see page 150).

To help children to make or draw maps, provide them with opportunities to:

■   observe and describe using common and collective nouns and adjectives to label and classify;

■   perceive *(e.g. check that the old chapel is not perceived as a school);*

■   memorise *(short- and long-term memory)* landmarks, nodes, routeways, topography;

- *construct mental maps (sequence landmarks, nodes, routeways and relate to topography);*
- recall;
- orientate *(match shape of mental map to paper)* relate to compass directions;
- scale *(size of first mark determines informal scale of map);*
- represent *(drawing, fine manipulative skills)* initially pictorial, but using map-making conventions when acquired: plan-shape, symbols, key, compass direction, scale;
- evaluate *(assess skills and accuracy).*

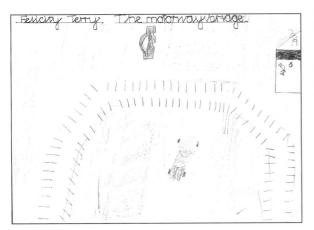
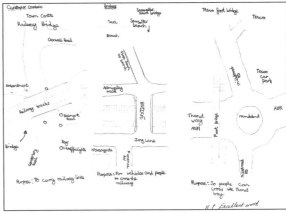

Children's developing concept of maps. Work: Felicity Terry and Christopher Goodwin.

If a child is unable to draw an appropriate (re. ability, experience, context) map of the route of a recent visit, say from school to the public library, any one or more of these skills may need developing. You should check which skills the child does and does not possess. When the children are drawing a map you should make its purpose and audience explicit, *e.g. is it a map to show a visitor how to get from school to the town centre, is it to show you, the teacher, how much the child knows about the area around school, or is it to show the relative direction and distance to neighbouring towns and villages?* Remind children of the graphicacy skills they have acquired and which you expect them to use.

Encourage children to:
- experience, observe and accurately perceive their environment;
- remember, recall and sequence landmarks, *e.g. specific buildings;*
- describe routes and road networks, *e.g. right/left turns and later north/south/east/west turns, uphill/downhill, angle of corners;*
- play memory games, *e.g. Kim's game (or memory tray), or variations of an a, b, c, game:
I walked along Exeter Road and I passed Boots.
I walked along Exeter Road and I passed Boots and WH Smith.
I walked along Exeter Road and I passed Boots, WH Smith and Tesco...
or
I walked along Exeter Road and I passed a chemist's, a bookshop and a supermarket;*
- construct then record structured sandtray play in pictures followed by maps,
e.g. make landscapes, islands, road networks;
- construct then record use of toys, in pictures followed by maps, *e.g. train set, farm and zoo animal, model lay out;*
- make sketch maps of the classroom, other areas of the school, short journeys;

- make maps to illustrate or accompany stories;
- (older children) make large-scale maps of the local area for younger pupils to use, *e.g. before and after a visit;*
- have frequent opportunities to draw maps of successively longer journeys or covering greater areas.

WHAT DO YOU NEED TO DO?

- check that there is a wide range of road and world atlases available in the school/class library;
- collect local maps and plans of all sorts, *e.g. school plans, street maps, brochure maps, parish maps, pictorial maps, OS maps of different scales and different dates;*
- collect map jigsaws and children's games that use a map (there are several including *Great Game of Britain, Journey Through Europe);*
- foster a love of, and interest in, maps *per se;*
- make sure you understand maps and their conventions;
- identify progression in the various discrete elements of maps (see Figures 2 and 3).

More wall and plan views –
changing the layout
of the classroom.
Photo: Kathy Alcock.

Figure 2:
Progression in the
various discrete elements
of maps at key stage 1.
Source: Catling, 1996,
pp. 101-4.

Children should normally learn to be able to do the following:

From 3 to 5 years:
- move toy vehicles, people and animals around large-scale playmat picture maps of different types of local environment, using roads and paths, and talk about what they are doing;
- create layouts of environments using toys, which are imaginary but increasingly imitative of 'real-world' layouts and use toys such as model furniture to make generalised layouts of familiar small-scale areas, such as rooms;
- draw routes between objects placed on large sheets of paper, such as a road between buildings, and navigate a vehicle along them;
- identify a variety of features on large-scale vertical aerial photographs of a familiar area and of places they do not know;
- talk about features and activities on, and trace journeys around, an area shown in a picture map;
- recognise a few features on a large-scale, full-colour abstract map of a small area about which they are talking with older children or adults;
- make journeys within their familiar environments and take others on these routes, talking about the features or landmarks they are passing;
- retrace routes along which they have walked and been able to observe landmarks and directions;
- use a large-scale map, drawn as a vertical view of the features, of a room or open space with a limited number of features in it, to find features they are shown on the map in that environment, especially when they have been helped to orient the map to the area;
- use colour-based co-ordinates to find items on a grid layout.

From 5 to 7 years:
- follow and give directions using terms such as 'left', 'right', 'forward', 'back';
- describe the relative location of features of environments they are in, using terms like 'in front of', 'nearby', 'behind';
- sort objects by their shapes and relative sizes;
- draw round the base of toy and life-size objects, remove the object and recognise that the shape left is its plan-view;
- make a model layout showing some of the features in an area they are familiar with and navigate a vehicle around the area;
- draw picture maps and maps using symbols of routes or small areas with which they are familiar;
- make a tracing of features on a large-scale vertical aerial photograph and identify those features when the photograph is no longer present;
- use a large-scale map of their own familiar environment to identify features and routes;
- use a large-scale map of a small, familiar environment to find their way around and identify named features;
- give locations on a grid system using alpha-numeric co-ordinates;
- estimate relative distances, using terms such as 'nearer than', 'further away', and relative sizes, using terms like 'larger' and 'smaller'.

Globes

Maps and pictures give us a two-dimensional representation, but the globe provides a three-dimensional representation or model of our three-dimensional world. We rely on our three-dimensional model or visualisation to understand many geographical (and scientific) phenomena, *e.g. day/night; phases of the moon; climate; world climate/vegetation zones;*

Children should normally learn to be able to do the following:

From 7 to 9 years:

- draw a moderately accurate free-hand map of such features as a table, a room and an outside area they can see;
- draw a free-hand map of a familiar area or a route that cannot be seen from one site;
- relate a large-scale map of a room, building or grounds to a familiar environment to find where features are and the way around;
- use a large-scale map and a street map of a familiar area that cannot be viewed at once to identify features and routes in the environment;
- use a large-scale vertical aerial photograph with a map of the same familiar area to identify features and routes;
- add features using pictures or symbols to a large-scale map of a room or the school grounds;
- begin to use some conventional symbols in making their own maps of real or imaginary places, and provide a key;
- measure distances in a room and in an open area using metre rules, tape measures and trundle wheels with reasonable accuracy;
- measure straight-line distances on a large-scale map using a scale bar;
- give locations on a grid system using four-figure co-ordinates;
- use a compass to find and give the four cardinal compass directions and the four intermediate directions;
- use the points of the compass when giving directions on a map when there is a compass rose present.

From 9 to 11 years:

- use plan shapes and symbols to show specific features on maps they draw, and include a key;
- draw a reasonably accurate free-hand map of a familiar area or a route that cannot be seen from one site;
- use the 16 points of the compass to give and follow directions;
- indicate compass directions in the neighbourhood;
- align a large-scale map of the school and neighbourhood, using landmarks and compass points;
- use a conventional large-scale map to find the way around an area and relate position on the ground to location on the map;
- understand the purpose of the information that surrounds a map, including the title, key, scale bar, grid co-ordinates and compass;
- begin to use six-figure grid references to locate points on maps;
- begin to have some sense of the real distance meaning of measurements made on large-scale maps of familiar areas;
- begin to draw reasonably accurate scaled maps of familiar areas, such as the classroom and school grounds, using measurements they have made;
- begin to make a moderately accurate scaled model of part of the local area showing features of the area;
- measure the straight-line distance between two points on maps of progressively smaller scales and begin to measure the winding distances along roads on maps;
- compare symbols for the same features on maps of progressively smaller scales;
- begin to recognise that the generalisation on maps increases with the decrease in scale;
- begin to appreciate that some symbols on small-scale maps are disproportionate in size to the real features they represent;
- begin to describe a route on a map from statements of direction and distance;
- recognise from the layer tinting and contour lines on maps that the landscape shown is not flat;
- annotate a sketch map of an area shown in a vertical aerial photograph to show the variety of features;
- begin to search for locations on atlas maps using longitude and latitude.

Figure 3: Progression in the various discrete elements of maps at key stage 2. Source: Catling, 1996, pp. 101-4.

Globes help young children to distinguish between land and sea.
Photo: Wendy Morgan.

relative sizes, directions of countries/holiday destinations; international time/date line; round-the-world sailing races. In adult life we may rarely use a globe (although computer-generated images of the globe are used on television to locate news events), but it is an essential image for us to hold.

Despite references to globes in the National Curriculum and other sources, and ideas for activities with globes, we are only now researching children's understanding of the globe. Nevertheless, because of the importance of internalising a three-dimensional model of the world, it is essential that children encounter this mode of representation from an early age, even if understanding does come later.

HOW CAN CHILDREN USE A GLOBE?

Encourage young children to:

■ play with an inflatable globe;

■ recognise that the colouring represents areas of land and sea;

■ accept that it models their world, the Earth;

then progress to:

■ recognise the shapes of the continents, and name them;

■ link the globe with atlas maps (see INSET Activity 3);

■ locate specific countries, oceans, locations, North/South Poles, northern and southern hemisphere;

■ more locational knowledge and detail;

■ learn the location of the 'imaginary lines': Equator, Tropics of Cancer and Capricorn, latitude, longitude;

■ know that the Earth rotates on its own axis, and around the sun;

■ understand the significance of the relative rotations: day/night; phases of the moon.

Older children should:

■ begin to recognise similarities in places at similar latitudes, and explain some differences between places in terms of latitude;

■ begin to recognise global patterns and explain them with reference to global location: polar climates, European-type climates, hotter-than-home and colder-than-home climates, the location of tropical rainforests, arid deserts;

■ understand the significance of the relative rotation of the Earth and sun: weather and climate, seasons, international time.

Placing continents on a globe.
Photo: Patrick Wiegand.

Atlases and globes should be used side by side. They are complementary, each providing some unique spatial information. Atlas maps provide more detail than globes, but globes provide information about relative size, direction and distance. Since the scale of maps is not consistent throughout an atlas, children can be confused. For example, in an atlas south west England often appears larger than Italy, Spain larger than Australia – how often do you, or the children, look at the scale in an atlas?

WHAT DO YOU NEED TO DO?

- have a range of globes (simple/detailed, political/physical, hard/inflatable) available;
- refer to a globe frequently, to locate topical events, places being studied, children's overseas holiday destinations;
- share with colleagues the importance of using a globe by engaging in INSET Activity 3 (see page 151), comparing information about a country obtained from an atlas and from a globe.

Mapwork and photograph interpretation skills should permeate geography, not be a 'bolt on' element. But, more than this, graphicacy should permeate the whole curriculum whenever and wherever opportunities present themselves, whenever and wherever it is appropriate to use maps, globes, atlases and photographs.

In conclusion, research shows that we underestimate children's mapping capabilities. Catling (1996) summarises research into children's spatial awareness and understanding, their ability to draw and use maps, models and aerial photographs (surrogate maps) and updates Boardman's (1983) framework for planning map programmes. His sequencing and structuring of the aspects of mapwork that children aged 3-11 years are considered to need is particularly useful, and integrates the aspects of graphicacy discussed here.

INSET Activities

ACTIVITY 1

Place a hoop on the ground to define 'a place':

1 Draw a map to record the location of the place (or hoop)

- *did you draw plan view, indicate scale and direction, and use words, pictures and/or symbols?*

2a Draw another map to record the detail of the place (i.e. within the hoop)

- *did you indicate scale and direction, did you draw pictures, or use colour or symbols and a key?*

2b Practise the familiar enquiry questions in the place *(Where is this place? What is it like? Why is it like this? How is it connected to other places? How and why is it changing? What do you feel about this place?).*

Imagine a three-dimensional cylinder defined by the hoop, extending as far down into the ground and up into the sky as possible:

3 Draw a diagram of this 3D space

- *did you include and explore the soil, humus layer, ground cover, canopy, sky?*
- *did you include a vertical scale and estimate the height of the trees?*

4 Identify movement or 'cycling' within the space and represent it in a diagram

- *what was moving down: precipitation, leaves, nutrients, air?*
- *what was moving up: plant growth, evaporation, air?*

■ *is it an open or closed system?*

■ *what is entering or leaving the system?*

5 Consider how it might be different at other times of the day/year

■ *how could you show this on a time-line diagram?*

ACTIVITY 2

Draw a sketch map of your school and grounds, then analyse how you did it. Identify the sequence of skills you used. Your response will be something like this:

> *'I visualised the school and its grounds. To do this I needed to have experienced and observed the area, perceived the components accurately (collection of evidence), remembered, created a mental map and recalled.' 'Then I transferred my mental map to paper. To do this I matched the shape of my mental map to the paper, orientated the paper, decided which component to draw first, where and how big to make the first mark on the paper (thus making a decision about scale) and used my drawing skills to complete my representation (Figure 4). Finally I assessed the accuracy of my map.'*

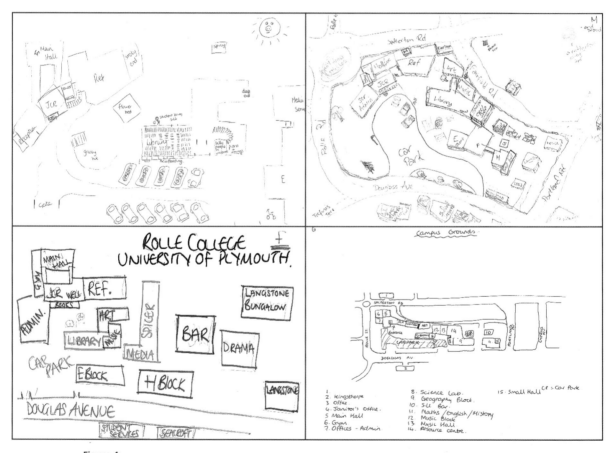

Figure 4:
The responses of four teachers to INSET Activity 2 are very different in their representations of Rolle School of Education, Exmouth.

ACTIVITY 3

Compare what you can find out from an atlas and a globe about, for example, Botswana.

Some year 5 children did this, and discovered:

From the atlas:
in Africa/near Africa/next to Africa
in south of Africa/on the bottom of Africa
near South Africa, Zimbabwe, Namibia
Atlantic and Indian Oceans around it
Atlantic Ocean not very close to Botswana
no sea round it/not near sea
Okavango swamp/Kalahari/sandy desert
no water? near salt pans
Capital: Gaborone
towns: Tshane, Molepolole, Serowe
lots of places in Botswana
1000m to 15000m high/above sea level, high ground
land gets lower as we move up the map
big/small: approximately 600 x 500 miles
strange boundary
Tropic of Capricorn going through it (imaginary line)
far from Kimberley, near Johannesburg, near Transvaal,
near Cape of Good Hope and Cape Town

From the globe:
it's in the southern hemisphere
south of the Equator
nearer the South Pole than to us
much, much bigger than Britain
not much further east than us
a long way from here
Africa's huge!

References and further reading

Barnett, M., Kent, A. and Milton, M. (eds) (1994) *Images of Earth: A Teachers Guide to Remote Sensing in Geography at KS2.* Sheffield: Geographical Association.

Boardman, D. (1983) *Graphicacy and Geography Teaching.* London: Croom Helm.

Catling, S. (1990) 'Beginning mapwork: ideas for developing mapwork in the reception class', *Primary Geographer*, 3, p. 6.

Catling, S. (1992) *Mapstart Books 1, 2, 3, OS* (second edition). Harlow: Collins-Longman.

Catling, S. (1996) 'Technical interest in curriculum development' in Williams, M. (ed) *Understanding Geographical and Environmental Education: The Role of Research.* London: Cassell, pp. 93-111

Chambers, B. (1996) 'Step by step', *Junior Focus*, April, pp. 2-4.

McFarlane, C. (1992) 'Photographs: a window on the world', *Primary Geographer*, 11, pp. 4-8.

Matthews, M.H. (1992) *Making Sense of Place.* Hemel Hempstead: Harvester Wheatsheaf.

Scoffham, S. (1997) *Atlas-Wise: Ideas and Themes for Atlas Work.* Sheffield: Geographical Association.

Chapter 11: Photographs, diagrams and maps: understanding and using them

The use of map, photograph and other visual images is essential to good geographical investigations. In the examples given these skills are applied to place studies and further developed in Section Five, and to various geographical themes in Section Six.

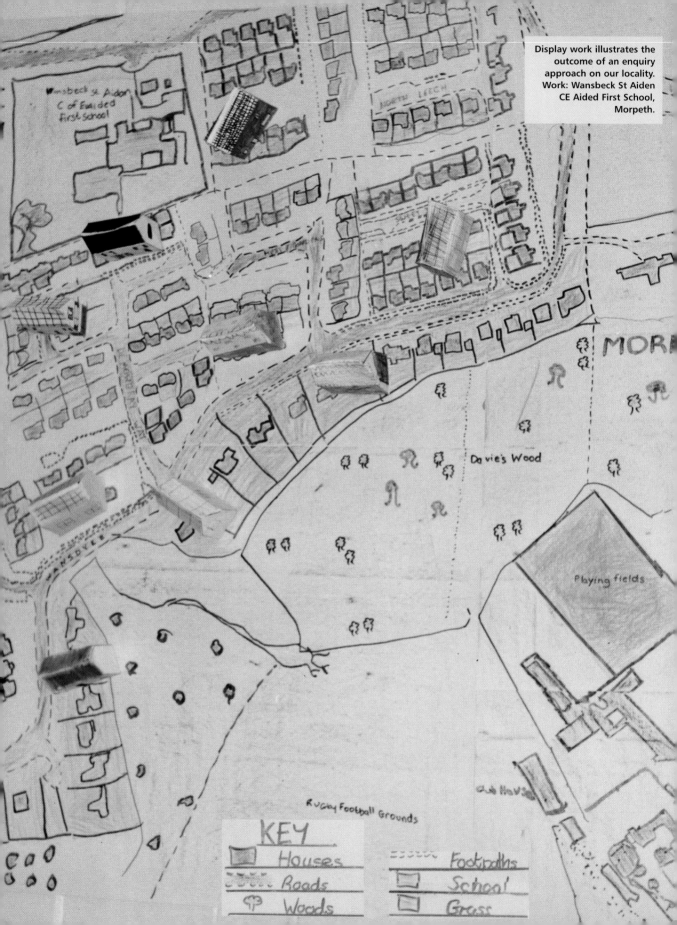

Display work illustrates the outcome of an enquiry approach on our locality. Work: Wansbeck St Aiden CE Aided First School, Morpeth.

Geographical questions and enquiry

Chapter 12

Geoff Dinkele

> 'An enquiry approach to geographical study may be defined as one in which the teacher assists pupils to develop the abilities to ask questions and seek to answer them through investigative work leading to sound knowledge, understanding and skill development' (DES/WO, 1990, p. 7).

Learning and enquiry

You might be rather surprised if, during an interview, you were asked how you think children learn. The most direct response I ever received was 'Somewhere between when I

tell them and when they want to!'. How would you answer the question? And how does your school's learning policy relate to its geography policy? This may sound like an inspection, but these are important questions!

Teachers have come to recognise the enquiry approach as an important strategy for children's learning. The research basis for this teaching strategy is that meaningful learning is found to occur when investigation is directed by a challenging question(s) and a solution and/or reasoned viewpoint is reached and clarified. Key questions are used as signposts to paths to understanding and, it is claimed, such an approach helps pupils to manage their own learning, handle issues objectively and use skills with a real purpose.

Specific reference is made to the enquiry approach in

Signposts to further understanding.
Photo: Paula Richardson.

Encourage pupils to think of their own geographical questions. Photo: Chris Garnett.

the Geography National Curriculum where point 1 of the programme of study emphasises the need to provide opportunities for pupils to investigate and to undertake studies that focus on geographical questions, and point 2 outlines a simple description of geographical enquiry under the general heading of Geographical Skills. Clearly, therefore, those responsible for the content of the curriculum were confident that geographical enquiry is a good strategy for teaching and learning; so let us investigate it further...

Asking questions

Educators have offered many classifications of questions posed in the classroom and it is patently obvious that geographical enquiry depends upon the teacher's questioning skills. How often are your questions posed clearly and succinctly and what is the proportion of closed to open ones? And do you set out to arrange your questions in a logical sequence to maintain coherence? How are you encouraging pupils to ask their own geographical questions? It is worth having a serious word with oneself, and with colleagues, about the use of questions in the classroom and their contribution to pupils' learning.

Asking questions is not restricted to cognitive matters; carefully and sensitively posed ones can also be effective for exploring the affective domain. Attitudes, beliefs and values are a vital ingredient of geographical studies, and geography offers many opportunities for considering the viewpoints of pupils and of others. Thus, it contributes to the development of tolerance and an understanding of contemporary issues.

Key questions

Effective geographical enquiry depends initially upon the quality of the key questions posed. The characteristics of these key, or leading questions, are listed in Figure 1. You will notice that they beg *more* questions and require *investigation* before an answer can be attempted. The origin of key questions must obviously lie in the intended learning outcomes of your curriculum and, for many, these will be those identified in the programme of study for each key stage. Key questions unlock the door to learning about the ideas implicit in the programme of study statements for Places and Themes (including issues). They also stimulate the development of the skills needed to enable investigation to be carried out.

Figure 1: Key questions.

The main characteristics of key questions are that they:
- are an immensely powerful way of planning a curriculum with structure;
- unlock the door to learning about key ideas and processes;
- give direction and structure to a topic, emphasising what pupils are investigating and why;
- are the driving force behind enquiry learning;
- demand enquiry, require investigation and beg more questions;
- may be awareness raising, descriptive, explanatory, speculative, moral/value based or reflective;
- should be shared with pupils;
- provide professional development for teachers generating them;
- stimulate skills development to enable them to be investigated.

The essence of a true key question is clear from the following example:
1 How many people live in Goodworth Clatford?
2 What is life like for the people living in Goodworth Clatford?

The second question requires sustained enquiry and some synthesis while the first is a closed one to which the answer can be found relatively easily using reference skills. To consolidate your thinking, consider the difference between the following two questions: (i) When did the Romans occupy England? and (ii) How do we know the Romans occupied England?

The precise phrasing of a key question will affect its place in the learning sequence; for example, 'Why are there differences in land use in our local area?' encourages a higher level of geographical thinking than the question, 'How is land used in our area?'.

Focused geographical enquiry

There is an important distinction between a focused enquiry route (see Figure 2) and general enquiry which permeates the curriculum. In Figure 2, notice how Stage 1a is an orientation phase when pupils relate their previous experiences and existing knowledge to the posed enquiry. This is followed by a focusing phase (Stage 1b) when initiative-taking begins in earnest and a range of enabling questions is raised as the enquiry process gets started.

Stage 1	a Awareness raising
	b Generating enabling questions
Stage 2	Collecting and recording information
Stage 3	Processing the gathered information
Stage 4	Drawing conclusions from the processed data
Stage 5	Sharing the learning and effective outcomes
Stage 6	Evaluation by all concerned

**Figure 2:
A framework for managing a focused geographical enquiry.**

Stages 2, 3 and 4 in Figure 2 mark the information phase and should be the time for intense and purposeful geographical activity. Factual statements and generalisations emerge during Stage 4 as pupils attempt to answer the current key question. Interpersonal skills are practised during the important Stage 5, the outcome of which can influence the responses during Stage 6 when feelings are revealed, including self-evaluation. These last two stages represent the reflective phase. Such a structured and substantial piece of work could be part of topic work or make up the bulk of the study unit.

An Enquiry Approach to Learning Geography (CCW, 1993) includes a framework for considering progression in enquiries; the suggested parameters are:

- the enquiry focus;
- the degree of pupil involvement in planning;
- the range of viewpoints considered in issues;
- the nature of the skills required for the investigation;
- the type and range of resources.

Add the progression in key questions and you have an excellent tool for monitoring this aspect of the curriculum throughout the key stage(s).

A well organised, well resourced and sharply focused geographical enquiry makes serious learning great fun for your pupils. Procedural skills are practised as the enquiry process moves into action and individuals and learning teams engage in activity based tasks.

General enquiry

Unlike focused enquiry, a strategy of general enquiry should permeate the geography curriculum in your school. Posing challenging and open questions encourages the investigative mode of thinking in the classroom. However, you should be aware of over-dependence upon this approach; it can become a predictable recipe and restrict the variety of teaching and learning strategies you employ. As one pupil reportedly advised a newcomer to the class; 'Don't look at anything in the room or she'll ask you a question about it!'. Many pupils learn a great deal through direct teacher transmission; it is how you tell them that is important and must be related to your own knowledge and experience.

An example of geographical enquiry: traffic problems in a school locality

BACKGROUND

In her book, *Plans for Primary Geography* (Morgan, 1995), Wendy Morgan recommends the choice of a local issue for an enquiry in years 5 and 6. So, with this in mind, Clatford CE Primary School (175 pupils), near Andover, Hampshire, decided to carry out an investigation into the traffic problems created in the school's vicinity by the arrival and departure of pupils. Here is an issue related to the pupils' own school and one in which they may well be personally involved. Of course, the problem is not unique to Clatford CE Primary and its village of Goodworth Clatford.

While the Clatford traffic problem itself is limited in both time and space, it is obviously related to the school's catchment area. Thus, in this case, the 'locality' is not just the immediate vicinity of the school, but extends into the area in which the pupils live.

Approximately 12 hours of curriculum time were allocated to the topic and links with mathematics, ICT and English were recognised and established. Opportunities to revise, practice and learn geographical skills were identified and teacher enthusiasm was channelled into the enquiry process.

THE KEY QUESTIONS AS A FRAMEWORK FOR THE ENQUIRY

Four key questions emerged from discussion of the learning objectives:
1 Why are journeys made?
2 Where do our pupils come from and how do they get to school?
3 What effect does our coming to and leaving school have upon the village?
4 What can we do to ease or solve the problem?

1 Why are journeys made?

The topic opened with an excursion into movements on the Earth's surface, spanning journeys within and beyond the classroom and within and beyond the home: helicopters passing over the school from nearby Middle Wallop, moles tunnelling under the school's playing field, clouds moving across the sky making shadows over the landscape, the River Anton flowing through the village, earwigs moving when a log is disturbed ... getting to school and back home again.

Reasons for such movements were discussed through questioning and many pupils began to grasp the following generalisations about journeys:

- they are made for a reason;
- can be of different lengths and distances;
- take place at different times;
- use varying modes;
- can have peaks or rush-hours;
- can occur on, above or below the Earth's surface.

It was decided not to include the key idea that routes, for various reasons, often deviate from the most direct path, with main routes tending to be more direct than minor ones.

2 Where do our pupils come from and how do they get to school?

Following this exploratory session, pupils mapped their journeys from home to obtain selected services, one map being produced for each service. The journey to school was then the focus of investigation and the second key question stimulated the crucial enabling

My picture map: Home to school.

Clatford CE Primary School pupils at work on traffic observations. Photo: Geoff Dinkele.

questions of 'What do we need to know?' and 'How do we find out?'. A simple questionnaire was proposed to obtain the raw data: origin of journey and route followed, mode of transport, possible sharing of transport and approximate time of arrival. The pupils soon realised the need for a simple format and agreed to observe anonymity by recording the year group only on the returns. In addition to ticking boxes, one section of the questionnaire invited parents/guardians to state their own feelings about taking and collecting pupils. Great excitement was generated by the distribution of questionnaires to each year group and returns were grabbed avidly for processing.

The total number of returns represented almost three-quarters of the pupils at the school and from such a representative sample it was possible to produce a summary which involved mathematical as well as drawing and design skills (see Figure 3).

The reported time of arrival at school revealed the fact that seven out of every ten pupils usually arrive during the ten minutes before the bell. With at least nine out of ten arriving by car and two of every three pupils coming along Village Street from the north, this led naturally into the third key question and the need to take a close look at things in the vicinity of the school gate.

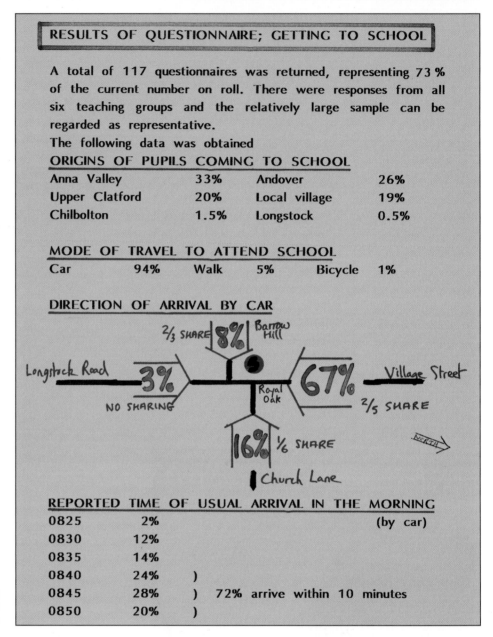

RESULTS OF QUESTIONNAIRE; GETTING TO SCHOOL

A total of 117 questionnaires was returned, representing 73% of the current number on roll. There were responses from all six teaching groups and the relatively large sample can be regarded as representative.

The following data was obtained

ORIGINS OF PUPILS COMING TO SCHOOL

Anna Valley	33%	Andover	26%
Upper Clatford	20%	Local village	19%
Chilbolton	1.5%	Longstock	0.5%

MODE OF TRAVEL TO ATTEND SCHOOL

Car	94%	Walk	5%	Bicycle	1%

DIRECTION OF ARRIVAL BY CAR

REPORTED TIME OF USUAL ARRIVAL IN THE MORNING

		(by car)
0825	2%	
0830	12%	
0835	14%	
0840	24%	)
0845	28%	) 72% arrive within 10 minutes
0850	20%	)

Figure 3:
Results of questionnaire on 'getting to school'.

Now came the time to organise a traffic count with a real purpose in mind and to establish the scale of the scene. The widths of the roads near the school were measured, and the amount of land available for vehicles in the Royal Oak pub's parking area opposite was calculated (the landlord offers this facility at dropping and collecting times). The average length and width of a car was also calculated. Pupils devised their own recording sheet for logging the arrival and departure of cars and organised the coverage of the study area on four consecutive mornings in early March from 0815 to 0850 hours (see photograph). It was raining the first morning!

Figure 4 presents data collected by the pupils on the four mornings. Pupils also reported events and human behaviour during their survey mornings (see Figure 5). They witnessed several examples of dangerous driving, illegal parking, lack of thought for local residents, lack of thought for other parents, a small example of gridlock, a relatively high density of traffic and the peaking of traffic.

Weather	rain	dry	dry/cold	dry
Day and date	Tu 4/3	We 5/3	Th 6/3	Fr 7/3
Total no. of vehicles logged	259	225	339	223
No. coming from Anna Valley direction	114	85	92	101
No. coming from Longstock direction	100	65	195	70
No. coming down Church Lane	45	75	52	52
No. using Royal Oak car park	22	20	48	30
No. parked in road outside school	64	65	111	84
No. parked in Church Lane	0	7	0	1
% of cars arriving after 0835 hours	83	94	84	70
% of cars parked more than five minutes in road	3	11	2	2

Figure 4:
Results of fieldwork
investigation into traffic
near Clatford CE
Primary School.

Cars parked across driveways of private houses, leaving the occupants unable to leave their property while the car was there. Many of these cars were left unattended for several minutes, some up to 10 minutes.

71 Longstock Road has had its garden spoilt with wheel marks where people have pulled in to the side to pass other cars.

People do U-turns at the T-junction.

People park on the zig zag lines.

Cars are parked outside the old people's bungalows for up to 10 minutes when parents take their children on to the playground and then stand and watch them play. This leads to other cars having to park even further up the village, thus increasing congestion.

During the period from 0830 to 0855, the road is reduced to single line traffic. When the buses arrive to take children to Stockbridge, there is a virtual standstill, as the road is totally blocked.

During this period mentioned, there can be as many as 19 cars per minute passing or parking.

One car was left unattended with its engine running.

One car was left unattended on the road with two small children inside.

Parents chat while their cars are parked on the highway which is obviously congested.

At no time was the Royal Oak car park full.

Figure 5:
Pupils' observations of
traffic problems at
Clatford CE
Primary School.

3 What effect does our coming to and leaving school have upon our village?

The key issue had emerged and most of the pupils in class 6 were part of it! One pupil deduced that the problem must be worse at the end of the school day when the infants depart at 1520 hours and years 3-6 all come out ten minutes later! 'At least other people are not coming home from work at the same time', said another. Most pupils grasped that all this traffic arriving and departing in such a short time has a clear impact on the school locality (see Figure 6). It was decided that, the following year, pupils could build upon these investigations and take a close look at the traffic situation in the afternoon.

4 What can be done to ease or solve the problem?

The final key question contributed to the reflective phase of the enquiry. Several residents had complained about traffic chaos in the mornings, how their drives were blocked and their own journey to work hindered. The Parish Council had debated the matter and contacted the County Highway Authority who stated that while there had been no reported accidents at or near the T-junction, they would agree to mark advisory white lines around the junction. Suggestions for alleviating the traffic problem included imposing a 20mph speed limit near the school, encouraging more pupils to cycle to school, raising awareness of the problem regularly in school newsletters to parents and improving the provision of school buses.

It was a salutary experience for the pupils to realise that problems of this kind cannot be solved in a trice and that some simple changes in adults' behaviour would go far towards mitigating the effects upon the village. The last word comes from Laura May, a year 6 pupil:

Movements compared

On class 6 maps showing journeys from home to buy groceries, clothes and for medical care, people travel in different directions, although they are moving for the same purpose. They have different destinations.

Although we travel for the same purpose to Clatford School, we don't go to different destinations. Instead we all converge on one place, although we may come from different directions.

This pattern of movement will lead to traffic congestion

Looking at traffic movement outside Clatford School.

Traffic coming from Longstock has been found to be greater than that of Anna Valley/Upper Clatford in our traffic survey. However, we have found out that most people coming to school come from Anna Valley/Upper Clatford, so we can only assume that the majority of traffic coming from Longstock passes school for a different reason than to drop of children there. This reason might be that they are coming along the Longstock Road and Barrow Hill, turning right and driving into Andover. However, this does make the traffic congestion outside Clatford School even though they do not park there. The busiest time is from 8:35 to 8:55.

The busiest day is a Thursday, when 14 cars pass the school per minute. We think that Thursday is the busiest day because it is market day in Andover. On Thursday 339 cars passed or stopped outside the school.

Unfortunately, most people park outside the school rather than in the Royal Oak car park. Because of laziness, people do not park in the Royal Oak. They could park on Church Lane, but not on the corner because drivers cannot see round the corner of Longstock Road.

As I have said, I think that it would be a good idea to put a policeman on duty between 8:35 and 8:55 at the T-junction outside school. We also could have a no-stopping-for-more-than-3-minutes rule on the road outside the school. The policeman could ensure this. It would be helpful to have 2 mirrors at the junction were Church Lane meets the Longstock Road and the road from Anna Valley/Upper Clatford, so that drivers could see round the corner.

Traffic Survey: Laura May, Year 6, Clatford CE Primary School, near Andover.

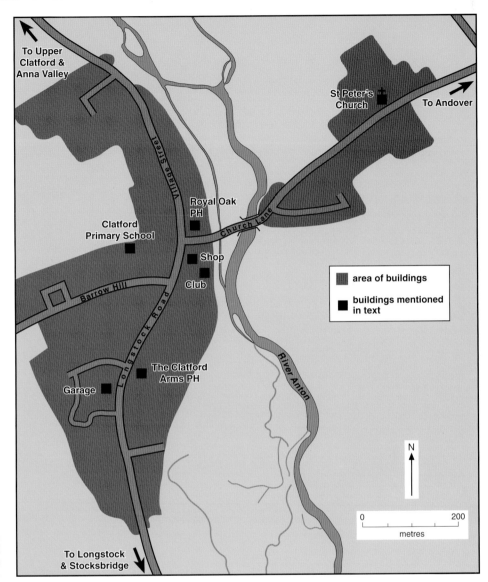

Figure 6:
Goodworth Clatford
showing the
places mentioned.

References

Curriculum Council for Wales (CCW) (1993) *An Enquiry Approach to Learning Geography at Key Stages 2 and 3*. Cardiff: CCW.

Department of Education and Science/Welsh Office (DES/WO) (1990) *Geography for Ages 5-16*. London/Cardiff: HMSO/WO.

Morgan, W. (1995) *Plans for Primary Geography*. Sheffield: Geographical Association.

Chapter 12: Geographical questions and enquiry

This chapter takes further the questions geography asks, as outlined by Margaret Smeaton in Chapter 1. The local issue described in the case study could well form an investigation within the local area (Chapter 16), or a contrasting UK locality (Chapter 17). It also reminds us that matters of environmental quality and improvement can usually be brought to children through local examples within their known world (Chapter 21).

My Home   Antony white

Outside

My house has one big rectangle and a small rectangle at the side of it. It is a red brick bungalow. It has red tiles for the roof. It has three chimneys. It has about ten windows. We have a big garage and two workshops. We also have a shed where we store things. We have a back lawn and a front lawn. The back lawn is about thirteen metres long. The front lawn is about five metres long. We have got twelve vegetable patches we've got five flower patches. We have got two trees.

Geography and language development

Chapter 13

Liz Lewis

> Once upon a time, a master and one of his most useful and well regarded servants began to have a deep discussion about their importance to one another.
>
> 'Aren't I really more important to you than you are to me?' suggested the servant, daring to be outspoken because he knew how much his master relied on him. 'Isn't it I who take you around and show you interesting places? And don't I provide you with so many things to talk about? However would you manage to be so interesting without *my* help?'. 'No, no, not so at all,' replied the master decisively. 'It is obvious to anyone that I am much more important to you than you are to me. After all I provide you with the means to exist. Without my support, you would not be able to go anywhere. You would lead an impoverished existence. It is I who feed you and clothe you, *and* I give you the freedom to say whatever you want – even to persistently ask questions, if you must!'.
>
> Fortunately, the pair were sensible enough to see that this kind of argument could have gone on for ever without either being deemed to have won it. So, being basically faithful allies in spite of their difference in status, they simply had to agree that they were indispensable to one another.

The last few years have seen similar discussions take place between teachers with curriculum responsibility for English and geography as they have tried to make sense of the relationship between their respective subjects in planning for the primary phase. The Dearing Report of 1996 clearly signalled a strong re-emphasis on the core subjects, and particularly on the development of basic English language skills. This has been significantly reinforced by the subsequent decision to release schools from the full requirements of the statutory Orders at key stages 1 and 2 in the foundation subjects, so that schools can pay more attention to the core skills if this is deemed necessary. Geography teachers are part of the solution, not the problem, in raising literacy standards. It is for us to demonstrate how geography not only provides important learning experiences in its own right, but also how it can provide rich contexts through which literacy (and indeed numeracy) may flourish. So it is timely for those of us who believe strongly that geographical work offers particular opportunities which are vital to the development of young children's understanding and thinking processes, to consider how our subject might be related to English, both in terms of a 'map' of the whole curriculum and in daily classroom practice.

This chapter sets out some of the important ways in which geography and English language can interact in primary classrooms. It begins from the premise that these subjects should not be viewed as master and servant, but as mutually supportive elements of a holistic approach to children's learning.

Where is geography on the curriculum map?

Geographers are renowned for their concern to define the position of their subject in the curriculum and to justify its existence to others who, perplexed by its sheer breadth, understandably ask some difficult questions. Is it an arts subject or a science? Is it a social science or economics? Why does it sometimes seem to be so enmeshed with history when we are studying our locality? How is it that it feels much more like mathematics when we are conducting a survey of litter or traffic? Why is some of the information we need in studying the landscape really geological, biological and technological?

Some writers have made sense of these questions by visualising geography as a bridge which links the arts subjects and the sciences, or even as the bridge of a ship from which the whole curriculum can be surveyed and navigated. Others describe geography as an integrative discipline, one which uses knowledge from many subjects and brings their ideas together to develop understanding of the nature of places. Understanding the centrality of geography on the curriculum map is crucial to realising why geography can offer abundant opportunities for language development. It is important in studying geography not only to use some technical and scientific language, of the kind that is used in discussing the physical world, but also to have descriptive, evaluative, aesthetic and emotive language to employ in aspects of human and environmental geography. Geographical work requires us to bring these different aspects of language together in the study of features, places and themes. Themes like environmental quality and change, for example, demand both scientific explanation and evaluative, possibly even emotional responses.

One child's personal response to an environmental issue. Work: Cathryn Epton.

At the heart of geography is the realisation that places are 'distinctive' or different from one another. The reasons for these differences can be traced to unique balances of human and physical characteristics and processes, not found in exactly the same assemblage in any other place.

How does English language work support geography?

Understanding the position and focus of geography in this way is important in considering its relationship to language work. When studying places geographers attempt not just to describe them, but to *explain* why they are like they are, searching out information by means of the 'enquiry approach'. While the process of enquiry regularly involves scientific reasoning and mathematical manipulation of information, it demands, above all, the ability to collect evidence from visual, written and spoken resources and to comprehend, mentally process and present that information as description, explanation or hypothesis. Not only do we speak, listen, read and write geography but the very processes of thinking, of developing new concepts, of refining ideas and testing them out on others to confirm understanding are heavily language dependent. The relationship between English and geography is not, however, a one-way dependence.

What does geography offer to English language development?

What geographical work can do for children's progress in literacy goes far beyond the very important, though rather limited, aims of the 'Use of language requirement' set out in the general section of the Geography National Curriculum, where we are reminded that in geography:

> *'Pupils should be taught to express themselves clearly in both speech and writing and to develop their reading skills. They should be taught to use grammatically correct sentences and to spell and punctuate accurately in order to communicate effectively in written English'* (DFE, 1995, p.1).

On account of its breadth of interest and its use of a variety of language-related resources, geography has particular value in providing exciting contexts and opportunities for literacy experience. Since the National Curriculum was introduced, school geography has benefited from a surge of activity in the production of new children's information books, geographical stories and poems, photopacks, audio, video, and CD-ROM resources.

LANGUAGE IN THE FIELD

Strong emphasis on the experience of fieldwork has also been instrumental in transforming the way that geography is taught in many primary schools, aided by local field centres with experienced specialist staff.

Outdoor work at first-hand has always been a powerful stimulus to self expression. The unsolicited writing in Figure 1 was written at the computer late one evening at a County Durham residential centre by a pupil with limited home opportunities for travel or literary support. She had been taken, during a geography field week, to see the spectacular waterfalls at High Force and Low Force for the first time. It is a committed emotional response to the landscape, partly descriptive but with some embryonic explanation. Yet it also contains elements of scientific comprehension, some newly acquired specialist

---

High Force

At first I felt frightend and worried then it started to grow on me. It was realy fun I loved it but the power of the water is amazing. How a 11 year old boy survived is unbelievible it is a miricle that he is alive today. The white spray is all over the place particularly over the plunge pool. What more can I say just it's fantastic. The height of the thing is high let me tell you. I'm only glad sir had a tight hold of me because I felt dizzy when Sarah took a picture. The force of the water is incredible the speed of the thing is fast it just zooms down. Thankyou sir for keeping a tight hold of me.

Low Force
Wynch bridge

Dirty water flowing down, the foam sticking to the rocks, the rocks at the side look like steps. The sound, sounds like when you run the tap but much louder. It was BRILLIANT
But some people find it scarey and are frightend but not me.
p.s I also felt surprized because the last time I came it was much cleaner some people do not care what they throw into the water.

Figure 1:
Pupil's writing on High Force.
Work: Paula Cook.

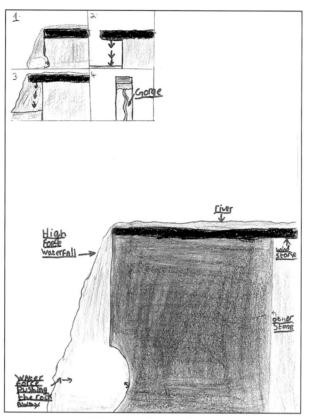

Work: Newbottle Primary School, Sunderland.

vocabulary, an element of story and a personal communication with her teacher. Within it there is ample evidence for those tracking her development of parallel progress in language and geography, as well as some indication of her immediate literacy needs. Best of all, being directly inspired by nature, it is written with spirit, a quality so very difficult to achieve in a book-based lesson.

It is important, when planning geography and English in tandem, to ensure appropriate time allocation for the two subjects. A day's fieldwork and follow-up may consume one half-term's geography time, yet there may be several different aspects of geography to address within that period. So we may be tempted to forget the fieldwork. However, if we can be more confident of saying precisely what language development is accruing from our work in geography then opportunities are opened up for deeper, more rewarding, more time consuming multi-purpose outdoor work. A good idea is to add to any planning sheets you use a new section or column in which to specify intended learning outcomes for English language, alongside the plan for geography. An example is shown in the 'Enquiry planner' (Figure 2), adapted from the Welsh Office's original *Non-Statutory Guidance for Geography* (WO, 1991). A sheet like this can be used for both medium-term and individual lesson plans.

The discussion which follows considers in more detail how the sequence of enquiry questions relates to particular language skills. It will help with the identification of specific language opportunities in geographical work. First, however it is necessary to reiterate some ideas about the use of geographical questions (see Chapter 12).

DEVELOPING LANGUAGE THROUGH GEOGRAPHICAL ENQUIRY

A recurring theme in this handbook is the planning of geographical work through a sequence of geographical questions (see Chapters 1 and 12, for example), sometimes referred to as the 'key' questions. The question sequence shown below is recommended in the National Curriculum and has been adopted by many teachers as a powerful planning tool, since it helps to identify the purpose of geographical study and indicates how progression in the subject might be tracked.

What is it?	– Naming identifying
Where is it?	– Locating
What is it like?	– Observing/describing
How did it come to be like this?	– Explaining
How is it changing and what might happen next?	– Hypothesising
What do I think/feel about it?	– Evaluating/caring

Focus for Enquiry					
Key stage	Year		Cross-curricular links		Time
Key questions	Learning outcomes – knowledge, skills, values and attitudes incude PoS coverage	Teaching/learning activities	Resources/Time Allowance per activity (approximate)	Assessment opportunities	Opportunities for Language development

Figure 2: Enquiry planner. Source: WO, 1991.

As a child moves up through school, this enquiry sequence is developed from simple recognition and description towards explanation and hypothesis by being continually revisited at different levels, in a range of geographical activities, e.g. local fieldwork, distant place studies, weather. From naming through to hypothesising there is a general increase in the difficulty of the thinking processes demanded by each question. But it is worth noting that the final question in the sequence stands alone for it demands an evaluative response, and that can be attempted even by the very young.

We can also envisage how progression might occur within the context of each question. For example, when very young children attempt to answer a 'What is it?' question, they are likely to use simple known words such as 'the water bends' whereas more experienced pupils could offer 'the river's channel is meandering'. The 'Where is it?' question may at first elicit only simple place references such as 'over there' or self-referenced ones like 'behind me'. But these might be expected to progress with teaching, from relative to absolute locations, as described in four- or six-figure grid references or latitude and longitude, by the later stages of primary or early secondary school. The overall implication of these two ways of tracking progress is that children operating at differing National Curriculum Levels may be encouraged to take part in the same enquiry at the same time but, through the judicious intervention of a teacher who is aware of their capabilities, can progress their understanding at an appropriate pace for them. It is worth taking time, perhaps as an INSET activity, to trace in detail the relationship between the skills demanded in the geographical question sequence and those defined as indicative of achievement at each level in the Level Descriptions.

Of course engaging in enquiry with children does not involve confronting them with a mechanical set of questions worded explicitly as above. It involves planning to help the children consider these *types* of questions, framed in ways which are understandable to them, taking care to use 'open' questioning techniques, i.e. forms of wording which freely encourage unselfconscious attempts to respond at the child's own level. The aim is, ultimately, to induct young children into the enquiry process so that they begin to ask *their own* questions and to research answers for themselves.

An excellent way of beginning any new geography topic, whatever the level of the children, is to elicit what the children already know and what they want or need to know. As well as defining starting points for the teacher it involves children in framing statements and questions and, with the teacher's support, refining and grouping these. If a list of 'What we know' and 'What do we need to know?' is compiled during the discussion, there will be modelling of the composing and writing process and an opportunity to discuss the structure and punctuation of statements and questions viewed together. Although it may have an ultimate geographical purpose, this kind of activity might be well presented as a 'literacy hour activity' and can certainly be justified as such.

Fundamental ideas about geographical questions have been re-addressed here because they also provide a useful organising tool to support analysis of the specific kinds of language opportunity offered by geographical work. In the section below a summary box indicates in brief the particular language focus of each of the key questions. This is followed by a brief discussion to raise research issues and support classroom practice.

What is it? **IDENTIFYING** **– geographical features and processes**	The development of **new vocabulary** progressing in range and complexity as pupils encounter an increasing variety of physical, human and environmental features and processes. **Stories, poems, information books and dictionaries** are important sources of words and ideas for all age groups.

Vocabulary

Geography is frequently criticised for having too much obscure specialised vocabulary. Unfamiliarity with the vocabulary of physical geography, in particular, is a very common anxiety among non-specialist primary teachers attending INSET courses. This need not be so, but it is important to ask how much specialist vocabulary is appropriate to primary children's needs and how we can go about introducing it. There are many children who might become quickly excluded from understanding by just one or two unfamiliar words, and in this respect a non-specialist may be more sensitive to their plight than a 'geographer' who is liable to slip technical words into a conversation unwittingly. However, there are other children who revel in terminology, if only to impress, and it would be a pity to stifle this enthusiasm. There are only occasional examples of technical words in the National Curriculum document, and there is little clear research to guide this issue, although a useful series of vocabulary lists was produced by Bridge (1993), Scoffham and Jewson (1993, 1994), and Scoffham (1998) in *Primary Geographer* to guide practice. Agreeing with colleagues a set of words to be developed within each topic, possibly with pre-defined levels of difficulty, is a profitable aspect of whole school planning.

We have little knowledge of what understandings children come to school with, although all teachers have come across examples of children knowing the same words but attaching different meanings. Patrick Wiegand notes (1993) that urban children often interpret the word 'hill' as 'slope', a two-dimensional concept rather than a composite three-dimensional feature, because they rarely see entire hills, unobscured by buildings. Devlin (1994) identifies homonyms as a particular problem in geography. Many of the words used in geography do have dual meanings. What children adhere to is the first meaning they have attached to the sound.

Thus, we might be surprised to find that in introducing river terminology to children, of the words 'source, channel, tributary, mouth', tributary, ostensibly the most technical word, may in fact be the easiest for them to absorb and recall simply because it is absolutely new to the child. The others are more familiar, hence 'source' conjures up a red bottle, a 'channel' is where you find a favourite television programme and a mouth is very useful for eating and talking! We therefore need to consider deliberately dismantling the known meanings before building the new understanding.

It may also help to be particular about terms. Using 'countryside' to refer to rural areas avoids confusion with 'country' in the sense of state until a child is mature enough to have the dual meaning of 'country' explained. We can also forestall misunderstanding by mentioning a more usual meaning whenever we introduce a new term – 'The top of a mountain is called the "peak", just like the peak of a cap.' We can also be deliberate about the spelling of words which sound the same. Finally, giving simple derivations of terms is possible for older juniors – 'cumulus' is like 'ac*cumul*ate', and 'tributary' is from the same root as 'con*tribute*'.

A fundamental need is for more detailed understanding of children's geographical vocabulary development, something that could be achieved for your school by keeping a shared notebook of piecemeal evidence of children's understanding to inform your shared planning and practice.

Where is it?	The understanding and use of **prepositions**
LOCATING PLACES AND FEATURES –	**of place** (in, beside, behind, under, etc.)
in the field and on pictures,	to describe relative locations, progressing
globes and maps.	to the **specialised vocabulary of absolute**
	location (compass points, grid references,
	latitude, longitude, northing, etc.)

Language and maps

Expressing position is a fundamental geographical skill which begins with the gradual acquisition of place language and progresses to sophisticated knowledge of mapping conventions, enabling the definition of absolute locations. Map reading itself has much to offer literacy skills. Skimming and scanning are necessary approaches to reading a map, offering a contrasting technique to sequential left to right reading, and so helping to develop awareness that in reading for information different approaches to text are needed.

Also, young children need to understand that places and features such as mountains and even farmers' fields have names just as people do. Maps are a tremendous resource for consolidating teaching about proper nouns and capital letters.

Locating skills also have an important link with story. The progress of events in a story is sequenced in place as well as time and, if we encourage children to map the story, their comprehension and visualisation of spatial relationships can be assessed. Children's own story writing may be enhanced by encouraging them to invent settings and make imaginary maps, and this in turn can support their ability to visualise sequenced events. Resources such as the Red Riding Hood picture map in Folens *Geography 1. Big Book* (Harrison and Havard, 1994) provide an excellent stimulus for this kind of work.

Language and pictures

Retrieving information from pictures is another essential geographical skill with implications for language development. Here, research shows that children pick out details relevant to their own immediate interest, such as animals, people, vehicles and other foreground details, rather than the surrounding landscape. We therefore need to develop strategies for directing their looking, for example by covering part of the picture, arousing curiosity by asking them to guess what is there, and then revealing it only when their attention is fully focused. It is also important to teach the vocabulary that will enable them to say where things are, e.g. near part, far part, distance, foreground, background, left and right.

What is it like? DESCRIBING – features and processes in the physical and human environment	The development of **descriptive language** from visual and other sensory stimuli, progressing through increasing clarity, **improved vocabulary and attention to detail** and through the **ability to describe and compare at an increasing range of scales.**
COMPARING	The practice of **comparative and superlative adjectives/adverbs.**

THE RIVER TEES

We were watching a video about the River Tees, from how it starts in the hills to the part where it reaches the North Sea. The part of the video that I found to be the most interesting was about the waterfall that is called High Force. The video showed us how a waterfall is made. There is a hard layer of rock that is called windstone, underneath this strong stone is a softer layer of rock called sand stone. The force of the water causes this softer rock to gradually wear away. After the sand stone has worn away the windstone will drop and form a gorge. On this gorge is normally a waterfall.

Work: Martina Capron and Robert Mustard, Newbottle Primary School, Sunderland.

Work: Peter Bee.

Using language to describe features and places

The ability to describe accurately is a general language skill which teachers are constantly monitoring as vocabulary grows. Outdoor work within geography can greatly enhance the skill of describing by deliberately focusing on the full range of sensory stimuli in the environment – 'Is it rough or smooth?', 'Does it have a smell?', etc. Even when secondary sources are the only ones at our disposal, studies of unfamiliar places, based on multimedia packs, can still invite descriptive writing which involves empathising with the experiences of people who live there.

Most teachers are well practised at 'taking children into a picture' by questioning that helps them imagine sensory experience: 'What do you think you could hear in this place?', 'Do you think you could feel the hot sun on your face?', 'What would happen here if the wind began to blow hard?'.

Activities like inventing islands and countries with imaginary geographies, culture, laws and customs give great scope to language development through descriptive invention.

Using story books and poetry

The use of picture story books in early geography is now a well documented teaching approach nowhere better evidenced than in the development of ideas about the weather and seasons in *Out and About* by Shirley Hughes (1988), or of environmental quality and change in Mairi Hedderwick's *Katie Morag and the New Pier* (1994). Reading extracts from novels for junior children to introduce geographical ideas is another way of stimulating curiosity and developing understanding in geography; *The Railway Children* (Nesbitt, 1906) (especially the description of the landslide) and *Earthquake* (Salkey, 1965) are both wonderful examples of powerful geographical description.

The special, evocative power of poems can also be harnessed to develop understanding of landscapes and processes, and children can be encouraged to respond to their own geographical experiences by writing their own poems (see Figure 3). If personal writing of this kind is shared through class reading, it can also be used to develop children's capacity to understand that places evoke human emotions which differ from person to person.

Using comparative language

In the progression from simple geographical description of one place or feature to more complex comparisons, the need to use comparative language arises. Geography gives children many opportunities to practise manipulating comparative forms such as 'smaller

By the Sea

The lashing waves,
Crash against the cliffs
And eat them away,
Never sleeping night or day.
At night the moon glistens on the sea
And makes the fish silvery
Under the waves they dash
In and out
Arrows of swift light.
On a summer day
Children play on the beach
Eat rock
And run along way
To reach the cool waves
To paddle, dip in toes
Splash
They never think these same waves
Crash on cliffs, and eat rock too-
                    Did you?

**Figure 3:
Poem written following a story experience based on the BBC *Look and Read* series, fieldwork in a coastal locality and modelling of poem composition in a whole-class English lesson. Work: Paula Mason, age 9.**

than', 'more industrialised than', 'not quite so cold as', etc., as well as introducing them to particular comparative hierarchies of words like 'dwelling, hamlet, village, town, city, metropolis', or 'hill, mountain, range, chain and system'.

How did it come to be like this? **What physical and/or human influences caused it to be like it is?** **EXPLAINING – geographical processes and patterns both physical and human.**	The skill of **sequencing an explanation** or hypothesis in writing or speech. **Effective weighing and ordering of ideas** so as to enhance meaning. **The language of tentative reasoning** in offering alternative explanations. The need to draw on an increasingly wide range of geographical factors in framing ideas demands **drafting and editing skills.**
How is it changing? **How might it change in future?** **PREDICTING/HYPOTHESISING –** about places, features, processes and patterns.	**Tentative language** is again useful in predicting, speculating and hypothesising about places and processes of change. This may include expressions of uncertainty, hope, anxiety, delight, anger, relief and persuasive language in relation to environmental issues. **Oracy through discussion, debate, drama and role-play.**

Using explanatory language

As geography progresses towards secondary level it begins to demand the skill of logically sequenced explanation and provides varied contexts for practising this. Although it is important to work towards clear written explanations we might expect explanatory language to be more frequently a characteristic of oral rather than written work in upper key stage 2. Therefore, varied approaches to classroom practice which give frequent

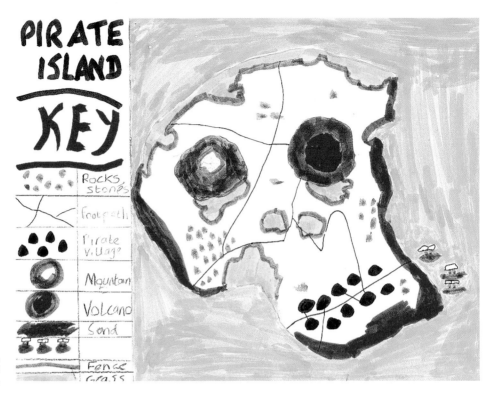

Work: Robert Lawton,
Ainthorpe Primary
School, Hull.

RIVER VOCABULARY

I was given a number of words about rivers with their meanings and I had to try and match them up. Here are my answers.

SOURCE The place where a river begins.
DELTA An area (usually triangular) between the branches of a river.
RAPIDS Part of a river where the water flows very quickly.
CANYON A deep valley, usually with a river running through it.
TRIBUTARY A river or stream that flows into a larger one.
GORGE A narrow valley with deep sides.
WATERFALL A place where a river or stream flows over a cliff or a large rock.
MOUTH The place where the river enters the sea.
ESTUARY The mouth of a large river where it flows into the sea.
SOURCE The river begins at a source.
DELTA The river ends at a delta.
CURRENT A current is a movement of water.
CHANNEL The part of a river near to its mouth where it flows into the sea.

Year 5 vocabulary.
Work: Sarah Elliott,
Newbottle Primary
School, Sunderland.

opportunities for spoken interaction and presentation are essential in primary geography. An ideal activity in this context is a role play in which children take on roles such as planners and developers, and propose changes to their environment, explaining and justifying their intentions and presenting ideas for class discussion.

Adopting the 'enquiry approach' implies a constructivist stance to learning geography, so we must be prepared for many early 'explanations' to be only partially tenable. It is vital for pupils to know that expressing uncertainty does not imply weakness in their understanding. Tentative language is a strong feature of all geographical explanation, even at high academic level, not only because of the range and complexity of the variables that influence places, but also because there are still many gaps in our understanding of the world. So the subject offers great scope for hazarding explanations: 'It might be because the weather ...', 'It could possibly make a difference to ...' 'Maybe it will be washed away or ...' Realising that there are often several possible and equally tenable explanations offers great comfort to non-specialist teachers too. In a climate of true enquiry there is no place for an all-knowing expert. The teacher's role is to apply the tacit knowledge and sharper logic of adult experience to the exciting task of helping children gradually to refine their own geographical reasoning. Within this process there is enormous opportunity for finely tuning meanings by careful attention to word choice and sentence construction.

Perhaps the greatest opportunity of all for self expression is offered by the final question in the enquiry sequence.

What do I/others think? **How do people feel about this place/ feature/process?** **EVALUATING** **Expressing concern and involvement about environmental quality, change or controversial issues.**	**Expressive language** has a strong role in aspects of geography involving evaluative, aesthetic and emotional responses to places, e.g. landscape appreciation, conservation, developing 'sense of place', experiencing awe and wonder or empathy. It may find expression in **factual writing, imaginative prose, poetry, opinionative and journalistic writing or in oral responses such as speech making.**

Using language in the context of environmental studies

Studies of environmental quality and change perhaps offer the richest arena for language practice in the geography curriculum because they invoke a personal viewpoint, engaging the emotions as well as the intellect. Children's own views may be presented through speech, drama, articles for class newspapers, letters, prose or poetry and will include opinion, persuasion, uncertainty, hope, anxiety, relief, anger and delight. The power of discussion in supporting concept development and refining understanding highlights oral language as an essential element of all environmental geography work.

Recently, pupils in years 5 and 6 from Lumley Primary School, County Durham, undertook a land use survey of their village and identified the four pieces of open land which might well come under pressure for development. In the roles of development and construction teams they set about planning new land uses for the sites following a discussion of what their village most needed – a supermarket, light industrial factory work, a leisure centre and a drive-in McDonalds! Having surveyed the sites and agreed on which environmental features were worth preserving they drew detailed exterior and interior plans manipulating a great variety of geographical variables from car parking space to noise pollution. A public meeting followed in which plans were presented orally and debated for their merits or otherwise. The heated argument which erupted from some proposals and the eloquence with which controversial issues – such as the removal of half the school field to accommodate the leisure facility – were debated was ample evidence of how a geographical context can be used to promote oracy. The activity was also one in which the children used geographical skills (map reading and map construction) and studied places (our immediate locality) and themes (settlement, environmental quality and change).

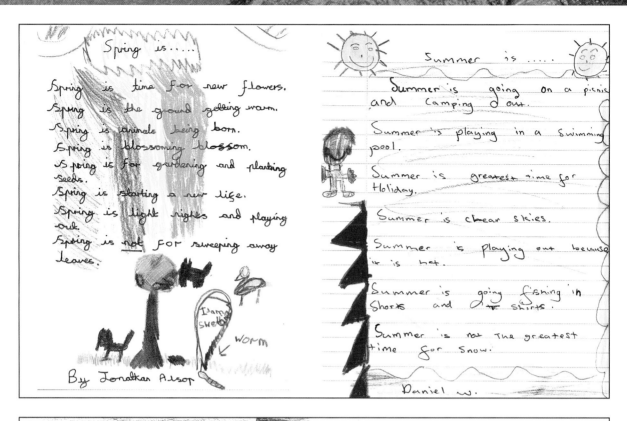

Spring is.....

Spring is time for new flowers.
Spring is the ground getting warm.
Spring is animals being born.
Spring is blossoming blossom.
Spring is for gardening and planting seeds.
Spring is starting a new life.
Spring is light nights and playing out.
Spring is not for sweeping away leaves.

By Jonathan Alsop

Summer is .....

Summer is going on a picnic and camping out.
Summer is playing in a swimming pool.
Summer is greatest time for Holiday.
Summer is clear skies.
Summer is playing out because it is hot.
Summer is going fishing in shorts and t shirts.
Summer is not the greatest time for snow.

Daniel W.

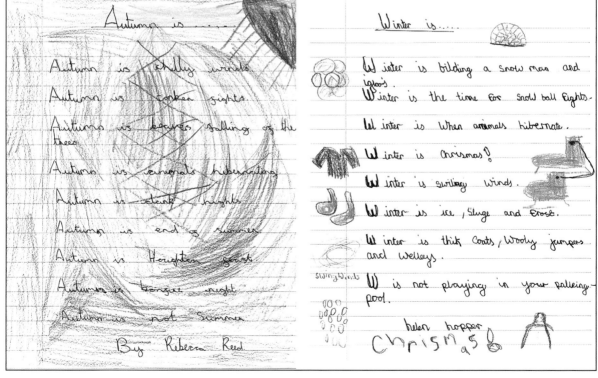

Autumn is .....

Autumn is chilly winds.
Autumn is conker fights.
Autumn is leaves falling of the trees.
Autumn is animals hibernating.
Autumn is dark nights.
Autumn is end of summer.
Autumn is Houghton feast.
Autumn is bonfire night.
Autumn is not summer.

By Rebecca Reed

Winter is.....

Winter is bilding a snow man and igloo's.
Winter is the time for snow ball fights.
Winter is when animals hibernate.
Winter is Chrismas!
Winter is swirling winds.
Winter is ice, sluge and frost.
Winter is thick coats, wooly jumpers and wellys.
W is not playing in your palleing-pool.

helen hopper
Chrismas

Seasonal poems.
Work: Newbottle Primary
School, Sunderland.

Developing a library for geography

Buying books is an expensive business, and resources for non-core subjects may be scarce. For this reason alone, there is a strong case for co-operative planning between the geography and language co-ordinators when buying books. There are other reasons too, as described below.

PICTURE AND STORY BOOKS

Of the many kinds of geographical stimulus mentioned in this chapter, books are still the most important resource in most primary schools and the maintenance of a library to support the subject is a priority for the subject co-ordinator. It should include as wide a collection as possible of children's fiction, organised where appropriate to support individual topics. Picture story books abound in which striking settings provide an ideal medium for developing geographical vocabulary and concepts. The essence of good story telling is, however, to enable the children to enjoy the stories in an atmosphere of relaxed anticipation, with no unwelcome geographical interruptions! It is a good idea, therefore, to return to particularly useful picture spreads later, and to invite the children to develop geographical ideas in follow-up discussion.

POETRY

Many poetry collections include poems with geographical potential which schools already have in stock. A pleasant way to locate useful examples would be to organise a co-operative search (during INSET time, perhaps) or run a competition for older children. A selection relating to different aspects of geography could be word processed in large print onto cards (a good job for parent helpers), illustrated by children and laminated for classroom use. Children's own geographical poems might also be added to the collection as time progresses.

INFORMATION BOOKS

Ideally, books with a range of different reading levels should be used to support each unit of work, but this may be difficult to organise, and it can be expensive. It is important to have a selection of books which have a contents page, glossary and index since these can be used for teaching information skills as well as geography. Question and answer formats are particularly helpful for geography since they reflect the enquiry idea. If the books are to be used by children themselves, they need to be strongly bound and attractive, with a variety of styles of presentation – text and pictures, comic strips, speech bubbles. Books referred to as 'faction', where characters to whom the children can relate and who act as guides through the information, also have wide appeal.

Before buying information books, it is important to vet them for outdated and stereotypical images, bias and prejudice. It is also important to be aware that some environmental texts contain images, of whaling for example, which many children find distressing.

SOURCES FOR SUITABLE MATERIAL

For obvious commercial reasons, publishers have difficulty in meeting the demand, sparked off by the National Curriculum, for information books about small localities in other parts of the world. Non-fiction, place-based series tend rather to concentrate on whole countries or continents, and while such books are invaluable sources of background material, they are not adequate in themselves for detailed locality studies. Alternative sources of support are the aid organisations, such as ActionAid, Oxfam and the Development Education Centres, and the Geographical Association, many of whose photopacks, posters, videos and software focus on localities world-wide, and in enough detail to foster empathetic understanding of other communities.

CLASSROOM DISPLAYS

Another source of reading material in the classroom is display. Most geographical topics provide inspiration for colourful assemblages of children's work and these can be ideal as resources for literacy development. Of particular value are interactive displays which provide things to do as well as things to look at. Participation can be invited by the use of bold captions based on geographical questions, which, if changed periodically will refocus attention and renew interest.

A locality study display.
Photo: Chris Garnett.

Finally, one should not forget the value of traditional geographical resources – globes, wall maps, atlases, aerial photographs of the school and daily weather charts – as sources of, and stimulus for, the development of geography and of language skills.

Planning the interaction of geography and literacy work in lessons

A number of suggestions are offered below, in which the session or topic time is deliberately organised to facilitate related geography and English language teaching.

1   A geography session leads into a creative writing follow-up such as writing a poem after fieldwork or writing a descriptive postcard from a distant locality.

2   A literature experience is used to stimulate a geographical enquiry, e.g. a reading of Philippe Dupasquier's *Dear Daddy* (1986) leads into an exploration of the globe and the plotting on a world map of all the connections between the class and other countries.

3   The language session is about reading for meaning but the context is part of the current geography topic and uses geography information texts.

4   The geography written work is designed for a particular audience, e.g. after researching weather stories, older children write stories about weather for younger ones, or prepare a display for a parents' evening.

5   A speaking and listening activity compares a geography video of St Lucia with an audio tape on the same theme.

6   A geography topic concludes with the making of an information book about it. Aspects of book production, page design, contents and glossary preparation extend the activity into language time, with an added ICT dimension.

7   Groups of children have been invited to invent a country and make a map of it. They consolidate geographical features vocabulary and learn about proper nouns while plotting imaginary towns, rivers and mountains. They explore ideas about what a country is by inventing a national flag, currency and language, and by writing laws, inventing folk tales and traditional recipes, and composing imagined biographies of the country's most celebrated inhabitants.

In 1996-97, SCAA decided to explore the language teaching potential of the foundation subjects. The fruits of this exercise, in which the Geographical Association took part, are now in schools. The summary below (Figure 4) is one of several contributions made to SCAA by the GA Working Party on Language and Geography. It offers a neat way of tracking the progression of language skills through reading, writing and speaking in geography. It is evident from this that geography can play a huge role in literacy development.

Planning for Progression

From:

writing in geography
- single words and phrases;
- writing with a simple single focus (e.g. describing a street scene);
- writing for a single audience (e.g. teacher).

reading in geography
- text with low readability age;
- text selected by the teacher;

- reading a text, all of which is relevant;

- texts from a single source (e.g. KS1/2 book).

speaking and listening in geography
- short answers to closed questions (one response expected);
- discussion in class or small groups;

- listening to or giving a narrative account (e.g. story of a journey);
- listening to and using simple vocabulary.

to:

- longer sustained pieces of writing;
- writing with several sub-sections (e.g. describing stages in a survey);
- writing for many different audiences (e.g. other pupils, local newspaper).

- text with high readability age;
- text found and selected by pupils (e.g. on CD-ROM);
- reading a text from which relevant information has to be extracted (e.g. entry in atlas);
- texts from many different sources, possibly conflicting (e.g. brochures).

- answers to open questions for which pupils explain their thinking;
- speaking aloud in front of a class in discussion or role-play;
- listening to or giving an analytical account (e.g. how the water cycle works);
- listening to and using specialised geographical vocabulary.

Figure 4:
Summary of use of geography in language.
Source: SCAA, 1997.

Summary

Photo: Steve Brace, ActionAid.

Attractive as it might be to teachers with overcrowded schedules to make time economies by combining English and geography, making curriculum economies is not what this chapter is about. Nor is there any intention to represent geography solely as a vehicle for language skills development.

Using language well is a vital life skill. It supports our understanding, brings alive our thoughts and gives expression to our beliefs. English and geography not only share a place on the curriculum map, they also share fundamental educational goals, for geography is also strongly concerned with communication. It nurtures our growing connections with fellow humans in other parts of the world and supports our ability to take part with them in informed debate about our shared future on the planet.

Geography does indeed provide a tremendous range of exciting real world contexts in which children can be offered an inspiring range of language experiences. But equally, to give them the best possible experience of geography we need to support its teaching with quality literary resources. We should also offer children the fullest possible opportunity for self expression in speech and writing within our lessons.

References and further reading

Bridge, C. (1993) 'Word sets', *Primary Geographer*, 15, p. 22.

Devlin, M. (1994) 'Geographical vocabulary in the junior school', *Issues in Education*, 2, 1, pp. 26-30.

Department for Education (DFE) (1995) *Geography in the National Curriculum (England)*. London: HMSO.

Dupasquier, P. (1986) *Dear Daddy*. London: Puffin.

Harrison, P. and Havard, J. (1994) *Folens Geography 1. Big Book*. Dunstable: Folens.

Hedderwick, M. (1994) *Katie Morag and the New Pier*. London: Random House.

Hughes, S. (1988) *Out and About*. London: Walker Books.

Nesbitt, E. (1906) *The Railway Children*. London: Penguin.

Primary Geographer 32 (January 1998). The theme of this issue is 'Focus on Language'

Salkey, A. (1965) *Earthquake*. Oxford: Oxford University Press.

Schools Curriculum and Assessment Authority (SCAA) (1997) *Geography and the Use of Language*. London: SCAA.

Scoffham, S. (ed) (1998) *Primary Sources. Research findings in primary geography*. Sheffield: Geographical Association.

Scoffham, S. and Jewson, T. (1993) 'A glossary of terms for key stage 1 geography', *Primary Geographer*, 15, p. 2.

Scoffham, S. and Jewson, T. (1994) 'A glossary of terms for key stage 2 geography', *Primary Geographer*, 16, p. 2.

Wiegand, P. (1993) *Children and Primary Geography*. London: Cassell.

Welsh Office (WO) (1991) *Non Statutory Guidance for Geography*. Cardiff: WO.

Chapter 13: Geography and Language development

The use of enquiry questions to structure geographical work permeates much of the book (for example Chapters 1, 3, 12 and Section Five). The interdependence of language skills and geographical understanding is referred to in Chapter 7. Readers will also see how these enquiry questions promote a similar approach to learning as that adopted in science.

The outcome of fieldwork
can take many forms.
A stained glass window.

Fieldwork

Chapter 14

Paula Richardson

Fieldwork is using outdoor experience to reinforce learning in the classroom by providing an environment to test out ideas and hypotheses, and allowing pupils to extend their understanding of the real world. Exposure to television, advertising and other media has extended pupils awareness of other places and environments, but they may nevertheless remain uncritical, unobservant and unchallenged. Even well-travelled pupils often make little use of observation skills or the experiences they have of their own locality.

Fieldwork gives pupils the opportunity, through a structured pathway, to become observant, to develop skills of recording, analysis and deduction and, hopefully, to develop enquiring minds. Over a hundred years ago the great geographical educationalist Sir Archibald Geikie made the important link between research enquiry using observation and recording in the field, and good practice in the primary classroom. Plowden (1967) also observed that 'exploration of the school locality as a teaching laboratory' is an essential part of developing children's geographical knowledge.

As adults we know that it is 'the doing' which can help us to reach a fuller understanding of things; for children the need is even greater. Fieldwork gives them real practical opportunities to see, hear, feel and understand for themselves.

Fieldwork often involves a class visit to a place and, as such, can be costly both in terms of finance and planning time. However, fieldwork can be organised in a variety of ways, including asking pupils to carry out work at home.

The organisation of fieldwork

There are three main ways of organising fieldwork, as shown below. The choice of method will depend on such things as finance, availability of staff, and so on. It is important that

Observation and recording in the field. Photo: Paula Richardson.

all pupils have a chance to experience all three types of fieldwork. While self-organised fieldwork is a good way of enriching pupil experience, it should not be chosen at the expense of, or instead of more formally organised fieldwork which offers different and equally important learning opportunities.

CLASS VISIT – MAJOR OUTING
This is usually to a specific place and is often guided, e.g. farm, museum. It can be in the local area or involve travel by coach/train to a more distant locality.

GROUPWORK
Groups might be working close together in a given area or at different times or at a variety of sites.

INDIVIDUAL WORK
This is done in the home or school environment.

For individual work, pupils might be asked to:

■ note things on their way to/from school;

■ do observational work on their own house or street (Figure 1 and Figure 2);

■ collect data for collation and analysis in school (see Figure 3 for a sample questionnaire).

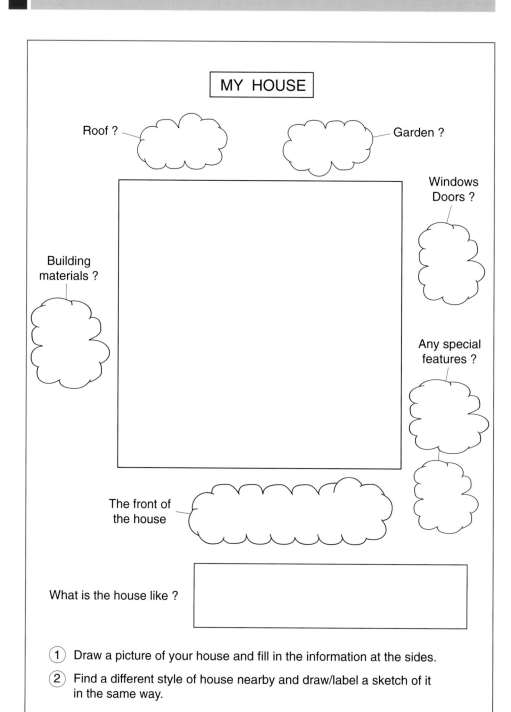

Figure 1:
An individual worksheet.

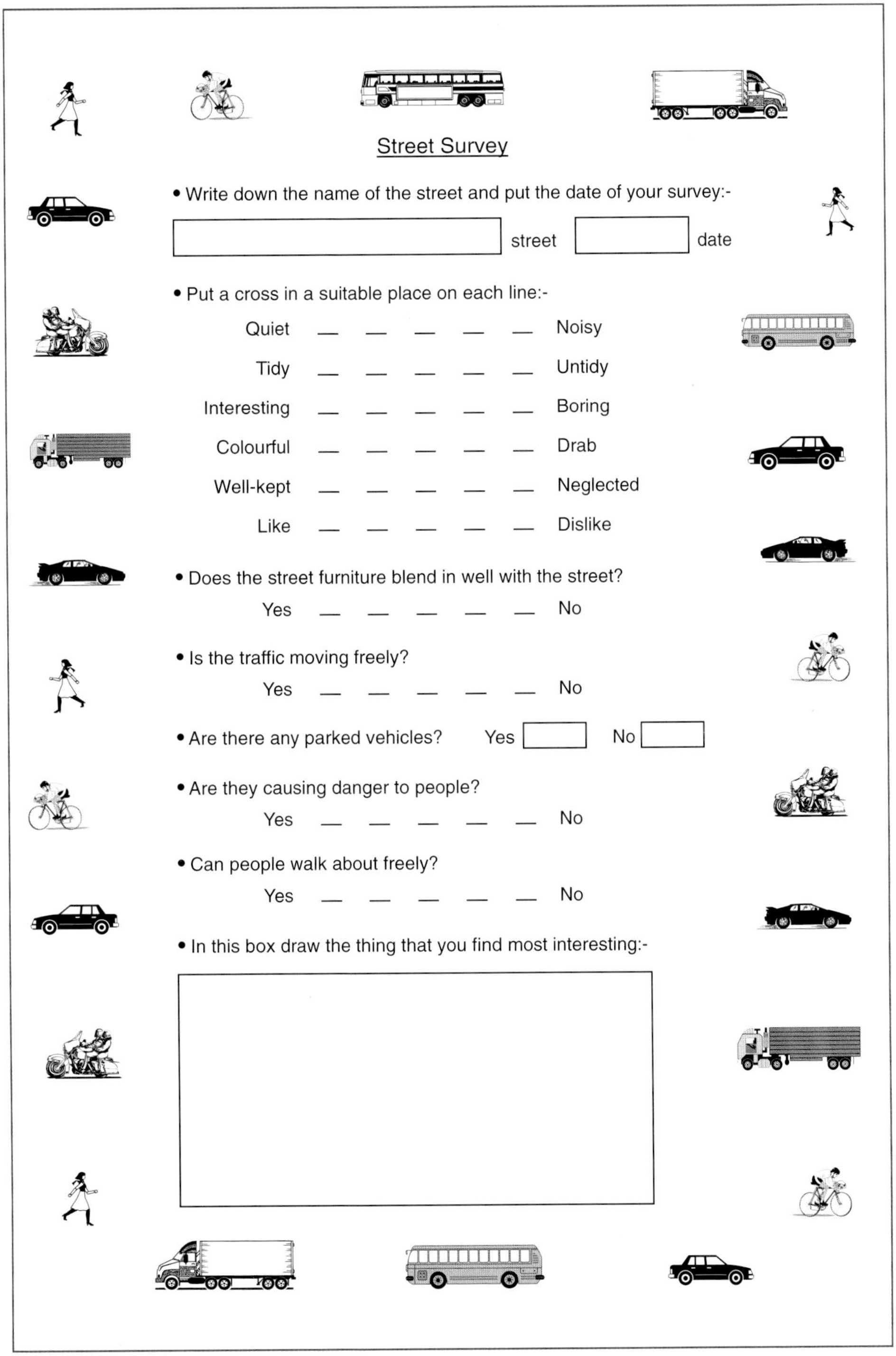

Street Survey

- Write down the name of the street and put the date of your survey:-

[   ] street [   ] date

- Put a cross in a suitable place on each line:-

Quiet	—	—	—	—	—	Noisy
Tidy	—	—	—	—	—	Untidy
Interesting	—	—	—	—	—	Boring
Colourful	—	—	—	—	—	Drab
Well-kept	—	—	—	—	—	Neglected
Like	—	—	—	—	—	Dislike

- Does the street furniture blend in well with the street?

Yes — — — — — No

- Is the traffic moving freely?

Yes — — — — — No

- Are there any parked vehicles? Yes [   ] No [   ]

- Are they causing danger to people?

Yes — — — — — No

- Can people walk about freely?

Yes — — — — — No

- In this box draw the thing that you find most interesting:-

**Figure 2:
Street survey.**

Most fieldwork is organised and supervised by teachers, and usually takes place in the locality or home region. However, pupils can also be encouraged to carry out investigations when they go on holiday. To help them to do this, it is a good idea to produce a small booklet to direct their enquiries.

This booklet could include the following questions for them to address:
- What is this place like?
- What is the weather like? (keep a weather record)
- What sort of facilities does your place/resort have?
- How do prices compare with those at home?
- What are the main differences between your holiday place and home?

The bottlebank questionnaire in Figure 3 is an excellent example of how data can be collected by individual pupils. The questionnaire responses provide a solid base of information which is ideal for the development of a database. Twenty-five pupils with four interviews each would provide 100 responses. Pupils will find that nearly all interviewees think that bottlebanks are a good idea, but actual use of them is variable. Answers to question 3 may be enlightening, offering reasons such as shortage of storage space or poor access to banks.

Recycling – Bottlebanks

We have done some work on recycling and we are now going to find out what people think about using bottlebanks.

Choose up to four people and ask them (politely) if they would mind answering a few short questions. (You could ask a member of your family/a neighbour.)

Male ☐   Female ☐

	P1	P2	P3	P4
1. Do you think bottlebanks are a good idea?	☐	☐	☐	☐

2. How often do you/your family use one? (tick one column)

	P1	P2	P3	P4
Weekly	☐	☐	☐	☐
Monthly	☐	☐	☐	☐
Not often	☐	☐	☐	☐
Never	☐	☐	☐	☐

3. If you don't use one very regularly can you say why you don't?

P1 _____
P2 _____
P3 _____
P4 _____

4. Which of these things do you collect/recycle?

	P1	P2	P3	P4
newspapers	☐	☐	☐	☐
milktops	☐	☐	☐	☐
stamps	☐	☐	☐	☐
Christmas cards	☐	☐	☐	☐
clothes	☐	☐	☐	☐
other, please say	☐	☐	☐	☐

Thank you for answering these questions

Figure 3:
A sample questionnaire to do with bottlebanks/recycling.

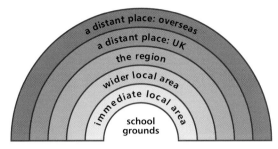

AREAS FOR FIELDWORK

Children's fieldwork experiences should start with their immediate surroundings and gradually broaden into less familiar territory, as they become confident with each area and have acquired some basic fieldwork skills. A simple 'nested hierarchy' of fieldwork areas is shown here, and the different potential of each area is examined in detail in the paragraphs which follow.

School grounds

These provide an initial stimulus for observing, recording and enjoying work outside the classroom, and a useful area to practise sketching, estimating and evaluating aspects of the environment. This means that when pupils are further afield time is not wasted in learning how to perform these skills; they can be put to use directly, and related to the work in hand.

Activities in the school grounds could include:
- finding different kinds of building materials;
- 'dating' the area on a map – which parts are older/newer?
- using map keys;
- finding pleasant/boring/warmest/coldest spots around the grounds;
- making up directions/routes round the site;
- sketching the views from the site;
- doing an environmental audit of the site;
- identifying the impact of seasonal/time changes on the site.

Environmental audit on the school playground produced by Broomley County First School, Stocksfield.

Observational work in the local area. Work: James Wiles.

Immediate local area

The potential of the local area will vary enormously from school to school but some of the following themes will be suitable for investigation:

- Streets, roads, buildings
- Local shops, corner shops
- Recreation – park areas
- Woodlands, fields
- Water features
- Transport links – car parks, traffic
- Local viewpoints
- Industrial estates
- Pupils' home areas
- New developments, e.g. building sites
- Service provision in the area

The local area has the benefit of being accessible and can therefore be visited frequently and for a variety of reasons (see Figure 4 for some lines of enquiry in both rural and urban areas). Also, groups can revisit to check evidence and observe changes over time. However, it is important that the study of geography is not seen to be restricted to the study of the local area on foot, while other curriculum areas, such as history, involve more exciting visits by coach to castles, famous houses and open air sites!

The wider local area and the region

Visits to both of these will involve travel and more time than local visits – half days or full days – but it is important for pupils to experience such visits so that they begin to see their own area in relation to a wider context, and can identify the inter-relationships which exist between them.

Photo: Roger Carter.

Photo: Paula Richardson.

Urban
Investigation of local street shopping parades/corner shops.
Comparison of buildings/designs/materials.
Assessment of litter problems, recycling issues.
Environmental walks to assess quality of the environment using an index.
Investigation of the impact of traffic in the area – How is parking/speeding controlled?, Is it effective?
Visit to a building site – monitor progress.
Identify and collect 'logo' signs – do patterns emerge in the provision of services?
Map the land use of the area using a key.
Map routes to school/pupils' houses.
Design/locate a leisure centre.

Rural
Complete a seasonal walk (four times per year to record changes).
Investigate the village/local services provided.
What is the effect of any closures, e.g. local shops?
Map the land use of the area using a key.
Identify/visit areas of change, e.g. a new building under construction, a road/bridge development.
Examine housing types/styles/ages.
Map where pupils live – routes to school – town.
Interview residents – What is good about living in the area? – What are the drawbacks? What changes would they like to see?
Walk to assess environmental quality of the area using an index.
Investigate traffic problems

Figure 4:
Lines of enquiry for
urban and rural fieldwork.

Examples of areas suitable for study might include:

■ the local town – town centre

■ a village outside the town

■ a water feature – river or lake

■ a contrasting physical environment

■ an industrial area

■ farms, leisure complex or airport

■ a seaside area

A distant place – UK/overseas

Finance and school organisation will play a major part in determining how often visits of this type will take place. However, it is important to allow pupils to have these experiences whenever possible, to broaden their horizons both curricular and social.

One way of setting up visits further afield is to make links with another school and offer return visits. The potential educational value is endless and financially attractive arrangements or packages can usually be found. For example, if each school hosts its visitors for the day, their only outgoings would be transport costs for getting there and back.

Many primary schools are now taking longer visits to a residential centre either in Britain or overseas, often France. These can be very exciting experiences for pupils, and for teachers too. However, it is also possible to have a one night residential stay, which is suitable for younger pupils and which can still be rewarding and exciting but without the greater financial commitment of a longer visit.

Fieldwork policy

In order to plan effectively for fieldwork throughout the school, it is important that a policy or guidelines are established. This will ensure that fieldwork becomes a part of the learning process and not an optional extra which happens occasionally during the summer term. The policy can be part of the geography policy or can be a stand-alone document. When it has been accepted by the governing body of the school, it becomes part of the accepted educational provision within the school.

Figure 5 gives a suggested outline of what the policy might include. Each element can be covered in a sentence or two, thus ensuring that the whole is concise as well as helpful to those who will need to read it. (This is dealt with in more detail in *Fieldwork In Action*, a series of books covering aspects of fieldwork in primary schools published by the Geographical Association (1993-98)).

To ensure progression and continuity, all schools should have a **School Fieldwork Policy.** This should not be a long, highly detailed document. It should be concise and easy to understand by those who need to refer to it.

It should include:

1   the philosophy of the importance of fieldwork

2   the aims and objectives of fieldwork

3   the minimum entitlement for each pupil

4   how fieldwork fits into the main curriculum plan – is it used as a stimulus visit or for consolidation of work already done?

5   suggestions of possible locations and activities suitable for each key stage

6   suggestions to show development and progression in fieldwork (progression might be identified through depth, breadth, locations, examples, etc.)

7   cross-curricular links

8   the Country Code/Outdoor Studies Code, etc.

9   health and safety statement/LEA guidelines

10 an equipment list and list of resources kept in school; reference to whether other equipment may be obtained

11 copies of letters to send to parents

12 Assessment of fieldwork in relation to:
    a pupil performance
    b suitability of location for the planned activities
    c suitability of activities for the pupils

13 presentation possibilities. Is a perfect finish needed for work done in the field? The concept of a fieldwork notebook.

Figure 5:
Towards a School
Fieldwork Policy.
After: May *et al.*, 1993.

Planning a visit: health and safety issues

PLANNING

Visits to places beyond the school grounds must always be planned with great care, and with close attention to health and safety issues. The following checklist highlights the essential elements of a plan, but detailed guidance on planning, management, and health and safety issues can be found in the *Fieldwork in Action* titles listed at the end of this chapter.

The following is a checklist for planning fieldwork visits:

1 Permission from headteacher ☐
2 Choice of location – aims, objectives, dates ☐
3 Refer to school/LEA documents, insurance, costings, etc. ☐
4 Book visit/transport, check timings ☐
5 Fill in required forms/letters to parents, medical forms ☐
6 Visit site, plan, book, do site visit analysis ☐
7 Prepare pupils – activities, clothing, equipment ☐
8 Brief staff and parent helpers ☐
9 Keep good accounts of monies collected ☐
10 On the day: leave lists of participants at school, know emergency procedures, brief staff, organise equipment and who is responsible for bringing it back ☐
11 Follow up: letters of thanks, payments, classwork, evaluate visit and note any changes to be made ☐

Health and safety, and risk assessment

One of the most important elements in pre-fieldwork preparation is a visit by the teacher to the chosen site, to access risks and safety issues, and to gain up-to-date information. A risk assessment should be undertaken for each new site or activity and previously-used sites should be reviewed as necessary.

There are five stages to good site assessment which, ideally, should be made not too long before the visit takes place:

1 Identify the hazards which could occur at the location.
2 Decide on what could happen as a result of the hazard and who might be affected.
3 Evaluate the risks involved and decide whether or not the precautions taken are sufficient or whether further ones are needed.
4 Record and date your findings, and find out whether or not there will be any significant changes before your visit.
5 Review the risk assessment before a further visit is made.

This exercise may sound very formal and complex but in reality is often very straightforward. It is important to know what the problems might be and how they can be solved or eased in some way. For example, if the fieldwork involves a survey of High Street shops, the points to consider in the site assessment might be as follows:

1 Hazards
■ narrow pavements
■ large number of people
■ constant moving traffic

2 What could happen?

■ pupils could be pushed off pavement

■ pupils could have difficulty crossing the road, etc.

3 Evaluation

■ not all the pavement areas are narrow, some provide better viewing areas than others. Note those that do

■ crossing the road will be very difficult, but pedestrian light crossings are available. Note their location and the need to remind teachers/pupils

4 Records

■ date of assessment

■ information on any extra hazards such as street market/digging up gas mains that may occur on certain days

5 Review

■ this environment will need a risk assessment at regular intervals, as changes are liable to occur quite frequently

It is vital to remember that teachers who accompany pupils on fieldwork trips should have at least a basic training in the essentials of first aid, and groups of pupils working away from school should always be accompanied by a sensible, reliable first aider.

Carrying out a hazard assessment before your pupils undertake fieldwork ensures that they work in safety.
Photo: Chris Garnett.

Progression in fieldwork

The local area in particular is relatively accessible and cheap to use for fieldwork and a pupil is likely to find himself/herself visiting the same area at different key stages in different schools. This often results in the area, or certain features in it, being overused – a pupil can be asked to study a local shopping area several times over, often using similar activities. For this reason liaison between staff at the various key stages is crucial.

Questions they need to address include:

■ How do you use the local area?

■ Which are the main areas/themes used by your pupils?

■ Which museums/farms/shopping areas do you use?

Typically, key stage 1 pupils will be asked to examine the quality of the local environment, while at key stage 2 they will progress to looking at changes in the environment, building on the skills and knowledge they have already gained.

Figure 6 shows an example of how a study of a local shopping parade/centre can progress from a simple analysis of the area (for lower primary) to a more in-depth exercise (for upper primary). Account is taken of children's increasing maturation in various ways, such as:

- a move from closed to more open questions;
- an increase in problem solving/decision making;
- movement from one to several variables;
- movement towards collaborative work and more independent learning.

Worksheets/activity sheets

While it is important to allow pupils to observe and use all the senses without too much distraction from worksheets, there will always be times when worksheets are needed. The following are some simple rules for making a worksheet as useful as possible.

1 The worksheet should be clear and well laid out.

2 The text should not be too crowded or contain too many tasks/directions.

3 There should be a variety of activities.

4 How?, Why?, Which?, When? produce better answers than Do.

5 Answers should require a variety of styles or response: draw, estimate, decide, underline, etc.

6 Vocabulary should be straightforward.

7 Pupils should be asked to use the senses where appropriate and safe: hear, see, smell, feel, taste.

The best test for a worksheet is to ask yourself if you would enjoy doing/be able to do it yourself.

Photo: Chris Garnett.

A shopping parade – lower primary age

1 On your base map, write in the types of shop, or colour them in and make a key in the margin.

2 What is the use of the floor above most of the shops?

3 Which types of shops are missing from here?

4 Is parking easy?

5 How many parking spaces are there?

6 How long do cars tend to stay here?

7 Why is this?

8 Where do you think the shoppers come from?

9 What can you do here besides shop? (telephone, recycling banks, postbox, etc.)

A shopping parade – upper primary age

One of the shops is empty. You have decided to rent it and open a
_____ (service or shop)

1 You need to decide what service or shop is needed here. How will you do this?
Question shoppers? How many? Look at other shopping possibilities in the area? What is the market for your service/shop?

2 You have to decide on a window display, signs layout, uniforms, opening hours.

3 Plan for your staffing – write an advert for staff (look at examples in local newspapers). Think about costs and rates of pay.

4 Plan your opening date. How and where will you advertise it? Local paper? Local radio? Free gifts?

5 How will you make sure your shop/service survives?

Figure 6:
Progression in
fieldwork tasks.

Resources for fieldwork

It is important to build up resources for local fieldwork, not least to help and inspire other colleagues. The resources should be centrally located and it is helpful to have several copies of the most useful items. It is also essential to keep adding to the bank of items with, for example, photographs of changes in the area, and newspaper cuttings.

Resources are divided into three types:
- Visual, written and other basic resources – for local fieldwork
- Equipment – for use in the field
- Information regarding places to visit

Visual, written and other basic resources

Maps	at scales of 1:50 000, 1:25 000, 1:10 000, 1:2500. Local street maps; theme maps
Booklets	local directories, e.g. *Kelly's*; guidebooks; leaflets about area
Photographs	ground based of selected places/items/festivals (see Figure 7); sequence photographs of, e.g. building sites; aerial photographs, both professional and amateur; postcards, newspaper pictures
Statistics	about weather (local information), traffic; environmental issues, conservation in local area. The last three, plus local Census data, are often available through local Borough/Council departments
Audio tapes	local people talking about changes/living in the area
Newspapers	cuttings about a variety of local issues
Previous work	data collected on previous fieldwork visits as evidence of change – and for making comparisons
Artefacts	relating to local geology/industry

Using resources at key stage 1.
Photo: Chris Garnett.

Equipment

Key stage 1

clipboards

tape measure

magnifying glasses

metre rulers

non-standard measures, e.g. foot

stop-watch/clock

compass

rock hardness testing equipment

thermometer

large-scale base maps

plans, e.g. school, shopping area

simple soil testing kit

simple hand-held anemometer

wind sock

rain gauge

soil profile in jars

Using resources at key stage 2.
Photo: John Hendy.

Key stage 2 – as for key stage 1 plus:

recognition cards for trees, etc.

quadrats

stop-watches

soil augers

water pollution testing kit

maps
(1:50 000 and 1:25 000)

noise meter

wind gauge

more sophisticated soil testing kit (to include chemicals)

anemometer

rain gauge/measure

cloud identification charts

clinometer

INFORMATION REGARDING PLACES TO VISIT, AND ACTIVITIES

It is useful to build a 'library' of information about fieldwork places in the area. These should be filed using a standard form such as the example in Figure 7. It may also be helpful to staff to have a 'library' of books with specific ideas on how to study the local environment.

Activities

Activities can be devised which help to focus attention on the area being studied and which develop skills of recall, thinking, prediction, sketching, and so on. Such activities also motivate pupils to take an active interest in their area. Below are two examples.

1 Take photographs of specific features in the immediate area, e.g. a church, traffic lights, shops, memorials.

   On a large, possibly hand drawn map in the classroom, ask the pupils to locate the photographs correctly around the map. Pupils can then check them on their way home, and on the following day a collective judgement can be made.

2 Take a series of photographs in the area and cut them in half. Ask pupils to sketch in what they think is missing. Again they can check on the way home or over a weekend, then, when back at school, be shown the full photograph.

Conclusion

Fieldwork offers the opportunity for interesting and innovative teaching and learning; we need to make the most of it to bring a real and practical dimension to our pupils' geographical experience. We should also remember that, for many children, a fieldwork visit may be one of the most exciting and memorable events of their lives (Chambers and Donert, 1996, p.14).

Location:

Address:

Tel:

Date visited:

Number of pupils:

Number of adults:

Year group:

Topic links:

Education facilities

Education officer

Educational resources/worksheets

Teacher's notes/guidebooks

Handling materials

Loans

Video/tape commentaries

Talks/activities

Practical details

Cost involved

Journey time

Parking facilities

Lunch room

Education room

Toilets

Shop

Aims of visit

On-site activities and organisation (enclose any material used)

Follow-up work

Evaluation/comments

Figure 7: Visit/fieldwork record sheet.

References

Chambers, B. and Donert, K. (1996) *Teaching Geography at KS2.* Cambridge: Chris Kington Publishing.

May, S. (1996) *Fieldwork in Action 4: Primary Fieldwork Projects.* Sheffield: Geographical Association.

May, S. and Cook, J. (1996) *Fieldwork in Action 2: An Enquiry Approach.* Sheffield: Geographical Association.

May, S., Richardson, P. and Banks, V. (1993) *Fieldwork in Action 1: Planning Fieldwork.* Sheffield: Geographical Association.

Plowden, B. (1967) *Children in Primary Schools.* London: HMSO.

Richardson, P. and Walford, R. (1998) *Fieldwork in Action 5: Mapping Land Use.* Sheffield: Geographical Association.

Richardson, P. and Whiting, S. (eds) (1998) *Fieldwork in Action 6: Crossing the Channel.* Sheffield: Geographical Association.

Thomas, T. and May, S. (1994) *Fieldwork in Action 3: Managing Out-of-classroom Activities.* Sheffield: Geographical Association.

Chapter 14: Fieldwork

Fieldwork opportunities outlined here show how practical work outside the classroom can enrich children's understanding of geographical places (Section Five), themes (Section Six), and skills (Section Four). There is also important advice for geography co-ordinators (Chapter 8) about organisational and safety matters.

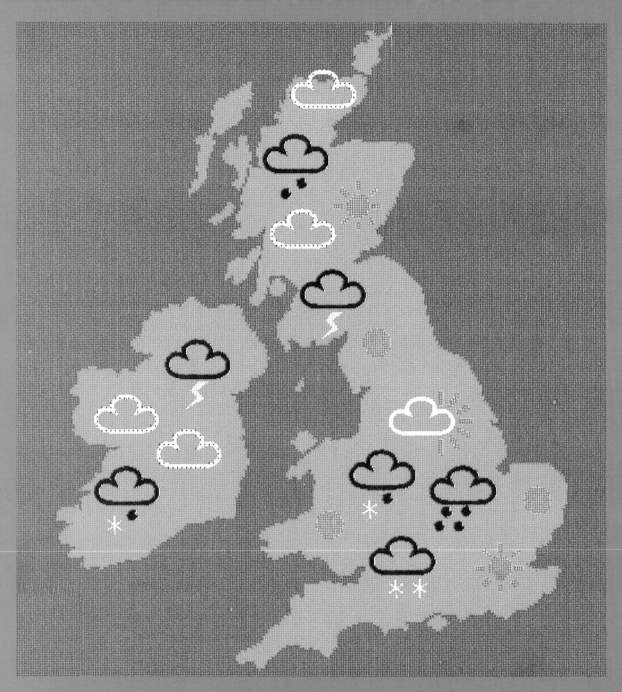

clanoiy   Thunder

Sunly   Showerey

rainiy   run and swy

    rain snowy

vuree suniy

Geography and ICT

Chapter 15

Kate Russell

The use of Information and Communications Technology (ICT[1]) has become firmly established in the primary classroom since the first computers were introduced in the early 1980s. ICT was incorporated into the National Curriculum in 1990 when ICT Capability was Attainment Target 5 of the Order for Technology. In 1995, a separate Order for ICT was published. This stated that ICT be set in a curriculum context and that:

> *'pupils should be given opportunities, where appropriate, to develop and apply their ICT capability in their study of National Curriculum subjects' (DFE, 1995a, p. 1).*

Recent changes in emphasis have placed ICT in the 'core' of the Primary Curriculum and schools are still required to cover all the National Curriculum Programmes of Study. There is a strong commitment to raising standards in the use of ICT; the National Grid for Learning will have an impact on all our schools by 2002. The Grid is an education network providing learning and teaching materials through a Virtual Teacher Centre. The Standards Fund will provide additional computer equipment to state schools in England and Wales in a rolling programme up to the year 2002.

Primary geography provides such a curriculum context for pupils to develop their ICT capability and apply their skills. At the same time, the subject will benefit considerably from the use of ICT, and teachers who integrate ICT with geography can be confident that the geography they teach will be much enhanced by its use. The strands relating to ICT that are currently identified by the National Curriculum are:

- Opportunities for ICT
- Communicating and Handling Information
- Controlling, Measuring and Modelling

If we consider each of these aspects of ICT in more detail, it will become clear how ICT and geography can be mutually beneficial subjects. The Geography National Curriculum for key stage 1 states that:

> *'In investigating places and a theme, pupils should be given opportunities to observe, question and record and to communicate ideas and information' (DFE, 1995b, p. 2).*

There is an expanded statement for key stage 2 geography, and a similar focus on the enquiry approach, and on information gathering and analysing can also be found in the ICT National Curriculum as outlined below.

The ICT National Curriculum

OPPORTUNITIES FOR ICT

The ICT Order states that pupils should be given opportunities to use a range of ICT equipment, including computers and software as well as various keyboards, programmable toys and devices such as digital cameras. They should explore the use of computer systems and control technology in everyday life and investigate parallels of their experiences of ICT with the use of ICT in the wider world, considering the effects of its use and comparing it with other methods.

COMMUNICATING AND HANDLING INFORMATION

Pupils should be able to generate and communicate their ideas in different forms, using text, tables, pictures and sound. At key stage 1 they should be able to enter and store information and then retrieve, process and display the information that has been stored. At key stage 2 it is expected that they will communicate ideas in a variety of forms,

ICT helps pupils to analyse their fieldwork data.
Photo: Kate Russell.

incorporating text, graphs, pictures and sound as appropriate, showing sensitivity to the needs of their audience. Pupils will increasingly need to be able to use the power of the software to organise, reorganise and analyse their ideas and information. They will also classify and prepare information for processing, checking for accuracy. They will check the plausibility of information stored and consider the consequences of inaccurate information. For this strand pupils will be using a variety of software including word processors, desk-top publishing, music composition software, drawing and graphics packages, databases and spreadsheets. All this is good practice in geography in terms of the enquiry approach to learning.

CONTROLLING, MEASURING AND MODELLING

At key stage 1 pupils will be taught to recognise that control is integral to many everyday devices; they need to give direct signals or commands and describe the effects of their actions and be able to use models or simulations to explore aspects of real and imaginary situations. There is no requirement to do any monitoring at key stage 1. At key stage 2 pupils will have to create, test, modify and store sequences of instructions to control events. They are also expected to use ICT equipment and software to monitor external events. They have to explore the effect of changing variables in simulations and similar packages, to ask and answer questions of the 'What would happen if ...?' type and to recognise patterns and relationships in the results obtained from ICT-based models predicting the outcomes of different decisions that could be made. For this strand pupils will be using programmable toys, and software which includes a programming language such as Logo, some simulations, data-logging equipment and software, and spreadsheets.

ICT and geography

All primary school pupils have an entitlement to develop their ICT skills and capability. Every primary teacher is a teacher of both geography and ICT and where the two can complement each other, then we should capitalise on the opportunity. ICT is both a National Curriculum subject in its own right and a cross-curricular tool for aiding teaching and enriching learning.

Over recent years there has been an increase in the number of computers available in primary schools, but there is an ongoing need to replace ageing equipment and to increase pupil access to up-to-date ICT resources. To be able to provide ICT experiences for all pupils in the class, a teacher should expect access to at least one computer system (including a printer) and appropriate software in the classroom. ICT does not just mean the use of computers, however, it also includes the use of other technological equipment such as programmable toys (Roamer, Pip and Pixie), tape recorders, cameras, fax machines, data-logging equipment, automatic weather stations, Internet and CD-ROMs, all of which are tools to aid learning. There are many ways in which ICT can be used to help teachers in their own work, for example administration, preparing worksheets, for reference and to aid display work. Using ICT in these contexts often helps to overcome some of the nervousness that teachers feel, and if they are supported in developing their own skills, this will in turn enhance the curriculum for the young people in their care. Resourcing and training issues of this kind will have to be addressed by the senior management team and governors, who should be review them regularly.

Curriculum planning is critical with ICT, to ensure purposeful activities reflecting continuity and progression of skills rather than an ad hoc approach. The geography co-ordinator should work alongside the ICT co-ordinator to plan for integration of ICT into geography in a meaningful way. A good starting place is to look at the current situation in school, to review how ICT is being used and to build upon it. Any gaps can be filled in over time – do not attempt to make too many changes at once. Try to introduce new activities slowly; if the changes are manageable then they are likely to be more successful as teachers will gain confidence in what they have achieved.

Planning should start with the geography curriculum, reviewing areas which will naturally be enhanced by ICT activities, rather than making forced links. The two co-ordinators will be able to work together to look for opportunities for using ICT in geography. Factors to consider will include current practice, resource availability and staff confidence.

In their joint publication of the leaflet *Primary Geography a Pupil's Entitlement to IT*, the Geographical Association and the National Council for Educational Technology (NCET) (GA/NCET, 1995) identified five ways in which ICT can help pupils' learning in geography in the primary school (see Figure 1). These are now considered in turn

Figure 1:
How ICT activities may contribute to a pupil's learning in geography.
Source: GA/NCET, 1995.

ICT can make a positive contribution to pupils' learning in geography by:
- enhancing their skills of geographical enquiry;
- providing a range of information sources to enhance their geographical knowledge;
- supporting the development of their understanding of geographical patterns and relationships;
- providing access to images of people, places and environments;
- contributing to their awareness of the impact of ICT on the changing world.

Enhancing skills of geographical enquiry

There is little enquiry-based work that cannot be enhanced with ICT (see Figures 2 and 3). For example, the use of databases, spreadsheets, data-logging equipment or the Internet will certainly be an advantage in cases where pupils are asking geographical questions, making observations, or recordings and investigating data from fieldwork and secondary sources. These tools can also enhance the study of the weather, a traffic or shopping survey, or a local river study. This sort of open-ended or generic software helps pupils to organise the information they have collected in a structured way; they can sort the information into a more appropriate order, search for patterns and produce graphs to illustrate their findings. Pupils who are fortunate enough to have access to a portable computer during fieldwork can enter data directly into the computer and, by using appropriate software, process and analyse the data on-site.

Geographical enquiries invariably involve creating, using and interpreting maps and again, ICT can provide relevant support. For example, pupils could use a concept keyboard

Ideas for teachers

1 In a geography display include some ICT generated work – even if it is just titles and headings.

2 Teachers can set high standards of presentation in their worksheets.

3 Build up a locality photo pack by having your photos stored on a photo-CD (a service available at many high street photo processing outlets) or using a digital camera – they are then in a very flexible format for incorporating with other documents and printing out.

4 Build up ICT resources alongside other resources for your topics (e.g. concept keyboard overlays and datafiles).

5 Build up a bank of cribsheets and manuals for the core software in school.

6 Teachers must have ICT skills if they are to pass these on to their pupils.

Pupil activities

1 Do not use a computer as an electronic typewriter to re-type hand-written work – allow pupils to draft, redraft and edit work for final presentation at the computer.

2 Aim for each pupil in your class to have used ICT with at least one geography activity during the year.

3 Teachers can create the structure of a database or spreadsheet in advance – pupils enter the data.

4 Some ICT activities are better suited to individual work, especially word processing, and can be time consuming.

5 Data handling is usually a group (or even whole-class) activity as pupils take it in turns to enter data and then analyse it.

Resources

■ Many CD-ROM disks are valuable as sources of information for the teacher as well as for pupils.

■ Ensure ICT equipment is in working order and that classrooms have access to the appropriate software and disks.

Figure 2:
Some suggestions to support good practice.

Does your school have these ICT tools?

The following is a list of resources which schools could reasonably expect to have access to:

Hardware and peripherals
■ Computer system and printer in each classroom
■ Programmable toy(s)
■ Concept keyboards and a bank of suitable overlays
■ Multimedia computer with CD-ROM
■ Data-logging equipment and/or automatic weather station
■ Access to the Internet and an e-mail address

Software
Generic software which is general purpose and suitable for the age of pupils it is to be used with:
■ Word processing (preferably with spell check)
■ Desk-top publishing
■ Graphics or drawing
■ Programming software (such as Logo)
■ Database (or graphing software for very young pupils)
■ Spreadsheet

Geography-specific software
■ Mapping software
■ Simulations or adventures which involve 'mental maps'
■ CD-ROM disks:
   Encyclopedias
   Atlases
   Providing images and information about places

Towards the future
■ Facsimile machine
■ Portable computers
■ A school web site
■ Video conferencing
■ An e-mail address per pupil

Figure 3:
Essential ICT resources checklist.

Photo: Kate Russell.

to investigate images of localities and develop map skills, and there are computer programs available to help them to produce maps for particular purposes.

When pupils are communicating the results of their enquiries in the form of text, pictures and graphs, there are many word processing and presentation programs to help them. The use of some ICT generated work, alongside materials produced using other media, is very effective. A worthwhile project would be for some pupils to produce a 'tourist' guide to their local area, which could be illustrated with photographs combined with text. Photographic negatives can be put onto a CD-ROM by your photographic developer, thus transforming them into a more flexible resource. Now that digital cameras are becoming more widely available, photographic images can be transferred directly from camera to computer, and once 'captured' in this way can be manipulated and positioned to suit the operator's needs.

Many schools now have their own web site on the Internet which is used to publish information about the school. This may include information about the locality, so there is an opportunity here for pupils to contribute material and information they have gained during geographical enquiry work. Electronic mail (e-mail) links with schools in another locality enable pupils to communicate with a wider audience; because of the potentially rapid response time facilitated by e-mail, pupils can enter into a dialogue with other pupils. Much of this dialogue could focus on finding out about features of the other locality and what it is like to live there.

Work: Leanne Burns and Helen Stiff, Esh Winning School, County Durham.

ST LUCIA'S HOTELS

All of the hotels in St Lucia have a sea view. They also are not very far away from a gorgeous, sandy beach. Our three most famous hotels are well recommended by many of our customers. Practically all of our customers have been satisfied with the way they were treated and have even come back again. There is a balcony and there are rooms for your family that will be just the right size.

ST LUCIA'S ENTERTAINMENT

During the day there is a swimming gala in most hotels early in the morning. On rainy days we will put on a kids show. Every day you can come to Fishys Kids Club. On a night they will have a kids disco leading on to entertainment for adults such as karaoke and many comedians. You can visit the volcano in the centre of St Lucia on a guided tour.

FOOD IN ST LUCIA

The food in St Lucia is really fantastic. It is healthy and has a lot of fruit. You are bound to find something to your liking.

L +H
HOLIDAYS

Providing a range of information sources to enhance geographical knowledge

Recent advances in communications technology have added both sources of, and means of gathering information to the already wide range of traditional sources used by geographers. The most powerful recent addition is the Internet, which enables pupils to communicate directly with people in different places as well as providing access to a vast amount of information. Electronic mail and faxes are also now available in many schools and help to generate links as well as routes to gathering information. As stores of stimulus material, such as photographs, videos, animations, sound and other information, CD-ROMs have particular value in the geography classroom, though, like books, they can soon become dated. For collecting material derived from interviews, e.g. with visitors about their jobs or about living in another locality, a tape recorder is a very useful aid; even young pupils will be able to operate the machine for both recording and playback.

Supporting the development of understanding of geographical patterns and relationships

As part of their geography pupils will be encouraged to recognise spatial patterns and make comparisons between places and events. A programmable toy, such as a floor turtle, can help by developing pupils' spatial awareness, especially if it is programmed to move around a large floor map or maze. While many computer 'games' have little to offer educationally, and may promote stereotypes or bad practice, it is worth looking at these for opportunities to develop spatial and other geographical skills. Examples include games where use is made of an on-screen map or where players have to develop a mental map or make decisions.

Databases, spreadsheets, some simulations and multimedia can help to provide an insight into geographical relationships such as weather patterns, causes and effects of water pollution or the movement of water through different soils.

ICT can help develop
spatial skills.
Photo: Chris Garnett.

Providing access to images of people, places and environments

Primary geography aims to develop pupils' awareness and knowledge of the culture and character of a variety of places. The use of ICT tools such as fax, e-mail, CD-ROMs and the Internet can assist in providing access to images and other information in a variety of forms, such as first-hand data, photographs, video and sound. Many publishers are entering the world of multimedia and some are producing materials on CD-ROM to complement textbooks and television programmes. Also now available are photo compact disks which enable schools to build up a collection of photographs of the locality and which could be exchanged with schools in contrasting localities in the UK.

Increasing awareness of the impact of ICT on the changing world

One requirement of the ICT National Curriculum is that pupils should 'investigate parallels with the use of ICT in the wider world, consider the effects of such uses and compare them with other methods' (DFE, 1995a, p. 3). Geography provides an ideal opportunity to study this aspect of ICT developments. For example, pupils can look at ways in which ICT has influenced communications, leisure and the world of work. They can also investigate how computers and other devices are used in travel agencies and supermarkets; for providing information from satellites; and to forecast the weather. They can observe the uses of ICT and control devices at home and at school.

During a geography fieldwork visit to a high street or local shopping centre, one task a group of pupils could undertake is to observe and locate the uses of technology and control and monitoring systems such as automatic doors, cash dispensers, bar-code readers and supermarket stock control systems, video surveillance cameras and traffic and pedestrian crossing lights. On a visit to an airport, one school focused on how ICT and control systems were used there. The airport staff were very helpful and showed the pupils the check-in procedures, the seat allocation system, the luggage security scanners and many other ways in which ICT has had an impact on the workings of a modern airport.

Lydd-Ashford Airport

Lydd-Ashford airport plays a leading role as a alternative airport for the South-East of England. Flying from Lydd Ashford is a potential saver of time fuel and money. The airport serves the South-East which covers the counties of Kent, Sussex and Surrey. The airport is already well served with a good road network. Travelling through Lydd-Ashford will then be a viable alternative to travelling through the London airports, even for those living in the Greater London area. 1500 metre hard runway and excellent terminal buildings, with a fast improving road service from London, services to Le Touquet continue Love Air, London Flight Centre Cinque Ports Flying Club

Work: Melissa Kennedy.

Planning

The key to success in the use of ICT to enhance geography lies in careful planning. This should be a process in which several people are involved – the geography co-ordinator, the ICT co-ordinator and the relevant class teachers. The planning process will be a cyclical one, undertaken periodically to take account of when geography activities change or there are new ICT resources in school. The main elements of the planning process are listed in Figure 4.

EVALUATE, PLAN, ACTION, MONITOR AND REVIEW

A good place to start in the planning process is to review current practice. If the activities used with pupils are successful and enhance their learning, then they should be written into both geography and ICT schemes of work.

The next step is to consider if you could put more ICT into the geography curriculum. As well as the ideas in this chapter, there are several publications (see **Resources** section at the end of the book) which offer guidance and practical ideas for activities. Among the issues to be considered at this stage are staff confidence and expertise, and access to hardware and software. It may be that these are lacking, but this need not be a barrier to implementing your ideas and steps can be taken to remedy the situation: if additional resources are required, then representation needs to made to the headteacher and governors and incorporated into the School Development Plan. If teachers lack the appropriate skills and confidence to undertake an activity, plans need to be made to address the training required, either with provision made within school or use made of a centre-based course.

1. Evaluate
Refer to the five entitlement statements.
What opportunities to you provide for using ICT in geography?
How is it enhancing your geography teaching and pupils' learning?
Is ICT included in curriculum documentation and planning for geography?
Could you do more?

Consider:
■ current practice
■ staff confidence and expertise
■ access to hardware and software
■ geography, ICT and assessment policy
■ progression and differentiation

2. Plan
Establish a development plan for geography which includes ICT.

Consider:
■ professional development needs
■ resource implications
■ responsibilities
■ a realistic time span (one or two years)
■ monitoring strategies and success criteria

Develop a scheme of work for geography to include ICT, which:
■ has clear objectives
■ has reference to NC programmes of study
■ demonstrates progression
■ gives clear reference to assessment and recording
■ is part of a whole-school approach

3. Action
Carry out the development plan.
Implement the schemes of work.

4. Monitor and review
Do pupils have opportunities to use ICT to:
■ support investigation and enquiry;
■ access different sources of information;
■ recognise patterns and relationships;
■ evaluate its effects on everyday life?

Are pupils able to:
■ ask and answer geographical questions;
■ identify, collect and classify relevant information;
■ analyse patterns and relationships;
■ talk about the impact of ICT?

What do pupils know and understand?
Has ICT contributed to this?

Figure 4:
Planning entitlement for
your school.
Source: GA/NCET, 1995.

It is important to ensure that pupils experience a broad and balanced range of ICT activities over a key stage. These need to be carefully worked out with clear regard to progression and differentiation, and be properly resourced. A few well-planned activities is better than several ad hoc ones with less clear objectives.

Once the activities have been planned, reference needs to be made in the relevant curriculum policy documents, showing the links between the subjects. After activities have been undertaken, it will be necessary to review them and then, if necessary, to modify them in the light of experience. The review process should make reference to the entitlement statements in Figure 2 to check the extent to which the ICT opportunities have supported pupils' investigations and enquiries. It should also reveal whether or not the ICT based activities have provided access to different sources of information, or have helped pupils to recognise patterns and relationships. Finally, it will show you if the pupils have been able to evaluate the effects of ICT on everyday life. Another method of monitoring the value of the activities is to consider to what extent pupils were able to ask and answer geographical questions. The purpose of the review is to highlight areas where action needs to be taken. If modification is necessary then this needs to be catered for and incorporated into the planning review.

Pupils with Special Educational Needs

All pupils can benefit from access to ICT, including pupils with learning difficulties. ICT can facilitate pupils' access to the curriculum, encourage motivation and develop skills. Word processors with spell-checking facilities and word lists for the insertion of words, and concept keyboards used with appropriate overlays will both support the development of literacy. Word processors with speech feedback can also be beneficial for pupils. Another useful resource for some pupils is CD-ROM software which includes sound, giving the option of having the text read to them.

For pupils with mild learning difficulties, especially those in mainstream schools, the starting point should be finding a means of using familiar equipment and resources to create activities for individualised learning, rather than considering the need for different resources. Pupils with moderate or severe learning difficulties can benefit from a range of specialised equipment, including voice recognition systems, which provide access to the curriculum. There are also several subject-specific learning programs with content presented at different levels of difficulty, thus offering activities for a range of individual needs.

ICT in a familiar primary topic

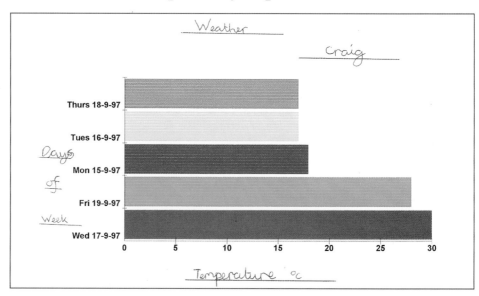

Work: Newbottle Primary School, Sunderland.

Weather is a popular topic in the primary geography curriculum, and has been chosen here to show some of the ways in which ICT can be incorporated into topic work. This exemplar demonstrates how a range of ICT applications can be used across the primary age range, with clear progression of skills. It is not, of course, intended that all pupils would have to undertake every activity!

USING ICT TO TEACH AND LEARN ABOUT THE WEATHER

SPRING IS ....

Spring is time for new flowers.

Spring is the ground getting warm.

Spring is animals being born.

Spring is blossoming blossom.

Spring is for gardening and planting seeds.

Spring is starting a new life.

Spring is light nights and playing out.

Spring is not for sweeping leaves.

Work: Christopher Hall, Newbottle Primary School, Sunderland.

In an **infant classroom**, pupils will make observations based upon their experience of the weather, including characteristics of the seasons. They will focus on questions such as 'What is it like?' and 'How does it make me feel?' and be encouraged to use correct terminology wherever possible. In work of this kind pupils will be able to make effective use of a concept keyboard and appropriate overlays to describe the weather they have observed during the week, or to match the weather with suitable clothes to wear. Alternatively, they could use one of the many graphing software programs available, to produce simple graphs as part of a display. Using a package with a base map or chart, they could copy appropriate weather symbols to compile a weather map or chart.

In the **early years of key stage 2**, pupils will extend their observations and will make recordings of weather data using simple instruments, including taking temperatures in the sun and in the shade. Data will be collected at several times during the year. They can devise their own indicators for measuring wind speed. Pupils should be given opportunities to store this data in a simple database in order to sort information and produce graphs. A display can be produced of their database graphs, accompanied by written (or word processed) accounts of the weather patterns which they have observed. These could perhaps be compared with newspaper forecasts.

Towards the **end of key stage 2**, pupils will make prolonged observations and will start to look for seasonal patterns. They will use a wider range of instruments, some of which they may have made themselves, including thermometers, barometers, raingauges, wind vanes and anemometers. Records can be kept from year to year in a database or spreadsheet, which can be added to by subsequent classes. Pupils will write reports of what they have observed, using appropriate word processing or desk-top publishing software, incorporating the graphs and charts which they have produced. They will also look for national and global patterns of weather, using data available from a variety of sources.

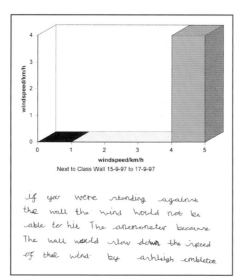

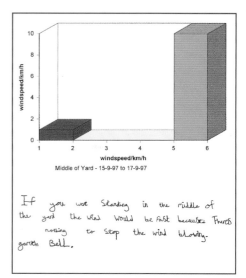

Work: Newbottle Primary School, Sunderland.

Some schools may have access to one of the remote weather stations available for recording weather data. Although these systems represent a substantial investment for schools, they have the advantage of recording data throughout weekends and holidays, as they store the data for a period. A snapshot of the 'weather now' can be produced as well as the prolonged records. It may be beneficial for primary schools to link with local high schools who have this type of equipment. A joint project could be established, with groups of primary pupils visiting the high school where the older pupils could explain how the system works. The data captured by the high school could then be given to the primary pupils as part of their topic on weather.

Who can help me?

ICT is essentially a practical tool, requiring a 'hands-on' approach. While it is hoped that this chapter may have provoked ideas and provided a context for development, you may still be left wondering 'Yes, but how?' (see Figure 5 for some suggested sources of help).

1 The ICT co-ordinator in school (he/she will be delighted if you take an interest in ICT!)

2 LEA advisers (ICT and geography)

3 Your local ICT centre

4 The Geographical Association Annual Conference (this is held around Easter and includes an exhibition of new materials as well as ICT workshops)

5 *Primary Geographer* magazine (published quarterly by the Geographical Association)

6 The BETT Show (in January) and The Education Show (in March) (these are both occasions when new materials are launched)

7 The British Educational Communications and Technology Agency (BECTA) which is the successor organisation to NCET, has useful publications to support ICT in the curriculum, and a free catalogue.

8 Local support in your school cluster (liaison between high schools and primary schools is important – ensure ICT is on the agenda. Start a local support network if one does not exist)

9 Micros and Primary Education (MAPE) (an organisation which organises regional events for teachers interested in ICT)

Figure 5: Sources of help in the use of ICT in your geography teaching.

A final word

ICT should be an active rather than a passive contribution to learning, and as such it is possibly the most difficult aspect of the National Curriculum to organise and manage. It is also expensive in terms of both resources and the time required for training and management. Because ICT is a relatively new requirement in primary schools, some teachers feel threatened by it, and the fact that their pupils may have greater expertise and confidence in using computers than they do. However, ICT is exciting and motivating and nearly every child will take to it with enthusiasm, irrespective of age and ability. Finally, and most important, is the fact that ICT has enormous potential for enhancing and supporting the geography curriculum so, provided you start in a manageable way, and follow the guidelines set out here and in the many other support publications now available (some of which are listed below), your chances of success are high. Good luck!

Note

1. The term Information and Communications Technology (ICT) is now often used rather than IT.

References and further reading

DFE (1995) *Geography in the National Curriculum (England)*. London: HMSO.

DFE (1995) *Information Technology in the National Curriculum*. London: HMSO.

Geographical Association (quarterly) *Primary Geographer*. Sheffield: Geographical Association.

GA/NCET (1995) *Primary Geography: A Pupil's Entitlement to IT* (leaflet). Sheffield/Coventry: Geographical Association/NCET.

GA/BECTA (1998) *Planning for ICT* (leaflet). Sheffield/Coventry: Geographical Association/British Educational Communications and Technology Agency.

NCET (1995) *Approaches to IT Capability, Key Stages 1 and 2*. Coventry: NCET.

SCAA (1995) *Key Stages 1 and 2 Information Technology: The New Requirement*. London: HMSO.

SCAA (1997) *Expectations in Geography at Key Stages 1 and 2*. London: SCAA.

Chapter 15: ICT and geography

Other chapters (e.g. Chapter 23 on weather and climate) consider ICT in relation to specific aspects of geography. In order to provide recurring opportunities for children to use ICT in geography work, it must be built in at the planning stage (Chapter 4), and with regard to children's growing capabilities (Chapter 5).

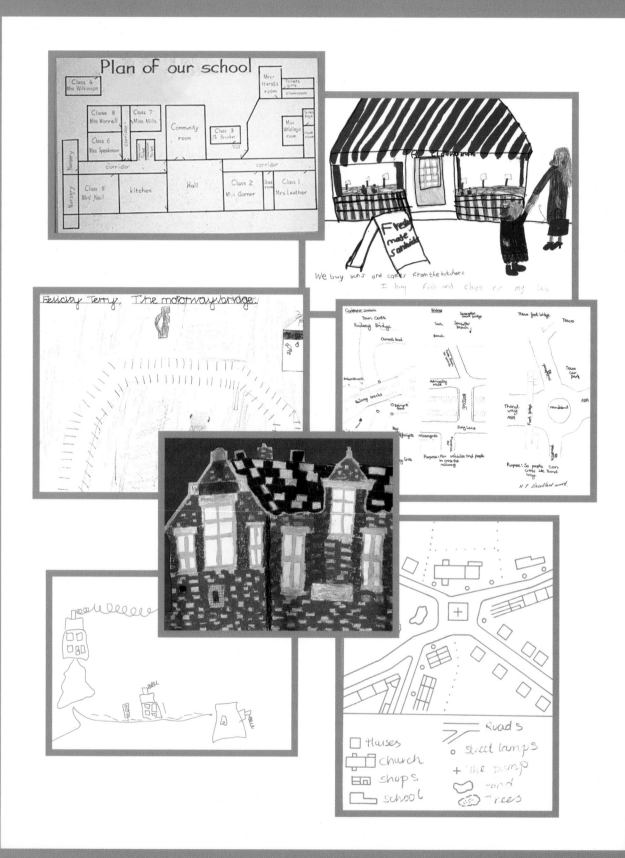

Exploring the local area:
1. Using the school grounds at key stage 1

Chapter 16

Angela Milner

> In this chapter Angela Milner considers how the school grounds can be used at key stage 1. The theme is developed by Wendy Garner, who describes how to make use of the larger area around the school with older children.

Why use the schools grounds?

Children learn best when activities revolve around their own interests and concerns. Young children are particularly curious about their own sphere of operations – the building and grounds of their school – and early years practitioners have long recognised the value of the school and its immediate environment to their pupils' geographical learning. In their reports, HMIs have consistently identified the best geographical work as that carried out within the immediate locality of the school, where practical fieldwork observations can most easily take place.

Within the school grounds, investigations can involve simple map making, early observations 'in the field' and talking to people about their way of life and the world of work. Pupils can also be introduced to the relationships between human and physical processes and between people and places. Children's developing environmental awareness can also encourage them to take responsibility for their school environment.

The three key geographical ideas – place, space and the environment – can all be developed within the school grounds and should provide pupils with a memorable, vivid, active and relevant outdoor learning experience.

Links with the Geography National Curriculum

In the past, good practical fieldwork could occur more or less spontaneously; followers of the Geography National Curriculum have to plan for it. The National Curriculum emphasises the importance of locality studies at both key stages. Much of the key stage 1 programme of study can be covered by the effective use of each individual school's environment, working in either a cross-curricular or a subject-focused way.

At key stage 1 the unique concept of place is developed through two locality studies, one of which has to be:

> 66 *'... the locality of the school ... this includes the school building and grounds and the surrounding area within easy access' (DFE, 1995).*

The other study has to be a similar-sized locality in the UK or overseas. A detailed study of the children's immediate environment will form a sound basis for comparision, enabling pupils to move (see Blyth and Krause, 1995) from *Little Geography to Big Geography*.

First-hand experience, work outside school and the involvement of pupils in investigations and enquiries are all essential to the school's geography curriculum. This first-hand experience requires the development of fieldwork techniques and encourages the use of ICT applications. Many aspects of the Geography National Curriculum programme of study can be delivered through locality studies based around the school grounds. Such work might include links with well-established geographical topics such as rocks, soil and landscape features, the weather, buildings, journeys, settlement studies, the provision of goods and services, knowledge of natural resources and the awareness of environmental change.

The school grounds provide opportunities for work in each of the three areas in the geographical 'cube' frequently used to depict the importance of the integration of skills, places and themes (see page 10). In the area of skills development there are opportunities for geographical enquiry (2), using geographical terms (3a), fieldwork (3b), following directions (3c), mapwork (3d and 3e) and secondary sources such as photographs (3f). The school grounds are a key requirement in terms of locality studies (4) and provide further opportunities to investigate both physical and human features (5a), consider similarities and differences with other places (5b), observe the effects of the weather (5c) and discuss land and building use (5d). It is also possible to address the thematic study as required in (6a) expressing views, (6b) noticing changes and (6c) looking after and improving the school grounds to address the investigational approach required in (1a); and to undertake studies based on key questions (1b).

Progression

Locality studies feature in the Geography National Curriculum at both key stages 1 and 2. It is important to ensure that continuity and progression occur both within and between key stages: all members of staff should share both a clear definition of 'the locality of the school' and a view of how it can be used as part of the geography curriculum. Pupils will return to this key resource throughout key stages 1 and 2. You and your colleagues will need to consider how progression can be planned for: should it be through an extension of the content covered, by increasing the scale of locality studies, or by demanding from pupils greater accuracy, a greater depth of understanding and an awareness of the issues?

Practical advantages

Using a small area within easy walking distance has many advantages. It is a small-scale, relatively safe environment to which short visits can be fitted easily into school sessions. As well as being easily accessible the school grounds also provide a safe environment from which to study the immediate locality, e.g. to undertake observational drawings of shops or houses across the road. All schools will have some distinctive features, inside and out, which are worthy of study.

Photo: Angela Milner.

The enquiry approach

Structuring geographical learning around the enquiry process (see Chapter 12 and elsewhere) enables effective investigational work to be undertaken in the immediate environment. Teachers (at key stage 1) and pupils (at key stage 2) should identify a place, theme or issue to explore and then consider appropriate questions to structure their investigation. Pupils will be involved in planning, collecting, analysing, evaluating and hypothesising. Ideally, the enquiry should focus on a real issue: for instance, 'Why is there a problem with litter in the playground?' or 'Where shall we site a new litter bin?'. The school grounds can be used as a focus for learning *about* the environment through the acquisition of knowledge, learning *through* the environment as a resource for study, and learning *for* the environment to consider issues, values and attitudes.

Outdoor work is an important aspect of the curriculum, offering opportunities for both independent learning, and for co-operation with others; children will respond to these forms of learning in different ways. With young pupils, such work is best done little and often. Short periods of between 10 and 30 minutes outside are best – even though with very young children it can take more time to get them ready to go out than they actually spend in working outside! Careful timing, allowing children to complete observations without getting bored, is essential. Unfortunately such work is always weather dependent and you need to learn to make the most of every possible learning opportunity – planned and incidental – and to have a wet weather alternative up your sleeve.

Planning

Any work outside the classroom demands careful planning and preparation. If more than one adult is available, and the class has had the activity explained beforehand, it is possible to work outside with a whole class. The ideal arrangement, though, is a small group with a dedicated adult. A number of small groups can cover different aspects of the study in a controlled learning context which allows individuals to exploit their own interests, with each group returning to the classroom when their tasks are complete. Different aspects of the study will need to be discussed beforehand both with your pupils and helpers; careful preparation of helpers will help to ensure that all pupils are supervised, but each group is allowed some independence. Ensure that all children know exactly what they are doing, have chosen a suitable resource or activity, can operate any necessary equipment and are physically comfortable. When pupils return to the classroom they must know where and how to store their findings, and time should be made available for groups of children to share their findings with others.

If you are well organised you will be more confident and better prepared to take advantage of the spontaneous opportunities which will inevitably arise when working outside and which frequently provide the high points of the study. All outdoor work must, of course, follow your school and LEA policies for fieldwork (see Chapter 14).

Suggested activities using the school grounds for developing geographical skills, knowledge and understanding at key stage 1

Blyth and Krause (1995) contend that every school is a 'Little geography' in itself and that it involves two elements: the immediate locality, and nearby places which are readily accessible. 'Little geography' will figure prominently in studies undertaken by the youngest children; a central feature will be the school and its locality. The following activities will help you and your pupils develop a greater geographical understanding of the school and its locality and ensure that the necessary progression occurs. Some of them can be built into your curriculum plans for geography; others can provide a focus for an in-service training day in your school.

INSIDE-OUT

Different features of the school buildings (inside) and the school grounds (outside) can be used as a basis for geographical investigations. Inside, at the simplest level the classrooms can be used for work on plans and models. As soon as children leave their classroom or base area they are involved in making a journey, following directions, taking a route, using their senses and taking part in elementary fieldwork activities. They will also meet other people who frequent the same environment, who can be interviewed as part of various types of survey.

School grounds work can start from producing plans and reasons for journeys around the school. Work: Lynette Brasier and Joni Barratt.

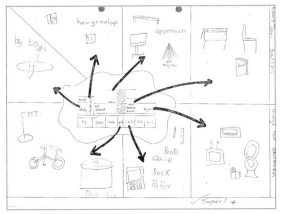

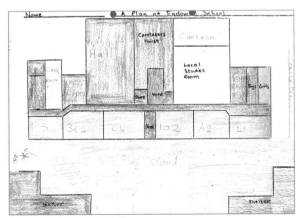

VOCABULARY BUILDING

Simple five-minute activities such as 'I-spy' can be based around key vocabulary associated with the school building and grounds. Using a wordbank, dictionary or alphabet display – particularly important when helping children gain access to secondary sources – you can focus on features associated with particular letters or sounds through the use of an index.

THE SCHOOL BUILDINGS

The buildings will have geographical connections. A close study can be made of building materials:

- What are they?
- Where do they come from?
- Why were they chosen for that part of the building?

Sensory activities can encourage children to explore textures, pattern, size, shapes and materials. Other questions about the school buildings that you could ask are:

- What are the different parts of the buildings called?
- What sort of place is it?
- Why is it built like this?

Photo: Wendy Morgan.

THE SCHOOL GROUNDS

The playground can be a useful space for directional games, such as using giant directional arrows, and to reinforce key vocabulary such as up, down, eye-level, forwards, backwards, right and left, overground and underground. A simple base plan of the playground can be used for activities and trails. Pupils could consider which parts of the school grounds are natural/built/green; what sort of habitats have been created in this place; who lives there and why.

ASSESSING ENVIRONMENTAL QUALITY

Children's environmental concerns can be explored and developed by asking questions such as:

- What do children think about their environment?
- Can they assess it using faces with different expressions or by describing their feelings?
- Could it be improved?
- Is there evidence of weathering, decay, pollution, or real problems that children can remedy through action such as litter collection?

SURVEYING

You can use the school building and grounds to help children develop simple survey techniques and learn to plot symbols on a base plan. For example, a simple land use survey could be carried out using a colour code system.

- Why do children think certain activities take place in particular locations?
- Are there better alternatives?
- Can the school building and grounds also be used for practising questionnaire and interview techniques?

For sampling specific locations for intensive small-scale study, use a PE hoop to delimit a sample area and focus the children's attention on a particular area for study.

COLLECTING DATA

The school grounds can be used for practical work such as simple collecting, counting and measuring exercises, e.g. counting or plotting the position of doors, windows, drainpipes, covers, grates, steps and flags; or in a weather topic to read a thermometer, measure rainfall, observe cloud formations and movement, calculate wind speed and direction or even to take a closer look at soil.

RECORDING – RUBBING, SKETCHING, WRITING

How do young children learn to record their findings in the field? Have you tried allowing them to make rubbings using large sheets of paper and chubby wax crayons? Try rubbing gratings and then locating the rubbings on a large base plan, marking their correct positions.

Photo: Angela Milner.

LOOKING UP, DOWN AND THROUGH

Learning to 'look down' is vital to the development of the plan view concept and mapwork skills. These and observational skills will be strengthened if children are clear about which direction they are looking in and the position from which field sketches have been made or photographs taken.

- What can they see when they look up? Down? Through an archway or door?
- Can they sketch what they see?
- Can they go and stand in the position that a photograph was taken from?

DIRECTIONS

Young children need to learn to look all around, not just straight ahead.

- Ask them to draw what they see straight ahead, and then what they see when they turn a quarter turn (90 degrees) to the right or left or by turning around to look behind.
- Do they understand terminology such as forward, back, right and left?
- What directional vocabulary can they use?
- Are they ready to make the connection with the four cardinal points of the compass?
- Are they ready to make an electronic toy such as Roamer or Pip move in a particular direction, or give others directions?

RECORDING THEIR FINDINGS

There are many ways in which pupils can record their observations: through talk and discussion; tape recordings; writing and presenting their findings to others by using plans, sketches, maps, a database; plotting and displaying information in graph and tabular formats; photographs; and through model making.

LINKING DIRECT EXPERIENCE WITH APPROPRIATE SECONDARY SOURCES

The teacher has a key role in this area. Large-scale Ordnance Survey maps and vertical and oblique aerial photographs of your school building and grounds should be used from an early stage. Have you tried producing base plans of your school building and grounds, and collecting or taking photographs?

SPOTTING CHANGES IN THE ENVIRONMENT

Give children a photograph of something in your school grounds.

- Can they find the place in the photograph?
- Is it still the same?
- Has anything changed since the photograph was taken?
- Is this place always the same – at different times of the day, on various days of the week, at different times of year?

Using simple orienteering skills. Photo: Flick Titley.

MAPPING

Mapping is a unique geographical skill, and every opportunity should be taken to practice and develop it. In the school building and grounds you have the most accessible and meaningful learning context for mapping skills as part of thematic work. In the school grounds children can relate their direct experiences to map making, map using and the identification of symbols and features identified on aerial photographs. Simple orienteering skills can be developed, based on trails using pictures or symbols as clues, or by following string to collect objects. Maps can also be used to follow and record routes and to identify locations, features and positions.

WEATHERWATCH

The weather affects everyone – particularly children. The school grounds provide a real context in which children can experience this phenomenon and make first-hand investigations and observations. Such as:

- When do they need to wear a coat outside? Why?
- Why does the school roof leak?
- Why do some window frames need to be re-painted or replaced?

Weather watching helps children develop a greater awareness of the factors influencing the weather.

- What is the weather like today?
- How does it change?
- What seasonal differences occur?

Everything from tracing the journey of a raindrop to the long-term effects of weathering can be followed and investigated in the school environment.

Photo: Angela Milner.

SENSING

One of the most meaningful types of local environmental work for young children is through using their senses: identifying what they can see, hear, smell and feel. The fifth sense of taste, for obvious reasons, is best avoided! Observation – learning to look carefully – is an important geographical and cross-curricular skill to learn and develop. Here are some ideas worth trying with your pupils:

- Going on a sensory walk.
- Blindfold activities, requiring children to feel and use language to describe and identify features in the school grounds. (Their sense of smell might also be used to help them identify where they are!)
- Spotting shapes and features, identifying likes and dislikes, brainstorming and composing word pictures, drawing a memory picture or mental map.

A SCAVENGER HUNT

- What can children collect (use plastic bags as gloves) without destroying the environment?
- Where did they find their items?
- Can they mark the locations on a base plan of the school?
- What do the items tell you about your school grounds as a place?
- Did other groups find similar or different things? Why do you think that is?

EYEBALLING

This combines observational and recording skills. Focus on a particular part of the school building or grounds, giving the children a photograph to focus their observations.

- Can they go to the spot and make an observational drawing of a specific feature, e.g. a door or window?
- Can children copy examples of writing in their environment?
- Can they make a field sketch or conduct a census to answer a key question?

Finding clues is a very motivating approach – ask the children to find signs of weathering, or a date stone, for example.

- What can the children see from different viewing points?
- Can they add information to base plans or drawings to record where they have found the clues?

LISTENING AND HEARING

What sounds can children hear?

- Do the sounds differ from place to place?
- Can they record the sounds they hear and explain what they are?

INPUTS AND OUTPUTS
Observe and record everything that comes into and goes out of the school grounds in a given time period.

- What goods and services are needed to make this place function?
- How is this place connected to other places?
- Where do the inputs come from and go to?

SPACE AND BARRIERS
Where are the spaces and barriers around the school grounds?

- What barriers exist?
- Are they all physical?
- Why do we need them?

Conducting a school locality appraisal

This will form an essential part of your school's geography curriculum planning. As teachers we are often guilty of failing to explore the school grounds and locality on foot ourselves; as a result we know less about them than our pupils do! It would be sensible to utilise a school in-service training day to identify collectively as a staff the following:

i. What are the key geographical features in your school environment?
Make an inventory of the particular geographical aspects of your school's locality. Consider the following:

- type and use of buildings,
- the leisure facilities,
- the types of land use,
- landscape features,
- physical features,
- examples of weathering,
- the layout and the main routes across the site,
- the journeys people undertake,
- any issues of concern or items which are changing in your school grounds.

Make a visual record of your findings and locate your results on a large master base plan of your school grounds.

- Would the children identify similar features?
- What would they see at their eye level?
- Are there any good viewing points for mapping and early compass work?

ii. What types of equipment are needed for fieldwork in the school grounds?
You need clipboards, collecting and measuring equipment, and field study boxes which any member of staff can use with their pupils. They need to contain everything pupils will need to work outside successfully; small self-sealing plastic food containers are ideal.

iii. Do you have an emergency fieldwork survival kit?
This should allow you to stay outside no matter what! It might include everything from a pencil sharpener to a plaster or spare clothing.

Year: Key questions	Term: Learning outcomes: knowledge, skills, understanding and attitudes	Enquiry focus: Teaching and learning strategies including ICT	Resources	PoS
Why is this place like this?	To develop pupils': ■ knowledge and associated language of their school both orally and in writing ■ identification and location of key features using secondary sources, i.e. photographs	Brainstorm children's thoughts about the school as a place, e.g. busy, large, bright Discuss why they have formed these thoughts – What clues led them to this conclusion? Give each child a piece of paper with a photograph of part of their school stuck in the centre. Annotate it with key words to describe it and ask the children to write a sentence to explain why it is like this. Sharing of ideas. Work placed around large outline plan of school in approximate locations	range of secondary sources	1a, b 2 3a, c, e 4 5a, d 6a
What is this place like?	To develop pupils' abilities to: ■ observe and describe features of the school grounds ■ compare and plot their findings ■ look carefully and use their observations to discuss their feelings about places and become more accurate in their use of vocabulary	Observational walk around school grounds to identify and label features. Group 1 take photographs of key features; Group 2 make a tape recording of sounds at key locations; Group 3 label the feature; Group 4 mark it on a base plan. Choose one location to complete an observational drawing – What do they like about this place? Use photographs, etc. – to add detail to a large base plan Look at photographs taken of the school – describe what it is like	camera, ground-based and aerial photographs, tape recorder, large outline base plan of the school building and grounds, individual base plans, clip boards	1a, b 2 3a, b, d, e, f 4 5a 6a
Where is this place?	To develop pupils' abilities to: ■ use geographical sources to recognise features from above and to record their findings ■ to link the 3D reality with 2D views	Look at a large-scale map and aerial photograph of the school – can children recognise it? Birds eye view ■ What is the same/different on each source? ■ What shape is it? Children to draw memory plan and label ■ Groups to model school from available construction materials and/or junk ■ Draw around 3D models to make 2D plans adding symbols or colours	large-scale maps, aerial photographs, construction equipment, junk for model making	1a, b 2 3c, e 4 5d
How is this place connected to other places?	To develop pupils' skills in: ■ identifying features on a map – school and home ■ relating addresses to simple letter/number co-ordinates ■ defining the class catchment area	Look at a local large-scale OS map. How does the school relate to other local identifiable features? What is the school address? Finding the school on a local A-Z street map How easy is it for pupils to get to school? Can they find their home, their school and finger-trace their route? How do they travel – foot/car/bus/etc? (graphs/ICT) Plot each member of the class's home on a street map to identify the class catchment area	large-scale OS map, local street plan	1a, b 2 3c, e 4 5a, d
What is it like to operate in this place?	To develop pupils' ability to: ■ think about the interaction of people, space and environment ■ talk to people about the world of work ■ recreate people's journeys to provide directions to others in a meaningful context	Take photographs of the people who work in school – Where do they work? What do they do? Talk to them about their work Produce an entry for the school brochure/photo display board Recreate people's journeys with model figures around construction models – describe the routes they take, direct others on journeys to find different people and where they operate from	camera, photographs, base plan, tape recorder, individual base plan of the school	1a, b 2 3b, e, f 4 5d
How is this place changing?	To develop pupils': ■ ability to recognise signs of change in the field and to compare the findings with other sources of evidence ■ ability to express their feelings about places and how they might be improved	Fieldwork: clue spotting of recent changes – redecoration, repairs, replacement; evidence of change from the past Recording photographically and in drawings. Compare with oral evidence and photographs from the past How could the school be improved in the future? – Children's ideas as plans, drawings or writing Is there anything children can do to improve their environment? Elicitation of ideas followed by practical action	camera, photographs, artefacts, previous pupils, staff	1a, b 2 3b, f 4 5b 6a, b, c
How is this place similar to or different from other places?	To develop pupils' ability to compare two different schools, to reason why they are similar and to account for the differences	Comparing findings with information on twinned school/school in different part of the world Groups working around key headings, e.g. playground, classroom, hall, building materials, equipment Spotting three things that are the same and three that are different and working out why they think the schools are different	secondary sources from twinned school or commercial pack	1b, c 2 3f 4 5a, b, c, d 6a, b, c

Figure 1: School grounds planning grid – key stage 1

iv. What safety issues arise?

Is there a school policy defining the organisational procedures and requirements and offering safety advice to colleagues?

v. How could effective use be made of other adults?

Do you involve them in your in-service training activities? Do you have a training programme for new helpers?

vi. What vocabulary can be developed and how?

Make lists of key directional and place related vocabulary. Look at activities planned in the school grounds at both key stages. Is there increased sophistication of language and vocabulary developed through fieldwork and active learning outside the classroom?

vii. What resources are needed to develop a useful series of secondary resources about your school grounds?

Do you have access to recent as well as older photographs of your school building and grounds? Plans, maps and memorabilia? Do you have large-scale Ordnance Survey map and aerial photographs of your school grounds? Have these been used to devise an A4 simple base plan of your school and grounds that everyone can use?

viii. Which parts of the National Curriculum can be covered by using your school grounds?

Make copies of the programmes of study – ask colleagues to highlight appropriate sections at both key stages. Are you covering all these?

ix. What sort of activities would be appropriate at each key stage?

This chapter should help – but it might be worthwhile brainstorming the available opportunities with your colleagues to ensure there is adequate and appropriate continuity and progression.

x. Which geographical and cross-curricular skills can be developed?

xi. How could your school grounds be used in other curriculum areas or your existing curriculum plans?

xii. Are you all maximising this valuable learning potential?

In engaging in these activities do you feel more confident in using the school grounds as a resource?

xiii. How does planning to use the school grounds relate to developing a sense of place through the key questions, developing a sense of belonging, development of values and attitudes?

Can you provide colleagues with an issue to explore through the key questions about place? How can they plan active learning to ensure progression throughout the school? Use the school grounds planning grid (Figure 1) to ensure you have considered geographical questions to structure enquiries, referenced this to the programme of study, provided appropriate pupil activities and identified the necessary resources required. What other columns might be useful at key stage 1 – assessment opportunities, learning opportunities, key vocabulary, etc.? Do you use a standard school proforma for planning geographical work in your school?

The opportunities are immense as each school's unique resource offers tremendous geographical potential. Skills can be developed, a locality explored and themes investigated within a meaningful and accessible first-hand resource. As teachers we need to be aware of how we can best exploit the potential of this valuable resource and to be able to plan appropriate structured activities based around it. This chapter is designed to help you and your colleagues to become increasingly confident in evaluating and making more effective use of your school grounds by exploring the geographical principles underpinning such work and by adopting good practice strategies for both geographical teaching and learning in this area.

Exploring the local area:
2. Venturing further

Chapter 16

Wendy Garner

Why do we use the local area and how do we define it?

The 'local area' is the area around the school which is relevant to, lived in and used by the majority of the pupils. All children are curious about their own surroundings and the space in which they operate. At key stage 1, the most relevant, safe and easily accessible environment is the school building itself and its grounds, as noted earlier in the chapter. At key stage 2, children are starting to operate more independently within their local area. At this age they are becoming increasingly mobile and often walk to school, to the local shops, to the park and to visit friends. These experiences help children to become more aware of the features in their locality and how they are organised in space. This evolving awareness has been described as 'spatial cognition' (Spencer and Blades, 1993) and develops 'through the gradual expansion of the area of a child's physical and social world' (Blyth and Krause, 1995, p. 11). This is illustrated by the children's maps in Figure 2.

Figure 2:
Routes to school drawn by primary aged children: (a) Reception, (b) Year 6.
After: Catling, 1978.

(a)

(b)

Given the above, at key stage 2 children should be given opportunities to draw on and consolidate their developing knowledge of the local area, including the school grounds. This will provide them with a relevant and vivid learning experience, and contexts in which many aspects of the Geography National Curriculum can be explored first-hand.

Geographical investigations in the local area provide a firm foundation for the study of localities further afield; both in the UK and beyond. Children develop confidence when investigating their own place – a place which is known to them. As they progress on to the study of less familiar places, they need to be able to draw on skills, knowledge, understanding and confidence gained from work in their local area.

Studying the area around the school.

The nature and extent of the local area is something which the geography co-ordinator will need to define. It is important that the area chosen allows for depth of study. For example, part of a suburb within which your school is located, rather than the study of a whole city. The following checklist may help in reaching a decision.

In defining the 'local area' the following might be considered:

Continuity – build on work undertaken at key stage 1, consider which aspects of the local area need to be re-visited. For example, local shops and services.

Progression between key stages – extend work undertaken at key stage 1. The local area at key stage 2 should be wider in terms of area coverage and features included.

Studies should also be in more depth. For example, progressing from identifying which way a river flows to increasing awareness of how flow rate varies at different points on the same river.

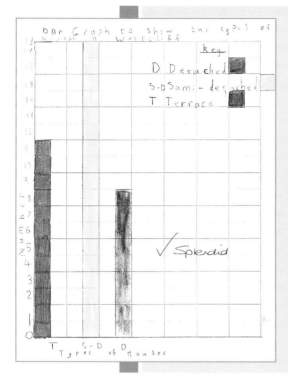

Progression between year groups – if the local area is visited twice at key stage 2, then consider extending the area for the older children. For example, if years 3 and 6 study the local area, the definition of the area to be studied could be extended for year 6. For urban children it could include a transect of their town or city, so that they have the opportunity to study the main characteristics of the whole settlement in more detail. For example, the location and function of the Central Business District. Examples of alternative definitions of the local area are shown in Figure 3.

Relevance to the children – include features which are relevant to the daily lives of the children. For example, where they live, shop and play.

Coverage of 'places' and 'themes' – the local area should provide the opportunity to study the main human and physical features which characterise the locality. For example, housing estates, slopes and streams. The area chosen should also provide the opportunity to study the four themes. For example, if possible, include a local river or stream and any areas which could be used as an example of environmental change.

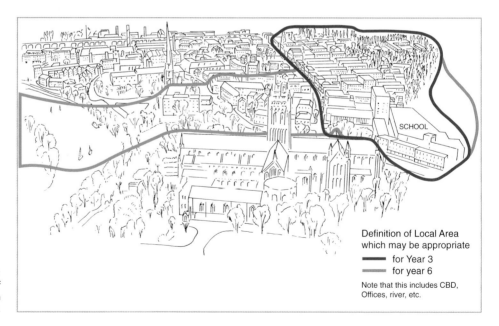

Figure 3:
Alternative definitions of the local area in a large city.

What resources do you need for your study of the local area?

The range and quality of resources used for the investigation of the local area will have a direct impact on the quality of teaching and learning (see Chapter 9). Stimulating, well chosen resources will help children to develop a sense of place.

There are three things which need to be considered when choosing resources:

1 Do you have a wide range of different types of resources?

   For example, maps, plans, diagrams, data, literature, photographs, video, artefacts ...

2 Are the resources of a high quality?
   For example, high quality colour photographs, as opposed to poor black and white
   photocopies.

3 Are the resources relevant to geographical enquiry?
   For example, photographs need to give a realistic, rather than a biased view of a place.

You can use the list of resources in Figure 4 as a guide, although it is by no means exhaustive. (See also Chapter 9)

Children working with local planners and architects. Photo: Wendy Garner.

How do you plan for work in the local area?

The three main components of the Geography National Curriculum are skills, places and themes. The School Curriculum and Assessment Authority (SCAA) recommend that these three components should be taught in an integrated way, as shown on page 11.

The skills defined in the programme of study should be learned and used by the children to investigate *real* places. As far as possible, the four themes (Environment, Settlement, Weather and Rivers) should also be explored within the context of *real* places. Therefore, the local area can be used as a context for skills development and for the investigation of aspects of places and themes.

Teaching and learning in primary geography should be enquiry based. The questions listed in Figure 5, are key geographical questions which should be used for the study of places. These key questions can be used to structure planning at both the medium- and short-term stage. An example of this can be seen in Figure 6. The photograph on page 227 shows children undertaking this work.

Resource	Co-ordinator's notes
Photographs/slides of your local area	Fixed point photography is useful for looking at short- and long term change. Think about photographing the same place in: different weather conditions, at different times of the day and at different times of the year. Remember, each photograph needs a clear geographical focus!
Maps of your local area *Range of scales/range of types*	Many authorities can produce digitised maps of the school and its locality. Alternatively you could collect a range of tourist, transport, thematic and street maps from tourist information and local shops. You also need to obtain some Ordnance Survey maps at the following scales: 1:2500 and 1:5000.
Aerial photographs *Oblique/vertical*	Try to ensure that your school is clearly identifiable on any aerial views purchased
Range of atlases	Atlases are expensive! Aim to have at least one full class set. It is useful to have a range of other atlases, even if you only buy one or two copies of each. A detailed UK road atlas is useful in terms of placing the local area in a regional and national context.
Globes	Ideally, each classroom should have a globe so that children can place their local area into an even wider, international context.
Compass	Using a compass is a skill which can be developed through geographical trails in the local area.
Simple weather measuring instruments *Rain gauge/thermometer/wind vane/anemometer*	These instruments can be purchased and/or made by the children. They are ideal for fieldwork in the school grounds.
ICT software *Mapping/data handling/CD-ROM*	It is useful to have a range of software which can be used to make comparisons between your local area and other places, e.g. spreadsheets for weather data.
Historical documents	These can be obtained from your local record office. It is worth looking at archival maps, directories, population figures, census data, artists impressions, written accounts, poetry and old postcards.
Planning documents	Your local planning department may be keen to involve children in proposals which will affect them in the future. Planners can provide maps and photographs of an excellent quality and it is well worth inviting a planner into your classroom (see photograph opposite).
Local/national newspapers	Visual images, clear headlines and simple data can complement work on weather and environmental issues in the local area.
Visiting speakers	Local residents, particularly if they have lived in the area a long time, are a valuable resource. They could lead a class discussion or be interviewed by the children.
Video of locality	You could make a simple video of the locality, recording evidence of short-term change. Such changes may not be seen by children on a short field trip. For example, high and low tide on a river.
Video snippets from local television programmes.	Keep your eye out for relevant items from regional news programmes.
Music/taped sounds	Music which has originated from the place is useful. Be careful not to use stereotypical music.

Photo: Julia Charlton.

Figure 4:
A practical guide to resource collection.

- Where is this place?
- What is this place like?
- Why is this place like this?
- How is this place connected to other places?
- How is this place changing?
- What does/would it feel like to live here?
- How is this place similar to/different from other places?

Figure 5:
Key questions for teaching and learning geography.

As can be seen in Figure 6, the key questions promote the coverage of skills, places and themes in an integrated way. Skills should be continually re-visited and used by the children in their enquiries, throughout the key stage.

Year group: 5				Locality chosen: Local area			
Key questions	**Programmes of study**			**Activity**	**Resources**	**Cross-curricular links**	**Assessment opportunities**
	skills	places	themes				
What is this place like? **Focus: RIVERS** To increase awareness of the main human and physical features of the locality.	–	5a	–	1. In the classroom, using maps of the local area, discuss and record main physical and human features. Find the river.	maps atlases	Speaking and listening	List of features
To increase awareness of how the locality is set within a broader geographical context.	–	5e	–	2. Using small-scale OS maps, locate the source and mouth of the river. List settlements passed by the river.	OS maps	Speaking and listening	Identification of source and mouth
To enable children to use geographical vocabulary associated with rivers and to develop an understanding of the processes of erosion and deposition.	3a	–	7b	3. Introduce, through physical modelling, the terms 'erosion' and 'deposition'. Visit a site on the river and discuss/attempt to explain features seen, relating back to experiences in the classroom.	sand tray water		Use/under-standing of geographical vocabulary
To enable children to undertake fieldwork activities.	3b	–	–	4. Children to produce field sketches of the river, noting where erosion and deposition occurs, with labels of other features seen.	clipboards paper pencils		Field sketches
To enable children to produce field sketches.	3c	–	–				

Figure 6:
A section from a medium-term plan.

If medium-term plans are drawn upon when writing short-term plans, then the key questions will also provide a framework for the focus of a particular lesson. However, at key stage 2 children should also be starting to organise their own enquiries, and opportunities for this should be built into lesson plans. For example, children may wish to ask more questions about the river being studied and will need the opportunity and appropriate resources to enable them to undertake their own enquiries.

What sorts of activities could you do with key stage 2 children?

The ideas in Figure 7 are intended to help you when writing schemes of work and planning activities for work in your local area. The activities outlined are generic and will need to be made relevant to your local area and year group. An attempt has been made to include examples of activities which focus on places and/or themes, but at all times, skills, places and themes have been integrated as far as possible. For each key question, one activity has been described as an example.

Children undertaking fieldwork by a river. Photo: Wendy Garner.

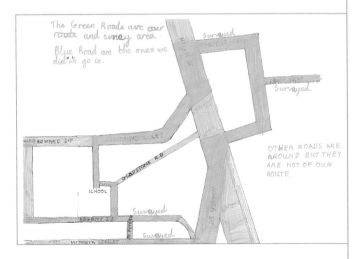

The Green Roads are our route and survey area. Blue Road are the ones we didn't go in.

OTHER ROADS ARE AROUND BUT THEY ARE NOT OF OUR ROUTE.

Fieldwork in the immediate locality.

Nadège Martin

		Maximal score	Street Name Middle Wall	Street Name Regent Street	Street Name Beach Alley	Street Name Victoria St.
1. LITTER	Refuse Collection, Litter Bins, Street cleanliness					
2. PAVING	Condition Variety, Appearance.	15	10	0	15	15
3. STREET FURNITURE	Seats, Lighting, Traffic signs, Post boxes, Gullies	15	10	0	15	15
4. WIRESCAPE	T.V aerials, Telephone, Electric wires	10	7	10	10	10
5. AIR POLLUTION	Smoke, Chimneys, Traffic fumes	10	10	10	10	10
6. Noise	Road, Industrys, School etc	5	2	0	5	5
7. BUILDING	Condition, Apearance	5	3	0	5	5
8. GARDENS	Attractive, Well Kept	5	3	3	5	5
9. GREENERY	Trees, Shrubs, Landscaping	5	5	0	5	5
10. TRAFFIC	Extent Amount of Heavy goods	10	9	10	10	10
11. TRAFFIC	Parking Safely	10	10	10	10	10
		10	8	10	10	10
TOTAL 327			100	94	33	100	100

Key stage 2   Locality chosen: Local area

Key questions	Programmes of study			Activity	Resources	Assessment opportunities
	skills	places	themes			
Where is this place? To increase awareness of links within a region To enable children to use maps To increase awareness that settlements vary in size and have a variety of functions	1d 3d –	– – –	– – 9a	1 Teach the use and purpose of: four-figure co-ordinates, measurement of distance and direction, interpretation of symbols and use of a key. Organise children into the roles of providers of tourist information so that they are required to respond, using the above skills, to the various scenarios presented to them. For example, the Brown family want to visit a rural village for a picnic before going for a walk by a river.	OS maps string compasses	Geographical skills of location, measurement of distance, use of symbols and a key
To enable children to use secondary sources of evidence	3e	–	–	2 Discuss what goes in a travel guide and why such guides are useful.	range of travel guides	
To enable children to make their own maps To raise awareness of how their locality is set within a broader geographical context	3c –	– 5e	– –	3 Children to produce a travel guide showing the route from a nearby settlement of their choice to their own locality. Children to produce their own map and to include information on distance, direction, location and alternative routes.	OS maps atlases string compasses information on transport networks; time and costs	Maps made, symbols and a key used, distance and direction measured
What is this place like? To enable children to record evidence in the field To enable children to use maps, secondary sources and geographical vocabulary	2b 3b 3a 3d 3e	– – – – –	– – – – –	1 Produce a trail of the locality, for use with children, including geographical questions, photographs and a large-scale map of the area to be explored. Children to stop when they have found where the photo was taken, answer the question and mark their location on the map.	trail photographs map compasses	Enquiry skills, use of maps, geographical vocabulary, secondary sources and use of a compass
To enable children to communicate and present findings, using ICT where appropriate To raise awareness of the main physical and human features of the locality and of how land is used.	2c 3f –	– – 5a	– – 9b	2 Children could help to produce a class display of route taken, including photographs, field sketches and written work. The range of land use in the locality should be highlighted.	display materials	Ability to communicate and present findings
Why is this place like this? **FOCUS: SETTLEMENTS** **(English Order)** *Economic activities (Welsh Order)* To enable children to use a variety of sources to answer questions To increase awareness of the main physical and human features of the locality To develop an understanding of the interaction of human and physical features	3d 3e – –	– – 5a 5c	– – – –	1 Children to look closely at historical and contemporary maps of the local area/settlement. Children to discuss ideas in groups why they think people settled here originally. For example, is the land fertile for farming, is it near to a river or the sea?	historical and contemporary maps historical documents atlases	Use of maps, atlases and secondary sources
To enable children to analyse evidence and communicate findings. To increase awareness that the nature of a settlement is largely determined by its function/the main economic activity	2c –	– –	– 9a (8b Welsh)	2 Write an advert, imagining that the area is devoid of human features, promoting the site and situation of the settlement in which the locality is located. Children can be asked to promote any economic activities which they think the area could accommodate. For example, if it is near a river, promote the possibility of a port area.	atlases showing relief contour maps historical directories	Knowledge and understanding of origin of settlement

Figure 7 continued on next page

Key stage 2 *(continued)* — Locality chosen: Local area

Key questions	Programmes of study			Activity	Resources	Assessment opportunities
	skills	places	themes			
How is this place changing? **FOCUS: WEATHER** To enable children to design and make fieldwork equipment	–	–	–	1 Children to design and make fieldwork equipment to measure wind speed, wind direction and rainfall.	variety of art and technology materials thermo-meter	Fieldwork equipment produced
To enable children to undertake fieldwork in the school grounds To raise awareness of how site conditions can influence the weather	3b –	–	– 8a	2 Children to test equipment in the school grounds in different, varying locations, recording results on base map. As a class, discuss differences in micro-climate and decide where the best place would be to site a wind vane.	base map of school grounds wind vane	Understanding of site conditions (micro-climates)
To enable children to collect and record evidence, while considering the need for fair testing To enable children to organise, present and analyze data To increase awareness of seasonal weather patterns	2b 2c 3f –	– – – –	– – – 8b	3 Discuss as a whole class the need for fair testing (same place/time each day), based on experience of micro-climates. Children to decide on the best place for their weather measuring equipment and data to be collected over time. Children to input data onto appropriate software and when there is a significant amount of data, search for patterns over time.	weather instruments data-handling software	Collection, organisation, presentation and analysis of data, regarding weather over time
How is this place connected to other places? To enable children to devise their own tool for collecting data	2a 2b	– –	– –	1 Children to undertake a survey, having devised the questionnaires themselves. They could ask parents, teachers and other pupils to complete the questionnaire, the main aim of which is to look at which settlements in the region are visited and why. Children could refer to an OS map to inform their research and could perhaps list settlements in their questionnaire, so that different types of settlements are considered (village, town, city).	OS maps	Ability to produce a questionnaire for fieldwork
				2 Children to organise and present findings, using data-handling skills.	data-handling software	Skills in data handling
To enable children to organise, present and analyse data	2c 3f	– –	– –	3 Children to analyse data, considering how settlement type relates to what people do there.		
To increase awareness of how settlement type and function relate	–	–	9a	4 A class display could be produced, showing links between the local area and the rest of the region. This could include photographs, possibly of people undertaking activities in each of the different settlements.	OS maps photographs	Skills in data analysis
To increase awareness and understanding of how and why the local area relates to other places in the region	–	5e	–			
What does it feel like to live here? **FOCUS: ENVIRONMENTAL CHANGE** To enable children to assess and record environmental quality To increase awareness of how features in the area affect the environment To increase awareness of proposed changes in the locality	1b 2b 3b – –	– – – 5a 5d	– – – 10a –	1 Choose an area where there is some sort of conflict in terms of land use. For example, an area of conservation is under threat of being developed into a car park. Visit the area with the children and undertake an environmental audit, focusing on information received through the senses. Children could draw a field sketch and note who they think would be most affected by proposed changes.	clip boards	Ability to complete an accurate environmental audit and field sketch

Figure 7 continued on next page

Key stage 2 *(continued)*   **Locality chosen: Local area**

| Key questions | Programmes of study | | | Activity | Resources | Assessment opportunities |
	skills	places	themes			
To increase awareness that land can be used in a variety of ways	–	–	9b	2 In the classroom, discuss how land can be used in different ways. Children could list ways in which the area of land visited could be used.	base map of area studied	Knowledge that land can be used in a variety of ways
To enable children to consider how and why people respond to environmental change To enable children to make informed decisions To enable children to use maps and secondary sources	– 3d 3e	– – –	10b – –	3 Children could use factual information, maps, letters from pressure groups, etc., to make informed decisions about how the land should be used. Children could pool their ideas and then debate, in roles as members of the community, which proposal should be pursued.	factual information relating to soils, plants and animal life, relief, surrounding features, etc.	Ability to understand different people's responses to environmental change
How is this place similar to/different from other places? To enable children to use maps, atlases and secondary sources To raise awareness of how two localities are similar/different To enable children to use geographical vocabulary	3d 3e – 3a	5a – 5b –	– – – –	NB: If at all possible, twin with another school, preferably within the contrasting UK locality studied at this key stage, so that data can be exchanged between pupils. 1 Children to locate the two areas on OS maps and in atlases. Children to compare photographs of two localities and to make notes under the following headings for each area: type of settlement, routes, occupation, leisure, landscape, land use.	OS maps atlases photographs of two localities	Knowledge and understanding of similarities and differences
To enable children to organise and present information in another form	2b 2c	– –	parts of 7, 8, 9 and 10	2 Children to prepare a brochure for another school (real or imaginary), to include information relating to the headings above. Children can add maps, plans, photographs, newspaper cuttings, etc.	wide variety of additional resources relating to the locality	Knowledge and understanding of own locality

Figure 7:
Examples of planning and activities for the local area.

How do you introduce local area work

Some activity ideas for co-ordinators in relation to school-based INSET are shown below.

ACTIVITY 1: INTRODUCING THE KEY QUESTIONS

1   Ask your colleagues to think of a place (settlement) which they have visited and that they liked. Talk to your colleagues about the seven key questions (see Figure 5) and ask them to apply the questions to the place chosen. When they have done this on paper, ask them to report back to the group.

2   Now give individual/small group of colleagues one of the key questions. Ask each individual/group to apply that particular key question to the local area of the school and to report back to the whole group.

This will help you to ascertain levels of expertise and will help your colleagues to feel more confident in using these questions.

ACTIVITY 2: INTRODUCING A PRACTICAL ACTIVITY

1   Devise for your colleagues (and for use with children later!) a simple photograph trail, for the purposes of exploring the local area. To do this you will need a set of photographs which have a clear geographical focus, a large scale map of the area to be explored and a set of questions which relate to each of the areas where the photographs were taken.

2   Walk the trail with your colleagues and ask them to follow the route marked on the map, looking for where each of the photographs was taken. When they find where each was taken, they need to mark the spot on their base map and answer the relevant question. This activity can be related back to INSET Activity 1 (above) by linking it to the key question 'What is this place like?'. The main aims of this activity should be to raise awareness of the main physical and human features of the local area, to provide colleagues with a practical activity which can be used with children and to highlight how this activity integrates aspects of skills, places and themes.

Summary

The local area is a rich resource for geographical enquiry as it builds on children's experiences, is highly accessible for fieldwork and has available a wide range of resources which help children to develop a sense of place. The local area (including the school grounds) represents the most meaningful context for the development of skills and for the coverage of aspects of places and themes. Its potential for practical and meaningful geographical work should not be underestimated.

References and further reading

Blyth, A. and Krause, J. (1995) *Primary Geography: A Developmental Approach.* London: Hodder & Stoughton.

Catling, S. (1978) 'Developing stages of cognitive map representation', *Teaching Geography*, 3, 3, pp. 120-123.

Catling, S. (1995) *Primary PGCE E880 Module 7 Geography.* Milton Keynes: Open University.

DFE (1995) *Geography in the National Curriculum.* London: HMSO.

Foley, M. and Janikoun, J. (1996) *The Really Practical Guide to Primary Geography.* Cheltenham: Stanley Thornes.

HMI (1989) *The Teaching and Learning of History and Geography.* London: HMSO.

Martin, F. (1995) *Teaching and Learning through the National Curriculum.* Cambridge: Chris Kington Publishing.

Mays, P. (1985) *Teaching Children through the Environment.* London: Hodder & Stoughton.

Mills, D. (ed) (1988) *Geographical Work in Primary and Middle Schools.* Sheffield: Geographical Association.

Scoffham, S. (1981) *Using the School Grounds.* London: Ward Lock.

Spencer and Blades (1993) 'Children's understanding of place: the world at hand', *Geography 78*, 4, pp. 367-373.

Chapter 16: Exploring the local area

Every local area is unique. The approaches commended in both parts of this chapter can be adapted to your own local circumstances (see also Chapter 14). Progression in local work is described in this chapter in terms of the range, scale and complexity of study. Other aspects of progression are detailed in Chapter 5.

A child's view of a village pond.

Studying a contrasting UK locality

Chapter 17

Greg Walker

> *'Mummy, you can tell when you're in the country because there aren't any pavements.'*
> *(Elizabeth Doull, age 6)*

This observation was made as a family travelled by car from their home in Tooting in south London to the child's grandparents' home in a village in Kent. It provides a simple, but graphic, example of how one child perceived the change between her own urban environment and one that was rural. It is an example of what Wiegand (1992) refers to as *'direct* experiences' with a place 'obtained through first-hand encounters'. On another occasion a class of year 3 children in an urban school were asked, before starting a study of a village in the UK, to draw what they thought they would see if they visited a village. Among a number of features that one girl drew was a child crying. When asked why the child was crying she replied:

> *'She's sad because people who live in villages are poor and they haven't got enough money to buy toys for the children.'*

Here the child seems to have little or no direct experience to draw upon. She seems to be relying on what Wiegand (1992) calls *'indirect'* or 'second-hand experience'. What these two examples do show is that young children have mental images of unfamiliar places that are the product of both direct and indirect experiences. The sources of those experiences have a powerful influence on their images of, and feelings about, places. Both types of experience combine to help children to develop their sense of place, that is a feeling for the 'personality' of a place, together with a sense of the range of diversity of places around the world (DES, 1990).

Children need to learn about the character of the place, this may be through observational drawings of houses.

Dircct experiences, e.g. family holidays or a visit to relatives or school trips, may be the most effective and 'real' for children but they are influenced more regularly by indirect experiences such as accounts of the travels of friends and family, through stories and, probably most significantly, television prog-rammes. What is certain is that children, while knowing much more about their own locality, are fascinated from an early age by places that are unfamiliar and different. We should therefore make opportunities to teach about such places in the UK, drawing on children's direct experiences while confronting their indirect, and often inaccurate or one-dimensional images. Because of such misconceptions it is important, therefore, before you start any place work, to find out your children's initial impressions. Brainstorm them through words and/or pictures, retain the information and return to it at the end of the project – this is an interesting exercise for both teacher and children.

Within the Geography National Curriculum, the programmes of study define the nature of the places to be studied as follows: They should be where 'the physical and/or human features contrast with those in the locality of the school'. The programmes of study also clearly state what 'pupils should be taught'. Key ideas are the 'character' of places, similarities and differences between places, land and building use, recent change, how the nature of a place influences what goes on there, and attractive and unattractive features of localities.

Before teaching a contrasting locality it may help to ask a series of questions such as those below.

WHAT CONSTITUTES A CONTRASTING UK LOCALITY?

You should feel confident about being flexible in your choice of locality. There is no need to search for a place that is *very* distant and *very* contrasting with your school locality. In fact a contrasting locality close to your own school may be particularly suitable. What the place *must* be is sufficiently contrasting to allow children readily to see differences but also to recognise that there are similarities.

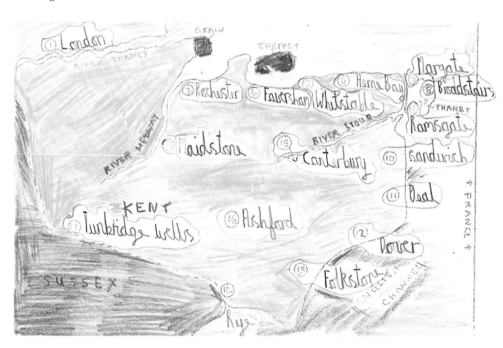

How localities are set within a broader geographical context.

WHAT IS THE SIZE OF THE LOCALITY TO BE STUDIED?

The programmes of study offer useful guidance here. In key stage 1 it should be similar in size to 'the school and its immediate vicinity ... within easy access'; in other words the neighbourhood of the school. In key stage 2 it should cover 'an area larger than the school's immediate vicinity' and it will 'normally contain the homes of the majority of pupils in the school'; that is, broadly speaking, the school's catchment area. Think about studying a village or *part* of a town or city. What it must *not* be, in either key stage, is the study of an area as large as a city or a region, although pupils should appreciate how localities are set within a broader geographical context.

WHAT CAN I DO TO SUPPORT A LOCALITY STUDY?

You have a number of options:

1 Use a locality pack that has been produced by the Geographical Association or another reliable educational publisher.
2 Produce your own locality pack, or combine with a small group of local teachers to do this.
3 Establish a twinning arrangement with a school in a contrasting locality.
4 Use the school residential visit as the context for the locality study.

There are serious time implications in options 2, 3 and 4 but vitally important in each option are the resources that you use. The children must find them exciting and relevant. They need to bring to life a place that the children may meet only indirectly but which may be a significant piece in their developing 'sense of place' jigsaw.

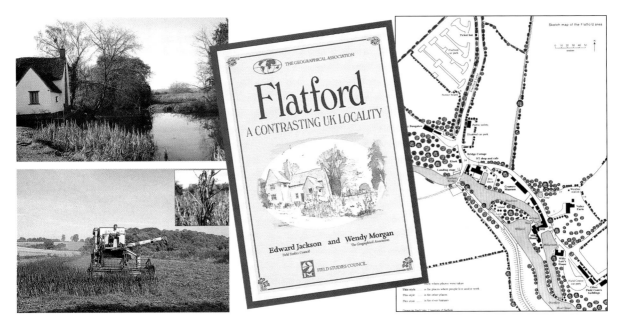

WHAT CONSTITUTES A GOOD RESOURCE FOR STUDYING A CONTRASTING LOCALITY IN THE UK?

Resources should include these fundamental elements:

Photographs

These are the foundation of any good locality pack and the resource that the children will be most influenced by, and gain most enjoyment from. Whichever option you choose there should be a large number, about 20, A4-size colour photographs of the locality. The images should present a balanced view of the physical and human characteristics of the place and should also be selected to allow children to notice similarities and differences between it and their own locality. Some should show evidence that the place is changing and there should be people in some of the photographs.

Look for photographs of the following:

■ the physical characteristics such as fields, playing fields, hills, rivers, and so on;
■ the human characteristics including (depending upon the nature of the place), the variety of homes (cottages, flats, bungalows, terraces); types of shops; significant buildings (town halls, police stations, churches);

- places where people work (factories, office blocks);
- places for recreation (play grounds, sport grounds, cinemas);
- a primary school, including its interior, and grounds;
- a 'feature family' in their home with primary age children who can be linked to the school;
- the place in the past to provide an historic perspective of change but also continuity.

The urban and rural photographs shown below and opposite are examples of suitable images for use in UK locality studies. Such photographs can be used in various ways, as described below:

1   A detailed examination by progressive enquiry questions. The nature of the questions will be determined both by the photograph content and the age of the children but some should allow the exploration of similarities and differences and feelings about places. A series of questions might be:

Sutton High Street, Surrey.
Photo: Greg Walker.

Key stage 1
- What can you see in this photograph?
- Was the photograph taken in summer or winter? How do you know?
- What do you think the people are doing in the photograph?
- How has this place been made attractive for shoppers?
- There is a big Woolworths shop in the background. What other kinds of shops do you think you would find here?
- In what ways are these shops similar to or different from your local shops?

Key stage 2
- Is this a big or small shopping centre? How do you know?
- You can see Woolworths and Burton's Menswear in the photograph. What other shops would you expect to find if you visited this high street?
- How has the place been made attractive and safe for shoppers?
- How do you think the people have travelled to this shopping centre?
- On the left is an entrance to the Times Square indoor shopping centre. What would be the advantages of shopping in this place?

Brockham village, Surrey.
Photo: Greg Walker.

Key stage 1
- What can you see in this photograph?
- Do you think this is a quiet or a noisy place? How do you know?
- What kinds of things do you think people do on the green in the front of the photograph in the summer? What would you like to do?
- If you stood in the middle of the green and closed your eyes what sounds do you think you would hear?

Key stage 2
- What kind of building is in the centre of the photograph? How do you know what it is?
- Do you think this photograph was taken in a town or a village? How do you know? What is similar to and what is different from where you live?
- What kinds of things do you think (a) adults, and (b) children, do on the green in summer?
- What other buildings do you think you would see around the green?
- Would you like to live in this place? Why?

2   After first giving the children unstructured time to look at the photographs, using information labels for each photograph can enhance their knowledge. Examples for the two photographs, differentiating between key stages 1 and 2, might be:

> **Urban photo**
> **KS1 label:** This is the main street in the busy town centre.
> **KS2 label:** This is the pedestrianised centre of the town with a pavement café and big shops.
>
> **Rural photo**
> **KS1 label:** This is the church by the village green.
> **KS2 label:** This is the centre of the village. It has a church, an old house and a village green with a road alongside.

3   Line drawings are useful to link key vocabulary with a particular image. Figure 1 is a line drawing of the photograph of the church with added vocabulary. To do this yourself, cover the photograph with an acetate sheet, use a suitable pen to outline the most important features and/or areas then photocopy your outline.

4   Excellent whole-class work can be done using a single photograph if you have a colour acetate made. Using an overhead projector you now have a huge enlargement, easily seen by the class, and ideal for detailed examination. The same principle applies for map extracts (but check copyright). The cost is the same as a colour photocopy.

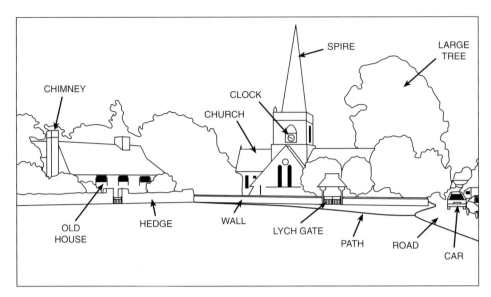

Figure 1:
Outline sketch of the Brockham village photograph.

Photo: Graham Butt.

Aerial photographs are unsurpassed as a resource for locality studies. They graphically show land use including large **patches** of land (housing areas, playing fields, woodland), the **lines** that separate (roads, river, hedges) but also the small **points** of land (roundabouts, ponds, tennis courts). You can purchase these for localities across the country from Wildgoose Publications (see references at end of chapter).

Maps

Any distant-place study must use a range of maps. They should be small-scale to locate the place relative to the children's own locality and large-scale, covering a small area in detail, to enable children to explore the locality in depth. Ideal for this purpose are OS 1:1250 (1cm represents 12.5m) and 1:2500 (1cm represents 25m) maps. The former cover urban and the latter rural areas and you can buy them from the Ordnance Survey (Tel: 01730 792960). Both are black and white and have great clarity, although the 1:2500 would benefit from enlargement. Figure 2 is an extract of the OS 1:2500 map of Brockham village.

Activities using Figure 2 might include:

■ Direction work, e.g. In what direction is Vicarage Cottage from the church?

■ Distance work, e.g. How far is it from the PO (Post Office) to South Lodge?

■ Creating a land use map using different colours, e.g. for houses, their gardens, the church and grounds, the roads, the PO, the village green, other open space. Carefully chosen colours and a key enables children to make their own maps.

There are also opportunities to link photographs and maps. The children might use Figure 2 to name the house shown in the photograph of a church on the previous page. They might also consider the direction the camera was pointing.

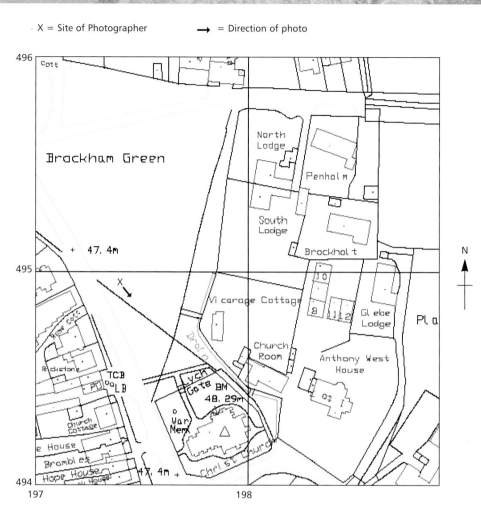

X = Site of Photographer ⟶ = Direction of photo

Figure 2:
OS map extract.
Reproduced from the
Ordnance Survey mapping
with the permission of
The Controller of HMSO
© Crown Copyright
Licence no MC841870M.

Case studies

Depending upon the nature of the place being studied, children need opportunities to study significant aspects of that place. These might include a study of:

1 the primary school in the place;

2 a significant workplace such as a farm, factory or large shop that helps explain that there is a reason why activities take place where they do;

3 an environmental issue that is of concern to the people in the place.

GENERAL BACKGROUND INFORMATION

You may have no direct knowledge of the place you are teaching about and any good resources should include basic information about the place including a brief history, some information about its physical site and situation, weather data which can be obtained from the Meteorological Office (Tel: 01344 854818) and detail about what is shown in each photograph.

Whichever way you choose to approach this part of the curriculum there are advantages and disadvantages, as shown below.

Using a commercially produced pack

Advantages

- the work has been done for you;
- the level of presentation including the photographs should be very high;
- the author(s) should be specialists and the geographical content and activities should be appropriate and varied;
- it need not be an expensive option.

Disadvantages

- you are limited to the localities studied in the published packs;
- the content may not suit comparison/contrast with those aspects studied in your local area;
- it is unlikely that you will be able to organise fieldwork at the place.

Producing your own pack

Advantages

- you can choose the most appropriate place and one that has fieldwork potential;
- you can develop resources over time;
- you can share the work with teachers from nearby schools who would also benefit from studying this place.

Disadvantages

- it is time consuming;
- it is more expensive than purchasing a commercial pack.

A twinning arrangement

Advantages

- you may be able to choose the locality;
- a link with another teacher is personal and should reduce the time taken to gather resources as you each collect for your own area;
- your children can help in information/data collection and they will be making personal links with other children;
- fieldwork may be a possibility.

Disadvantages

- collecting resources is time consuming;
- you may find that the two-way process ends up one-way to your disadvantage;
- to keep the links meaningful you need contact each year, perhaps with a different teacher and class in both schools (who may lack the interest of the original participants).

Using a residential visit

Advantages

- fieldwork will be integral to the study;
- more time should be available.

Disadvantages

- not all children go on residential courses;
- the study cannot all be done on site;
- geography may not be the main focus of the trip and the desired outcomes therefore not easy to complete.

HOW CAN I GO ABOUT DEVELOPING RESOURCES FOR MY OWN PACK?

The key is an easily accessible contrasting locality, although you might agree with Blyth and Krause who suggest that the place should 'not be so socially contrasting as to raise complex conflict questions before children are mature enough to handle them' (Blyth and Krause, 1995, p. 53). Visit a number of places to see if they meet your criteria. Make your choice and return to consider the features you intend to photograph. Visit the library or local book shop for historic information and local maps. Try to make contact with the primary school as they may be pleased to support your work (twinning opportunities?).

Try to include distinctive features that are unique to your chosen locality. Photos: Paula Richardson.

Take your photographs on a bright day, preferably in the summer when the content of gardens, open spaces and so on is more interesting. Take more than you intend to use so that after developing you can select the most appropriate twenty or so. If you want to contrast old and new then select the old images before the visit and photograph the area as it is now. Once chosen, get the photographs colour photocopied to A4 size, and laminated.

Case studies may take more time but a farmer, or factory or shop owner may be happy to supply you with information. Once you have their agreement, think about what you want to find out and send your questions in advance so that answers, data and so on can be prepared. If an issue is causing conflict the local school may alert you to its nature and back-copies of the local paper will fill in the background.

This guidance is the same for the 'Twinning' and the 'Residential visit' options shown above where the greatest problem may be the ease and convenience of gathering resources if the locality used is some distance from your school.

The key to each approach is the photographs. With these, a range of maps, some background information and fieldwork you can achieve excellent results. Over time you can enlarge the range of resources to fill in any gaps.

WHERE SHOULD THIS CONTRASTING UK LOCALITY BE PLACED IN THE SCHOOL'S LONG-TERM PLANS?

If you choose the contrasting UK locality in key stage 1 then its best place is probably in year 2, summer term. It has the advantage of allowing a variety of local geography to be undertaken in terms 1 to 5. The same ideas can then be followed in the contrasting UK locality study, encouraging the identification of similarities and differences. In key stage 2 the UK locality study might well come in year 4 after further local work in year 3 that expands on that completed in key stage 1. If you choose to link the contrasting UK study with a residential trip this may result in a delay in coverage until the summer term of year 6. This does not, however, mean you would do no UK studies before this topic; there are plenty of opportunities for using UK contexts in the thematic studies of Rivers, Weather, Settlement and Environmental change.

HOW CAN PROGRESSION BE ACHIEVED?

Progression can be achieved in a number of ways. A UK study lends itself very effectively to the enquiry process: in key stage 1 key progressive questions should be, 'Where is this place?', 'What is it like?', 'Why is it like it is?' and 'In what ways is it similar to and different from my place?'. The same questions should occur in key stage 2 plus others such as: 'How is it connected to other places?', 'How is it changing and should this change be taking place?', and 'What would it feel like to live in this place?'. There is a progression in the complexity of the questions, the introduction of abstract ideas and an acknowledgement of values and attitudes about other places.

The urban and rural photographs in this chapter have shown how progression can be applied to a single image, including appropriate vocabulary. Further opportunities for progression exist in the complexity of phenomena studied; the tasks set, including fieldwork; the precision required to complete those tasks; and the developing skills used, particularly map skills.

If you choose to study a contrasting UK locality in both key stages 1 and 2 you must consider progression in your key stage 2 locality. Look for one at a wider scale, in other words more distant from the home locality and, as Foley and Janikoun (1996) suggest, one that is 'a different kind of environment', and one of a slightly larger area than that studied at key stage 1 – to allow a greater range of phenomena to be studied.

HOW CAN I ASSESS THE CHILDREN'S GEOGRAPHICAL LEARNING THROUGH THIS UK PLACE STUDY?

Assessment tasks within a study of this nature can be many and varied and you can find several examples in *Expectations in Geography at Key Stages 1 and 2* (SCAA, 1997) that

The Lake District Locality
Study display.
Photo: Chris Garnett.

lend themselves readily to meeting requirements of the Level Descriptions. Taking Level 2 as an example, the photographs will allow pupils 'to describe physical and human features of places, recognising those features that give places their character'. Carefully constructed questions will encourage pupils to 'express views on attractive and unattractive features of the environment of a locality' as well as giving opportunities to 'use appropriate vocabulary'. Map work at different scales will help pupils to 'show an awareness of places beyond their own locality'. The variety of resources presented to pupils will help them to 'select information from resources' and to 'use this information and their own observations to ask and respond to questions about places'. Carefully planned fieldwork activities would support all of these expectations.

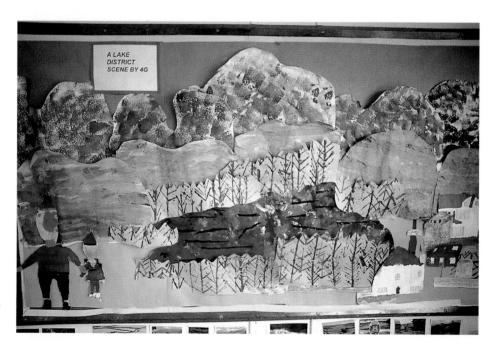

A Lake District scene –
whole-class work.
Photo: Chris Garnett.

WHAT OPPORTUNITIES ARE THERE FOR CROSS-CURRICULAR LINKS?

These are abundant for all subjects and for the cross-curricular themes. Links with English are through reading and written and spoken presentation; with maths in aspects of map work and data handling; with ICT in handling, classifying and presenting data; design and technology through model making; and with history through studying how places change over time. The cross-curricular theme of Environmental Education can feature in the study of environmental issues, Economic and Industrial Understanding through economic activities in a place, and Citizenship through the consideration of similarities and differences allied to a sensitive consideration of values and attitudes towards other places.

The ultimate aim of your teaching should be to enable the pupils to consider 'What would it feel like to be in this place?', not from the perspective of a short visit but from that of a child for whom that place is home.

References

Blyth, A. and Krause, J. (1995) *Primary Geography. A developmental Approach.* London: Hodder & Stoughton.

Cheshire County Council (1992) *Cheshire Twinning.* Chester: Education Services Cheshire CC.

Department of Education and Science (DES) (1990) *Geography for Ages 5 to 16.* London: HMSO.

Department for Education (DFE) (1995) *Geography in the National Curriculum (England).* London: HMSO.

Foley, M. and Janikoun, J. (1996) *The Really Practical Guide to Primary Geography* (second edition). Cheltenham: Stanley Thornes.

School Curriculum and Assessment Authority (SCAA) (1997) *Expectations in Geography at Key Stages 1 and 2.* London: SCAA.

Welsh Office (WO) (1995) *Geography in the National Curriculum (Wales).* Cardiff: WO.

Wiegand, P. (1992) *Places in the Primary School.* London: Falmer.

SUPPLIERS OF RESOURCE PACKS

Folens Publishers, Albert House, Apex Business Centre, Boscombe Road, Dunstable LU5 4RL. Tel: (01582) 472788.

The Geographical Association, 160 Solly Street, Sheffield S1 4BF. Tel: (0114) 296 0088.

Scholastic Publishers Ltd., Westfield Road, Southam, Leamington Spa, Warwickshire CV33 0JH. Tel: (01926) 887799.

Wildgoose Publications, The Reading Room, Dennis Street, Hugglescote, Leicestershire LE67 2FP. Tel: (01530) 835685.

Chapter 17: Studying a contrasting UK locality

Geographers ask the same questions when exploring a contrasting locality as when working locally (Chapter 16) or indeed beyond the UK (Chapter 18). Therefore Chapters 16, 17 and 18 adopt similar approaches. Chapter 19 explores ways to connect learning about different places.

Homes in Kenya

The Huts were made around a wooden frame with laced bamboo strips. The gaps are filled with soil and water mixed together to make a thick Paste which hardens in the sun. The huts are thatched with grass grown locally.

The wider world

Maureen Weldon

Why study distant places?

The 1991 Geography National Curriculum provided children with an entitlement to study distant places for the first time. For many primary teachers, half of whom had 'dropped' geography at 14 and who had received little or no INSET since, it was a daunting prospect. But for some primary teachers it was seen as a wonderful opportunity to extend their children's world, helping them to move towards a better, richer understanding of real places and people. Studying other places provides great opportunities to capitalise on children's natural interest in and curiosity about people and places, and this alone can make it a very satisfying and enjoyable experience for both teachers and children. But there are many other good educational reasons for studying other places (including overseas) with young children, as Figure 1 shows.

1	Uses and develops their interest and natural curiosity about places.
2	Provides opportunities for them to explore ideas and skills.
3	Develops their existing knowledge and understanding of places, environments and cultures.
4	Helps them to examine and clarify their existing experience and awareness of places.
5	Develops spatial awareness towards a global scale.
6	Helps them to recognise their interdependence with the rest of the world.
7	Builds positive attitudes towards other people around the world.
8	Builds a global perspective that extends their present perspectives.
9	Helps them to value diversity in places, environments and cultures.
10	Combats ignorance, partiality and bias, thus helping to avoid stereotyping and the development of prejudice.

Figure 1:
Ten good reasons for studying other places with young children. Adapted from: Catling, 1995.

Distant localities: size and geographical context

From the definitions given in the Geography National Curriculum for key stages 1 and 2, and from descriptions in Chapters 16 and 17, we know that a distant locality study is not the study an area as large as a country or region, rather, it is likely to be a village, part of a town or city, or perhaps a small island. What is important is that the size of the chosen distant locality is such that it allows children to compare and contrast it with their own school locality, is manageable to understand, and easy to relate to.

In all locality studies, children need to become aware of how the locality they are studying exists within a broader geographical context. When a distant locality is being studied, they need access to maps and globes to locate the position of the chosen locality within a country and continent, and to enable them to view it alongside their own home/school locality. General place knowledge, and specific knowledge relating to the Geography National Curriculum maps A, B and C, can be learnt through games and other

Photo: Chris Garnett.

'fun' activities or with reference to items in the news. A short, regular slot is probably best for this type of work (see Catling, 1995b).

It is essential to have some background information about the country in which the locality is set so that you can discuss its main physical and human features (e.g. its climate and the location of its capital and major cities) and how the chosen locality relates to or is influenced by them. In addition, we should build on children's own experiences of different places and tap into the knowledge and experience of adults associated with the school.

How do I choose a 'distant' locality?

At key stage 1, studying a locality overseas is optional within the National Curriculum so schools can select a 'distant' locality in the UK, rather than overseas, as long as either the physical or human features of the chosen locality, or both, contrast with those of the locality of the school.

When considering which locality to choose, the following questions need to be addressed:

- What distinctive features does the locality have?
- Will the chosen locality provide a contrast with our locality?
- Do we want to visit the locality? If so,
- Could I use the local school as a host base?
- Will the locality allow opportunities for fieldwork on site?
- How appropriate is the locality for an enquiry?
- Which localities are being studied at other key stages?
- Will there be variety over the six years?
- What secondary sources are available to sustain and develop the study?
- What potential is there to link the skills and themes of geography with the locality?
- Which localities am I, as the teacher, interested in?

Photo: Paula Richardson.

At key stage 2, one locality has to be in the UK and one in a country in Africa, Asia (excluding Japan), South America or Central America (including the Caribbean). When choosing a contrasting locality in the UK, consider whether you can visit it. Although this takes time and effort to prepare and plan, the benefits are significant; it will allow opportunities for fieldwork, enquiry and map work, so vital to budding geographers. Children enjoy the first-hand experience of a different place, seeing for themselves the features of the locality. You may decide to make a residential visit, using a field centre with 'experts' on hand to help you develop the geographical aspects of your study (Chapter 17).

As it is unlikely that your children will be able to visit the overseas locality at key stage 2, it is essential you consider what sources are available to you before you undertake the study, as these will affect the extent to which you can address the geography programmes of study. There is a growing number of resources available to schools, some of which are more useful than others. Figure 2 sets out the main advantages and disadvantages of using the different types of sources for locality studies.

Source	Main advantages	Main disadvantages
Account or talk by other adult, e.g. person from a distant place	Recent information and a good starting point. Interesting, particularly if combined with photographs, slides, artefacts, etc.	Often little follow-up material available. Doesn't always focus on one distinct locality. Talk may not be pitched at right level or include sufficient geography.
Personal knowledge of the locality chosen	Your first-hand experience can bring the locality 'alive'. Photographs, slides and artefacts from the locality can enhance the study.	You will need to prepare appropriate activities for the children to undertake. It takes time to put together.
Commercially produced pack (usually includes photographs and some activities)	Can reduce planning time. Usually cheap as a relevant resource.	Often more material than is required, so need to be selective about which parts you use. Not always video or slides intended for key stage 1. Activities may not be geographically focused and lead to 'topic drift'.
Slides of a locality	Whole class or group can view at one time. Useful as a focus for discussion with the teacher. The most interesting slides are your own.	Needs setting up. Teacher needs clear information about slides. It is difficult to talk about other people's slides. Not readily available for all localities. A 'static' view of a locality.
Video of a locality	Usually an interesting addition to a study. Whole class can view at one time.	Talk not always pitched at right level. Doesn't always focus on geography requirements. Difficult to find – often has a country or regional approach, not locality.
Photographs of a locality	Allows individual children/groups to 'see' the locality in some detail. If good quality, then can be very interesting. Easy to organise.	Selective and therefore may indicate bias and stereotyping.
Locality in the news	Interesting, topical, relevant. May have different accounts of the news of a locality, with some photographs.	Not always appropriate for KS1. Often insufficient detail for the study. May present an unbalanced view. Focuses on the unusual, rather than everyday life.
Book/story	Can be a good starting point. Can easily refer back. Usually high quality photographs. Useful for reference or as an additional source.	Few focus on a locality – usually a country or regional approach. Not always intended for KS1. Selective material, sometimes subject to bias/stereotyping in pictorial evidence. Usually an overview in insufficient detail. Single copy in class unmanageable.

Figure 2:
Some advantages and disadvantages of sources for locality studies.

What does an integrated approach to planning mean?

When planning activities for your children, an integrated approach to the three elements of geography – skills, places and themes – is ideal, and consistent with good geographical practice. This means that an activity should aim to increase a child's knowledge and understanding of a place through studying a thematic aspect of that place (i.e. when looking at the physical, human or environmental geography) and at the same time develop the child's geographical skills (e.g. from following a route on a map and studying photographs of the roads and means of transport, children discover that a vehicle is needed to get to the nearest town) (Figure 3).

Locality studies are most valuable when:

■ the *local area* and other localities are compared, so that:
   – the *character* of a distant place becomes clear;
   – pupils become aware of *similarities* and *differences* between the localities;
■ the *context* of the locality is developed – its place within the country;
■ the *locational* framework is studied – where in the world is it?
■ there is proper *depth* to the study, to develop *skills* and *understanding* sufficiently.

Figure 3:
The value of locality studies.

The skills identify a way of working: they are what geographers do and children should be involved in the development of these skills when undertaking any geographical study. Geographical questions are essential to help children gain a greater understanding of a locality (see 'How do I study another place geographically?'). Consideration should be given to opportunities for the development of ICT capability and the role of ICT in geography. Geography offers an increasing number of opportunities for children to be involved in ICT. There are increasing numbers of useful secondary sources for information, such as CD-ROM, e-mail, CDi, and mapping packages, in addition to open-ended software such as word processors and spreadsheets. These need to be included at the long-term planning stage to ensure appropriate coverage.

At key stage 1 the thematic study (investigating the quality of the environment) must be in the context of a particular locality – but that can be your own locality, the one chosen as a contrasting locality as part of the 'places' studies, or another locality entirely. Geography co-ordinators should encourage key stage 1 colleagues to include an overseas locality in their planning. The recent increase in, and improvement of, resources for overseas studies at key stage 1 make this an interesting and exciting option for both teachers and their children.

The National Curriculum states that the four geographical themes at key stage 2 may be studied 'as part of the studies of places' (DFE, 1995 p. 89), if you choose, so you may decide to do this for some of the themes. Some of the programmes of study lend themselves better to this approach than others, but whether you do study the themes as part of your locality studies or not, you will need to be sure that your planning allows work at a range of scales and a range of contexts, including the UK and the European Union, over the key stage. You will also need to allow for the development of knowledge and understanding by 'revisiting' a theme; this is most easily done through your place studies. Some possible options for consideration when planning are set out below:

■ You may decide to build some of each theme into every locality study over the key stage, allowing the children to cover the programmes of study in a range of contexts.
■ You could choose a locality set alongside an important river such as the Nile or the Rhine, where further information is available about the river.
■ Your school could 'adopt' a river, stopping off at a number of settlements along the way. This approach, with a major river, would allow opportunities to develop much of the geography work in an integrated way.

- Each locality chosen will potentially provide work about settlements. You may decide to look at a range of sizes and types of settlements over the key stage, comparing settlements in the UK, in Europe or in more distant locations.
- Consider choosing a locality where weather data is available or can be obtained. This can be compared with world-wide data printed in some national daily newspapers, or data from the television. Ideally the places chosen would be those with which the children are familiar, perhaps through news stories.
- Much early environmentally focused material took a regional or country-wide view, but more recently produced material is available for a specific locality or, for example, a named river. Care needs to be taken with making value judgements about other places. Using drama to explore ideas of how environments change can provide an interesting route to better understanding of the issues in decision-making processes.

What should I consider when teaching about distant places?

The study must develop children's knowledge and understanding of places. The children need to be taught about the main physical and human features that give the locality its character (both key stages) and also about its environmental features (key stage 2). These features will include, for example, river landscape, hills, woods, weather, type of housing, land use, uses of buildings, where people shop, and what people do. At key stage 2 it will extend to local environmental issues and links with other places.

Rural and urban Kenya.
Photos: Maureen Weldon.

One of the difficulties in studying distant places is the very real risk of presenting a misleading, inaccurate or biased picture. Geographers have an important role in providing opportunities to promote understanding, and in challenging ignorance and prejudice. A focus on a distinct locality, rather than a country or region, can help to avoid misleading generalisations which may be the basis of many prejudices. For example, by looking at travel brochures alone of, e.g. Kenya, children could conclude that Kenya is a hot country, mostly desert, with big game and lots of hotels. It is, however, equally important to consider the location of a locality within its country-wide context, otherwise children may have a distorted view of that country, assuming that it is all like the locality studied. For example, without looking at other material on Kenya, children might assume that all of Kenya is like the locality of Kaptalamwa: farmed land on steep hillsides with forested areas and no piped water or electricity.

A locality study will be a manageable size and so easier to comprehend. It can also be about real people with real lives, therefore engaging children's interest.

Children need a broad, balanced picture, rather than a one-sided viewpoint, so consideration should be given to rich as well as poor, urban as well as rural, female as well as male. Beware of over-emphasis on poverty accompanied by simple and dogmatic explanations of the causes of poverty abroad. We must help children to appreciate and value other cultures, ways of life and ideas. A distant-place study should stress that spiritual values are more important than material values for millions of people in the poor – and in the rich – world.

Even before they reach school age children will have attitudes, beliefs and values about other peoples and places. Some of these may be positive but others may be negative and critical. Indeed, we each have our own attitudes, beliefs and values about other peoples and places which we have not visited. Ideas and images come from a range of media sources such as television, articles in newspapers, holiday brochures, travel literature and films. Unfortunately these can, and usually do, present a very distorted view because of their selection for communication. They present unbalanced and incomplete images which may be reinforced within the home environment. We must beware of inflaming prejudice and increasing any tendency towards racial discrimination.

Schools should ask themselves:

- Will our personal images of a place give the right messages to our children?
  For example, describing a place as 'primitive' or 'simple' is unhelpful and biased.

- Do we misinform because of our own ignorance of particular places, or because we use terms incorrectly? An example might be using the word 'country' to describe Africa.

- Do our texts in school describe some places as 'problem areas'? For whom are they said to be environmentally problematic? For example, in the rainforests of Amazonia, the indigenous populations have lived there for centuries in equilibrium with their environment, but problems for these areas have come since the relatively recent settlement by Europeans.

It can be helpful to consider distant localities alongside your own locality – How would your locality appear to a visitor? What would you want a visitor to see? How would you present their locality to a visitor from abroad? You might also consider exploring visitors' ideas about other parts of our country – plenty of stereotypical images abound still. Consider also our traditions and culture in relation to how people from abroad might view them – bonfire night is an interesting one! Of course, all images have their limitations and in overcoming one set of stereotypes new ones may be created. However, by using a wide variety of images and providing plenty of opportunities to question and discuss them, it should be possible to build up a more rounded picture of life in a distant locality. The important thing is to be aware of these pitfalls so that we can make sure we do not fall into them and so that we can help children to develop an informed and balanced view of other people, places and cultures.

How do I study another place geographically?

When studying another place, we need to ask the same key geographical questions about it as we would for our own place:

- Where is this place?
- What is it like?
- Why is it like this?
- What is the landscape like?
- What goods and services are available?

- Where do people go to shop? What work do the adults do? How do people travel?
- What is it like to live there?
- What links does it have with other places?
- What is the weather like there?
- How is the place changing?
- Why is it changing? How do the people feel about the changes? How is the locality similar to/different from our locality/other localities we have studied?

Key

1. Maloca
2. Clearing and burning the forest
3. Newly planted chagra
4. Chagra ready for harvesting
5. Almost abandoned chagra with fruit trees and jungle growing up around it.
6. Totally abandoned chagra

Farming the Forest

Chagra is the Indian name for garden. To make their chagras the Indians clear patches of forest near the Maloca (a communal house).

They burn the tree stumps and plant their crop in the ashes. When the crops have been harvested a chagra is abandoned and slowly turns back to forest.

After about 15 years the site has grown back all its goodness and can be used again.

This kind of farming is called "slash and burn" and lots of Amazonians white and Indians do it.

Work: Christopher Hill and Robert Browning.

How should I start my locality study?

Some options:

- Start from where you are (more suitable for key stage 2 children) Identify where you are on maps and globes and locate your chosen locality. How would you get there? Consider various options – land, sea, flights, direct/following a particular route.
- Use a story from the country. What does it tell us about that country? What else do we know (or think we know!). Discuss how we can find out about a country or place.
- Use a partially covered photograph from the locality. Discuss the part of the photograph the children can see. Consider what might be outside the limits of the part they can see. Show the children the remainder of the photograph. Were they surprised? As a whole class devise questions which will provide starting points to help them to find out more about the locality.
- Show the children an artefact. Choose something which will capture the children's imagination – What is it? What is it used for? Who uses it? Where has it come from? What is it made from? What can it tell us about the place and people it belongs to?.

If you start from the locality, remember that you will need to set the locality within its country, its continent and within the world, using maps and globes.

What about using a television programme?

There is no doubt that television programmes can significantly increase interest in a place. The moving image is attractive and our children live in an age where the media is pre-eminent. As more programmes become available we need to consider the following:

■ Does the programme focus on a specific locality and aspects within it which are relevant to your studies? (The programme may not have been made with these in mind.)

■ Does the programme have a positive commentary? (Children are not sophisticated viewers – the commentary needs to be exact, precise and true.)

■ Does the programme show extremes or exceptions, highlighting the unusual or different? (Powerful images stay with you – the commentary is often forgotten.)

■ Are there suitable resources which can be used to follow up the programme?

Children today are bombarded with images and information, but don't have the skills to appraise them critically. Although a programme may be used to introduce a topic, it is often better used along the way. In any event, always record the programme so that the pause facility can be used, and always view the programme beforehand to check its suitability.

Can I design my own locality study?

Ideally, the chosen locality should be one which you have visited, or one that particularly interests you and for which you have collected plenty of relevant information and other materials. The information needs to be:

■ recent
■ accurate
■ relevant
■ interesting
■ unbiased

If possible, collect information and resources relating to the following features/aspects of the chosen locality:

■ the location (include local maps)
■ landscape
■ weather (include local data if possible)
■ the people and their way of life
■ homes
■ work
■ access to services (water, for example)
■ transport
■ health
■ recent and current changes

You may also wish to collect information about other aspects of the locality such as religion, customs, food, the local school and leisure pursuits. Although these are not essential to meet the programmes of study for geography, your children are likely to ask you questions about all of these and more! The information needs to be collated in a way that enables children to gain access to it easily. If the locality cannot be viewed at first-

Emma Pomeroy

Thursday, 18th June

Life in Chembakoli Village

These are some of the advantages and disadvantages of living in the Chembakoli Village.

The water is free, but people have to walk for about an hour to get to the well.

Children's parents can teach them all they need to know, but if they want to become something very different, like a business person, they would need to go to school, but the nearest school is in the next village.

The older people in the village are looked after by their children.

The farmland is passed down through the family, and the people can grow nearly everything they need on the farms.

If people cannot read, their landlord sometimes cheats them, so he gets more money than he should.

The people get very tired working in the fields, and carrying water from the well.

The doctor lives about 30 km away from the village.

Herbs from the forest can be used to make medicine.

The people don't have to buy fuel because they can get free wood from the forest.

Good, thoughtful work.

Work: Emma Pomeroy.

hand by the children, then visual aids are vital. A range of clear photographs (prints or slides), showing the landscape, housing, the people and their lifestyle would be particularly helpful, as would a video, even an amateur one, to make the place 'come alive' for the children.

What maps will I need for a locality study?

Suitable maps and plans of the locality are essential. If these are too detailed for young children to use, you could draw simple outline maps to include only the information that is necessary, and in a form which relates to the level of the children's mapping skills (see Figure 4). Your map should have a title, an indication of direction (perhaps an arrow pointing north) and a scale (even if only approximate). A simple key may also be included.

Photos: Maureen Weldon.

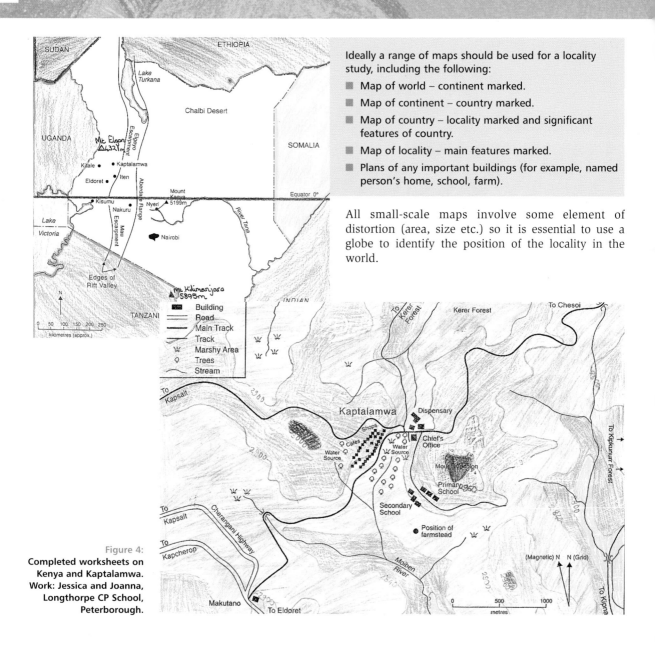

Ideally a range of maps should be used for a locality study, including the following:

■ Map of world – continent marked.

■ Map of continent – country marked.

■ Map of country – locality marked and significant features of country.

■ Map of locality – main features marked.

■ Plans of any important buildings (for example, named person's home, school, farm).

All small-scale maps involve some element of distortion (area, size etc.) so it is essential to use a globe to identify the position of the locality in the world.

Figure 4:
Completed worksheets on Kenya and Kaptalamwa. Work: Jessica and Joanna, Longthorpe CP School, Peterborough.

To enhance the study, displays can be made, and artefacts from the country made available, e.g. stamps, maps, food and products, coins, items of clothing, the national flag, a newspaper, stories, travel brochures and other pictures of the country. Art work from the locality, and recordings of local music can also add colour and atmosphere to the study (see photograph).

Should we link with our overseas locality?

There are obvious benefits to being able to make a direct link with your chosen locality. Forming overseas links has the potential to develop in children a sympathetic and caring attitude towards other peoples and ways of life, as well as a sense of responsibility for the environment, both locally and globally, and helps to counteract prejudice. Your children may wish to contact people in the chosen locality and so may ask you whether they can

Classroom display of African artefacts. Photo: Maureen Weldon.

write to children in the local primary school, for example. This may not always be easy, especially if the locality is in a remote part of Africa, Asia or South America. The language differences may be overcome, but unless there are fax or e-mail links, it may take weeks or even months for replies to arrive. If the locality you have selected is the subject of a commercial photopack, then many schools, perhaps hundreds, may be finding out about it, or making links. It makes sense, therefore, to try to find out where these schools are, and to make links with them too. The schools' linking movement is growing and there are many cases where links are very successful, particularly when the chosen locality is unique to a school and where there is a long-term commitment to the link.

References and further reading

Catling, S. (1995a) 'Wider horizons: the children's charter', *Primary Geographer*, 20, pp. 4-7.

Catling, S. (1995b) *Placing Places* (revised edition). Sheffield: The Geographical Association.

Development Education Centre (DEC) Birmingham (1986) *Hidden Messages – Activities for Exploring Bias.* Birmingham: DEC.

Department for Education (DFE) (1995) *Geography in the National Curriculum (England).* London: HMSO.

Weldon, M. (1994) *Discovering Distant Places.* Sheffield: Geographical Association.

Weldon, M. (1997) *Studying Distant Places.* Sheffield: Geographical Association.

Chapter 18: The wider world

Geographers ask the same questions when exploring a contrasting locality as when working locally (Chapter 16) or indeed beyond the UK (Chapter 18). Therefore Chapters 16, 17 and 18 adopt similar approaches. Chapter 19 explores ways to connect learning about different places.

Looking after the rainforest

The rainforest covers an area about the size of the united states. Many birds and animals live in these forests but their homes and lives are in danger because man destroying the forest for its timber and land to grow crops. If he continues he may create deserts (and is therefore a fool to himself.

If we want to survive we must make long-term plans not just think of the present-time. Your children would like to be able to live a healthy life too.

Today's pupils will grow up in a world facing challenges.

Making connections

Chapter 19

Steve Brace
Taahra Ghazi
Alison Rudd

> The death of Diana, Princess of Wales brought to a global television audience of 1 billion images spanning land-mine victims in Angola, a cancer hospital in Pakistan and Aids charities in America. Such images serve to remind us of the interconnectedness of events in today's world.

It is geography's role to help primary pupils navigate through the blizzard of information about the wider world. This is a world with enough resources to support all its people and yet a world in which one in four live in absolute poverty, 1.3 billion people have no safe drinking water or sanitation and 130 million children do not attend primary school. As Simon Catling argues:

> *'The future of our earth depends on concerted community commitment, in our local community and our global community ... (and this) involves commitment from early childhood to geography for people, places and the environment' (Catling, 1993 p. 357).*

Introducing global perspectives

Most primary school pupils already have some knowledge of the world beyond their home locality, but much of this is likely to be partial, inaccurate or confused – as exemplified by a key stage 1 pupil who associated Pocahontas with the 'Indian' village of Chembakolli (BBC, 1997). There is clear evidence that young children have not only inaccurate, but stereotypical images of 'distant' places, particularly if those places are rarely visited by them:

> *'The overwhelming perception of primary children in Britain is of 'Africa starving' or 'primitive Africa'. A primary school class was asked what images came to mind when the word 'Africa' was mentioned. They listed the following: deserts, trees, food-sacks, sand, Band Aid, Ethiopians, poverty, hungry, no houses, sun, heat, suffering, crying, hospitals, food, fields, insects and vultures' (Law, 1994).*

Global perspectives through photographs

Photographs, usually in the form of photopacks, are frequently used in primary schools to bring a global perspective into the classroom. Typically, a photopack will be based on a named locality, within which named people can be identified, thus giving a 'familiar' feel to the resources. While the camera might never lie, what children *see*, and what they *perceive* when confronted with photographic images of this kind are two very different things. For example, a key stage 2 pupil found it very difficult to reconcile the photograph of Salamatu Aberake, from Chereponi in Ghana (see photograph), with his own perceptions of life in Ghana, which was that all children living there would be unhappy.

Salamatu Aberake,
from Chereponi.
Photo: ActionAid/
Liba Taylor.
Source: ActionAid, 1996.

In this context, a useful activity is to ask pupils to identify what they already know about a specific place before introducing any photographs of it. Their ideas and perceptions can be returned to at the end of the piece of work to see what new information they have learnt and whether or not they found any evidence to support or contradict their original comments.

While it is important for pupils to see photographs which help them to investigate life within a specific locality, they should also be shown photographs which help them to place that locality within its regional and national contexts, illustrating the diversity that exists. Using such a range of images will enable pupils not only to make direct comparisons between their home and the distant locality, but also to identify features and issues which connect the two places. In this context, a useful exercise is to ask pupils to label features on photographs of a distant locality, then identify and name those features which can also be found in their home locality. This can be extended by using a Venn diagram to highlight those features which are specific to the two places and those which can be found in both (see Figure 1).

Photographs provide a powerful medium for the investigation of global perspectives and it is for this reason that teachers need to be aware of the issues of omission and bias when selecting and presenting images for young children. For example, while a locality

DESERTS
DESERTS LACK RAIN

PLAINS FLOOD AFTER
RAIN WATER EVAPORATES
SALT LEFT

STRANGE ROCKS
MAY BE ALL
THATS LEFT
OF OLD
MOUNTAINS

AFTER RAINSTORMS
SAND AND STONES
ARE WASHED FROM HILLS

AN OASIS WHERE
PLANTS AND
TREES GROW

FEW PLANTS AND ANIMALS
LIVE HERE. IT IS TOO
DRY.

NOMADS ARE PEOPLE
WHO LIVE IN THE
DESERTS.

photopack may apparently lack 'bias', because it typically contains no more than about 30 photographs, it is inevitably limited. In exploring the issue of omission, it is useful to ask pupils to select a small number of pictures that 'sum up' their home locality. Such a process is likely to involve the pupils in debate over which are the 'best' or most 'realistic' images, and raise the question of how strangers to the area would perceive it through these images.

A development education compass for exploring the world

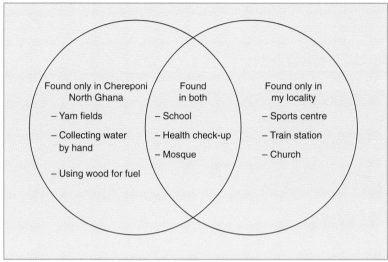

One development education aid which is particularly useful for geographers is the Development Compass Rose, developed by Birmingham DEC (DEC(Birmingham), 1995). This investigational framework replaces the points of the compass with four headings and related questions of relevance to the geography of places (Figure 2). Between the main compass points, there is overlap between the four different areas; thus, at the position 'north-east', there is interaction between Natural (environmental) and Economic processes.

Pupils can use the Development Compass Rose to investigate how different processes affect a given locality and its people. It can also be used at different geographical scales – local (this being a locality anywhere within the world), regional, national and international – and in association with photographs and other visual images as well as written descriptions.

Figure 1:
Venn diagram used to highlight similarities and differences between a UK locality and Chereponi, northern Ghana.

Natural
These are questions about the environment – energy, air, water, soil, living things, and their relationships to each other. These questions are about the 'built-as well as the 'natural' environment.

Who decides
These are questions about power: who makes choices and decides what is to happen, who benefits and loses as a result of these decisions and at what cost?

Economic
These are questions about money, trading, aid and ownership.

Social
These are questions about people: their relationships, traditions and culture, and the way they live. They include questions about how, for example, gender, race, disability, class and age affect social relationships.

Figure 2:
The Development Compass Rose.
Source:
DEC (Birmingham), 1995.

Global perspectives through literature

Stories are an ideal medium for making links between the lives of people living in different localities; it is through stories that many young children first learn about places outside their direct experience. Many such stories are centred around a main character – often a child – and so encourage readers to explore new worlds through the eyes of someone they can relate to. Thus, stories can provide a context for the development of empathy as well as positive images of unfamiliar cultures. As Professor David Milner argues:

'It is possible to demonstrate that positive images of black people in children's books positively affect the racial attitudes of black and white children alike' (Milner, 1994, p. 9).

Many stories contribute to the development of geographical understanding; they may evoke a strong sense of place, describe geographical themes such as environmental change, or highlight physical and human features through their illustrations. Stories set in contrasting areas within a country can be used to challenge pupils' perceptions and to introduce them to the variety which exists within a country in terms of its landscapes, lifestyles and people.

> The following stories, which illustrate a range of Kenyan environments, are good examples of this kind:
> - *The Village in the Forest by the Sea* (Birch, 1995) – a coastal environment;
> - *Masai and I* (Kroll, 1994) – a rural Masai settlement; and
> - *Mcheshi Goes on a Journey* (Mathenge and Miranda, 1993) – the journey from the capital city Nairobi to the island of Lamu.

Further, stories which move between Britain and a distant locality are ideal for examining similarities and differences between countries and localities and highlighting people's different perspectives. Good examples include *Grace and Family* (Hoffman, 1995), which follows a young girl's journey from England to the Gambia where she meets her father and his new family, and *Jazeera in the Sun* (Bruce, 1996) in which a young girl returns to her original home in India from her new home in England.

An introduction to the use of literature from overseas in geography is provided in *Hadithi Nzuri (A Good Story)*, published by ActionAid in 1997, which reviews 200 storybooks set in Africa, Asia and Latin America.

Think globally, act locally

The challenge to 'think globally, act locally' will have particular resonance for teachers of primary geography. It demands that the pupils' own locality is placed within the context of global perspectives, encouraging the investigation of those issues which connect the

two. Their locality, and indeed their school, will already have countless connections to the wider world. These may be through family ties, journeys, holidays, and goods and services. In this context, it is important to recognise that global perspectives are not just things 'out there', but are firmly rooted in the pupils' own experience of growing up in Britain's multicultural and globally interdependent society.

Trade with other parts of the world.
Photo: ActionAid/Liba Taylor.
Source: ActionAid, 1996.

In investigating trade with other parts of the world pupils need to move beyond the perspective of 'India grows tea for us in Britain' to understanding how local consumption patterns are linked to the wider world. They could examine not only the geographical conditions which make some areas of the world suitable for growing tea but also the circumstances of those involved in its production. For example, as the *Village Life in India* (ActionAid/CUP, 1996) materials make clear, for people who earn 50p a day picking tea, their poverty is due not simply to the lack of resources but also to their lack of access to, and control over, resources. (Note: now that 'fair trade' tea is widely available, pupils can take an active role in not only exploring, but also tasting, global perspectives!)

Exploring global perspectives.
Photo: Wendy Morgan.

It is important to recognise that inequality is not evenly distributed across the Earth's surface or even within its countries. India, for example, contains one of the largest concentrations of poverty in the world (including those picking tea for 50p a day). However, India is also home to a middle-class population of 200 million people, which dwarfs the combined *total* populations of the UK, France and Germany.

Conclusion

Fifty years ago, a driving force behind teaching British pupils about the world was that half of the world map on their classroom wall was shaded 'colonial red'. Now it is the increasing interdependence of our world which both drives and which requires the exploration of global perspectives.

Today's pupils will grow up in a world facing challenges, many of which directly connect a pupil's own locality to localities on the other side of the world. Our increasingly globalised world demands both an understanding of, and response to these circumstances at a local, national and international level. As Professor Michael Barber argues:

> *'If the ethics of teachers do not promote world understanding, who will? If teachers are not among the first to become, in effect, citizens of the world, who will?'* (Barber, 1997, p. 237).

In drawing on the support of development education, teachers of primary geography will play a key role in enabling pupils to understand the world they will inherit and to meet the future challenges which will face them (see Chapter 20).

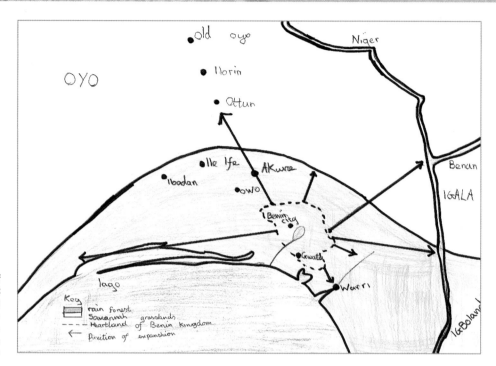

Becoming a 'citizen of the world' can start from an understanding of other countries. Work: Matthew Dransfield, Sharrow Junior School, Sheffield.

Development education organisations

Development education organisations can provide invaluable support to primary geographers. Development education is an approach which enables pupils to investigate issues in a global context, while also identifying those processes which link their locality to the wider world. This approach has particular relevance in relation to the Geography National Curriculum which requires pupils to study a distant locality and (at key stage 2) a set of themes – Rivers, Weather, Settlement and Environmental change – in a range of contexts in different parts of the world.

Global Perspectives in the National Curriculum: Guidance for KS1 and KS2 (DEA, 1995) provides an introduction to development education approaches in the primary geography classroom and is an invaluable starting point. The Development Education Association (DEA) sees development education as encompassing the following principles:

- enabling people to understand the links between their own lives and those of people throughout the world;
- increasing understanding of the economic, social, political and environmental forces which shape our lives;
- developing the skills, attitudes and values which enable people to work together to bring about change and take control of their own lives;
- working towards achieving a more just and sustainable world in which power and resources are more equitably shared.

Development education organisations include the development charities and 50 local development education centres (DECs). Teachers can get a contact address for their nearest DEC, whose services include providing resources for sale or loan, through the Development Education Association – see below.

References

ActionAid (1996) *The Big Families Pack – Ghana.* Chard: ActionAid.

ActionAid (1997) *Hadithi Nzuri, Children's Literature from Africa, Asia and Latin America.* Chard: ActionAid.

ActionAid/Cambridge University Press (1996) *Village Life In India.* Chard/Cambridge: ActionAid/CUP.

Barber, M. (1997) *The Learning Game: Arguments for an Education Revolution.* London: Galleons.

BBC Education (1997) *Teaching Today – Distant Places.* London: BBC Education.

Birch, B. (1995) *The Village in the Forest by the Sea.* London: Bodley Head/Random House.

Bruce, L. (1996) *Jazeera in the Sun.* London: Mammoth.

Catling, S. (1993) 'The whole world in our hands', *Geography*, 78, 4, pp. 340-358.

DEC(Birmingham) (1995) *Development Education Compass Rose – A Consultation Pack.* Birmingham: DEC.

Development Education Association (1995) *Global Perspectives in the National Curriculum: Guidance for Key Stage 1 and 2.* London: DEA.

Hoffman, M. (1995) *Grace and Family.* London: Frances Lincoln.

Kroll, V. (1994) *Masai and I.* London: Picture Puffin.

Law, T. (1994) *Primary Children's Ideas About Economically Developing Countries*, unpublished MA thesis in Primary Education, Institute of Education, University of London.

Milner, D. (1994) contribution to *A Multicultural Guide to Children's Books*, London: Books for Keeps.

Mathenge, J.W. and Miranda, R. (1993) *Mcheshi Goes on a Journey.* Kenya: Jacaranda (available in UK from Letterbox Library).

Organisations

ActionAid, Chataway House, Leach Road, Chard TA20 1FA.

DEC(Birmingham), Gillett Centre, 998 Bristol Road, Selly Oak, Birmingham B29 6LE.

Development Education Association, 29-31 Cowper Street, London EC2A 4AP.

The DEA can provide details of your school's nearest Development Education Centre and other development education organisations.

Chapter 19: Making connections

Teaching about unfamiliar 'distant' (overseas) localities presents a number of challenges, not least being the selection of appropriate resources. In looking at the links between local and distant places, this chapter overlaps with the content of Chapters 16-18, but extends it to consider aspects of development education, and ways of using resources such as stories to encourage a global perspective. It therefore provides a useful bridge between earlier chapters in Section Five and the final chapter on Exploring Futures (Chapter 20).

Vision of the future.

Exploring futures

David Hicks

> 'In urging that we teach a geography of the future, I do not mean to say that we should give up teaching the geography of the past: but we should make that past the servant of the future. If the future is unavoidable, let us at least not walk backwards into it' (Walford, 1984, p. 207).

Teaching for tomorrow

A geography of the past or a geography of the future, which shall we choose in school? Backward looking geography deals with the issues and problems of the late twentieth century, the agenda that teachers themselves grew up with. Forward looking geography explores the issues and dilemmas of the early twenty-first century, the agenda that our pupils will have to live with. Will we choose the new century or the old?

Should the task of meeting such needs seem difficult, geographers might recall the key role that exploration played in the evolution of their subject during the nineteenth century. Early geographers often gained their credentials as explorers mapping unknown territories. Such spatial exploration played a key role in understanding this planet and its peoples. A forward looking geography also requires what one might call temporal exploration, i.e. mapping the possible nature of short and longer term futures. To turn our backs on the future is to avoid taking responsibility for the consequences of our choices and actions in the present.

Hopes and fears for the future

Children are, of course, very interested in the future. After all, they are going to spend more time there than their teachers will. Yet we do not often ask them what they think and feel about the future or consult them about their hopes and fears for the future. We have some evidence of what these may be from a study carried out by Hicks and Holden (1995) with nearly 400 pupils from rural and urban schools in south-west England. Just over half of these children were of primary age. All were asked to identify their hopes and fears for the future: personally, locally and globally. The main local issues that concerned them are shown in Figure 1.

Hopes for the local area		Fears for the local area	
Less pollution	56%	More crime	41%
Better amenities	36%	More pollution	36%
Less crime	30%	Terrorism	29%
Greater prosperity	25%	Unemployment	22%
Less traffic	25%	Homelessness	9%

Figure 1:
Pupils' hopes and fears for their local area.

As Figure 1 shows, children's hopes and fears often mirror each other. From this evidence it is clear that children's concerns fall into three broad categories: the environment, personal safety and quality of life.

How we might respond to these in our geography teaching is by asking pupils:

- to list some of the things that they like and dislike about their local area;
- to identify individually three hopes they have for the future of their local area;
- then to identify individually three fears they have about the future of their local area.

We might then ask ourselves how many of these relate to geographical themes? How do they help us to understand our pupils' relationship to their community?

Figure 2:
Pupils' hopes and fears for the global future.

Hopes for the global future		Fears for the global future	
Peace/no war	49%	Disasters natural/human	46%
Less pollution	45%	More wars	35%
No poverty/hunger	32%	More pollution	20%
Good relationships		More poverty/hunger	17%
between countries	19%		

Figure 2 tells us that the pupils' hopes and fears for the wider world also mirror each other. It is also interesting to note that primary aged children are clearly aware of the major global issues of environment, war and peace, poverty and hunger.

How we might respond to these hopes and fears in our geography teaching is by asking pupils:

- about some of the events going on in the wider world that they are aware of, and how they feel about these;
- to list individually three fears that they have in relation to the future of the planet;
- then to list individually three hopes that they have for the future of the planet.

We might then ask ourselves how many of these relate to geographical themes? How does it help us to understand our pupils' perceptions of the world they live in?

A futures dimension

It is generally agreed that one of the prime tasks of education is to prepare pupils for adult life. Thus Section 1 of the Education Reform Act 1988 placed a statutory responsibility upon schools to 'prepare pupils for the opportunities, responsibilities and experiences of adult life' (NCC, 1990, p. 1). Children in school now will live well into the latter part of the twenty-first century, therefore teachers have a statutory responsibility to prepare them for life then, not just for when they leave school! The curriculum thus has both a spatial dimension (local-national-global) and a temporal dimension (past-present-future). In schools, however, we generally find a 'temporal imbalance' in the curriculum – most time is spent on study of the present and the past with very little explicit exploration of the future. The question then becomes: What does a future-orientated perspective look like in the curriculum?

While it is widely recognised that geography has a major contribution to make to the spatial dimension of the curriculum, it also has a significant contribution to make to the temporal dimension. Geography has, of course, always been concerned with time in that it is interested in the nature of change, both natural and human. This is clearly set out in the Geographical Association's publication *Programmes of Study: Try This Approach* (Rawling, 1992) which includes the following in a list of key geographical questions:

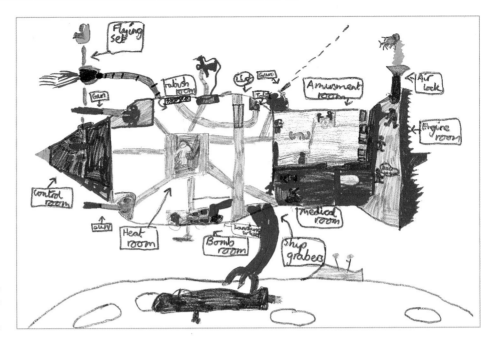

Exploring futures can mean designing a space ship! Work: Jonathan Lamb.

■ *What might happen? With what impacts? What decisions will be made and with what consequences?*
Predicting how the place or situation might change; analysing how decisions will be made; evaluating the impacts and consequences of these changes.

■ *What do people think about this and why? What do I think and why?*
Becoming aware of what a place or situation might be like in the future, and of how it may affect people; evaluating alternatives for the future; developing a personal response and justifying this.

The Land Use-UK 1996 Survey offered many pupils the opportunity to consider and record changes in their local community. Photo: Chris Garnett.

We need to look, therefore, not only at how places have changed in the past, but how they are changing now and how they may change in the future. We need also to look at how the environment has been changed in the past, how human activity is changing it now, and how it might be changed in the future. Amongst other things this will give us opportunities to address many of the concerns pupils have about both their local and the global community. It means that we will be helping children think more critically and creatively about the future and therefore helping them to develop some of the skills of responsible citizenship.

Future geographies

Many teachers are becoming increasingly interested in how they can educate their pupils more effectively for the future (Fountain, 1995). This applies to all age phases and all subject areas of the curriculum. What follows are specific suggestions as to how this interest can be activated within geography. They are drawn, in particular, from a resource book for teachers entitled *Educating for the Future: A Practical Classroom Guide* (Hicks, 1994).

LOOKING AT CHANGE

Change is an ever present theme in geography and children find this most interesting when it is brought out into the open and examined explicitly. Figure 3, for example, invites pupils to consider and record changes that they are aware of in their own lives, their local community, in Britain, and the world.

Things that are changing:			
in my life	locally	in Britain	in the world

Figure 3:
Things that are changing.

Questions About The Future

1. Will they cut down any more trees?
2. What will I be doing when I am 20?
3. Will there be more nature?
4. Will we find out more about Sea life?
5. Will I be more popular?
6. Will there be less nature?
7. Will Tony Blair Still be prime minister, and win every election?
8. Will there be pollution in the Sea?
9. Will I not have to wear glasses?
10. Will I be more mature?
11. Will I be prime minister?
12. Will I be dead?
13. Will there be peace in the world?
14. Will England Split in half?
15. Will there be an earthquake?
16. Will there be a bigger population?

One child's questions about the future.

Simple sketches together with a keyword are put in each box and the resulting posters can create a really eye-catching display. This activity will provide you with an interesting snapshot of how children perceive their changing world. Alternatively this matrix can be used to explore change in one particular locality or in relation to a specific theme such as the environment. A variety of questions can be used to initiate wider discussion. For example, 'Which changes interest pupils most and why?', 'Where do they get their information from?', 'How accurate is it?', 'What are the causes of these changes?', 'Who benefits from these changes and who loses?' and 'Are they changes that pupils welcome or not?'.

- Use the matrix shown in Figure 3 to find out what sorts of change your pupils are most aware of. What are their sources of information? What is it that interests them about these changes?
- Devise a similar matrix to record recent and current changes in the local area, e.g. in relation to roads and buildings, the environment, rivers and weather. Explore the differences between natural and human change.
- Repeat this activity for a contrasting area in the UK. How similar or different are the changes that are occurring? What are some of the reasons for these changes?

Having accustomed pupils to observe change more closely it is then possible to set this within the wider framework of past, present and future. One way of doing this is with the idea of the 'extended present.' Thus in many communities today there will be some people who are 100 years old and there will also be babies born today who may live to be 100. In our own and other communities we can therefore stretch out and touch both past and future across a 200 year period – the extended present. This most readily comes alive when shown as the relationship between generations (see Figure 4).

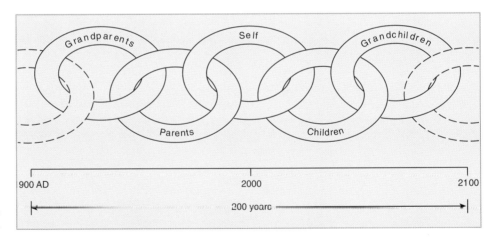

Figure 4:
The extended present.

While not all pupils may know their parents/grandparents the emphasis here is on the changing generations. What stories can they each tell of this place? What photographs, artefacts, memories would they like to share? Studying the past of a place in this way – how it became as it is today – is not unusual, but the extended present idea takes this further. What changes might occur in the future if present trends continue? When might pupils themselves become parents or grandparents? What responsibilities do we have towards future generations? Change is not something that just happens to us. It is something to which we also contribute, whether by our actions or inactions. If an out-of-town supermarket is planned, with all the consequent impacts on local shops and traffic, we can support it, oppose it or do nothing. Doing nothing, of course, is always a vote for the most powerful group in any situation.

- What does farming look like in a particular locality over the last 200 years to present? How and why has its form changed (crops, markets, pesticides, mechanisation)? How may it change in the future and why?

- What does transport look like in a particular locality over the last 200 years to present? How and why has it changed its form (type, efficiency, routes, volume)? How may it change in the future and why?

- What does your own community look like over the last 200 years to present? How and why has it changed its form (size, function, land use, industries)? How may it change in the future and why?

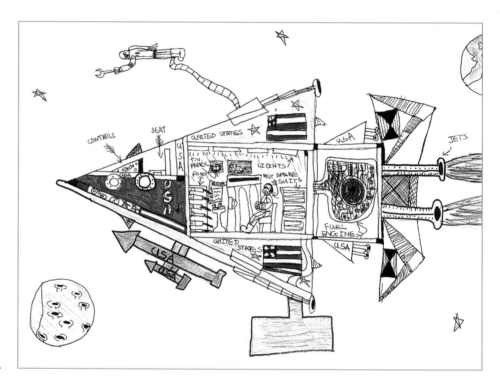

Work: Adam Weller.

USING TIMELINES

Looking at change and the future does not necessarily have to cover a 200 year period. A simple timeline can be drawn to map change in the present and the future. This might cover a year, a decade or longer. The important point is that timelines can be used to explore future possibilities, i.e., the consequences of change. One way of doing this is to look at current trends - e.g. to do with land use, employment or migration – in a locality or in relation to, say, an environmental issue. How might these trends affect the future of this place/issue? The possibilities can be sketched onto a timeline with dates and annotations.

Drawing future timelines immediately raises a major question for pupils. They will want to know: Is this the future that we think is *likely* to happen or is it the one that we *want* to happen? This question highlights one of the most crucial differences in thinking about the future. On the one hand we have probable futures, i.e. all those which seem most likely to come about because of current trends. Probable futures focus on what people most expect to happen in a given location or in relation to an issue. By contrast preferable futures are all those that we would most like to come about. Preferable futures reflect our deepest values, wishes and priorities. Probable and preferable timelines can be drawn separately or together, as shown in Figure 5.

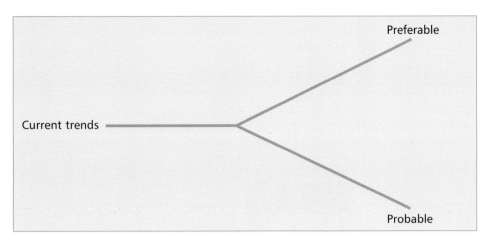

Such a diagram could be used to map probable and preferable futures for your street or your town or indeed any other location. If doing both it is best to complete the probable timeline first. Older pupils' probable futures sometimes reveal a degree of concern because they presume not much will change. My own probable future concerning the issue of traffic in Bath would show congestion, air pollution and respiratory diseases getting worse, because I presume that current trends will continue. My preferable future, by contrast, would show all sorts of alternatives to reliance on the car, including a mix of buses, pedestrianised areas, tram routes and more cycle ways. This leads to the question: Who else in my town is interested in this sort of future? Investigation then reveals that all sorts of organisations are concerned about traffic and the local environment. This means that pupils can then learn about positive change at grassroots level in their own and other communities. Finding out about, and being involved in, local action for change can go a long way in assuaging children's concerns for the future.

1 Take a particular environmental issue that the class has been studying and ask pupils in pairs to draw a probable timeline to show its future development. What changes do they predict and how might these affect people?

2 For the same issue ask pupils in pairs to draw their preferable timeline for its future development. How is this different? What needs to be done to bring such changes about?

3 Ask pupils to draw probable and preferable timelines for a distant locality that they have been studying. Which future influences do they think are local to the area and which are global in affecting that place?

USING SCENARIOS

A further way of examining what might happen and with what consequences is through the use of scenarios. Scenarios are like maps, sketches or short stories about the future. Their purpose is to catch the attention and the imagination by highlighting different aspects of possible futures. Thus while any number of futures is actually possible for a given locality, it is useful to identify say four quite different scenarios. These can then be used to explore how different decisions in the present will lead to different futures coming about. The point of scenarios is to show a range of possible futures. One of my favourite examples was a leaflet, *Landscapes for Tomorrow*, from the Yorkshire Dales National Park (1989). This included a series of sketches showing different future landscapes for the National Park. Each had an accompanying paragraph which explained what decisions had been made in the present to bring that particular future landscape about.

If we take society more broadly, popular views of the future tend to fall into four broad categories, as shown in Figure 6 (see Hicks (1994) for more details of this). Each view of the future is summed up by its title: More of the same; Technological-fix; Edge of disaster; Sustainable development.

It is possible to 'visit' each of these futures and to carry out 'fieldwork' investigations by asking the following questions:

- Do you think people like living in this possible future?
- What are some of the good things about it?
- What are some of the difficult things about it?
- Who will benefit and who will lose in this future?
- Say why you would or would not like to live in this future?

Work: Adam Summers.

Such scenarios are much more than fanciful thinking. They are a widely used tool for assessing options and weighing up alternatives. You may wish to draw your own scenarios or let pupils come up with their own. The purpose of such scenarios is to encourage more forward-looking thinking, consideration of alternatives and consequences, so that wiser choices can be made in the present. It is about helping pupils develop skills of foresight for use in their own lives and as responsible citizens. As stated earlier such aims are at the heart of good geography teaching: predicting how a place or situation might change, evaluating the impacts and consequences of changes, evaluating alternatives for the future, developing a personal response and justifying this ...

- Pupils draw up alternative scenarios for the future of their classroom and/or the school grounds. (If you choose this it needs to be a real exercise in which pupils have an actual say about the changes.)
- Alternative scenarios could be drawn up for the local shopping centre, a revised transport system or the local community as a whole. Who is already doing this sort of work in the community?
- Scenarios could be drawn up for a contrasting locality, e.g. to show different possible impacts of tourism in an area like the Lake District or the consequences of different aid projects to a developing country.
- Scenarios could be drawn to explore different energy options for the future, especially in relation to energy efficiency and renewable sources, or in relation to global warming.

Figure 6:
Four scenarios for the future
(a) more of the same,
(b) technological fix,
(c) edge of disaster,
and (d) sustainable development.
Source: Hicks, 1994.
Reproduced with kind permission of the Worldwide Fund for Nature.

Lessons for the future

We need to help children think more *explicitly* about the future because:

1 we live in a world of rapid change where yesterday's certainties are no longer an effective guide to tomorrow;

2 developing foresight, the ability to think ahead more clearly, is increasingly a vital survival skill;

3 we need to be aware of the range of alternative futures, both probable and preferable, that may be open to us;

4 we need to think much more carefully about the consequences of our actions today on others in future time;

5 this will help us make more considered and thoughtful choices here in the present.

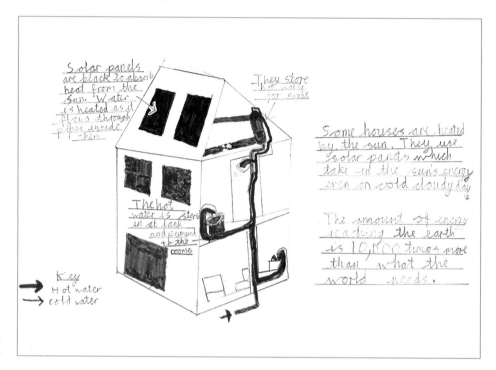

Alternative energy.
Work: Nigel Browning.

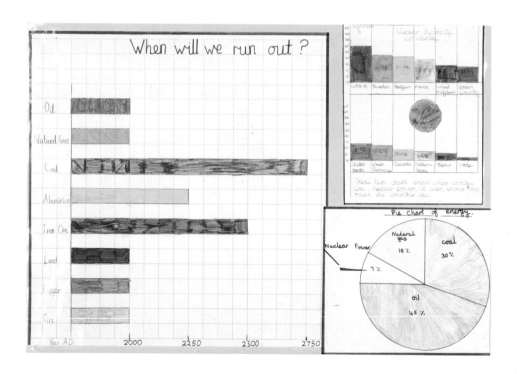

Photo: Centre for Alternative Technology, Machynlleth.

The 1997 debate about the effectiveness of the Rio Earth Summit five years on is a reminder to teachers that issues of environment and development will be on the global agenda for much of the twenty-first century. The global agenda is also the local one and many exciting initiatives are taking place under Local Agenda 21 programmes. Children *need* to explore positive and inspiring case studies of change since sustainability is not an abstract concept best left until secondary school. It is rightly part of primary geography and can be brought alive in a variety of ways (Chambers, 1995; SCAA, 1996). It is future geographies such as these that we should be helping our pupils to explore in schools which, as Whitaker (1997) has shown, need to become more futures-orientated in their own right.

- Find out about Local Agenda 21 initiatives in your area. In some places children have been involved in the process of planning the future of their community.

- Take your class to visit the Centre for Alternative Technology near Machynlleth in Powys (CAT, 1995). They take school parties for both day and week visits. Or maybe there is somewhere similar in your own region.

- One of your tasks as a teacher is to help your pupils think more critically and creatively about the future. How have you helped them to clarify their visions for a more sustainable future?

References

Centre for Alternative Technology (CAT) (1995) *Crazy Idealists! The CAT Story.* Machynlleth: CAT.

Chambers, B. *et al.* (1995) *Awareness into Action: Environmental Education in the Primary Curriculum.* Sheffield: Geographical Association.

Fountain, S. (1995) 'Change and the future', *Education for Development: A Teacher's Resource for Global Learning.* London: Hodder & Stoughton.

Hicks, D. (1994) *Educating for the Future: A Practical Classroom Guide.* Godalming: World Wide Fund for Nature UK.

Hicks, D. and Holden, C. (1995) *Visions of the Future: Why We Need to Teach for Tomorrow.* Stoke-on-Trent: Trentham Books.

National Curriculum Council (NCC) (1990) *Curriculum Guidance 3: The Whole Curriculum.* York: National Curriculum Council.

Rawling, E. (1992) *Programmes of Study: Try This Approach.* Sheffield: Geographical Association.

School Curriculum and Assessment Authority (SCAA) (1996) T*eaching Environmental Matters Through the National Curriculum.* London: SCAA.

Walford, R. (1984) 'Geography and the future', *Geography*, 69, 3, pp. 193-208.

Whitaker, P. (1997) *Primary Schools and the Future.* Milton Keynes: Open University Press.

Yorkshire Dales National Park Committee (1989) *Landscapes for Tomorrow.* Skipton: YDNPC.

Chapter 20: Exploring futures

Children may be encouraged to consider possible and desirable futures both in relation to places studied near and far (Chapters 16, 17, 18 and 19) and especially in relation to environmental geography (Chapter 21).

The Ozone Layer

The ozone layer is a thin covering made up from lots of different chemicals. It covers the world.

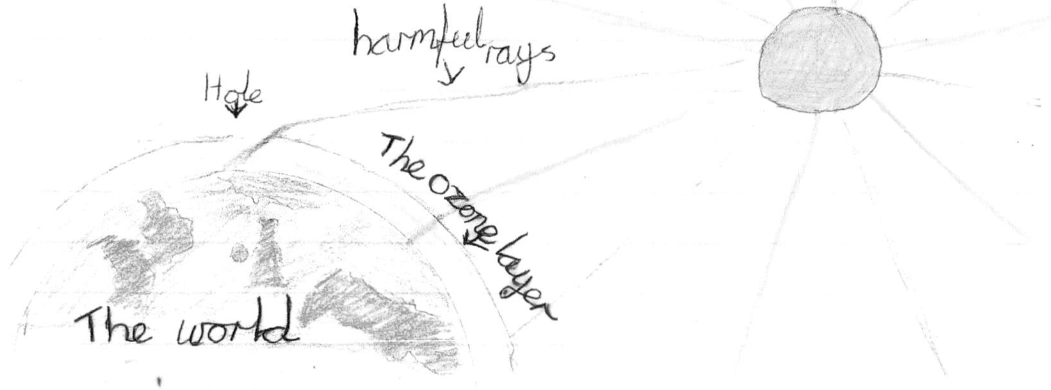

Hole

harmful rays

The ozone layer

The world

The ozone layer protects the world by stopping the suns harmful rays which can give us skin disease.

Near the Arctic a hole is forming in the ozone layer this is caused by air pollution. CFC is the chemical which is causing most of the damage. It is found in airisole cans and fridges. There are now ozone friendly airisole cans.

If we did not do anything about the hole this is what would happen.

The suns rays would melt the ice at the Arctic, this would cause tremendous floods. The greenhouse afect is similar to this

Environmental geography

Chapter 21

Liz Essex-Cater
Steve Rawlinson

> 'Never has there been a greater need for young people to be aware of the necessity to look after the environment. They are its custodians, and will be responsible for the world in which, in turn, their children will grow up. It is essential that all those with influence over the environment work together towards its conservation and improvement' (NCC, 1990, p. 1).

This chapter is concerned with teaching environmental geography within the context of good classroom geography. While offering suggestions for teaching environmental geography as required by the National Curriculum, we do not feel that teachers should be limited by the programmes of study which, in our view, should be regarded more as starting points for the development of children's geographical education than as ends in themselves.

There are two underlying considerations that we wish to highlight:

1 Fieldwork is fundamental to all geographical education. Involving children in activities outside the classroom is especially relevant to the effective delivery of environmental geography.

2 Environmental geography is an extremely useful vehicle for appreciating other people's attitudes and values and for encouraging children to express their own opinions, develop tolerance of alternative opinions and their own ability to analyse and reconsider their own stance on a particular issue.

What is environmental geography?

Environmental geography uses both geographical skills and knowledge to raise individual awareness of the issues affecting the quality of life on Earth. It requires knowledge and understanding, but also involves attitudes, values, opinions and provides an ideal opportunity for all children to contribute to real issues that are of concern to them.

Environmental geography should be seen as one of the component parts of environmental education. This cross-curricular theme has broader aims and objectives and can encompass all subjects of the primary curriculum (see NCC *Curriculum Guidance Document Number 7 Environmental Education* (1990) and the more recent (1996) SCAA documentation). Since its inception the Geography National Curriculum has recognised the strong links between environmental education and environmental geography. Three main strands were identified in the 1991 Order:

1 The use and misuse of natural resources.
2 The quality and vulnerability of natural environments.
3 The possibilities for protecting and managing environments.

(NCC, 1991)

There is obvious potential for using environmental education topics as a vehicle for delivering *all* National Curriculum subjects and in particular literacy and numeracy; however, it is essential that teachers produce clear schemes identifying the **geography** within any environmental education taught. It is all too easy to lose the geographical focus and drift into other subject areas when addressing environmental geography. The teacher, and indeed the children, must be clear in their own minds where the geography appears in any activity they undertake.

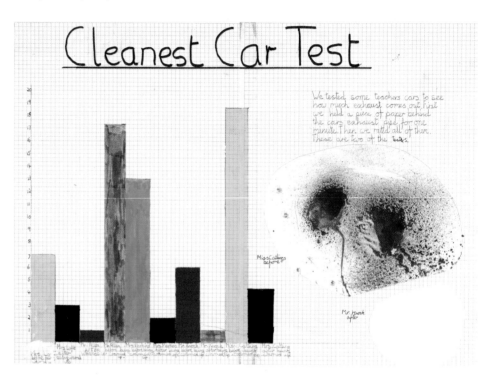

Projects offer scope for cross-curricular activities.

Environmental geography should start with the immediate environment.
Photo: Steve Rawlinson.

How can environmental geography be delivered?

GENERAL PRINCIPLES

The study of environmental geography should start with the child's own environment and expand out from that to the wider world. Within the Geography National Curriculum, local area studies feature in key stages 1 and 2, and the study of more distant environments in key stage 2 (though this does not preclude their inclusion in key stage 1).

The local environment is a **primary resource** with the unique quality that the children can interact with it (see Chapter 16). It has the advantages of being:

- free;
- accessible;
- familiar; and
- local people are usually willing to be involved in the children's learning process.

Children can collect their own **primary data** through, e.g. questionnaires, tape recordings, surveys, field sketches, photographs. **Secondary information** can also be collected to support the study of more distant localities through CD-ROMs, atlases, photographs, newspapers, magazines and the Internet. The information collected in these ways can then be used to draw conclusions.

This process could involve:
- the creation of databases to manipulate quantitative data;
- discussions based upon qualitative data with general trends identified;
- analysis of visual material.

Environmental geography is also about **communicating ideas.**

This may be achieved through:
- the production of a newspaper;
- role play within the class or for wider audiences, e.g. assemblies, parents' evenings;
- interviews with people involved in particular environmental issues;
- drawings, photographs and other art work to produce exciting wall displays;
- the production of a simulated television programme.

The **enquiry process** is one of the most effective ways of delivering geography, as recognised in the National Curriculum, for key stage 1:

'...in investigating places and a theme, pupils should be given opportunities to observe, question and record, and communicate ideas and information' (DFE, 1995, p. 2).

For key stage 2:

...in investigating places and themes, pupils should be given opportunities to:
- *observe and ask questions about geographical features and issues;*
- *collect and record evidence to answer the questions;*
- *analyze the evidence, draw conclusions and communicate findings*
(DFE, 1995, p. 4).

Which of these features do you have?
Ideally you need at least one from each category for local area work for children aged 5-11. A starter vocabulary (Figure 2) is also essential for local area work.

Water features
Stream, pond or lake, river, estuary, coastal area

Landscape features
Hills, valleys, cliffs, mountains (showing evidence of erosion or deposition by water, wind or ice), woods

Physical features
Slopes, soil, rocks

Climate work sites
For weather surveys, micro-climate work (usually school grounds)

Local issues
Bypass, road-widening scheme, out-of-town shopping development, new housing estate, new reservoir, rubbish tip site, local improvement scheme

Sites showing the origins of settlement
Crossing point of a river, a route centre, a defensive site, site where water became available, old core of modern settlement, evidence of growth, development, decline

Buildings
House, cottage, rows of houses, housing estates, groups, rows of buildings with different functions

Transport
Safe place for traffic survey, bus station, bypass, airport, railway station

Industry
Farm, business, small manufacturing unit, warehouse, factory

Shops
Single shop, parade of shops, supermarket, hypermarket, shopping mall

Leisure facilities
Library, museum, park, swimming pool, leisure centre, golf course

Settlements
House, hamlet, village, town, city (including suburbs)

Services
Fire, police, ambulance, hospital, doctor, dentist, refuse collection, recycling plant

Figure 1:
Features for study at key stages 1 and 2.
Source: NCC, 1993.

The strength of this methodology is that it can effectively deliver almost any aspect of geography, including environmental geography (Figure 1).

Some suggestions for key stage 1

In Curriculum 2000, environmental geography remains an important element of the programme of study at key stage 1.

'In this study pupils should be taught:

a   to express views on the attractive and unattractive features of the environment concerned;

b   how that environment is changing;

c   how the quality of that environment can be sustained and improved'

(DFE, 1995, p. 3).

Work: Peter Adcock, age 7, Sharrow N&I School, Sheffield.

POSSIBLE TOPIC TITLES

Within the above context, topic titles might include:

Looking after our school
Here children could be encouraged to express opinions about what they feel is attractive and unattractive about their school and its campus. Through writing and drawings they can be encouraged to plan for improvement.

Planning playground renovations at Broomley County First School, Stocksfield.

Airport	Forest	Office	Slope
Autumn	Frost	Park	Snow
Beach	Gentle	Path	Soil
Bridge	Hill	Pavement	South
Building	Hospital	Pedestrian	Spring
Bus	House	Place	Steep
Canal	Housing	Plan	Storm
Car	Ice	Pond	Stream
City	Island	Position	Summer
Cliff	Jobs	Quarry	Town
Cloud	Journey	Railway	Train
Country	Lake	Rain	Transport
Desert	Land	Right	Up
Down	Left	River	Valley
East	Level	Road	Village
Environment	Map	Rock	Weather
Estate	Materials	School	West
Factory	Mine	Sea	Wind
Far	Mountain	Season	Winter
Farm	Near	Settlement	Wood
Field	North	Shop	Work

Figure 2:
Appropriate geographical starter vocabulary.
Source: NCC, 1993.

Caring for animals

This could initially involve an appreciation of what the children's pets require to survive and could then be developed through a farm study, where the children can formulate their own opinions on the way farm animals are kept. There are also opportunities to study endangered wildlife habitats.

Looking after our water

Children could consider the various uses for water and the absolute necessity for clean drinking water. This, of course, may lead to a consideration of water supplies in other countries, encouraging children to empathise with children in distant lands and different cultures.

Trees

Ways of teaching environmental geography through this topic are detailed below.

Some of the clean water goes into the pond. There are fish and swans in there too. It shows that the water is clean enough for the wild- life to live

Photo: Colin Bridge.

Trees as a key stage 1 environmental geography topic

Trees provide the focus for an exciting and wide-ranging topic. Possible aims are as follows:

- **raising awareness** of the value of trees to the environment, e.g. the production of oxygen, the source of alternative medicines, and aesthetics;
- allowing children to express and develop their own opinions on forest-related issues, e.g. coniferous monoculture, rainforest decimation;
- appreciating that there are **different attitudes** relating to the value of trees.

DEVELOPMENT THROUGH A LOCAL STUDY

This could involve:

- mapping the school campus and/or local area to show where trees already exist;
- identifying, through discussion, the opportunities for enhancement of the environment by tree planting;
- a visit to either a local park or woodland and/or, through a 'local expert', enabling the children to identify a suitable variety of trees for their school.

THE ENQUIRY PROCESS

Armed with this knowledge and the opinions of a variety of people the children have consulted, the project could be advanced using questions such as:

- Do we want trees?
- Why do we want them?
- What trees will we plant?
- Which trees will grow in our environment? (This links to a consideration of weather and climate.)
- How do we look after them? (Identify what things trees need in order to survive.)
- How do we get the trees we want?
- Who will plant them?
- How will we plant them?
- Where will we plant them?
- Who will look after them?
- How do we pay for them?

Photo: Julia Charlton.

If these questions were to be formulated into a scheme to plant more trees in the school, in order to achieve their aim the children would then need to develop their own ideas for raising the money, perhaps by writing letters to appropriate organisations seeking sponsorship, and organising money raising events such as jumble sales, sponsored walks, 'swim-athons' and map quizzes. This could involve them in a series of community activities which would forge community/school links. These activities could culminate in a high-profile event where a local dignitary takes part in the tree planting ceremony.

DEVELOPMENT THROUGH A DISTANT LOCALITY

This project can be developed further to bring in studies of **distant and contrasting localities** as identified in the National Curriculum. For example:

- the destruction of rainforests
- the creation of a coniferous forest monoculture

Such an approach would require reference to secondary source material to resource the activities. This can be obtained from various organisations (see the list at the end of this chapter), many of whom have 'tailor-made' materials for just such a topic. Using such materials, the children might be encouraged to ask and find answers to questions such as:

- What and where are the rainforests?
- What is happening to them?
- Is this a problem? For whom?
- How can we influence what is happening there? (This raises major issues of empowerment.)
- What is it like to live here? (This would encourage the children to empathise with a different culture.)

Once again, this means using an enquiry approach to address the thematic investigation as described within the National Curriculum.

Other activities for environmental geography in key stage 1

1   Use of stories, e.g. *The World that Jack Built* by Ruth Brown, and *Dinosaurs and all that Rubbish* by Michael Foreman.

The early stages of creating a butterfly garden at Hope Primary School. Photo: Joan Crookes.

2   Use of poetry, e.g. *When Dad Cuts Down the Chestnut Tree*, by Pam Ayres.

3   Create a trail in a rural area (see the Ebchester School example on pages 288-293. This attempts to integrate many of the principles discussed).

4   Create a trail in an urban area.

5   Children create a play area for themselves, using resources like, for example, bark chippings. (This has been successfully introduced into a South Tyneside school to avoid mud being brought into the school buildings.)

6   Create a butterfly garden with the help of older pupils.

7   Make nesting boxes for birds and site them in appropriate areas.

8   Make attractive fences and boundaries. (A fence bordering the Tyneside Metro was transformed by a series of murals, with help from the Passenger Transport Authority and the Groundwork Trust.)

9   Improve the inside of the school with, for example, plants, signs, sculptures, paintings.

These ideas may be regarded as mini-projects and may provide a sound basis for further development in key stage 2.

Some suggestions for key stage 2

In key stage 2, the programme distinctly sets out seven investigations, three of which focus on place, and four on themes. One of these themes is Environmental change, and environmental concerns may well permeate other topics.

 'In investigating how environments change, pupils should be taught:

a how people affect the environment;

b how and why people seek to manage and sustain their environment'

(DFE, 1995, p. 6).

The local area will often provide some excellent issues which the children can investigate first-hand. As well as the examples suggested in the documentation, below are some more ideas which teachers could develop with their children and which also allow children to explore contrasting localities in their own country and in distant localities, as specified in the National Curriculum.

POSSIBLE TOPIC TITLES

Tourism

There are many examples of where tourism has had both a positive and a negative impact on the environment, and these can be used to raise a variety of geographical issues. For example:

1. Intense visitor pressure on National Parks and mountain environments. People who visit such areas often contribute to the destruction of the very thing they have come to experience, i.e. unspoilt landscape, peace and tranquillity.

2. Pressures of tourism
   This is well exemplified by, e.g. southern Spain, where small coastal fishing villages have been inundated by numerous foreign visitors who stay in the large tower-block apartments built to accommodate them. Torremolinos is an excellent example.

Bypass construction

In 1996 the Newbury bypass highlighted the contentious nature of this issue and the opposing views of various factions in the locality. There are many examples of where local road building schemes have raised opposing feelings.

Rivers/coasts

The abuse of our rivers and coastal waters through misuse can, unfortunately, be all too readily studied, e.g. oil spillage, agricultural waste, sewage waste and chemical discharges.

Green belt land

The building on green belt land is a dilemma facing most urban areas and one which impinges directly on rural areas.

Quarrying

Depending on the school's locality, resources and access to sites, quarrying can be the focus of geography topics set in a variety of place contexts, for example:

- an open cast coal mine within a predominantly agricultural landscape, such as Northumberland;

- limestone quarrying within the Peak District National Park;

- chalk quarrying in southern England;

- precious metal mining in an Equatorial rainforest, such as the Amazonian rainforest in Brazil;

- iron-ore mining in Scandinavia.

Equatorial rainforests

These provide a topical, though perhaps overused, context within which children can learn about our inability to sustain natural biomes. Mining and quarrying of minerals and metals in such an environment raise issues of sustainability and conflict. This opens up a wealth of views about the development of these distinctive regions.

If carefully selected, examples such as these will satisfy the National Curriculum requirement that:

> *'one locality should be in the UK and the other in a country in Africa, Asia (excluding Japan), South or Central America (including the Caribbean)' (DFE, 1995, p. 5).*

Case study: open-cast mining in Northumberland

Open-cast coal mining in Northumberland is a fascinating topic, highlighting many issues relating to environmental change in a UK locality.

Possible aims are as follows:

- **raising awareness** of the impact of open-cast coal mining on the environment;
- allowing children to **express and develop** their own opinions on a contentious issue;
- appreciating that there are **different attitudes** relating to open-cast mining in a rural area;
- development of a variety of **geographical skills and techniques**.

Children visiting a quarry.

DEVELOPMENT THROUGH THE ENQUIRY PROCESS

The aims of this study could be met by considering the following questions:

- What types of coal mining are there?
- Why is open-cast coal mining being carried out specifically in Northumberland?
- What does an open-cast coal mine look like?

- How many jobs does the industry provide and what do these jobs entail?
- Is the quality of the environment more important than the provision of jobs for local people?
- To what extent do people living around the area of coal extraction benefit or suffer from this activity and in what ways?
- To what extent do the owners of the quarry ensure minimum impact in the locality?
- What representation have the local people made about the effects of this industry, and to whom?
- How is the landscape reinstated after mining?
- Is the reinstated landscape better than the original?
- Has the land use changed?

ACTIVITIES

These could include:

- Whole-class discussions on the nature of coal and how it may be extracted. These discussions may be reinforced through children's own research on coal using books, CD-ROMs and information from coal companies.
- The use of map skills involving the use of acetate overlays to delineate the mining area and to show the extent and nature of the development. Children can then draw their own conclusions about land use before mining took place, and develop their own opinions as to the impact the mining has had on this landscape. They can also identify the dwellings and settlements in the immediate vicinity of the coal mines and can imagine what it would be like to live in that locality.
- A site visit. Before the site visit, children could work in groups to develop questions that they might choose to ask their guide. During the visit, they could take photographs, make field sketches and make tape recordings (e.g. of their interviews, or the noise of lorries).

  Part of the visit may also include a period of time spent in one of the settlements close to the mine. Children could collect a variety of additional information that might include, for example, interviews with local inhabitants, observations on the visual and aural impact of the mine, a dust survey (using dust plates), a traffic count. The use of LOGITs could enhance this study and address ICT requirements.

  If a site visit is not possible, secondary sources such as photographs and videos could be used

FOLLOW UP ACTIVITIES

These might include:

- Making a display of photographs, maps, newspaper cuttings, field sketches and graphs of the results of the surveys. The children can use these as a resource and as a focus for the classroom activities.
- Having a class discussion on what the children have discovered about people's attitudes towards open-cast mining.
- Creative writing activities in which the children express their opinions and attitudes about what they have seen and interacted with. This could take the form of the front page of a newspaper and involve the use of a desktop publishing package.
- Designing and mapping a landscape that would enhance the environment after the mine has closed. The children may choose to transform the hole into either a water park with wildlife habitats or a lake for recreational purposes; they may wish to return the area to an agricultural land use or develop a country park with woodland walks. Given current trends, they may decide to build a mountain bike track with all its attendant facilities.

■ A role play exercise centred on a proposal to start an open-cast coal mine in a new area, close to the school. The cast of characters in this scenario could include:

– a local MP

– a town planner

– a conservation group representative

– members of the parish council

– a village shopkeeper

– an unemployed parent of three children

– an 8/9 year old child

– the mine owner

– the haulage contractor

– a farmer

This role play could take the form of a studio discussion for a television programme. It might be possible for a person from the local planning department to chair the meeting and draw together the threads of the debate. Such a person would be able to provide the children with a considered decision as to whether or not the open- cast coal mine should go ahead.

If the role play is videoed the children can use the video as a resource to stimulate discussion concerning the issues raised by open-cast mining.

The very nature of environmental geography means that many of the topics, such as open-cast mining, are contentious ones. Feelings about these environmental issues can run very high and it is up to the teacher to develop the topic with appropriate sensitivity. The teacher therefore has a critical part to play in providing a role model for the pupils when they too are handling these ideas.

Whole school approach: case study

Ebchester Church of England Primary School in County Durham provides an excellent example of how environmental geography may be delivered via a whole-school approach. The rural location of this school is clearly an advantage, but the same principles may apply to, or be adapted by, schools in urban locations.

'The children are cared for, taught to care and in turn care for each other and their surrounding environment. In this context "their" world progresses from the reception class children to the year 6 pupils, who not only pass on their skills and knowledge to younger children, but also have a touchstone on which they can base their own decisions' (Richard Coombes, Headteacher).

The enthusiasm and commitment of the headteacher was the driving force behind this undertaking. Richard Coombes saw the learning opportunities within the school environment, in particular the woodland, the stream and a substantial open grassed area. His enthusiasm for using the environment encouraged parents, unemployed local people, local businesses and the pupils to work as a body. Together, the adults and children have worked to conserve and develop wildlife habitats in the local environment. This has provided an exciting, ongoing learning experience for all those involved, forging strong links within the community.

The children were central to the decision-making process and so learnt a great deal from the interaction with adults and from planning the developments. This is an excellent example of the value of empowering children by giving them ownership of a project.

The project involved enhancing the school grounds by conserving some existing features, and creating new ones.

Ebchester School Herb Garden.
Photo: Steve Rawlinson.

These included the following:

- woodland area
- weather station
- pond
- sandpit area
- butterfly garden
- herb garden
- structured play area
- wild flower meadow
- compost area
- organic vegetable garden (with produce prepared in the school dining room)

ACTIVITIES

The activities given below formed part of the Ebchester School project and provide ideas for activities that other schools could undertake to enhance and develop environmental geography.

The creation of trails

Different areas of the school grounds, such as the butterfly garden and woodland area, were linked together by the creation of all-weather paths made from renewable materials. This has provided or improved access to and between the areas throughout the year.

The trails (e.g. a bird trail and a tree trail) and the various site developments were all planned by the children who used their own knowledge and imagination to draw the plans, with the help of local experts (see Figure 3)

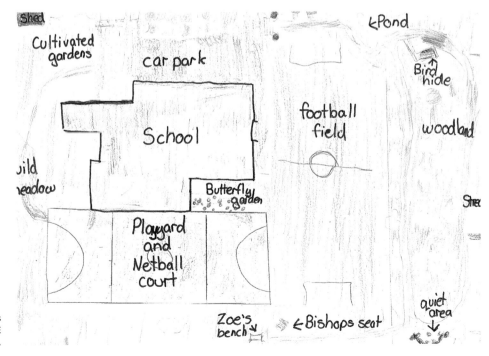

Figure 3:
Trails devised by pupils of Ebchester CE Primary School.

Interaction with other schools

Initially, the project was quite parochial but, as the plans came to fruition, Ebchester School began to involve other schools and to enjoy the resulting interaction.

Children are appointed as wardens to escort visitors around the various trails and areas, and are given a warden's badge. This gives children:

- the opportunity to communicate information
- confidence
- the chance to express themselves

'All of the children benefit from their interaction with children from visiting schools and take great pride in sharing their school with others (the high self-esteem of the children is important to the school). This also gives them an appreciation of their geographical situation and is of great value when studying contrasting areas' (Richard Coombes).

Worksheets

Worksheets are developed by the children themselves for use by visitors from other schools (Figure 4). These worksheets, and the planning activities, enable the teacher to address geographical skills, e.g. in key stage 1 'the use of geographical terms in exploring their surroundings' and in key stage 2 'make plans and maps at a variety of scales using symbols and keys' (NCC, 1995, pp. 2 and 4).

Figure 4: **Worksheet for visitors, produced by Ebchester School children.**

Find Three Colours

What To Do

1) Take a little bit of the three colours you want.

2) Stick them on the three bits of sticky tape.

3) Tell me where you found them.

_____   _____   _____

4) Draw the whole object.

    1   2   3

CREATURES

Go down to the woodland and see what insects are down there. Draw the insects that you have seen.

Pick out which one you like the best.

Next, draw which one you picked out.

Cut out the pictures of the insects.

Put them on a piece of paper.

Write down the names of the insects.

Our area

Each class was assigned one area of development. It was their task to ensure the continued progress of the project, which they did by discussing, drawing and planning it. They also identified improvements which would enhance their area in the long term. This initial planning stage then led into decisions about what was wanted, and final plans were produced. The plans provided the basis for the children to communicate their ideas to those people who could help to realise them, e.g. parents, local businesses, volunteers, experts. (Note that communication of this kind can involve the use of ICT: an overlay plan of the proposed development could be laid on a concept keyboard, and when parts of this are pressed, the children's ideas are displayed on the screen.)

In a project like this, continuity of all the activities can be ensured by involving the lower school at an early stage. It is a long-term, ongoing developmental process which changes in emphasis from year to year because of variations in, for example:

- the children's interests and enthusiasm;
- availability of resources;
- expert help;
- parental input;
- curriculum developments;
- contemporary environmental issues.

Photo: Paula Richardson.

LINKS WITH THE NATIONAL CURRICULUM

Today, Ebchester School has a curriculum which, for the most part, can be covered within the boundaries of the children's own environment and, as a consequence, enables all subjects within the National Curriculum to be addressed in a practical and meaningful way.

> *'The children not only learn geographical facts but, because there is a real purpose and interest in the acquisition of this knowledge, it can be used and applied to other areas of the curriculum which leads to an enquiring approach to learning in real-life situations. This is taken into their secondary education and, hopefully, through to adulthood'* (Richard Coombes).

Listed below are those parts of the Geography National Curriculum that have been addressed by the developments at Ebchester School. Environmental geography is covered in both key stages, as are other aspects of geography. The examples given in the National Curriculum documentation have been replaced (in bold type) by those referring specifically to the experiences gained by the children at the school.

KEY STAGE 1

Skills

In investigating places and a theme, pupils should be given opportunities to observe, question and record, and to communicate ideas and information. Pupils should be taught to:

a. use geographical terms, **e.g. stream, woodland, valley**, in exploring their surroundings;

b. undertake field work activities in the locality of the school, **e.g. locating the weather station;**

c. follow directions including the terms up, down, on, under, behind, in front of, near, far, left, right, north, south, east, west, **e.g. laying out trails around the school grounds;**

d. make maps and plans of real and imaginary places using maps and symbols, e.g. drawing up plans and designs for the butterfly garden, the bird hides, the vegetable plot

(DFE, 1995, p. 2).

Thematic study

The quality of the environment is the only thematic study within key stage 1. Through this child-centred development at Ebchester School all three aspects of this study can be addressed.

In this study, pupils should be taught:

a. to express views on the attractive and unattractive features, **e.g. absence of a place to reflect quietly, and read**, of the environment concerned, **e.g. the school field, stream and the woodland;**

b. how that environment is changing, **e.g. pollution in the stream and improved accessibility;**

c. how the quality of that environment can be sustained and improved, **e.g. creation of a pond and wetland area, butterfly garden, meadow area, planting of new trees**

(DFE, 1995, p. 3).

KEY STAGE 2

Skills

It is important to note that the methodology referred to under the sub-heading of 'skills' in key stage 2 develops further principles established in key stage 1. So number 2 of the programmes of study in key stage 2 is developed to include:

■ analyse the evidence, **e.g. water quality;**

■ draw conclusions, **e.g. choosing the correct environmentally friendly material for the paths;**

■ and communicate findings, **e.g. children act as wardens escorting visitors around the school** (DFE, 1995, p. 4).

Further opportunities for the coverage of geographical skills comes under PoS 3a, where vocabulary might include: **habitat, currents, regeneration, aspect.**

PoS 3c demands that children make plans and maps at a variety of scales using symbols and keys **e.g. a more detailed plan of how the school grounds would be developed.**

PoS 3f, which identifies the ICT requirements, was addressed by the children at Ebchester School through the **production of a newsletter detailing the on-going developments of the project.**

> **Themes**
>
> Clearly, 'Environmental change' is the most relevant theme in the case of this project.
>
> In investigating how environments change pupils should be taught:
>
> a. how people affect the environment, **e.g. by working together as a community considerable improvements can be made and positive attitudes engendered. By making places more accessible through the use of boardwalks and bark chippings, damage was avoided and people were encouraged to enjoy the area;**
>
> b. how and why people seek to manage and sustain their environment, **e.g. by managing the woodland the children created a more diverse habitat for wildlife which they were then able to learn from and enjoy'** (DFE, 1995, p. 6).

The experiences at Ebchester School show how delivering environmental geography may be done in an imaginative and stimulating manner. It is possible to adapt this approach to your school situation and offer children benefits that amply justify the time and effort involved.

Summary

The teaching of environmental geography is enhanced by the use of resources, whether these be primary, in terms of fieldwork, or secondary, such as books and teaching packs. There is a plethora of attractive and valuable resources available to teachers which often focus upon environmental education as opposed to environmental geography. It is therefore easy for teachers to be drawn along this environmental education avenue without fully appreciating the wealth of **geographical** opportunities that lie along this route.

In order to make environmental geography relevant to children, the value of local issues, supported by such resources as newspapers, local news footage, planning applications and photographs, collected over a period of time, must not be overlooked. This could be a child-centred activity with the children identifying the issue they want to look at and organising the resources relating to that issue themselves.

Dealing with environmental issues obviously requires the teacher to handle a multiplicity of **feelings** within the class with sensitivity and understanding. This is a skill which is not always explicitly acknowledged or addressed. Many teachers are able to operate in this sensitive area as a matter of course, but we must all appreciate that this is a skill that needs to be carefully cultivated.

ACKNOWLEDGEMENT
The authors wish to thank Richard Coombes and the staff and pupils at Ebchester Church of England Primary School, County Durham.

References and further reading

Ayres, P. (1990) *When Dad Cuts Down the Chestnut Tree*. London: Walker Books.

Bowles, R. (1993) *Resources for Key Stages 1, 2 and 3*. Sheffield: Geographical Association.

Brand, J. (1991) *The Green Umbrella*. Guildford: WWF/A&C Black.

Brown, R. (1991) *The World that Jack Built*. London: Red Fox.

Cade, A. (ed) (1991) *Policies for Environmental Education and Training: 1992 and Beyond*. Peterborough: English Nature.

Chambers, B. *et al.* (1995) *Awareness into Action; Environmental Education in the Primary Curriculum*. Sheffield: Geographical Association.

Curriculum Council for Wales (1992) *Environmental Education; a Framework for the Development of a Cross-Curricular Theme, Advisory Paper 17*. Cardiff: CCW.

Department of Education and Science (DES) (1991) *Geography in the National Curriculum.* London: HMSO.

Department for Education (DFE) (1995) *Geography in the National Curriculum (England).* London: DES/HMSO.

Foreman, M. (1972) *Dinosaurs and all that Rubbish.* London: Hamish Hamilton.

Gadsden, A. (1991) *Geography and History Through Stories.* Sheffield: Geographical Association.

Howson, J. (1993) *Going Green at Home and School.* Brighton: Wayland.

Joicy, H.B. (1986) *An Eye for the Environment.* London/Guildford: Unwin Hyman/WWF.

Masheder, M. (1990) *Windows to Nature.* Guildford: WWF.

May *et al.* (1994-98) *Fieldwork in Action* (series of six books – to date). Sheffield: Geographical Association.

Mayes, P. (1985) *Teaching Children Through the Environment.* London: Hodder & Stoughton.

Morgan, W. (1995) *Plans for Primary Geography.* Sheffield: Geographical Association.

NCC (1990) *Environmental Education: Curriculum Guidance 7.* York: NCC.

NCC (1993) *Teaching Geography at Key Stages 1 & 2: An INSET Guide.* York: NCC

Neal, P.D. and Palmer, J. (1990) *Environmental Education in the Primary School.* Oxford: Blackwell.

SCAA (1996) *Teaching Environmental Matters Through the National Curriculum.* London: SCAA

Stoker, B. and Brawn, T. (1993) *From Giant Sweets to Sponge Floors: A Schools Ground Design Guide.* Chester: Cheshire CC.

Thomas, G. (1992) *Science in the School Grounds.* Exmouth: Southgate.

Van Matre, S. (1979) *Sunship Earth.* Martinsville, IN: American Camping Association.

Williams, R. (1989) *One Earth Many Worlds.* Guildford: WWF.

Useful contacts

Centre for Alternative Technology, Llwyngwern Quarry, Machynelleth, Mid-Wales SY20 8DN. Provides useful teaching materials.

Council for Environmental Education, School of Education, University of Reading, London Road, Reading RG1 5QA. Excellent library and regular newsletter.

Council for the Protection of Rural England, Warwick House, 25 Buckingham Palace Road, London SW1 0PP. Useful publications on rural issues.

Countryside Council for Wales, Plaf Penrhos, Penrhos Road, Bangor LL57 2LQ. Useful newsletter.

English Heritage Education Service, Keysign House, 429 Oxford Street, London W1R 2HD. Can arrange free visits to English Heritage sites.

English Nature, Environmental Education Section, Northminster House, Peterborough PE1 1UA. Useful newsletter.

Friends of the Earth, 26-28 Underwood Street, London N1 7TQ. Produces posters, packs, etc., on topical issues.

The Geographical Association, 160 Solly Street, Sheffield S1 4BF. Publishes many excellent teaching guides and materials.

The Green Teacher Co-operative Ltd, Swn Y Mor, Pen Yr Angor, Aberystwyth SY23 1BJ. Tel: 01970 626478. e-mail: djr28@tutor.open.ac.uk. Publisher of *Green Teacher.*

Groundwork Trust, 85/87 Cornwell Street, Birmingham B3 3BY. Can provide practical advice and help on developing school grounds.

Learning Through Landscapes, 3rd Floor, Southside Offices, The Law Courts, Winchester SO23 9DL. Excellent advice on developing school grounds.

National Association for Environmental Education, Walsall Campus, University of Wolverhampton, Gorway, Walsall WS1 3BD. Resource information and support.

Oxfam Education, 274 Banbury Road, Oxford OX2 7DZ. Resources for Third World issues.

Scottish Natural Heritage, 12 Hope Terrace, Edinburgh, EH9 2AS. Useful newsletter.

Shell Better Britain Campaign, Red House, Hill Lane, Great Barr, Birmingham B43 6LZ. Possible source of sponsorship for grounds improvement.

The Tidy Britain Group, The Pier, Wigan, Lancashire WN3 4EX. School based projects to raise environmental awareness.

The Tree Council, 35 Belgrave Square, London SW1X 8QN. Information and teaching packs.

Watch Trust for Environmental Education, The Green, Witham Park, Lincoln LN5 7JR. Excellent practical projects and information.

The Wildlife Trusts (London), Central Office, 47-51 Great Suffolk Street, London SE1 0BS. Produced the *Create a School Wildlife Garden* – described as an interactive teaching package for developing school grounds.

The World Wide Fund for Nature, Panda House, Weyside Park, Goldaming, Surrey GU7 1XR. Teaching resources on a variety of issues.

Chapter 21: Environmental geography

Since fieldwork is 'especially relevant to the effective delivery of environmental geography' the connection to Chapter 14 is important. Readers are reminded of the importance of urban environments (see Chapter 22) as well as rural ones. Studies of environments at different scales and locations are built into Section Five.

An Arab

Head
protected
by a head
dress
Body
protected by robe
feet protected by sandals

Human Geography

Photo: Chris Garnett.

The children in your class all come to school with many experiences of human geography. They live in a dwelling. It may be an isolated farmhouse, a tower block, a terraced house or perhaps even a narrow boat. They will live in one of many types of settlement. Home may be in a small village or a large city of a million people. Some of them will walk to school, some will cycle, others will be brought in a car and a few may travel by train. Even those who walk to school will all have different journeys because their homes are in various locations. I believe they will all have feelings about their journeys and the effects of the human and physical landscape: they may dislike having to walk to school when it is raining hard but love their journey in the snow. Some may enjoy the noise and excitement of their city while others will be scared and confused by it.

They will all have varied experiences of their locality and the wider world. Some of them may have lived all of their lives in one village or town. Others will come from families who have lived in many places. Some of them may have families and friends who all live very close and visits between them may make up the majority of journeys made by the children. Others will have friends and family located in many different places and may have experience of travelling to see them.

All your pupils eat foods of different kinds. The bread in their lunch boxes may be baked around the corner from the school, but the flour may have come from a distant continent. A pot of yoghurt in the same box may be from a local organic farm, but could easily come from another European country. The food for their lunch could have been bought from the corner shop or an out-of-town hypermarket.

Work: Joanna Firth, Newton Infant School, Stockton on Tees.

When your class are out of school, they will have varied experiences of the wider world. One child may have a parent who is a long distance lorry driver and who tells stories of the journeys they make. Some children may have relations in Asia who they visit once a year. Others may have grandparents who have always lived in the schools' locality and can tell them about all the changes which have happened there. Some will have books and computers with access to the 'information superhighway', while others have little opportunity to read at home. However, these same children may know every corner of their locality and know every detail of how it is changing. Alternatively, some children may have limited experience of exploration because of parental concern for their safety in the modern world.

The things the children own all have links with the wider world. Their trainers may have been manufactured in the far east; they may have a collection of dolls from around the world; bedroom furniture from sustainably managed forests; an ornament which is perhaps a memento of a holiday in a distant place. They see television programmes made in different countries which portray a variety of lifestyles, and they may make contact through the Internet or e-mail with people in contrasting localities all around the world.

This may seem to be a long list at the start of a chapter, but it should help you to begin to focus on what human geography is at key stages 1 and 2 and how you can begin to build on the children's experiences as you plan your geography curriculum. Their lives are a part of the many patterns we can see in human geography.

Human geography deals with:

■ how and where people live and work;

■ the way people use the land;

■ the links between people:
- shopping, trade, etc.;
- communications;

and how all of these are affected by the physical environment.

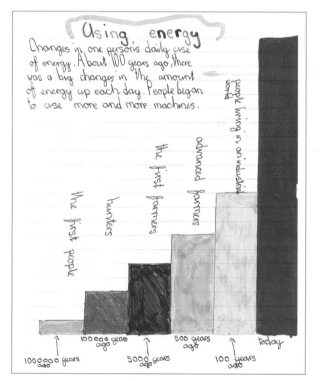

Changing the world through the way we live.

People live in different types of home in many types of settlement. They make journeys for different reasons by various modes of transport. New forms of communication are changing our lives, whether it is the Channel Tunnel or e-mail. We all use different facilities for shopping and recreation. People are employed in many types of work, or do not work at all. In our modern world we are very closely linked and interdependent with wide ranging effects: we buy coffee from South American co-operative farms and cars from transnational companies; some of our industrial pollution contributes to acid rain across parts of Europe. Most of our human activities are affected by the physical world: our homes mainly have sloping roofs because of the rainfall; your children may raise money for earthquake victims in distant countries (human geography) and yet see how little we can control natural forces (physical geography). You may also discuss with them the evidence for global warming and how people may be changing the world through they way they live.

This is all human geography. But some of the ideas in the previous paragraph may seem complex, confusing and distant for primary children. It is important to begin with things they have direct experience of, and with enquiries they develop with your help – How much traffic really travels through our village high street in one day? Is there more than there was ten years ago? Where is it coming from and going to? – these are important lines of geographical enquiry in primary schools. By doing their own surveys, looking at old photographs and asking for data in local council offices, they may be able to establish just how much the traffic has increased.

An important consideration when planning your geography curriculum is to ensure that children do not develop a view that towns, regions or indeed any place is isolated, but rather that they are connected in different ways with their immediate surroundings and the wider world. Studying changes in the local traffic can lead to more global ideas of transport and communications. This is reinforced at key stage 2 when pupils should be given opportunities to:

> *'become aware of how places fit into a wider geographical context, e.g. links within a town, a rural area, a region'* (DFE, 1995, p. 88).

Key stage 1

Many important concepts in human geography can be introduced to children at key stage 1. The National Curriculum programme of study lists geographical skills, places and a thematic study. The most effective planning will occur when these three areas are built into appropriate topic work. Imagine them, perhaps, as three spotlights on a stage (Figure 1). They can all move and overlap in varying amounts. Sometimes one spotlight may dominate and another not be used. The area of overlap represents each topic you choose

Figure 1:
Skills, places and themes under the spotlight.

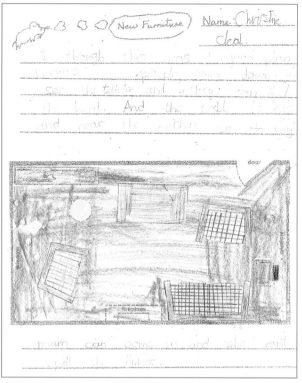

**Homes and houses.
Work: Christine Cleal.**

to develop geographical enquiries with young children.

If you and your colleagues are revising or developing your whole-school planning, it may be worth looking carefully at the topics you currently use at key stage 1. Some may (still) be excellent vehicles for human geography: 'journeys' and 'houses and homes' for example. Others may need to be changed so that your topics make the best use of the time available. Some of this work will be blocked while other parts will be continuing (SCAA, 1995, p. 11). A topic on 'houses and homes' might be an effective unit of blocked geographical work, featuring a contrasting locality, while work on 'weather' may need to develop through key stage 1 in various topics where relevant and as a continuous activity to develop key concepts of data collection and change. Geography can be planned to integrate with other subjects, but the key question to ask is 'Does the integration help young children to understand better the world in which they live?'. A key stage 1 topic on 'the clothes we wear' could benefit from links between science, geography and art, but may not need music or history, as concepts in those subjects may best be covered in other carefully planned topics.

PLANNING A HUMAN GEOGRAPHY-BASED TOPIC: JOURNEYS

**Rosie's Walk.
Work: Peter Adcock,
Sharrow N&I, Sheffield.**

A number of key points need to be considered in planning a geography-based topic at key stage 1. These can be drawn out by looking at the planning of a topic with a strong human geography focus: Journeys.

Key points when planning a geography-based topic at key stage 1
- Enquiry
- Skills development within place studies
- Development of vocabulary:
  - descriptive
  - positional
  - directional
- Contrasts/comparisons between places
- Patterns
- Aspects of:
  - physical geography
  - human geography
- Environmental considerations where the two meet

Enquiry is central to effective geography. At key stage 1 it involves 'studies that focus on geographical questions' and gives opportunities to 'observe, question and record, and to communicate ideas and information' (DFE, 1995). Working with the children, you will be able to develop a range of questions which they will understand and want to investigate:

1 Why do we make journeys?
2 How do we travel for different journeys?
3 What do we feel about the journeys we make?
4 How can we measure or describe different journeys?
5 What do we send on journeys?

These five enquiry questions are just some of the possibilities, but they have been chosen to illustrate particular planning points.

Reasons for journeys: travelling to Mecca. Work: Peter Adcock, Sharrow N&I School, Sheffield.

Why do we make journeys?

By working with examples from their own lives, and perhaps stories such as *Rosie's Walk* (Hutchins, 1992) and *Winnie-the-Pooh* (Milne, 1926), children can begin to understand that people and animals make journeys for different reasons. Sometimes we want to visit people. Some journeys are to take things to another place. Geographical skills such as questioning, observing and recording, fieldwork activities and making and using maps could be developed from these starting points. A journey might take us to a different type of place, developing the opportunity to make comparisons with the school locality, and to look at how the land is used in that place.

How do we travel for different journeys?

We can walk, go by car, boat, train or even plane. This question will help develop a wide range of geographical vocabulary and provide opportunities to see how major geographical features can affect how and where we travel; various sorts of map can be used.

How do we feel about the journeys we make?

Pupils are to be taught to express views on the attractive and unattractive features of the environment. What happens when a lot of cars use a road at the same time? Is a train journey more exciting than a walk?

Environmental quality could be explored with this question and perhaps the use of questions could be extended by talking to other people about their journeys, e.g. people who deliver goods (milk, mail, etc.), a doctor or a farmer. Children could also think about the places at the end of the journey to extend their understanding of places. To explore the inter-relationships of human geography, personal, social, moral and cultural issues could be considered by talking about how people enjoying a journey by jet plane may be affecting the lives of people living near the airport.

How can we measure or describe journeys?

This question can lead to the development of practical skills, and might involve using non-standard measurements or simple equipment such as a trundle wheel. Simple map making can be introduced, as well as ideas about how long a journey takes: a walk up a steep hill or through a crowded place may take longer than one on level ground, or in a quiet place. Activities and ideas such as these will involve developing key geographical vocabulary (particularly 'directional' words), as will describing journeys through talk and simple recording. There is plenty of scope for using ICT in this context, for example pupils could plan and run a journey for a 'Pixie' or 'Roamer' programmable toy.

What do we send on journeys?

You and your children will be able to make many enquiries like this, depending on pupils' experience and the opportunities of the locality. How did a certain letter arrive in school? Where did the food for a school dinner come from? Why are some astronauts going on a space shuttle journey and what will the world look like from space?

This last example is perhaps quite a telling one to make the point about the range and scale of places which can be included within the geography curriculum. In a world where many children do see images of other countries on television and video and see satellite photographs on weather forecasts, we need to take this huge range of stimuli and help them begin to understand the many patterns and contrasts which exist in the world.

Schools today have to have clear and detailed plans for many reasons. The most effective plans will allow teachers some flexibility and encouragement to include topical events within their geography teaching: an erupting volcano gives an excellent opportunity to reinforce or assess previous human geography you may already have covered; a space shuttle launch is a meaningful chance to look again at pictures of the world from space; the siting of new recycling bins near the school could let you and the children extend work from a thematic study on the quality of the local environment; the annual school summer fair also provides a topical opportunity to plan human geography (see Figure 2).

USING THE LOCALITY

In these examples, geographical skills, places and a thematic study have been linked together in relevant ways to develop geographical understanding. The primary curriculum is still very full of content so it is important to make effective use of time spent in every subject. In geography this will be helped if you and your colleagues have a clear knowledge and understanding of the opportunities offered within the locality of your school. If you are able to plan in the study of another locality at key stage 1, consider whether somewhere in the UK, a European locality, or one from further afield will provide children with an interesting range of similarities and differences to compare with what they find from enquiries in their own locality. Make full use of contacts and resources you have when deciding on the second locality, as well as considering the nature of the localities the children will study at key stage 2.

Your knowledge and understanding of the locality of the school will help you to plan appropriate geographical skills and place concepts within your chosen topics and indeed suggest suitable themes for human geography. Using part of an INSET day for staff to appraise a locality can be time well spent (Figure 3).

It is important for key stage 1 children to have opportunities to use secondary sources to obtain geographical information. These may be new and old postcards to show how buildings and land are used (and how these have changed), aerial photographs to help identify features and extend geographical vocabulary, and sources based on ICT.

USING INFORMATION AND COMMUNICATIONS TECHNOLOGY

It is important to remember that the definition of Information and Communications Technology is broad. It includes not only using computers to record and interpret data, for example about local traffic or pupils' likes and dislikes about their environment, but also the use of:

- a programmable robot (Roamer or Pixie) to send on journeys;
- a heat and light sensor to map the hot and cold parts of the classroom using simple colour keys;
- CD-ROMs to search for photographs of homes in other countries to compare with those in the locality.

Making a class video or audio recording about a local environmental issue is another example of planning ICT into the geography curriculum.

KEY STAGE 1: SUMMARY

Effective geographical work at key stage 1 will create important foundations for future enquiries. Children need to develop geographical skills as they follow simple lines of enquiry. These need to be firmly located within studies of real places, such as the school locality and one other. The best planning will include clear details of the geographical vocabulary which children will be learning or reinforcing. The 'journeys' example above would include words for types of transport, various means of communication, directional terms and associated vocabulary to help them interpret the world – e.g. railway station, port, travel agent, signpost. Geographical skills will be taught and developed within these studies of places and the thematic study.

Some topical opportunities to plan human geography units may already be very close to you in school. Involving children in planning where all the attractions in the school summer fair will be positioned on a school field lets them explore many of the mechanisms involved in human geography in miniature. For example:

Locating stalls and attractions
For obvious reasons the 'welly wanging' may be best located near the edge of the field, while the ice cream stall needs a central position.

Services
If the ice cream stall is in the centre, how can the electricity supply to the freezer be safely connected? Where should the six portable litter bins be placed in the field?

Land use
How wide should the aisles between stalls be? Should all of the stalls needing a supply of water be sited together?

Journeys
How easy will it be for our visitors, young and old, to get all to all of the attractions? Is there room for a car park? Did our advertising bring people from further afield?

Environmental links
Should we use disposable catering materials to save work? Will the noise and influx of visitors annoy local residents? How can this be reduced?

Information and communications technology
Sensing equipment could be used to measure wind speed/direction around the field, and surveys could be made using a computer, e.g. mapping places where raffle tickets have been sold.

Figure 2:
Planning a summer fair: some examples of related human geography studies.

1 What types of housing are there in the locality?
2 Where do people work?
3 What is the land used for?
4 What various types of transport can you find near the school?
5 What shopping facilities are there?
6 What parts of the world do local people come from?
7 How is the locality linked to other places?

Once you begin these enquiries, you will begin to collect a wide range of resources to develop the human geography in your school at key stages 1 and 2. They will also highlight the possibilities for first-hand experience of fieldwork for the children.

Figure 3:
Questions to ask when appraising a locality.

Key stage 2

The work in key stage 2 takes the key stage 1 introductions to understanding our world and builds upon them.

Settlements are a major feature in human geography and are one of the four thematic studies at Key Stage 2. The purpose of this section is to provide clear guidance on how to plan a human geography study unit focused on the theme of Settlement. The main planning considerations will be discussed and you will be able to apply these to your school's particular location and needs.

WHOLE-SCHOOL PLANNING

The key stage 2 programme of study sets out geographical skills, places and thematic studies in separate sections. However, it is clearly stated that the themes:

> *'may be studied separately, in combination with other themes, or as part of the study of places' (DFE, 1995. p. 89).*

It may be worth thinking about how your curriculum design will affect the understanding children develop of the world. If a Rivers study unit is taught in one term and Settlement in another, will they have the opportunity to learn the many links between the two? Will you ensure that the connections between rivers and settlements are clearly made? If your school's locality is a village with a river running through it, will you separate the two or develop plans which help children to understand that the river has an effect on the village and the people in the village influence the nature of the river? The key to whole-school planning is to design topics which will allow you to select sections from the programme of study and build them into a series of experiences which will allow children to learn geographical concepts.

At key stage 1 the children may have visited the local shop to see what is sold in it and they will have been introduced to some geographical vocabulary relating to journeys, people's jobs or shops. At key stage 2 they may re-visit the shops or shopping parade in year 3 to survey where customers come from or in what parts of the world some of the goods are produced. This activity will help to link the locality to the wider world. In year 6 they may compare this local shopping centre to the one in their contrasting UK locality during a field visit there. Each visit will have an extending range of geographical skills built into it and help children understand that settlements have different types of shopping facilities and that patterns can be seen in different settlements.

Urban study in the market.
Photo: Steve Watts.

Good planning, therefore, will blend skills, places and themes within geographically focused topics. Not all of your topics need to have an equal balance of them, but if they are carefully chosen they will be effective vehicles to teach specific skills and understanding. This will strengthen progress and continuity. It does reinforce the need to audit the school locality because you will find out what parts of the geography programmes of study can be taught through the locality and what needs resources from other places. For example, if your school is in a small market town some way from a large city, you may decide that the contrasting UK locality should be within a major built-up area. When you are choosing any other locality do remember that 'contrasting localities should be similar in size to the locality of the school' (DFE, 1995). This is good practice regardless of whatever legal requirements are currently in force.

Given this, you will only need to select a part of the city to study. The contrasting locality does not have to be a huge distance from your school. Indeed, if it is reasonably easy to reach, this will make a field visit simpler and cheaper to run and allow your children to develop geographical skills through first-hand experience. If you are not able to visit the settlement in your chosen contrasting locality, making a link with a primary school there can be an ideal alternative. If they agree that your locality would be suitable as their contrasting locality, then not only is the collection of relevant resources made much simpler, but there is further impetus given to the study if pupils know that they are sharing their results with another school. If both schools can obtain two copies of every geographic resource, they can be exchanged. This approach allows a dialogue to develop between children which could produce valuable work for the English and ICT parts of your curriculum. Perhaps best of all, it allows your children to study human geography by working with the people in their localities.

This raises the question of the quality and range of resources available to your children for the study of human geography. If you plan one of the school links suggested above, you might be able to involve your children in researching and producing locality resources

Collecting first-hand evidence.
Photo: Chris Garnett.

for the children in your linked school; this way they will have a purpose for conducting their own locality study. Also, they will then be faced with the need to select materials and evidence which reflect their own locality. This will develop skills which help them analyse and select secondary sources of evidence.

STUDYING A CONTRASTING LOCALITY OUTSIDE THE UK

The study of a contrasting locality in a country beyond the UK will probably be based on secondary sources. When you are choosing this locality, keep the school and contrasting UK locality in mind, so that the three together help you teach a full range of National Curriculum requirements. It is likely that this place study will include enquiries about settlement. A carefully chosen locality will also provide evidence of how the physical environment affects the way people live; homes in hot climates are built in particular ways, often using materials available locally; some buildings in earthquake zones are designed accordingly. Studying these will help children think about their own locality and make comparisons.

Banana farming in St Lucia.
Photo: Steve Scoble.

When these contrasting localities are being planned and taught it is easy to think only of the differences between them. An important aspect of our studies in human geography is to enable children to develop empathy for people in other countries. While there clearly are many differences in settlements and ways of life, enquiry questions should also be planned which help children see the great many similarities between peoples: human beings all need shelter and food and they share all the human emotions and feelings. Geographical questions such as 'What is this place like?' or 'How is it changing?' can help children develop empathy as well as greater knowledge about places. Your contrasting locality in another country may include a farming community which grows crops we import, for example bananas from St Lucia. What are the lives of the farmers like? Are they controlled by the major banana shippers? Or perhaps your locality has suffered from war. What might it be like to have to leave your home and land? Where are people going? Such questions need sensitive handling but all help to introduce children to thinking about the lives of other people and, in some cases, how our lives are interdependent, as in the case of the St Lucia banana farmers.

DESIGNING A HUMAN GEOGRAPHY STUDY UNIT

When you are designing a human geography study unit, it will probably be one of a number of units which children study at your school. Look at the overall provision to check that a range of contexts are included over the whole programme. One range will be the mix of settlements children study. If you are able to use examples from hamlets (see Figure 4) to major cities, children will gradually build an understanding of the patterns and nested hierarchies found in human settlements. Try to select places which come from a variety of UK and global locations. If you have followed the guidance in the programmes of study about the range of places to use, this should be straightforward. Variety of context also means including settlements which have different functions; capital cities, farming communities, new towns, ports and commuter villages are examples you may plan for. This will also help childrens' growing understanding and use of correct geographical vocabulary at key stage 2.

As children study more about the variety of settlements and what happens in them, they will begin to learn that 'land in settlements is used in different ways' (DFE, 1995, p. 90).

Changes to a village 'green'

At the time of writing, residents in the author's home village of Stonesfield, Oxfordshire, had just received outline plans from the local council for improvements to be made to the small village 'green'. It has not been a green for some years, and consists of a hard surface used as a car park. A mature tree grows from the centre of this 'green'. Most of the village residents use their cars to travel to and from work in other settlements, mainly Oxford and London. Villagers are being asked to comment on the proposals and suggest their own ideas.

The issues include:

- residents park their cars on the 'green' under and around the tree because their cottages do not have garages or front gardens;
- visitors need to park here for access to the church through the gate and along the path;
- some cars stop outside the post office to post letters, adding to the congestion;
- people who wish to use the post office or post box often need access on foot, but there are no footpaths and the village lanes are narrow. Cars parked close to walls cause extra problems for pedestrians.

Focusing on a particular part of the issue offers the opportunity for different types of learning, for example, the fact that some people live in villages and commute to work in urban areas helps children to understand how places are connected with the wider world. They would also learn that this rural settlement has very few residents with rural jobs. There would be many opportunities for children to use and make plans and maps at a variety of scales, for example, a large-scale plan of the 'green' would be needed, while smaller scale maps could be used to plot where people work.

This also offers an excellent, topical example of a human geography settlement study, with an active focus on changing land use. It also includes environmental change, because it raises important questions about how the quality of the 'green' may be improved, while still retaining parking facilities.

- By examining old photographs, children could ask enquiry questions about how the place has changed and why these changes have occurred.
  (The photographs show the village green today and as it was in the 1920s.)

A 'local issue' study of this kind creates opportunities for children to study their schools' community and work alongside adult 'experts' such as a local planning officer and an architect.

Figure 4:
An example of a local planning issue.

Photo: John Halocha and © Oxfordshire Photographic Archive, DLA, OCC..

GENERAL CONSIDERATIONS

- It is important to remember that all of the thematic studies at key stage 2 should use **case studies** – and all of these will give opportunities to link with aspects of human geography.

- It may be appropriate to plan relevant **curriculum links** with history when your enquiries look at 'How environments change' (DFE, 1995) in order to study changes in land use in settlements. Topical material can often be included (see Figure 4).

- Pupils' social development and partnership with parents and community are examined in **school inspections**. If you are able to show how these are planned into your curriculum, the 'quality of education' judgements by OFSTED may well be raised. Inspectors have to consider the extent to which pupils 'take responsibility, participate fully in the community, and develop an understanding of citizenship' (OFSTED, 1995, p. 82).

  In a broader context of human geography through the study of other people and places, you will also be able to help: 'pupils to appreciate their own cultural traditions and the diversity and richness of other cultures' (OFSTED, 1995, p. 82).

  Even if work like the 'green' development (see Figure 4) takes place well before an inspection, a set of photographs showing children working in the community with people, along with pictures of some of their work, can help provide evidence of the quality of education you provide.

- **Topical examples** such as the 'green' development (Figure 4) are not always available and do not exist forever, but there must be few localities where change and key questions in human geography are not happening. This is why it is important to know your school locality well and keep up-dating your information. Once people know the school is interested, it is surprising how easy it is to find suitable materials and sources of information. A lot of this topical material does not suddenly appear and a good local knowledge, for example, reading the local newspapers or talking to the road crossing warden, can give you advance notice of relevant issues for human geography. This can then help you plan such units of work into the whole-school plans being developed in many schools.

Summing up human geography

Human geography can help children begin to understand how people interact with the physical world, in addition to understanding how groups of people inter-relate.

 'Children gradually need to confront issues relating to their own national identity as well as understandings of the wider world' (Wiegand, 1992. p. 4).

Children today are regularly confronted with images of people and events from all over the world. They have increasing access to communication systems which allow them to contact people in a variety of places. Many of them explore locally and some have travelled the world before they leave primary school. By developing some of the ideas in this chapter in school, you will give your pupils some of the skills and understanding they will need to live in an increasingly complex world where communications bring humans from every continent into closer contact than they have ever been in the past. You will be helping them to explore and enjoy the huge range of human activity, ways of life and ideas which they will experience as they live their lives in the twenty-first century.

References and further reading

Chambers, B. *et al.* (1995) *Awareness into Action: Environmental Education in the Primary Curriculum.* Sheffield: Geographical Association.

Department for Education (DFE) (1995) *Key Stages 1 and 2 of the National Curriculum.* London: HMSO.

Foley, M. and Janikoun, J. (1996) *The Really Practical Guide to Primary Geography* (second edition). Cheltenham: Stanley Thornes.

Hutchins, P. (1992) *Rosie's Walk*. London: Bodley Head.

Kimber, D. *et al.* (1995) *Humanities in Primary Education*. London: Fulton.

Milne, A.A. (1926) *Winnie-the-Pooh*. London: Methuen.

Norris Nicholson, H. (1996) *Place in Story-time: Geography through Stories at Key Stages 1 and 2* (revised edition). Sheffield: Geographical Association.

Office for Standards in Education (1995) *Guidance on the Inspection of Nursery and Primary Schools,* London: HMSO.

School Curriculum and Assessment Authority (SCAA) (1995) *Planning the Curriculum at Key Stages 1 and 2*. London: SCAA.

Spencer, C. and Blades, M. (1993) 'Children's understanding of place: the world at hand', *Geography*, 78, 4, pp. 367-373.

Wiegand, P. (1992) *Places in the Primary School. Knowledge and Understanding of Places at Key Stages 1 and 2*. London: Falmer.

Chapter 22: Human geography

This chapter on planning and teaching aspects of the primary curriculum that fall within 'human geography' has many links with earlier chapters relating to planning (Section Two), to developing skills (Section Four) and to teaching about places (Section Five). The focus on units of work relating to journeys and to settlements helps to illustrate how the many strands of places, skills and themes can be brought together and taught in ways that relate closely to children's experiences in their own environment.

Sunny

Foggy

Thunder

Raining

Windy

Weather and climate

Chapter 23

Rachel Bowles

This chapter shows how observing and keeping regular weather records from the earliest classes can enhance understanding of the impact of weather and climate on the environment and on human activities in that environment.

Weather studies

Weather is one part of the world about us which affects every aspect of our lives – clothes, food, buildings, the way we feel, what we see and hear, and so on. Daily variations in the weather provide material for small-talk to ease a difficult situation and for developing precise language on quantity and quality. The results of accurate observation and measurement are distilled and transmitted daily at regular intervals into our living rooms by the weather people, in language we can all understand. In short, weather is a cross-curricular topic, combining elements of English, mathematics, science and geography, and presenting opportunities for improving music, art and drama.

There are five aspects to learning about the weather:
1 Observing and recording weather conditions and the effects of these on human activities.
2 Making weather instruments and recording data.
3 Observing seasonal patterns.
4 Finding out about weather conditions and patterns around the world.
5 Considering the causes and effects of unusual weather conditions.

Weather and the National Curriculum: key stage 1

Curriculum 2000 does not require weather and climate to be studied as a separate theme in the primary curriculum. However, aspects of weather will always feature in locality studies.

'What is the weather like today?' is often the first question in class discussion time and can be used to prompt children to think about daily weather changes, as well as introducing them to an enquiry approach. You could start by focusing upon what Teddy is, or should be, wearing to develop observation skills and to remind the children that they need to wear clothing which suits the weather. The regular completion of a daily weather diary is an ideal activity for encouraging children to observe, question and record, and to communicate ideas and information. Personal diaries and stories are also valuable in helping children to select appropriate vocabulary to describe both the quality and quantity of sun, rain and wind. By year 1, practical measurement is possible; charts and graphs can be made and used to note changes during the day, between days and also weeks, months and eventually years.

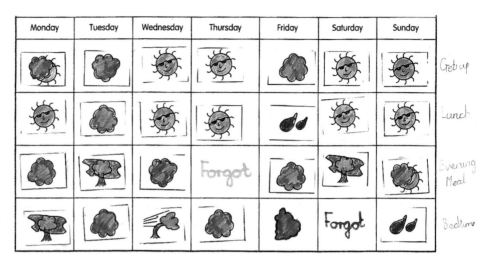

| | Monday | Tuesday | Wednesday | Thursday | Friday | Saturday | Sunday | |

Developing practical
measurement.
Work: Claire McAlpine.

Observing and recording the weather on a regular basis from the earliest moments of a child's school life provides an important foundation for developing awareness about the wider world and is vital to an understanding of hot and cold places. The use of secondary sources such as pictures, stories and photographs is also important in this respect; by illustrating such things as clothes and vegetation these can help to show how hot or how cold other places are in relation to home. Often, the pictures illustrate an environment as a whole, e.g. *A Balloon for Grandad* (Gray and Ray, 1991) shows the change from well-watered green Britain to the drier places of the Mediterranean thus providing an opportunity to use weather in the context of the environment theme.

Weather is one of those experiences you can focus upon at the time of happening. The children could take photographs of, for example, the pond frozen over, or an unwatered tub of flowers looking like a desert after a dry holiday, and attach them to their weather record for that day or week. Direct evidence of this kind can be used when looking at other places, in particular places which contrast with the home locality. It will help the children to remember the effects of weather on themselves and their local environment when studying the effects of weather on people and their surroundings in other places, thus encouraging empathy as well as making it easier to identify similarities and differences between places.

By the end of year 2, children should understand the difference between the seasons and how seasonal changes are reflected in the landscape. At the end of key stage 1, they should also be able to relate consequences to causes and processes, for example a flooded playground is the consequence of a heavy rainstorm. From observing and recording a local weather incident such as this, children could progress to looking at the water cycle.

Weather studies for infants

VOCABULARY, STORY, PICTURES AND FEELINGS

Nursery rhymes (e.g. 'Incey Wincey Spider', 'Dr Foster', 'Rain rain go away'), sayings (e.g. 'Red sky at night …') and stories, (e.g. *Postman Pat* by Cunnliffe and *Caribbean Tales* by Salkey) contain a wealth of inspiration for continuing discussions on the daily weather and what it feels like on different days and in different places. As well as considering the way daily weather affects the clothes we wear, children can look at what is happening to plants and trees. They could bring in fruits, leaves and flowers, noting how each season has distinctive colours, often related to temperature (e.g. red leaves are a reaction to cold, white blossoms appear as the temperature rises, an abundance of green reflects regular rainfall, yellows reflect harvest and dry grass – and so on). The variations from day to day and week to week can be used as starting points to develop a vocabulary and literary repertoire. Gradually repetition and change will become apparent.

What would you add to each scene to show the changes in the four seasons?

Noting the seasons' different colours.

Seasonal topics can be developed in each term; these all lend themselves to cross-curricular work and can be revisited with increasing detail and complexity according to the development of the class. Figure 1 indicates the kind of vocabulary needed and possible by the end of year 2. A weather word book and weather word bank could be compiled using computer software.

Elements
wind, breeze, gale, sun, rain, snow, ice, frost, clouds, raindrops, hail, mist, fog, thunder, lightning.

Seasons
summer: hot, boiling, dry, warm, humid, sunny, bright, showers, storms, calm, downpours, pouring, cloudless, drought, shine, fresh, light.

winter: cold, freezing, frosty, wet, cool, snowy, crystals, chilly, severe, rainy, floods, gales, foggy, dull, overcast.

spring and *autumn:* changeable, spitting, drizzling, damp, dew, frosty, splash, puddle, strong, gentle, mild, spell.

Terms
temperature, thermometer, rainfall, gauge, weather/wind vane, wind sock, wind rose, wind direction, anemometer, shelter, shade, diary, record, chart, symbol, period, season, moisture, heat, polar, tropical, temperate.

Sayings
rainbow, dawn, dusk, thunderbolt, squalls, crunchy snow, bitter wind, cats and dogs, mackerel skies, mares tails.

Figure 1:
Weather vocabulary appropriate for the end of year 2.

OBSERVING AND RECORDING

Level 1

Observing and talking about a familiar place on a regular basis emphasises the idea that weather changes from day to day. Once a class is settled, more systematic observation and ways of recording can be developed. Take specific weather types, e.g. warm weather, cold weather, wet weather, windy and foggy weather. In the autumn term a late warm spell (Indian summer) can link with holidays past and to come (many members of ethnic groups visit their homeland in December/January). As the weather is changing, symbols can be devised and used (see Figure 2). The symbols can be matched to pictures for each kind of weather. Have ready clothes suitable for dressing a cardboard figure or teddy for each season, to help the understanding that weather influences what we wear. The children's understanding of changes in weather can be assessed by matching the clothes to the symbols at the end of the week.

Start using a thermometer by year 1 – there are specially large ones for infants. Look at the daily newspaper report to see if any other places had the same temperature. In Britain, the north cools down more quickly than the south in autumn, and spring temperatures are correspondingly later in rising. In winter the west is usually warmer than the east and vice versa in summer. These ideas can be developed by looking at children in different climates and talking about the weather and what to wear in hot and cold places (see Kindersley and Kindersley, 1995). Locate these places on the globe and relate to the Poles and Equator.

As number work becomes more secure, measurement can begin with more precision and questions asked about the element measured. Collect rain in a wide container, then measure it in a tall, narrow container - this maximises the smallest shower! Use consistent, non-standard measures, e.g. one jam jar per day. Decide which way the wind is blowing – use the playground compass to show that the direction is from where the wind is coming.

Understanding suitable clothing!
Photo: John Dominy.

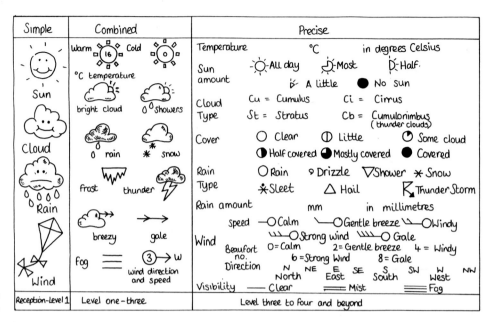

Figure 2:
Progression in
weather symbols.

Stand with backs to the wind and look at the way hair and clothes are blowing. Most winds are from the west or south west so the most sheltered place in the playground will be on the east side. Shadows help – they point to the west in the early morning, to the north at midday, and to the east at home time. At first, location language will be 'in front', 'behind' and so on but the four compass points can be casually introduced. Practice location language to describe the wettest, driest, hottest, coldest places at school, locally, in the world.

The elements produce different reactions, and we respond to them with all some of our senses: snow and frost are bright, cold and crunchy, and snow crystals make patterns. The following are questions that can be used to direct the children's learning about the various elements:

Rain and snow

- Why do we protect ourselves (and plants, buildings, etc.) from rain and snow?
- What is waterproof, and what waterproof materials are there?
- What happens to rain after it has fallen? (Compare trays of sand/soil, one covered with plastic to represent tarmac.)
- What happens to puddles? (Watch what happens to water in a saucer placed on a sunny window sill.)
- Why are roofs often different shapes in wet/dry places? (Look at sloping and flat roofs.)

Wind

- In what ways is the wind useful? Can it push things - us, sails, boats, mills? (Make a toy windmill.)
- What does wind do to litter in the streets?
- In what ways is the wind harmful?

Sun and shelter

- What is shelter? (Use a terrarium and a box model to consider the differences between greenhouses and ordinary houses.)
- Why do we wear shady hats and sun creams?
- How do animals and plants adapt to the sun and heat?

Level 2

By year 2 the ideas that rain and temperature can be measured, that weather has patterns and that different clouds are associated with different weather can be supported by more detailed and regular measurements using home-made equipment (see Figure 3). Plan to make reasonably accurate measurements of rain, temperature and wind for at least one week, three if possible, in more than one season.

Measuring wind direction. Photo: Elaine Jackson.

Level	Rain	Temperature	Wind	Air pressure
1/2	Collect in wide bowls, measure in narrow, tall jars, one per day.	Thermometers should all be alcohol filled. Giant ones make reading easy and develop good recording habits.	Use home-made wind vanes showing four compass points, and wind speed indicators which give higher readings the stronger the wind.	
3	Collect in a straight-sided, level-bottomed jar with a scale in millimetres facing inwards. Record the reading in mm each day at the same time.	Maximum-minimum thermometers (from good hardware stores or garden centres) show temperature is an ongoing change.	Hand held anemometers and ventimeters (more robust) measure wind speed. The best of three readings should be recorded.	Use a sensitive home-made barometer with a scale graduated between high and low pressure.
4	Collect in a jar placed inside a cylinder sunk into the ground (the cylinder, e.g. tall coffee tin, acts as a shield for the rain collection jar). The rain is collected via a 12.5cm diameter funnel resting on the top of the jar and measured in a standard science measuring cylinder, as with official gauges.	Wet and dry bulb thermometers allow humidity to be measured – the more humid the air the more equal the readings, and the more uncomfortable the air! Cheap thermometers/hygrometers from garden centres give similar results.	Anemometers can be connected to a digital recorder for constant readings. Link wind speed readings, taken at the same time as other observations, to the eight points of the compass and the Beaufort Scale (Figure 4). Record on a wind rose.	Use an aneroid (banjo) barometer and link the readings to Radio 4 shipping forecasts. The concept of rising and falling pressure becomes interesting when considering storms at sea and the lines of equal pressure (isobars) shown on weather maps.
graph	Bar *Discontinuous data*	Line *Continuous data*	Circular *Directional data*	Line *Continuous data*

Figure 3: Progression in measuring techniques.

The following are some suggestions for activities at this level:

- Link weather observations with myths and legends (e.g. 'Persephone and the wind' from Legends of the *Sun and Moon*, Cambridge University Press) Weather poems (*Hot Dog and other Poems*, Penguin).
- Make picture maps.
- Role play as weather forecasters.
- Use different words to describe moisture from dew, fog, mist, rainspots, showers, drizzle to downpours, storms and blizzards (thus making links between English and geography).
- Combine and extend weather symbols (see Figure 2).
- Use grid plans of the playground and neighbourhood to locate the best places for sun, shade and shelter, and refer to the four compass points.
- Use fair tests to show evaporation from puddles or containers left outside.
- Show how steam from a jug kettle condenses on to a cold surface.
- Use two plants, water one only, to show the importance of rain to growth.
- Link wind with clouds - are all the clouds moving in the same direction as the wind (usually this is so)?
- Use a toy windmill to measure winds of different strengths.
- Translate the Beaufort Scale into pictures (see Figure 4). The children could make felt shapes from the pictures, then sew or glue them onto card as part of a display about the weather.

Force No	Symbol	Name	Wind speed kph	mph	Effect
0		calm	0	0	Smoke rises straight up
1		light air	1-5	1-3	Smoke drifts. Wind vane does not turn
2		light breeze	6-11	4-7	Leaves rustle. Wind vane moves
3		gentle breeze	12-19	8-12	All leaves move. Flags flutter
4		moderate breeze	20-28	13-18	Small branches move. Litter blows
5		fresh breeze	29-38	19-24	Waves on water. Small trees sway
6		strong breeze	39-49	25-31	Large branches move. Wires whistle
7		near gale	50-61	32-38	Trees bend. Umbrellas useless
8		gale	62-74	39-46	Branches break. Difficult to walk
9		strong gale	75-88	47-54	Tiles blown off. Fences down
10		storm	89-102	55-63	Trees uprooted. Buildings damaged
11		violent storm	103-117	64-70	Widespread damage (rare in UK)
12		hurricane	118+	71+	Devastation to everything (not in UK)

Tick on symbol shows direction. Feathers increase by half a feather per stage.

Current weather reports give speed in mph. Wind measurer scales are in mph, kph or metres per second.

Figure 4: Beaufort Scale.

Progression in measuring techniques

It is helpful if there is a whole-school policy about the kind of weather symbols to be used, and the progression of those symbols (see Figure 2). There should also be agreement on progression in the use of measuring equipment (Figure 3 shows the ideal development for the main elements). Finally, agree on when detailed weather observations will take place and the audience for whom they will be useful.

Weather and the National Curriculum: key stage 2

Key stage 1 work provides a good foundation upon which more precise observations can be made, leading to the recognition of patterns and the analysis of evidence. Evidence can be collected in the school grounds, collected as part of a study of a contrasting locality, and collected through using a fax and other information and communications technology. What is important is that the evidence is integrated with the study of places and other themes such as environmental change. In the context of locality studies, weather can be identified as an important contributor to the character of a locality and therefore as a characteristic to be used when comparing one place with another – in this place, rain falls mainly in daily thunder storms throughout the year; in that place, droughts happen for months rather than weeks, and so on. In turn, these characteristics influence human activities and can, in the case of prolonged drought, for instance, lead to profound changes.

Weather information about places around the world can be gathered from daily world reports in newspapers, and used to help develop children's understanding of climate. Newspapers, and other news media, are also useful as sources of information about world events which may be directly or indirectly related to weather conditions. So, for example, a volcanic eruption or earthquake, while not being directly related to weather, raises questions concerning shelter and warmth for victims of the events. Similarly, children's appreciation of seasonal weather patterns could be fostered by asking them to think about what clothes an aid worker might take when visiting places where disasters have occurred.

An insight into the ways in which micro-climate may influence land use in a locality can be developed through work in the school grounds. For example, measurements taken of the amount of rain, sun and wind in different parts of the playground can lead to discussions about the siting of vineyards on south-facing slopes, or of forests or ski slopes on north-facing ones.

YEARS 3/4

The lower junior child should be able to recognise that weather not only changes from day to day but also during each month and year. Combining more precise observations serves to show that sunshine does not always mean high temperatures and that rainy days can be mild – depending upon which way the wind is blowing. In order to study variations over time and space, the daily recording sheet needs to become more specific (see Figure 5).

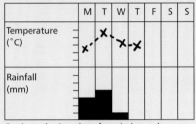

Year 3/4
Record for three or four weeks, at the same time each day.
With a young, inexperienced class start with symbols.

Progress from pictogram graphs to linear (temperature), bar (rainfall) and circular (cloud and wind) graphs.

Week beginning		Term							
		Mon	Tue	Wed	Thu	Fri	Sat	Sun	
Temperature	°C °F								
Rainfall									
Cloud cover									
Wind speed									
Direction									

	M	T	W	T	F	S	S
Temperature (°C)							
Rainfall (mm)							

Begin gathering clues for wind speed from a Beaufort Scale (see Figure 4).

Figure 5:
Progression and differentiation in recording at key stage 2.

Which way the wind blows.
Photo: Wendy Morgan.

With weather data from around the world available in the daily papers and on Ceefax/Oracle, responsibility for collecting data for several places can be delegated to 'roving reporters'. Ceefax can be recorded, and the weather maps and information from several papers brought in on a daily basis. These in turn will stimulate class discussions upon the design of symbols as well as providing information about contrasting localities and other places of significance. Weather forecasting encourages accuracy in estimating temperatures and amounts of rain and involves children thinking about the importance of being able to predict the weather for people in different occupations. Design technology can be used to make reasonably accurate measuring equipment (see Figures 6, 7 and 8), and science can contribute towards understanding weather phenomena through simple experiments (see Chapter 15 for more ideas on the application of information and communications technology).

Wind

Wind is air moving from one place to another; it brings heat and moisture from the place it has just left. Consequently it is named after the place from which it is travelling. The west wind usually brings cool, wet weather to the British Isles, picked up over the Atlantic often in a series of low pressure conditions; the north wind, regardless of the time of year, brings cold, clear or stormy conditions from the polar regions; easterly winds in winter bring snow, frost and fog, coming as they do from a continent that is very much colder than our islands. In summer, this position is reversed, with long spells of hot, dry winds, and heat waves in July and August, for now Europe and further east is very much hotter than Britain. In each season the air pressure is usually high.

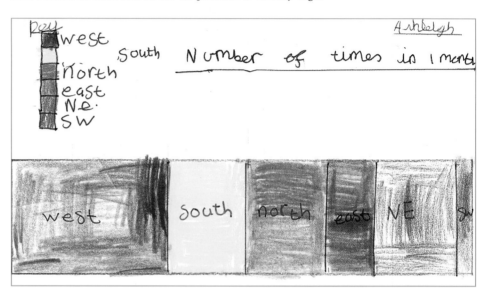

Charting wind direction. Work: Newbottle Primary School, Sunderland.

Sometimes the British Isles are engulfed in warm, humid air – very welcome in winter, unpleasant in summer. This air has originated over the Tropics, in the region of the Azores. Britain's weather can often be explained as a battle between cold air from Polar regions meeting warm air from tropical regions.

In teaching about wind it is important to discuss how the source of wind affects its character. Work with globes can be used to support discussions about television and radio weather reports, which usually refer to wind bringing weather, and science experiments can be used to help explain why land and water cool and warm up at different rates. Wind direction can be observed from the way dust, litter, leaves or tissue streamers blow in relation to the playground compass, a weather vane or wind sock. It can be recorded on a wind rose (see Figure 6). Use the UK map to mark on the wind directions in relation to your school. Do the winds cross land and sea? Could they have become drier before reaching you? Are winds from the west always wet?

Wind speed is a measure of the strength of the wind (see Figure 4). You could make several different wind measurers, such as a yoghurt pot anemometer (see Figure 6), and refer to an official ventimeter (school supplies or ship's chandlers) or anemometers (school scientific suppliers) and adjust the scales so that all measurements relate (calibrate). Using such instruments you could measure wind speeds in different parts of the school grounds noting, for example, if there are differences around corners, or between the top and bottom of a slope. You could also discuss how wind affects certain people, e.g. pilots, sea captains and athletes. Wind-generated electricity is a topic which has links with 'energy' in science and technology and which can be used to introduce ideas about the pros and cons of siting wind farms in scenic areas.

Look at the daily weather chart in a newspaper and relate wind speed to the distance between isobars. The isobars link places of equal pressure: close together means high speed winds; far apart means light winds or calm.

Studies of the kind suggested above will involve children in observing and recording, and their competence in these skills should be assessed, as should their understanding of wind direction and the character of winds.

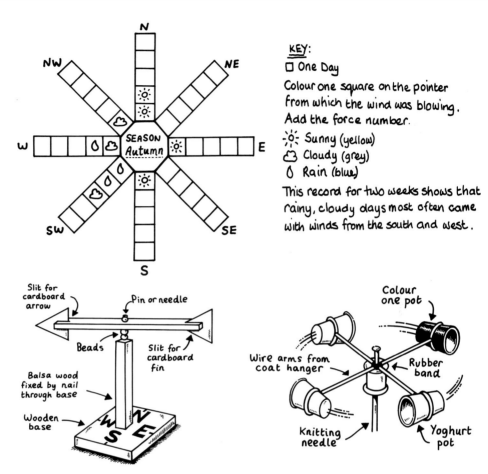

Figure 6:
Wind strength and direction (a) a wind rose, (b) a wind vane, and (c) a simple anemometer.

Rain

Wind brings moisture, usually in the form of rain. Fog and dew may occur when warm humid air meets colder conditions, as when the ground has cooled during the night. Clouds are the result of the same process at higher levels – which is why the tops of mountains are often shrouded in mist, while valleys are clear and sunlit. Condensation on a glass of iced water illustrates the formation of dew and fog, and clouds can be created by blocking a glass jar containing hot water with an ice cube. The water vapour from rising, warm, moist air cools to form a cloud under the ice. Rain falls when the droplets of condensed moisture are large and heavy enough to drop through the rising air beneath the cloud. They can be small (drizzle) or as large as hailstones. All the different forms of 'rain', including snow, are known as precipitation.

Measuring rain can be frustrating and disappointing – even when it rains heavily only a small amount will collect in a gauge (see Figure 7). This is why the longer the observation period the more probable it is that significant data will be collected. Gauges can be positioned at contrasting sites round the school (such as under trees, at the foot of an east-facing wall (sheltered from rain-bearing westerly winds), in a puddle area, in a 'dry' area) and similar and different results noted, with reasons.

National forecasts predict rain at home and elsewhere. Their accuracy can be checked against actual measurements, and the relationship of precipitation to other features such as wind and amount of cloud cover noted. Photographs and reports of the effects of prolonged rain or prolonged drought (both at home and abroad) could be collected, and discussions held about the consequences of such extreme conditions for, e.g. farmers, tourists and water suppliers.

Work: Ainthorpe Primary School, Hull.

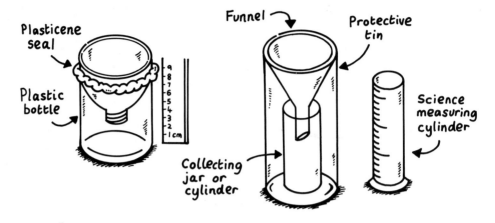

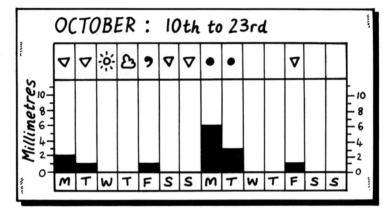

Total mm divided by number of days recorded or total for each of seven days divided by seven, then sum totals for each week and divide by the number of weeks, e.g. 4 weeks 0 monthly average.

Figure 7:
Measuring and recording rain.

Clouds

The appearance of clouds, and the patterns they make, are good indicators of weather to come and there is a rich vocabulary associated with their description (see Figure 8).

When recording the type of cloud and amount of cover, it is important to use the same window each day and to estimate cover in terms of either quarters or eighths (oktas). When learning cloud types, choose a week when lows, depressions or 'unsettled weather' are forecast coming in from the west, and make it an end-of-morning or afternoon game. Connect the weather observations with forecasting. Can the children forecast the afternoon weather from the morning observations?

Language	Description	Type and abbreviation		Height	Weather
Wispy, mares' tails, curls	High streaks fanning out ahead	Cirrus	Ci	High	Often more wind; usually storms after good weather
Sheet, layers, blanket	Blanket of low grey cloud which can reach the ground	Stratus	St	Low to high	Drizzle, fog which can become steady, wet, rain
Billowy, fluffy, heaps	White, flat-bottomed clouds which look like cotton wool	Cumulus	Cu	Low	Small – fair and sunny Large – showers
Dark, towers, castles	Large, dark clouds from ground to the highest level	Nimbostratus	Ns	Medium	Heavy rain or snow
Dark base, billowy towers	Marked, dark base which gets darker as rest of white cloud billows up to anvil shape	Cumulo-nimbus	Cb	Low to high	Very heavy showers with hail, thunder, lightning. Move away at speed

Figure 8:
Cloud characteristics.

A changing seasons weather display. Photo: Steve Rawlinson.

Temperature

When studying 'hot places' and 'cold places' it is important that children understand the temperature variations that occur in these places either between day and night, or between seasons. For example, even in hot deserts the soaring heat of the daytime may be replaced with sub-zero temperatures by the end of the night, and Polar regions can be as hot during the day in summer as places much nearer the Equator.

There are specialist thermometers which can be used to develop understanding of temperature variations over time. For example, maximum-minimum thermometers, which record and 'save' the lowest and highest temperatures (Figure 9), are used regularly by gardeners to monitor changes between night and day temperatures. Using, or describing such thermometers will help children to understand why 'tender' plants used to Mediterranean conditions, e.g. geraniums and busy lizzies (*Impatiens*), have to be kept indoors until late May or June when all danger of the night temperature falling below zero (frost conditions) is past. Readings from these thermometers can be matched with cloud observations: Was there a blanket of cloud overnight, preventing the loss of warm air, or could the stars be seen? With what night-time cloud conditions are morning hoar frost or heavy dew associated? Predictions about such temperature changes can be part of the class weather forecast.

Figure 9:
Measuring and recording temperature.

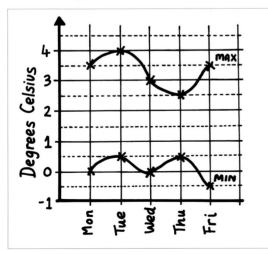

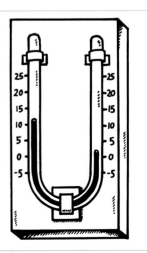

Ask questions:

- What was the highest temperature you recorded?
- When did this occur? Where?
- What was the lowest temperature?
- How much cloud cover was there?
- What was the range of temperature?

For at least one day each season record the temperature every hour for as long as possible and make charts and graphs to compare the daily and seasonal changes. (Thermosticks and digital thermometers use electronic probes which can be used to measure ground temperatures as well as air temperatures, so if you have access to either or both of these it is worth using them to compare recordings made by different instruments.) Extend the exercise by measuring the differences between south- and north-facing sites in the school grounds at each season. Graph the results and compare them with records from other seasons and other places. Experiment with different sites round the school building, putting the thermometer in full sun, shadow and the same place in different classrooms. Make a map and link recordings to compass directions – which way do the warmest rooms face? Remember that all 'official' readings are shade readings and are therefore lower than readings made in full sun.

Year 5/6: Increased detail in observing, in number of observations and in number of locations.

Key	Monday		Tuesday		Wednesday		Thursday		Friday	
Temperature °C	min	max	min	max	min	max	min	max	min	max
Sun: ○ all day ◐ most ◑ half ◔ a little ● no sun										
Cloud cover: ○ clear ◕ little ◑ some ◔ much ● covered										
Cloud type: Ci Cu St Cb										
Visibility: clear mist/haze fog										
Rain type: ○ rain drizzle ▽ showers ❄ snow △ hail sleet Thunder										
Rain mm										
Pressure: ⇧ rising ⇩ falling										
Wind strength calm gentle windy strong gale										
Beaufort speed										
Wind direction: N, NE, E, SE, S, SW, W, NW										

Groups can collect specific data, e.g. **temperature** and sun, **cloud** and visibility, **rain** and pressure, **wind speeds and direction**. Over four weeks, using a carousel system, everybody could have a chance to collect all types of data. Those elements in bold type are for younger or less able children and could all be collected by one group.

Figure 10:
Progression and differentiation in recording at key stage 2.

Weather records
The types of temperature reading suggested above measure temperature extremes. The temperatures given for places in general are average readings, usually of midday temperatures (note that the news weather reports give the time of observation for all the readings).

Figure 10 shows a sample recording sheet. Before using such a record sheet, take one lesson to explain and demonstrate how to take readings and discuss why the site(s) need to be away from walls and corners, on flat ground and protected from sun and wind. Thereafter allow 10 minutes per day for group measurement and 20 minutes for entering the data onto the record sheet or a database. The start of school, lunch time or just before the end of school are the least disruptive times – but must be the same time for each day for results to be valid. With practice this becomes quicker – encourage the 'spare' time to be used to compare current with previous readings and the newspaper and Ceefax readings. At the end of each week plan a reporting session where the weather patterns are discussed and forecasts made for the coming weekend and week ahead. Link to football, festivals and other newsworthy events. Consider if weather-sensitive work such as window cleaning high buildings, foot deliveries, road or air and sea transport will be affected by 'bad' conditions. This can be extended to include discussion of holidays and other first-hand experiences.

YEARS 5/6

Weather and climate

Upper juniors who regularly observed and recorded weather earlier in their school career are in a good position to consider weather patterns at different scales and contexts beyond the school grounds and local area. Comparisons with other places and contrasting localities will have been built up over the years making a foundation for the study of seasons and climates on a global scale.

Weather is the condition prevailing at a moment in time in a particular place. The pattern of weather over time in a particular place is its climate, or 'average weather'. In general distance from the Equator is the key factor in determining climate, with distance from open water a close second and finally the influence upon seasons of the Earth's tilt and orbit (Figure 11). Upper juniors should be aware of these patterns and their global distribution, and should make comparisons between the climate in their own locality and others around the world.

Good school atlases have sample climate graphs for rainfall and temperature in locations around the world. Using these graphs, children can be asked to find the hottest, wettest, coldest, driest months selected in regions. The climate maps of each country can be used to locate your contrasting locality and to decide what weather changes to expect over a year. If possible obtain a satellite view of the world which shows the major areas of natural vegetation and discuss how these are related to climatic conditions.

It must be understood that climate figures are averages of daily weather figures. Use your own records to demonstrate average temperatures/rainfall for each week of observations in the school year. Repeat for a whole month if possible. Gather together information on precipitation and temperature for your region for a whole year. It is possible to do this from the daily newspaper weather data, which includes weekends and holidays. Other sources are the local weather centre, the local reference library (which keeps back issues of most newspapers), the Meteorological Office or a local secondary school. Average each month of the 'official' records, i.e. average 30/31 records or four average weekly records per month. Discuss whether the hottest, wettest and other extreme readings are obvious. Make a climate graph for your own locality and, if possible, for your contrasting localities. Because the figures are averages, comparisons are much easier. Relate the differences observed in climate to such things as farming, holidays and clothes.

Members of the class could act as foreign correspondents who report back on weather conditions in your contrasting localities. This works particularly well if their locality or its region is prone to extreme conditions such as tropical storms (hurricanes), monsoon flooding, severe snow falls or season-long droughts when the rains fail. Reports can also include reference to the lack of spring and autumn in tropical lands, and the 12 hour day; in these areas, where the sun rises each day at 6.00am and sets at 6.00pm, the seasons are identified by differences in the amount of rain that falls rather than by extremes of temperature.

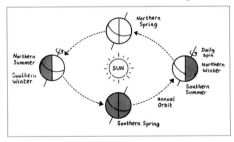

Figure 11:
Why there are seasons. Demonstrate the movement with a central light and small globe on its stand (this keeps the tilt).

Microclimates

The use of more than one site in the school grounds to show variations caused by different conditions has already been mentioned. For upper juniors the number of sites can be extended to at least four, relating these to compass points or to plans for locating new seating, flower tubs, animal hutches or a pond (Figure 12). You may be able to broaden the study into the local area for similar projects - a sheltered corner for elderly people to rest, a suitable site for a greenhouse on the allotments, the construction of bus shelters against the wind and rain. Temperature, amount of sun, type and amount of rain, and speed and direction of wind all have significance. At this level readings should be made from accurate instruments with the emphasis on making precise readings. This enables comparisons to be made with official and other automatic readings.

Name:	Date:		Day:	
Elements	**Location 1** name	**Location 2** name	**Location 3** name	**Location 4** name
temperature				
rainfall				
wind direction				
wind speed				
shade/sun				
other observations, e.g. dryness of ground; litter; vegetation; height of nearby buildings; slope; near water, e.g. lake, stream; current land use.				

This data can be entered on a spreadsheet to facilitate analysis. If working in a small area, one group per day can visit all sites in the same period and obtain immediate feedback on the contrasts.

Work in groups of three (two observers, one recorder) on a rota. All readings to be made in the same part of each day.

If working in the locality (home or contrasting) divide the observations by element: one group takes temperature readings; another considers wind features; another the light conditions, using a light meter (this covers both shade and sun in different aspects). Rain observations will have to be qualitative or based on humidity (i.e. degree of dryness). The compass direction (aspect, i.e. facing which way?) should be noted for each site and related to the wind observations. (All these observations will benefit from the use of portable logging devices linked to pocket computers.)

If possible look at the different locations for at least a week at different seasons. After the first set of observations, estimate the kind of changes to expect in the new season, particularly in cases where the observations are connected with an environmental/community issue such as the siting of a bus shelter or other feature.

Figure 12:
Recording on more than one site.

The variations found between sites can be used to explain differences at larger scales in the landscape. For example, in mountainous regions forests often grow on north-facing shadowed slopes while the south-facing slopes are used to grow hay and pasture to feed animals from the warmest spring days to late autumn. You could also look at how long, narrow, deep valleys funnel winds, leading to damaging gales as in the case of the Mistral winds of southern France. Note also how trees, hedges, and walls all affect wind speed and direction, and can therefore be used to protect crops and buildings.

Air pressure

Winds, dry or wet, are the consequence of different air pressures at the Earth's surface. This can be demonstrated on a small scale by observing how air spirals over warm radiators, and by asking why hot air balloons rise, and why cold air is felt coming from the bottom of a fridge or freezer. All illustrate the principle that hot air rises and is replaced by cold air. Thus, air at the Equator, where the sun's rays are concentrated (because of the curvature of the earth) becomes hot, rises and spreads north and south in the upper atmosphere. It is replaced by colder air moving at lower levels from the Poles which are less warmed by the sun. The surfaces of land and ocean, which heat up and cool at different rates (replicate with soil and water under a heat element in science), lead to inequalities in air pressure resulting in the movement of air masses from place to place.

When studying television and other weather maps, notice how wind arrows point outwards from those areas marked high pressure, often over central Europe. For us in Britain this usually means dry, settled weather. That dry air is often replaced with damp winds moving inwards as centres of low pressure, bringing rain into the Mediterranean or, on a larger scale, bringing the monsoon rains into south-east Asia. Similar conditions operate between the Sahara high pressure and low pressure areas bringing in rain from the south Atlantic. Sometimes, because of unusual pressure conditions, the rain bearing air masses fade away (fail). In Britain the resultant drought leads to hose pipe bans, in the Sahel region of West Africa it means harvest failure and famine for cattle and people.

To engage children, and to bring relevance to studies of air pressure using barometer readings and automatic readings (see Figure 13), you could try the following role play exercise. First make a tape recording of a shipping forecast (broadcast on Radio 4 at 6.00am, 2.00pm, 6.00pm and midnight). These forecasts include pressure readings and say whether pressure is rising (a low pressure, rainy spell ending) or falling (a high pressure, settled spell ending). Wind direction is given, followed by strength, then force, and the changes likely, then precipitation and visibility are described. The forecast starts in the north east (Viking) and moves clockwise around Britain.

Divide the class into groups, and allocate one area to each. Each group is given the role of a sailor in a yacht. Listen to the tape, several times if necessary, noting details for the selected areas. Most areas can be located next to their mainland name: Forth, Tyne, Humber, Thames, Dover, Wight, Portland, Plymouth, Lundy (Bristol Channel), Irish Sea, Malin (North Ireland), Hebrides. Using a UK map, plot the wind direction and direction of pressure movement observed by each group. Look at your own pressure readings from an aneroid barometer (see Figure 13) and decide from which way and what type of weather is coming – in from the Atlantic or off mainland Europe. Look at your own observations and the newspaper report and discuss how each 'sailor' would be affected by the weather changes that were forecast. You could also discuss how the weather would affect fishermen, and various coastal and inland activities.

Extreme weather conditions

Tropical storms (hurricanes), monsoons, tropical droughts, bush fires and heavy snow (blizzards) all represent deviations from usual climatic patterns and all receive special mention in reference books, information software, atlases and on the world wide web. Gather together groups to work on specific topics to make presentations on these topics, using ICT packages. These presentations can be made at assemblies or in the form of special displays for open days, using a world satellite map as the focus. Assessment could be via question and answer sessions with peers and visitors.

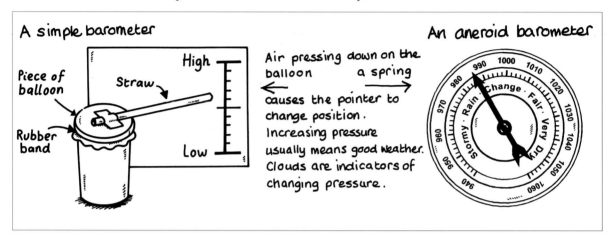

Figure 13:
Equipment for measuring air pressure.

Recording for the future

Weather studies in the primary curriculum offer many opportunities for developing and using skills in recording and observation. In addition, they encourage children to think about the reasons behind some of the similarities and differences between areas around the world, and to empathise with those whose lives are dependent on or directly affected by weather conditions. Also, by keeping and maintaining weather records over long periods, children are part of a long and valuable tradition of weather watching that goes back at least as far as Roman and Greek times.

While the increased detail and accuracy of modern weather observation has obvious benefits for us all, even simple methods, such as those we use in our schools, still enable us to make useful predictions. And our records, which may span many years or decades, are things of value which, in future years, will provide a rich source of information about past patterns and changes.

References and further reading

Chambers *et al.* (1989) 'Viewing the earth from space', *Primary Geographer*, 1, pp. 7-10.

Cowcher, H. (1990) *Tropical Rainforest*. London: Picture Corgi

Cunnliffe, J. (1983) *Postman Pat*. London: Hodder.

Gray, N. and Ray, J. (1991) *A Balloon for Grandad*. London: Orchard Books.

Hadley, E. (1983) *Legends of the Sun and Moon*. Cambridge: Cambridge University Press

Harrison, P. and Harrison, S. (1997) *Time and Place*. London: Simon and Schuster/Stanley Thornes. (The teachers guides in the series show progression and differentiation in a cross-curricular context at specific levels and with many practical ideas.)

Harrison, S. and Havard, F. (1997) *The Weather Book for Primary Teachers*. London: Simon and Schuster.

Kindersley, B. and Kindersley, A. (1995) *Children Just Like Me*. London: Dorling Kindersely/UNICEF.

Manley, G. (1952) *Climate and the British Isles (New Naturalist Series)*. London: Collins. (A readable explanation of weather in different places in Britain. Obtainable from libraries.)

SCAA (1997) *Expectations in Geography at Key Stages 1 and 2*. London: SCAA.

Morgan, W. and Bunce, V. (1992) 'Landscapes and weather, volcanoes and hurricanes', *Primary Geographer*, 9, pp. 6-7.

Morgan, W. and Bunce, V. (1995) 'Devastating Debbie (a hurricane)', *Primary Geographer* (St Lucia special), 22, pp. 28-29.

Salkey, A. (1980) *Caribbean Folk Tales and Legends*. London: Bogle L'Ouverture.

Primary Geographer (1997) number 31. Sheffield: Geographical Association. (This issue focuses on weather.)

Smeaton, M. (1991) 'Project Thailand: a study of a tropical locality', *Primary Geographer*, 6, p. 2.

Warren, N. with Cambier, A. and Ranger, G. (1997) 'Geography meets French in the classroom: a contrasting locality study at key stage 2', *Primary Geographer*, 29, pp. 20-21.

Wright, K. (1982) *Hot Dog and Other Poems*. London: Puffin.

Useful addresses

Meteorological Office, Marketing Services, Sutton Building, London Road, Bracknell, Berks RG12 2SZ. Tel: 01344 854818. (Supplies details of fax and satellite services, and specific help on weather studies including weather forecast logging maps.)

INFORMATION AND COMMUNICATIONS TECHNOLOGY

Advisory Unit, Computers in Education, 126 Great North Road, Hatfield, Herts AL9 5JZ. Tel: 01707 266714. (Supplies *Weather Reporter*, an automatic weather recorder and guide.)

(BECTa/NCET), Sir William Lyons Road, University of Warwick Science Park, Coventry CV4 7EQ. Tel: 01203 416994. (Supplies data packages and literature.)

SECC, Church Lane, Hixon, Stafford ST18 0PS. Tel: 01889 271317. (Supplies weather files for *PaintSpa* and other ICT information.)

SoftTeach, Sturgess Farmhouse, Longbridge Deverill, Warminster, Wiltshire BA12 7EA. Tel: 01985 840 329. (Supplies *Weather Watch* which automatically dates data entries on a rolling spreadsheet for each month, includes a file with data from a school in Bath for 1992. Graphs include wind roses. The teachers notes are clear and helpful.)

TAG, Freepost TU 823, Great Western House, Langport, Somerset TQ10 9BR. Tel: 01458 253636. (Supplies *Weathermapper* which allows weather maps to be drawn from collected data.)

WEATHER MEASURING EQUIPMENT

Thermometers, rain gauges, anemometers and weather vanes are available from:

Griffin and George, Bishops Meadow, Loughborough, Leics LE11 0RG. Tel: 0116 233344. (Also sensors for LOGIT)

Invicta Plastics, PO Box 9, Oadby, Leicester LE2 4LB.

MJP Geopacks, 92-104 Carnwath Road, London, SW6 3HW.

TTS Ltd, Unit 4, Holmewood Fields Business Park, Park Road, Holmewood. Chesterfield S42 5UW.

Chapter 23: Weather and climate

The content of this chapter lends itself to ICT applications (Chapter 15), to work in and around the school grounds (Chapter 14) and to cross-curricular links with, for example, science and technology (Chapter 7).

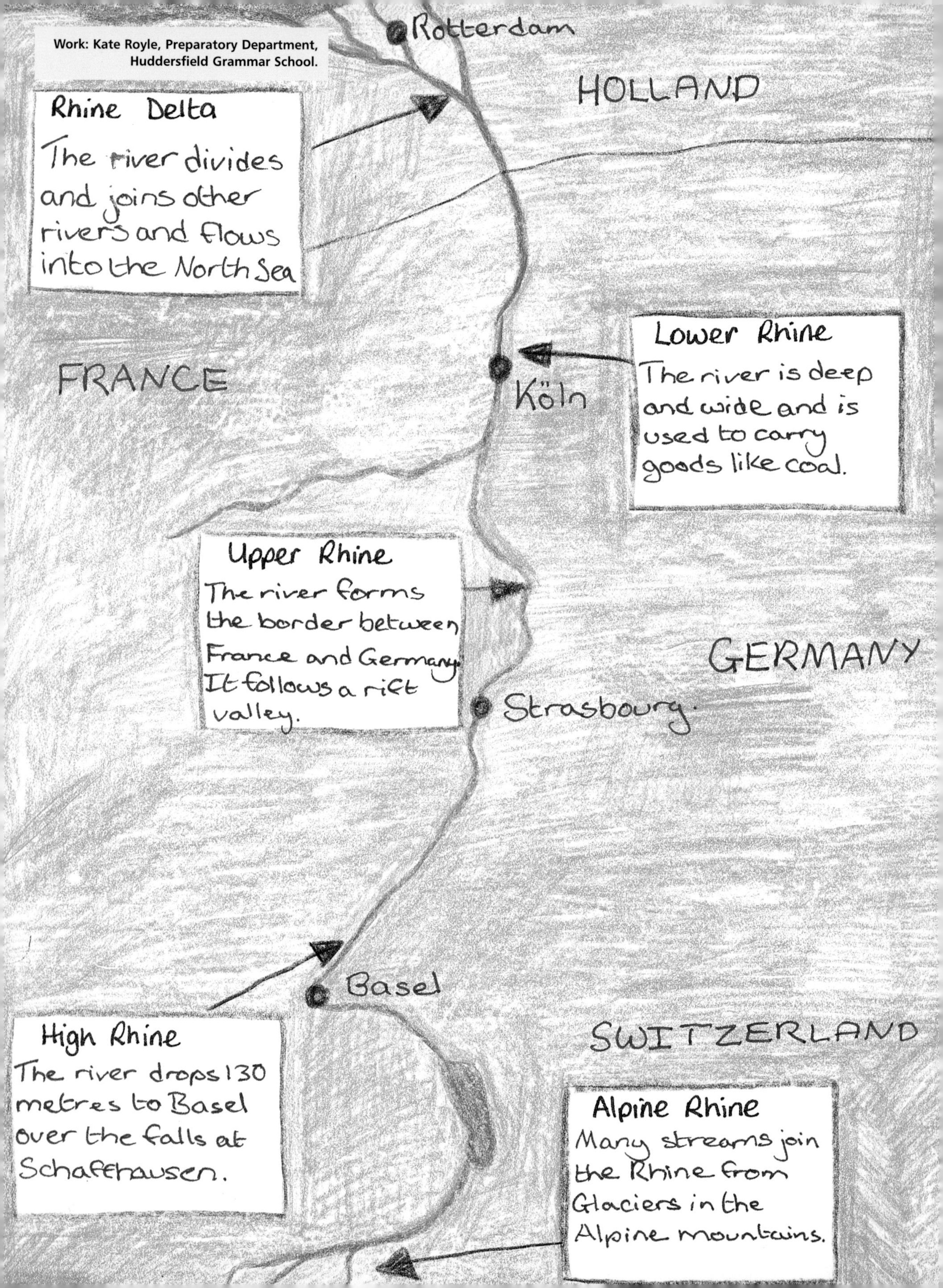

Rotterdam
HOLLAND
Rhine Delta
The river divides and joins other rivers and flows into the North Sea
FRANCE
Köln
Lower Rhine
The river is deep and wide and is used to carry goods like coal.
Upper Rhine
The river forms the border between France and Germany. It follows a rift valley.
GERMANY
Strasbourg.
Basel
SWITZERLAND
High Rhine
The river drops 130 metres to Basel over the falls at Schaffhausen.
Alpine Rhine
Many streams join the Rhine from Glaciers in the Alpine mountains.

Work: Kate Royle, Preparatory Department, Huddersfield Grammar School.

Rivers

Chapter 24

Liz Lewis

The delight all children have in playing by the water's edge provides an excellent starting point for teachers planning work in physical geography, and remembering our own childish explorations of the physical environment can be a powerful tool in the designing of appropriate activities. For it is surely in the children's best interests that we begin by attempting to view the features we want them to investigate, through their freshly enquiring eyes and not our own more knowledgeable and jaded ones.

This may well be less difficult for a non-specialist teacher than it is for a more experienced 'geographer'. It is all too easy for those with an enthusiastic interest in the formation of physical features to slip into the use of specialist terminology and to try to communicate detail about erosional and depositional processes in ways that the children are not yet ready to accept. Someone to whom the work is new, on the other hand, may not only be able to gauge the children's starting points more aptly, but can also share in any subsequent enquiry more sincerely. It is also comforting to the non-specialist to realise that at this early stage in geographical education successful induction into that process of enquiry is at least as important as any factual knowledge gained from it.

Geography as a subject is essentially investigative. Physical geography is less a series of facts to be learned than a series of questions about the processes shaping the environment which can be explored at a level appropriate to the learner. This is recognised in the National Curriculum when it advocates direct experience, practical work, exploration, investigations based on fieldwork, and above all, the idea of teaching through 'geographical questions' which underpins the entire programmes of study.

Happily, these requirements make it essential that we undertake some work in the field, and this immediately raises the profile of geography in children's eyes! Like all outdoor activity, river investigation will need careful planning, especially to ensure safety, but if it is to be truly investigative it should not demand any greater depth of teacher knowledge than is included here.

This chapter is intended primarily to support field study to develop understandings relating to water in the landscape. Since it is acknowledged that for financial reasons school-based teaching will need to supplement, and sometimes even replace, field experiences, the suggestions for key stage 1 are based around and within the school grounds. Initial understandings which underpin the rivers theme in key stage 2 can thus be built within early studies of the immediate locality and local weather.

It is in key stage 2 that a focused study of rivers becomes appropriate. But this study need not be either very detailed or very specific; it can be accomplished by developing work around one or two very locally visitable field locations. Since the work could also be part of either an immediate or contrasting locality study, in which we are reminded to study the physical as well as the human characteristics of the chosen place, the key to both curricular and financial economy appears to lie in some judicious choices being made at whole-school planning level.

Pupils of Frosterly Primary School raise questions in an investigation of the Bowlees waterfalls in Teesdale. Photo: Liz Lewis.

Developing field opportunities

In most parts of Britain there is the possibility of encountering some running water within the local environment. Each school can, as part of its general 'locality appraisal', investigate this local water for its potential to help understanding in physical geography. By far the greater part of the physical geography input, and references to the work of rivers in particular, are now in key stage 2 and this chapter is, therefore, principally directed to supporting the successful teaching of that work. However there is still some opportunity to teach a little physical geography at key stage 1. It seems wise to do this in a way which can progress towards the more difficult ideas embodied in the junior curriculum.

First ideas about rivers

At key stage 1 the physical geography relating to landscape, i.e. 'the main physical features – e.g. rivers, hills' should be included within each locality study. So where the area local to the school, or the chosen contrasting locality, happens to includes a river or stream some general ideas about flowing water and some simple vocabulary such as 'river, stream, river bank, river bed, flow, bend, upstream and downstream' could be established as a valuable basis for later work. We might also encourage children to think about how humans make use of rivers and why valleys are important routeways.

Ourselves

Work about the effects of weather on ourselves can also assist the development of fundamental concepts about flowing water. Most children are aware that walking in the rain can be uncomfortable and that we need special clothing to keep dry. Beginning with the question 'How does waterproof clothing work?', children can be encouraged to explore the waterproof properties of materials as part of their science/technology work, but also, and more relevantly for geography, they can explore how water behaves on the surface of waterproof clothing, and how the shape of the surface directs its flow into creases and down slopes. The study of a sou'wester-style hat, whose shape directs water to flow down the back of the wearer, an umbrella whose spokes drip well away from the user, and plants whose leaves direct the water to drip onto the root base are also useful foci for enquiry. Young children might also be encouraged to study their own faces and think about how water flows over their body in the shower, how the eyebrows form a barrier which directs water around the eyes, and how we change the shape of our bodies by walking with heads down to protect our faces from the impact and discomfort of trickling water. It is a short step from here to understanding the behaviour of water on the uneven surface of a landscape.

Our stories

Judicious use of picture story books can be invaluable in this context too. Good examples include Jill Dow's *Webster's Walk* in the *Windy Edge Farm* series published by Frances Lincoln, which describes the effects of a drought on the ducks, and draws a very clear distinction between the still water of their pond and the moving water of the river; and Benedict Blathwayt's *Be Quiet, Bramble*, published for Sainsbury's by Walker Books, the story of a brave cow who saves her friends when they are marooned on a tiny patch of higher ground when the river suddenly floods. *Come Back Hercules* by Rob Lewis, a delightful rhyming saga published by Macdonals, is a bored goldfish who escapes via the loo to his local river and eventually finds his way down to the sea. Usefully, he passes many features of geographical interest on the way. I have seen this story colourfully retold by a class of infants and their teacher in a long thin wall 'map', detailing the sequence of the story and naming the important geographical features of Hercules' journey downstream.

Making rivers in the classroom

The wet sand tray is another valuable asset to early work on rivers. Hilly landscapes can easily be shaped by hand and valleys identified (Figure 1). It is quite difficult to demonstrate runoff simply by sprinkling 'rain' from a watering can, because the loose sand is so porous. But after trying this to show that water sinks into some surfaces, the landscape could be 'water-proofed' with thin polythene and the experiment repeated. A sprinkling of dry sand over the polythene should show that when streams develop they are capable of carrying loose material away, and depositing it somewhere else. Ponds or lakes can be engineered too. Teachers of older infant classes, who might not have a sand tray on hand, will find a length of plastic guttering and a selection of sands and gravel of different grain sizes useful for creating investigations into water flow and its capacity to move things (Figure 2).

Making land and waterscapes in a wet sand tray at key stage 1. Photo: John Dominy.

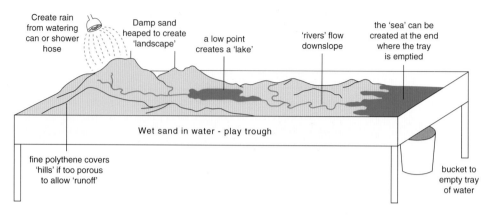

Create rain from watering can or shower hose

Damp sand heaped to create 'landscape'

a low point creates a 'lake'

'rivers' flow downslope

the 'sea' can be created at the end where the tray is emptied

Wet sand in water - play trough

fine polythene covers 'hills' if too porous to allow 'runoff'

bucket to empty tray of water

Figure 1:
Creating a river landscape in a wet sand tray.

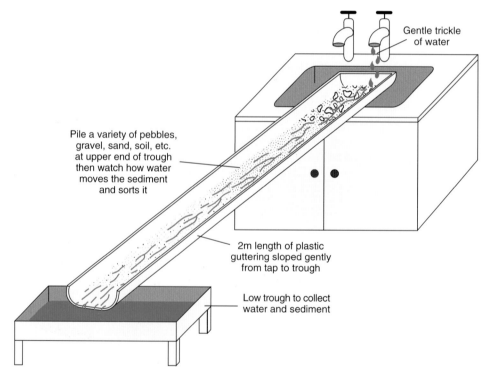

Gentle trickle of water

Pile a variety of pebbles, gravel, sand, soil, etc. at upper end of trough then watch how water moves the sediment and sorts it

2m length of plastic guttering sloped gently from tap to trough

Low trough to collect water and sediment

Figure 2:
Guttering is used to show how running water can move things.

Rivers in our school

Since the very existence of rivers is an 'effect of weather on our surroundings', river work might equally begin from a study of water and how it moves around the school. Whether your school has a flat or sloping roof there is some system for transferring rainwater to the ground. Leaky flat roofs, a scourge of many modern school buildings, can become a temporary asset, giving a good focal point for discussion of how surface water finds its way down. Models of flat, sloping and arched roof buildings could be undertaken as a technology project and evaluated for their effectiveness in shedding water.

A sloping roof amply demonstrates the idea of a watershed, in this case the roof ridge, which separates the flow on one side of the roof from that on the other. In exactly the same way, a ridge of high ground in a real landscape directs water down into one river system or another. A simple pictorial diagram could be made from observation of your own

Creating a temporary river.
Photo: Angela Milner.

school, to show the progress of the water via gutters and drainpipes to the ground. Where a flow of fresh water from a drainpipe (or any other source) can be directed onto the surface of the playground, children can watch what would happen if there was no organised drainage system (Figure 3). Finding an unobstructed path, the stream of water will create a temporary river flowing down to a low point and will possibly meander on the way. Overfilling existing puddles and watching where the water goes is another interesting source of discussion. Children might make detailed observations of puddles forming and disappearing and map puddles (Figure 4) and the likely courses of excess water in the playground with which they are already very familiar.

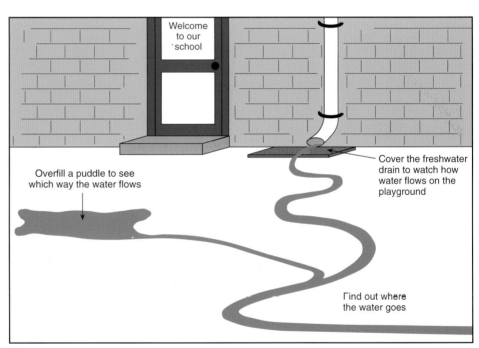

Figure 3:
Where water goes in the playground.

Welcome to our school

Overfill a puddle to see which way the water flows

Cover the freshwater drain to watch how water flows on the playground

Find out where the water goes

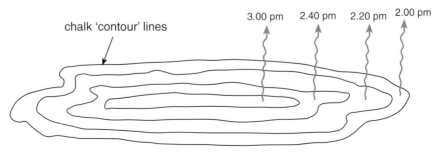

Figure 4:
How a disappearing puddle can be used to demonstrate evaporation and simple contour patterns.

chalk 'contour' lines

3.00 pm   2.40 pm   2.20 pm   2.00 pm

draw round drying up puddles at intervals
to discover how fast they evaporate

Our locality

If there is a very local small stream or river in your immediate area an opportunity to observe this will be part of the physical component of your locality study. Whilst young children should obviously not be encouraged to throw things into the water to see how they behave, they could conduct a simple experiment in which a floating biodegradable object is released into the current and its speed and path observed. If the river floods from time to time, the absence of houses near the river or the construction of flood protection barriers might form a good discussion point which links the human and physical aspects of local study.

The study of a riverside environment, such as a small park, nature reserve or public footpath, might also form part of the work specified under the 'quality of the environment' theme, within which simple visual investigations might be carried out into how clean the water is, whether people throw rubbish into the river, who uses the riverside and how this environment might be cared for or improved. Some schools in the Sunderland area have 'adopted' sections of the recently created 'River Wear Trail' giving even very young pupils an opportunity to engage with conservation and planning issues at first hand. Ruth Brown's strikingly illustrated picture story *The World that Jack Built*, published by Red Fox (1991), would be an excellent support for such work.

**Recording data near a canal.
Photo: Paula Richardson.**

The transition to key stage 2

It would be unwise to assume that any of the knowledge and understanding suggested above will be part of the usual repertoire of children just entering junior school. As all teachers are aware, concept development can be a long drawn out process which bears much revisiting and repetition of ideas. Consequently any of the above ideas for practice might apply equally well to the lower years of the junior phase. In any case, it is still the **local** river or stream which should form the ideal starting point for the key stage 2 physical geography theme. In the lower junior years this might again be first approached as part of the immediate locality study, and then given more depth in years 5 and 6, in the thematic study itself. If you have no local river then you will need to consider how this work can be covered by your choice of a contrasting UK locality, hopefully a visitable one.

What should I teach at key stage 2?

> In studying rivers and their effects on the landscape pupils should be taught:
>
> a   that rivers have sources, channels, tributaries and mouths, that they receive water from a wide area, and that most eventually flow into a lake or the sea.
>
> b   how rivers erode, transport and deposit materials, producing particular landscape features, e.g. valleys, waterfalls.

But these are not the only opportunities to develop understanding about river systems. The possible connection between the rivers theme and the immediate locality study has already been noted, as well as the opportunities for skills development offered by river work. In addition paragraph 5a of the key stage 2 programme reminds us that this theme could be extended through raising awareness of physical features (e.g. valleys), in studies of contrasting localities in the United Kingdom or overseas, and through further development of this theme into a European and, at the discretion of the teacher, a wider world context (paragraph 6).

The study of rivers is thus a good example to show that although the content of a particular theme may, at first, appear to be confined to a single paragraph of the document, 'the teacher's approach should be to use the whole of the geography programme of study in planning for progression through this work'. After all, it is unlikely that a single exposure to learning about rivers will be sufficient to teach what is required. A suitable plan for revisiting the topic in the course of key stage 2 might look something like Figure 5.

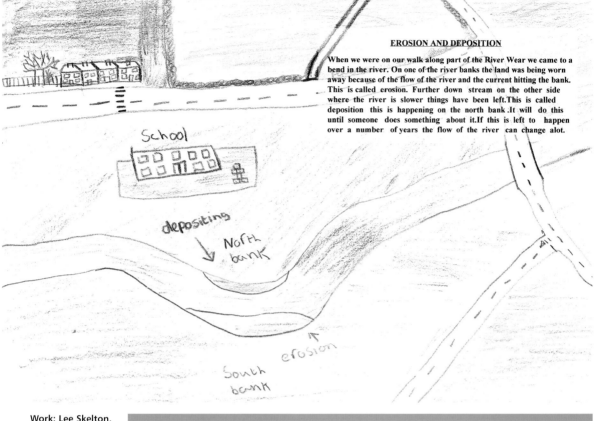

EROSION AND DEPOSITION

When we were on our walk along part of the River Wear we came to a bend in the river. On one of the river banks the land was being worn away because of the flow of the river and the current hitting the bank. This is called erosion. Further down stream on the other side where the river is slower things have been left.This is called deposition this is happening on the north bank .It will do this until someone does something about it.If this is left to happen over a number of years the flow of the river can change alot.

Work: Lee Skelton, Newbottle Primary School, Sunderland.

Figure 5: Key stage 2 plan for revisiting 'Rivers'.

Year	Activity
3	Looking at what happens to water in the school and its grounds. (Part of a science based topic.)
4	Land use and conservation of a local river is studied as part of an immediate locality study.
5	The rivers theme is explored through local fieldwork, with an emphasis on investigating physical features and processes.
6	The features and importance of the local river are compared to a river in a contrasting locality studied from secondary sources (e.g. a locality pack) or during a field visit to a contrasting place.

Cross-curricular considerations

Rivers are not only powerful shapers of physical landscapes but also exert powerful influences on human decisions about land use – where to site a capital city or a chemical plant, where to graze cattle rather than grow crops, which is the best route for a new motorway, or even just where to spend next Sunday afternoon. They are part of the natural water cycle, vital to industry, trade, factories and farming, needed for public water supply and transport, attractive as havens for wildlife sport and tourism, beautiful, calming and mysteriously appealing, but also dangerously powerful and terrifyingly destructive in times of flood.

So, as well as providing bridges across the geography curriculum, the study of rivers also offers convenient routeways into other subjects. The rivers theme may thus serve as a fruitful focus for more wide ranging cross-curricular study. From this point of view, a good addition to resources is to make a collection of picture books, story extracts, video-clips, news bulletins, newspaper extracts, photographs and artists' work in a number of styles which will support your work on rivers. This is obviously a long-term goal but the suggestions in the section below will help you to begin.

First steps into the field

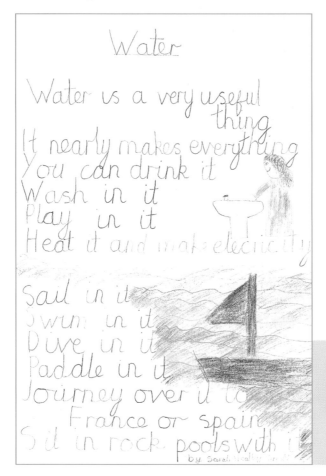

Water

Water is a very useful thing
It nearly makes everything
You can drink it
Wash in it
Play in it
Heat it and make electricity

Sail in it
Swim in it
Dive in it
Paddle in it
Journey over it to
    France or spain
Sit in rock pools with

by Sarah Healy

Work: Sarah Healey-Smith.

Undertaking independent fieldwork on rivers without the help offered by an experienced warden in a well-equipped field centre may seem daunting to anyone who does not regard themselves as a 'geographer'. It need not be. There is a ready source of excellent advice on all aspects of fieldwork planning and management in the Geographical Association's *Fieldwork in Action* series (see Chapter 14), and it is the intention of the remainder of this chapter to address other questions which primary teachers would need to ask about riverside work – in particular, questions such as:

■ Where should we begin?
■ What on earth do all these geographical words mean?
■ What subject knowledge do I need?
■ How will it feel in practice?

Where should we begin?

IN THE SCHOOL GROUNDS

Running water within the school grounds – in guttering and drains, overflowing from puddles and trickling down slopes, both natural and constructed – provides an initial focus for the study of running water. The children may well have encountered some experiences of this kind as part of their weather work in infant school, but in key stage 2 it can be given a different slant and develop into a more detailed study of what happens to rainwater when it reaches the ground.

As explained on page 332 the ridge of a roof sheds rainwater down one side or the other exactly as a ridge of land in a landscape does. Such a ridge in the landscape is aptly called a 'watershed'. In the case of a roof the water is shed into gutters, directed into down-pipes and disappears down freshwater drains into an underground drainage system which carries it to the nearest natural stream. Waste water and sewage, on the other hand, is transferred to a purifying plant before being released into the natural drainage system.

After children have seen how buildings cope with running water (asking for a drawing of where the water goes around their own homes is a good extension activity) an investigation into what happens on other surfaces around the school can be initiated. A survey to predict the distribution of puddles and small streams of water, and checking these predictions after rain has fallen, provides a good opportunity for adding detail to the familiar school plan and for comparing this to the aerial photograph in a search for other

Photo: John Dominy.

evidence of surface water. Major slopes could be marked on the map as coloured arrows and sloping areas scrutinised for signs of rainwash, as a simple introduction to erosion. Although this work may be similar in content to that described above for key stage 1 it is different in that it focuses on developing a more sophisticated set of geographical skills, making diagrams and maps, predicting and hypothesising, and beginning to draw attention to processes of erosion and deposition.

Children should be taught that in the landscape rainwater can become direct surface runoff, or seep into the soil where it is either used by growing plants or finds underground paths through permeable and porous rocks, either to be stored in underground reservoirs or to re-issue as a spring and resume its flow over the surface to the sea. But probably the most important single understanding in this work is that water flows downhill. This may seem to be too obvious to mention but is critical to any understanding of river systems. Many children entering secondary school believe, perhaps because they have seen a tidal river, or have been asked where a river 'rises' or have not fully understood the maps they have come across, that rivers 'begin' at the coast. The word 'mouth' adds to this confusion; after all, in the limited and personalised experience of young children, things usually do go in via mouths rather than come out!

BEYOND THE SCHOOL

A study confined to the school tells only part of a story; juniors need to pursue this towards a fuller understanding of how all water is returned ultimately to the sea. Nevertheless we have begun from local and first hand experience and so both children and teacher have taken significant steps towards field based enquiry. We need, next, to look for a visitable 'riverside locality' and consider its potential to support our geographical work.

This might vary from a small trickle in the local park to a vista of a major estuary like the Thames. In either case it is a useful learning environment. A deepening understanding requires us not only to teach children all about 'our river' and how it affects the immediate locality, but also to help them to view 'our river' in the whole context of river systems generally. If we are close to a busy river mouth, or a navigable and industrialised river, the starting points may be more appropriately grounded in a study of land use – the 'settlement geography' theme – but this can then be pursued into a consideration of why the river is there, where it has come from and what it is like upstream.

Studying a small
local stream.
Photo: Steve Rawlinson,
University of Northumbria
at Newcastle.

Conversely, if the school is well inland, an insignificant trickle of water on a local hillside can be pursued on foot and through mapwork towards its destination, in a programme of work that begins with local physical detail and progresses towards the human use of the downstream area. Good primary geography considers the human and physical worlds together and weighs up the influence of each on the other. It is natural that features which exist together in place should be considered together in the curriculum. As geographical work progresses in the junior school, from naming, describing and comparing towards explaining, the 'integrated geography' approach embodied in the 'cube diagram' becomes increasingly important.

What do all these 'geographical words' mean?

Already in this section a large number of geographical terms have been used which may not be immediately familiar, and which you may consider too difficult for the children you teach to be exposed to. Terms like 'upstream', 'tidal' and 'estuary' are not part of most children's usable vocabulary and we do need to tailor our use of terminology carefully for fear of alienating some children, or even colleagues! Nowhere is technical and commonplace vocabulary richer than in the description of water features – stream, burn, beck, falls, force, ghyll, puddle, pool, pond, mere, tarn, etc. Such is the variety of river sizes and features that even giving a name to your local water can be problematic. Exploring water feature names, distinguishing the local examples, locating these and agreeing the range to be used in different stages of the teaching is a worthwhile staff planning exercise.

For example, is the stretch of running water you have identified a 'stream', a 'tributary', a 'river', an 'estuary' or what? Instead of any of these it may have a local, colloquial name such as 'beck' or 'burn'. It is quite legitimate to ask when and where does a stream become a river, or a river an estuary? But you are unlikely to find a precise answer. There are no 'official' sizes at which these terms apply. Indeed, if there were a precise definition, say in terms of a flow rate of 'so many cubic metres per second', would it mean anything to an observer? Even converted to 'so many Olympic swimming pools per minute' it defies immediate visualisation. What these terminological uncertainties do imply, however, is that teaching children to name features is really an issue of inducting them at their own level into the whole nomenclature debate. 'What do you think we might call a feature like this?' is therefore always an essential 'key question'. Like any good 'open' question it has an expectation of a variety of answers and discussion of all possible answers is necessary to refine vocabulary and understanding.

Many children, quite apart from not being able to employ a vocabulary of comparative sizes, may not even be familiar with the idea that physical features have 'proper' names like people do. We may need to be very conscious of saying 'the River Trent' rather than just; 'the Trent' in the early stages of any work. Adding the three longest rivers, named in the National Curriculum, your own local rivers, and any others the children know about, to an enlarged UK map (making sure that you draw them in from source to mouth) is a simple way of raising this awareness and a good way of initiating discussion about sources, tributaries and mouths.

All questions of terminology become easier to grapple with, of course, the more regularly the children are exposed to new examples on different scales. It is a case of being alert to the opportunity to 'drip feed' additional ideas whenever the chance arises. The use of appropriate stories or newspaper cuttings can greatly assist this work so the Literacy Hour is a good time to support geographical learning. You could, for example, ask the class to make up a name for a river that is unnamed in the story, and to relate the features of this river to what they have been learning by drawing an imaginary map to show where they think it begins and ends and where along its banks the story is set. Freed by the imaginary setting from the constraints of achieving locational accuracy, the children will be able to show you what they know about rivers and maps, a useful interim assessment opportunity. It is essential, however, that we are well prepared to support their understanding of real rivers too, and this involves developing our own subject knowledge.

From time to time opportunities arise to join courses which involve subject knowledge induction at an appropriate level. Most of these offer a chance to develop understanding in the field, which may not have been part of our own school learning. Whilst it may seem daunting

---

Basic understandings to support river work at key stages 1 and 2

- water flows downhill
- water has the power to carry a 'load'
- a lot of water can carry more than a little water
- fast water can carry more than slow water
- when water slows down it carries less (drops some of the 'load')
- the 'load' is important as a scraping tool, it helps the river to erode the banks and bed
- rainwater is not pure because it picks up chemicals as it falls through the atmosphere and is therefore a weak acid (carbonic). So river water can dissolve soluble rocks
- some rocks (e.g. limestone, chalk) are soluble in a weak acid
- the pebbles in the river are carried by the water. This makes the pebbles roll or jump and, as they grind against each other, they become smooth and rounded

**Teachers on 'Rivers' INSET.
Photo: Chris Garnett.**

to take on new learning of this kind, especially if we have a personal stereotype of the big-booted hearty 'geographer', those who run the courses are very conscious that fieldwork for this purpose need not involve exhausting treks across country. Teachers taking part frequently comment that a bit of gentle induction has greatly enriched their own appreciation of the natural landscape and added enjoyment to their own excursions as well as confidence to their practice. When we are teaching physical geography to young children the enrichment of *their* contacts with the physical environment, aesthetically and spiritually as well as intellectually, should, similarly, be one of our prime aims.

It is helpful, especially for those teaching at the top end of key stage 2, to know that in secondary geography the approach to river work is still likely to include local field experience. In the case of schools which may use the same local field resource as the secondary school there is a good case for some liaison, not only to avoid direct overlap but to ensure that the approaches are complementary. The notion of the river as a 'system' features in the original Programme of Study for geography and is prominent in current geographical practice and textbooks in secondary education. It is therefore helpful for primary teachers to have a feel for this way of looking at the work of rivers too, if only because a secondary textbook can be a good source of help.

So what does looking at the river as a 'system' imply? If we can consider the characteristics of another 'system', more familiar to us as teachers, that may help. In our education 'system' there are 'inputs', teaching itself being the most important, and 'outputs' measured in children's learning. The term 'system' implies that all the component parts – finance, policy making, administration, curriculum development, etc. – all work together, harmoniously and efficiently one hopes, to achieve the desired end, a nation of enlightened citizens or an efficient workforce, depending on the current view. All 'systems' can be described like this in terms of '**inputs**' and '**outputs**'.

A river system is, thankfully, much more straightforward than the education system. The inputs are rain, snow and hail (collectively called **precipitation**); the output mechanisms of **evaporation, percolation** (seepage) and **run-off** are the means by which that water is returned as efficiently as possible to the atmosphere or oceans. Each of these mechanisms has a distinctive role in achieving that output. As a naturally harmonious system it constantly adjusts itself so that it can operate efficiently. Provided its capacity is not exceeded (in which case, of course, there will be a flood) the river basin achieves a carefully adjusted water transfer operation from the hills to the sea. Many of the physical features that are of interest in a river basin can be seen as by-products of the system's effort to adjust to current circumstances and maximise its efficiency. For example if it encounters an obstacle, in the form of either a natural feature or something dumped in the river, it will attempt to remove it by 'erosion'. Conversely, if something slows the current so that it is attempting to carry more sediment than its volume and speed will allow it will simply drop any excess as 'deposition'.

Looking at rivers as 'systems' in this way represents a shift in perspective for those of us whose geographical education pre-dates the systems approach. It transfers the main focus of interest away from landscape features created by rivers and towards the climatic context in which they operate. It views the river in context as a component in the water cycle. So, we need to explore how these two aspects can be appropriately tackled together in junior work.

By the time most children have reached upper junior level they should already have grappled with the water cycle idea in a number of contexts, from wondering where the puddles go, to developing simple explanations of clouds and rain. The grafting of the river system idea onto their existing schemas seems a logical next step. The technical

MALHAM TARN

Malham Tarn is a lake high up in the Pennines. It disappears into the hills. It reappears again in the valley below the village that is called Malham. There are lots of underground streams and rivers in this part of the country. It is important to know that streams and rivers can disappear into a hillside or valley and reappear somewhere else as we can see from Malham Tarn.

Work: Marc Cairns, Newbottle Primary School, Sunderland.

terminology, however, may serve only to obfuscate the essence of an issue which is essentially very simple. When rainwater reaches the ground it either evaporates directly or seeps in, the rate depending on the type of surface, or it runs off if the surface is impermeable (or impervious or waterproof). In either case it finds its way underground or overground to the most convenient drain or stream and back to the sea. It may be used by plants and returned through transpiration to the air, or it may be drunk by animals or captured and fed through the public water supply and disposal systems, in which case, after suitable treatment, it still finds its way back into the oceans.

Much of this understanding can be built up gradually, assisted by good classroom resources and the use of the school buildings and grounds. A large sand and gravel tray or outdoor 'pit' which can be raked up to form a mountain area and 'rained on' with a spray hose, will reveal some of the features of that developing system. A selection of grades of soil, sand, gravels, small pebbles and larger stones banked up in a length of guttering along which water can be poured from a tap, and the pressure varied, will demonstrate practically how water moves and sorts its sediment load (see Figure 2). The introduction of a waterproof layer (plastic or polystyrene sheet) will demonstrate the principle of springs. Those who live near beaches can study river systems in miniature (Figure 6).

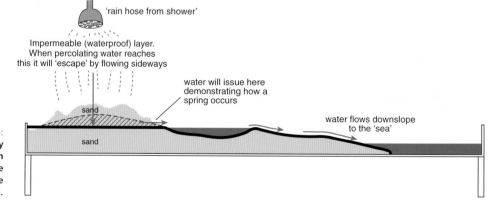

'rain hose from shower'

Impermeable (waterproof) layer. When percolating water reaches this it will 'escape' by flowing sideways

water will issue here demonstrating how a spring occurs

water flows downslope to the 'sea'

sand

sand

Figure 6: The wet sand tray (Figure 1) in cross-section showing extension of the activity to demonstrate how springs form.

Photo: Elizabeth Pearson.

Large picture resources (years 3/4) or a good video sequence such as *River Landscapes* in the BBC series Resources Unit 11-13 Geography (years 5/6), will do much to draw the practical experiments into a real context. It is not so straightforward, however, to communicate understanding of the timescale over which the system develops and operates or to consider the formation of river features inside a classroom. It is logical, then, that where fieldwork is possible it should still focus on investigating physical features with an emphasis on looking at their scale and variety of detail, and gradually on beginning to understand river (or 'fluvial') processes through enquiry and experiment.

In summary, then, wherever we are when we look at a river with children, we will need to be able to help them place it in the context of the whole system. Without overburdening them with terminology, we will want both to help them grasp general ideas about what the river is like upstream and down, and to help them to consolidate and extend their understanding of 'their' river as part of the water cycle. Whether the study of a textbook example can profitably precede practical experience is a matter for each teacher's professional judgement. Factors to consider include where the children live and what previous knowledge of rivers they have, the quality of resources available and their level of interpretative skill with maps, diagrams and photographs. A few well chosen photographs for discussion, a time set aside to brainstorm what we already know and what we would like to know, and a good river based story or two are probably more effective forms of initial contact than exposure to technical textbook coverage which may be quite incomprehensible to some pupils.

How will the fieldwork feel in practice?

The development of successful river studies which include fieldwork and which incorporate additional elements of geographical skills, such as the development of investigative skills and the building of understandings about the distinctiveness of places, will have three equally important stages: the planning, the field experience itself and the follow-up work.

A FRAMEWORK FOR PLANNING

A happy solution to the uncertainties of preparation for both children and teachers is to adopt a 'key questions approach'. This is recommended as a planning framework in many publications by the Geographical Association as an approach particularly accessible to non-specialist teachers:

- What/where is it?
- What is it like?
- How did it get like this?
- How and why is it changing?

This is how a question based framework might operate in relation to planning a local field experience for a class of juniors.

The teacher's questions

First, the questions which the teacher hopes to work on can be framed from interest and personal knowledge of the site gained on a pre-visit and in consultation with the National Curriculum documents. Since elements of the work on rivers are likely to need revisiting across the key stage, it is worth considering a whole-staff approach to this element of the planning.

You might begin by putting together as many questions as you can relating to rivers and their work. A convenient riverside venue will help you to do this with more conviction if you can manage to spend part of a planning day in the field. If you use a pad of reminder stickers to record the questions individually they can then be sorted in a variety of ways.

1. Sort them into three columns labelled thus:

A. Geography	B. Not geography	C. Geography and ...

Columns B and C will help you to think about the cross-curricular opportunities offered by the rivers theme, as well as focusing discussion on how to define geography and generally encouraging a shared vision of the subject within your particular form of curriculum organisation.

The questions in Column A can also stand closer scrutiny. You might consider whether they are 'physical geography' (P) or 'human geography' (H) or both.

You can also ask whether they contribute to the developing understanding of a locality (L) and whether they contain any element of skills acquisition (S). It is also useful to consider the extent to which a question demands specific knowledge (SK) or whether it is open to discussion and debate. So the end result of the analysis of Column A might look something like this:

- Why are rivers sometimes brown? (P) (SK)
- Why is the bridge built here? (P) (H)
- How many kinds of pebbles are there? (P) (S)
- Is the river polluted? (S) (H) (L) (SK)
- Where is the current fastest? (P) (S) (SK)
- How deep is the river? (S) (P)
- What do local people use the river for? (H) (S) (L)
- What changes are taking place on the river bank? (P) (H) (L) (S)

Looking through the whole set of questions will help you in a variety of ways. It could, for example, suggest what would be the most suitable starting point for enquiry in your particular locality, or that there are several lines of enquiry (at differing levels of difficulty perhaps) which might be tackled by different groups of children. It will tell you what you need to know more about, and give an indication of what resources you might need to provide – water containers, floats, questionnaires, etc. It will also help you to determine how many issues can be tackled in the field and what can conveniently be left for the classroom.

The children's questions

At the beginning of the unit of work the children can be involved in devising their own questions. This is an important step in giving children a sense of ownership of the enquiry, which should increase their commitment to it. It helps to 'play professionals', letting them visualise themselves as researchers; if a real community purpose can be found for the results of the survey so much the better. An example of just such a list follows.

Prior to the visit questions will be spontaneous and will not overtly reflect geographical purposes, let alone specifically National Curriculum ones! Nevertheless they are worth having for they signal to the teacher the fantasies, anxieties, misconceptions and real interests that will attend the visit, and are thus a vital prelude to more effective interaction. By matching the children's preoccupations and interests against the programme of study mutually agreed starting points can be discovered. Usually when the children's questions are carefully unravelled they are found to relate much more closely to the purpose in hand than at first appears, as the bracketed classification indicates.

In the list below, for example, those in bold type would form the starting points for the imagined field experience which follows.

Photos: Julia Charlton and Paula Richardson.

- **Will it be safe to paddle?** (P)
- **Is it very deep?** (P)
- Who does it belong to? (H)
- **Where does the river come from?** (P) (L)
- **Why does the water get dirty?** (P)
- **How fast does the river go?** (P) (S)
- How long is the river? (P) (L)
- What would happen if you fell in? (H)
- Are there any fish in the river?
- Will we see otters and things?
- What happens if you go gallivanting about on a river bank? (P) (H)
- Where does the water go to? (P) (L)
- **Why do rivers bend and twist?** (P)
- Where does the water come from? (P)
- Are there any boats on it? (H) (L)
- **How wide is the river?** (P)
- Why does the river dry up sometimes? (P)
- Does it flood over the edges? (P)

One thing is always certain; the closer and more involved their contact with the water, the better pleased the children will be!

A FIELD STUDY IN PRACTICE

Photo: Steve Watts.

When choosing a fieldwork location bear in mind that it should afford as many of the following opportunities as possible:

- A guided walk along a stretch of riverbank, ideally incorporating a photograph trail.
- Opportunities to identify, describe, sketch and label landscape features while seeing the real thing, and matching it to the trail photographs.
- A chance to locate features/follow the route on large-scale maps and/or on aerial photographs.

Group	Field activity	Follow-up work
1 Level 2/3	Measure the width of the stream by making a human chain across it and its depth by marking the water level on their wellies with a chinagraph pencil. Investigate and describe pebbles collected across the stream bed. Find places where the current is stronger and weaker by observing floating objects, e.g. twigs.	Present their results pictorially. Talk/write about discoveries (using comparatives and superlative forms of strong, weak, deep, shallow, fast, slow, large, small, etc.). Discuss/compare results with Group 2.
2 Level 3/4	Measure the width and depth at one metre intervals using metre sticks and a measuring tape. Make a sketch plan to show where the measurements were taken. Investigate, describe and compare pebbles collected across the stream bed. Is there a relationship between pebble size and the strength of the flow?	Present results by drawing pictures, simple cross-section diagrams and sketch maps. Describe their investigation by talking and writing about their methods and results using comparative language as above. Compare and discuss results with Group 1.
3 Level 4	Investigate current speed along a measured straight stretch of the river by using measuring tape, a biodegradable float (cauliflower florets) and a stopwatch. Take a number of measurements of the speed the float travels over a set distance and average them, start the float at the sides and in the middle. Observe and describe the behaviour of the float. What does it tell us about the water flow (current)? Check on direction of flow by observing the direction in which a red ribbon tied to a stick extends when placed in the water. Investigate pebbles as above.	Describe and *explain* their investigation in words, pictures, diagrams or sketch maps. Show evidence and *explain* findings orally to the rest of the class. Help other groups to *explain* their pebbles by telling them what was discovered about the current.
4 Level 4/5	Investigate depth, width, current speed and pebbles (load) as above, but around a bend in the river (meander). Draw and label sketches of the outer side and the inner side of the bend. Make a list of differences between the outside of the bend and the inside.	Make a frieze showing the bend investigated and the equipment used. Explain how it was done. Describe and explain what happens at a bend in the river using words, pictures, sketches and simple maps. Present discoveries orally to the rest of the class.

Figure 7:
Suitable differentiated river activities for group enquiries.

- A stopping point which gives a vista over the whole area.

- Safe locations at which to investigate the river at first hand, e.g. by wading and measuring.

- A chance for groups of children to do their own investigation under adult supervision.

- A place to have lunch, visit the lavatory and play safely to give everyone a break from work.

Photo: Steve Watts.

It is useful to visualise the fieldwork as operating on three levels.

1 At the whole-class level, the teacher will wish to plan essential shared input in the form of opportunities for questions and explanations during the guided walk.

2 At the level of the individual child it is profitable to provide each child with a photograph of a feature to find and investigate along the route. This helps considerably to sharpen observation and maintain interest. Children with similar photographs can later be grouped for follow-up activities.

3 First hand investigations of the river are best done in groups, each supervised by a well-briefed, responsible adult helper. This enables close supervision, discussion of methods and results and differentiation of tasks by ability. Figure 7 gives a brief impression of suitable activities for group enquiries.

You will need:
- clipboards and pencils
- biodegradable floats (cauliflower florets)
- metre rules/depth gauges
- ribbon on pole
- chinagraph pencils
- stopwatches
- measuring tape (10m +)
- laminated maps and photographs (see below)
- washable felt pens that will write on laminate

You will also need to take account of differentiation (see Figure 7).

What else do I need to know about river processes and features?

A little more information about the processes of erosion and deposition will support our answers to children's spontaneous questions in the field. As the current swings round the outer bend, especially when the river is high, the full force of the water is thrown against that outer bank. All rivers carry debris – stones, soil, sand, twigs, branches and litter, for example – referred to as the '**load**', or '**bedload**'. The stronger the current the larger and heavier the load that can be carried. The current and the load are together responsible for 'erosion', the wearing away of the banks. When the current throws its load against the outer bank it has a scouring effect on it, loosening the soil or wearing away rock so that this bank is undercut (see Figure 8a). Water itself has little effect on solid rock unless the rock is soluble, like limestone or chalk, so the importance of the bedload as a scouring tool needs to be highlighted once the children begin to recognise the erosion process. The vertical bank cut on the outside of a bend is called a 'river cliff' and can be anything from a few inches in height to a spectacular feature. The particles of sand and rock which have been removed become part of the load. In time the overhanging section will become unstable and collapse into the stream (see photograph on page 335), will in turn be added to the load, and the current will renew its erosive action further back. The smoothing and rounding of individual pebbles is caused by their

Recent erosion on the outer bank of a meander on this stretch of the River Petteril near Carlisle shows undercutting of soft clay and collapse of the grassy surface. Photo: Liz Lewis.

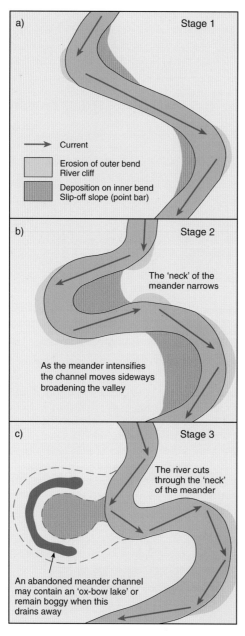

Figure 8:
How erosion and deposition can lead to the formation of an ox-bow lake.

constant grinding against each other in the river bed as the current shunts the load along. A stream cannot of course keep on collecting all the debris indefinitely; it would simply have too much to carry. Dissolved substances and tiny particles (silt), held in suspension in the water, may remain and be carried right to the sea. But larger items like coarse sand, gravel and pebbles will be dropped again if their quantity exceeds the carrying capacity of the current. Some will fall to the bottom only to be picked up again in a flood. Alternatively, they may be carried along for a short distance and deposited elsewhere along the banks. The clearest examples of deposition occur on the inner sides of bends where sandy, gravelly or pebbly '**beaches**', known as '**slip-off slopes**' are found (see Figure 8a). The field investigation above showed this to be the part where the current is weakest. The material on this little beach may show evidence of sorting by the current into patches of small, medium and large grain sizes.

In summary, then, whilst the outer edge of a meander is wearing back, the inner edge is creeping forward; in other words the river is very gradually changing its course (see Figure 8b). It is these processes of sideways erosion and deposition which, over the very long term, have created the flatness of the valley bottom. Occasionally, if a meander develops into almost a full-circle bend, a more spectacular change of course can take place. Figure 8c shows the development of a '**cut-off**'. While the abandoned meander contains water it is known as an '**ox-bow lake**'; more typically, however, it drains, leaving a curving patch of boggy ground (see photograph opposite).

FOLLOW-UP AND EXTENSION ACTIVITIES

The intended follow-up to the field day is the children's presentation of the results of their investigations as indicated in the description of the field visit. Much of this needs to be completed quickly, while the experience is fresh – and a large and varied display will result. This will amount to a working display because it will spawn comparative work, foster discussion and provide factual material for the children's presentation on river safety. The promise of a real audience for the work should sustain the interest for long enough to achieve the desired learning outcomes.

This is probably sufficient to draw from one field experience. Prolonged follow up never generates the enthusiasm of the real event and can simply cause the children to become sick of the subject. We can however reinforce and build upon what has been

This boggy hollow, colonised by water loving reeds, indicates a previous course of the River Petteril. The edge of the present floodplain is marked by a terrace just in front of the farm which is wisely built on higher ground. Photo: Liz Lewis.

achieved in the field in the short- and medium-term planning. By seeking out related issues we can construct subject-specific activities that might serve as brief revisits to the work on rivers and help 'fill in' aspects of the programme of study in which our particular field location was lacking. It helps if these 'extra' activities are linked to the original study, have some intrinsic interest or excitement that can be tapped into, and can be pursued by absorbing practical activities. One which all children will find relevant would be the planning of a riverside park. This draws attention to mapping skills as well as physical landscape features. It also demands consideration of the possible human users of the park, their needs and their capacity to alter the land use and environmental quality of the riverside. It is a topic brimming with potential across the geography programme.

Since some children are beginning to understand the role that running water plays in the developing landscape, suitable themes which focus on the power of water should also secure their interest. We are reminded in the programme of study that contexts for the rivers theme should include the UK and European Union and that they should be set within actual places and use topical examples (paragraph 6). Floods and waterfalls are examples of two possible free-standing follow-up activities both of which can also be linked to work in other curriculum areas, particularly the use of non-fiction texts in English. They are essentially extensions to the fieldwork, which can be taught about in class provided that the initial exposure to river processes has been done in the field.

Summary

I hope this chapter has illustrated that it is not a case of undertaking all this river work in pursuit of one theme, but rather of pursuing it for its benefits across the programme of study, to English, maths, science, and skill development generally, much of which is transferable learning. With experience, the time taken to set up work in imaginary contexts is short, and needs to be considered against the teacher preparation time needed to teach 'the facts' in a more formal way, bearing in mind that not all the children in a particular group will be ready to work to the same level. The ideas suggested here could operate well as groupwork, with some children working only at a descriptive level whilst others approach explanation and hypothesis. Active and involved enquiry, engagement and presentation will ensure that the important geographical issues and arguments have a chance of surviving long term in the minds and imaginations of our pupils.

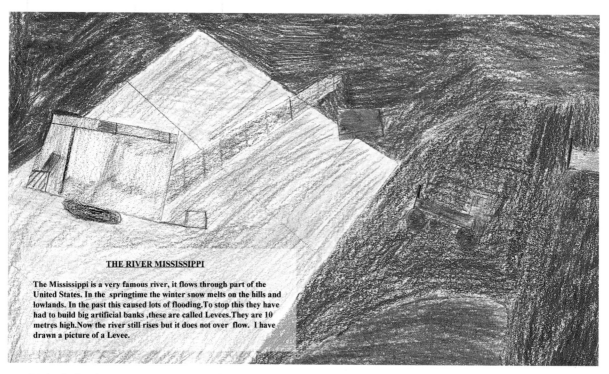

THE RIVER MISSISSIPPI

The Mississippi is a very famous river, it flows through part of the United States. In the springtime the winter snow melts on the hills and lowlands. In the past this caused lots of flooding. To stop this they have had to build big artificial banks ,these are called Levees. They are 10 metres high. Now the river still rises but it does not over flow. I have drawn a picture of a Levee.

Work: Nicola Whyte, Newbottle Primary School, Sunderland.

DOING GEOGRAPHY – THE ENQUIRY OPPORTUNITY

I have tried, with reference to the rivers theme, to combine an introduction to some essential understandings in physical geography, with a vision of the enquiry approach in action, some advice about fieldwork, and some suggested children's activities. I have avoided matching individual activities to particular age groups because I don't believe it is possible to be prescriptive about this with any real credibility, especially in the context of someone else's class. As teachers we are all best placed to judge the capabilities of individuals in our own teaching groups and to select well matched activities to extend their learning. Some schools may intend to develop a single programme of work on rivers, others to integrate the work with locality studies or other curriculum areas, and yet others to visit and revisit the theme throughout the junior years in differing contexts. All these modes of organisation are possible given the flexibility of the National Curriculum.

I have concentrated on the broad vision of field based *enquiry* in the knowledge that there are already numerous published resources to assist the design of classroom based work, and individual activities, many of which can also be easily adapted to support the outdoor opportunities encountered in your own particular locality or region. For me as a teacher the beauty and strength of the enquiry approach is its open-endedness. Once the broad context of the investigation is set, and the issues of interest defined, by children and teachers working together, then individuals can enter that enquiry at their own level and proceed within it as far as they are able.

Although the investigations considered here begin from a physical geography focus, they contain elements which are human and environmental and so they can be extended to span several elements of this broad and relevant subject. Any enquiry that is worthy of the title 'geographical' must incorporate both physical and human elements. It can achieve this by examining, in the context of real places, those relationships which are at the very heart of geography – the effects of the world's varied physical conditions on human activities and of humans on their sensitive physical home, the earth. By raising awareness of and fostering thoughtful responses to the many important and often politically sensitive environmental issues with which our world is currently struggling, we shall be providing the kind of learning that an informed and sensitive next generation will desperately need.

In planning for geography, then, taking time to develop with colleagues a broad subject philosophy and an overview of how the recommended content interlinks at each level, may be more important than amassing a vast bank of factual knowledge and collecting a thousand activities to have at our fingertips. Developing understanding of the physical landscape is in some ways the most difficult aspect. But it is very worthwhile because that understanding can enrich appreciation of the natural environment and so feed the desire to protect and conserve it thoughtfully. Pursuing a broad understanding of processes, and having the nerve to hypothesise about local features in the light of this growing understanding, can be more useful than being able to describe classic textbook examples of physical features which have no immediate relevance to our lives, or those of our pupils.

Learning by doing it is not only for children but teachers too. As we *do* geography, and evaluate what we have achieved, our understanding of the aims of the subject will gradually grow, and then we can progressively cast a more critical eye on the resources and activities developed by others and begin to design our own more confidently.

Sir Halford Mackinder, the prominent educationalist and pioneer of academic geography, who seems to have harboured a healthy scepticism about the sterile rote learning of the 'capes and bays' tradition, had this to say about school geography in the 1920s:

> *'You cannot have taught them much by way of facts, but if you send them out curious, seeking to learn, and with an idea that there is order in the world and that their experience must fit into a corresponding order in their minds, you have done all you can hope to do' (Mackinder, quoted in Garnett, 1934).*

This liberating thought, although, of course, it predates chaos theory, represents a traditional value in geographical education, and is the kind of thought from which the enquiry philosophy has sprung.

Our role in primary physical geography, then, is not to present our pupils with a watered-down version of our own half-remembered, or recently resurrected, senior school experience. It is rather that, inspired by our own local landscapes and supported by well chosen secondary resources, we should invite and nurture the natural curiosity they all have about their own world. All primary teachers, whatever their subject orientation and expertise, can surely embrace this role with confidence.

References

BBC Education *River Landscapes* (part of the Resources Unit 11-13 Geography). London: BBC Education.

Blathwayt, B. (1989) *Be Quiet, Bramble.* London: Walker Books.

Brown, R. (1991) *The World That Jack Built.* London: Red Fox.

Dow, J. (1990) *Webster's Walk.* London: Frances Lincoln.

Garnett, O. (1934) *Fundamentals in School Geography.* London: Harrap.

Lewis, R. (1988) *Come Back Hercules.* London: Macdonalds.

Chapter 24: Rivers

Covers aspects of progression and differentiation (Chapter 5), and work on the Rivers theme at a variety of scales (**Section 5**). Is there a convenient and safe stretch of water to study within your local area (Chapter 16)? The language of river studies also connects with Liz Lewis' work (Chapter 13) on geography and language.

Photo: John Sharp.

Resources

Maps

ORDNANCE SURVEY MAPS

Note that detailed lists of these maps can be obtained from the Ordnance Survey (see address list), from local OS agents and, in some cases, bookshops.

1:1250 (formerly the 50" map) Available for large urban areas. Essential for the school area and local and contrasting locality studies. Check availability with your LEA and also regional OS map agents. In terms of progression, this is the one to start with, with younger children. Each map covers an area of 500m by 500m. These maps are computerised and easily updated, but arguably are aesthetically less pleasing than the earlier large scale versions. In some OS agencies you can get the maps centred on your local school.

1:2500 (formerly the 25" map) Available for areas outside towns and cities (apart from remote upland areas). Contains a similar level of detail to the 1:1250 map, and equally useful. You may well find your local library stocks the last edition of the 1:2500 for your urban area. Includes not only the immediate surrounds of the school, but also a wider neighbourhood, and therefore useful for key stage 2 locality work. Each map covers an area of 1 square kilometre.

1:10 000 (formerly the 6" map) Another black and white map, but with brown lines to show contours. Again important for locality work as it covers a larger area of a town or city than the maps above. Shows the pattern of roads well, and gives names of streets and of main buildings. Ideal for land use survey and was used in the Geographical Association's Land-Use UK initiative of 1996. Each map covers an area 5km by 5km.

1:25 000 (formerly the 2½" map, known now as the **Pathfinder** series). Shows even more detail than the classic Landranger series (see below). Includes field boundaries. Ideal for walking. Somewhat simpler to follow for key stage 2 children than the Landranger series. An absolute mine of information, and essential for place coverage in the British Isles. Local area 1:25 000 maps can be purchased at good booksellers and tourist agencies. Cover an area 10km by 10km.

1:50 000 (formerly the 1" map, known now as the **Landranger** series). The most popular OS series and certainly accessible to children at the top of the primary range. Very useful for an overview of the features of the region in which the school is found. It is recommended that your own area's 1:50 000 maps are laminated and mounted so the children can constantly interrogate it (or them). Like other OS maps, sometimes more than one is needed to centralise your school on the map as a whole. Available in all good bookshops. Cover an area 40km by 40km.

Small-scale maps produced by the Ordnance Survey include:

Travelmaster maps on sheets of:

- 1:625 000 (two for the country) or
- 1:250 000 (eight for the country)

These are good for motoring and planning routes.

Outdoor Leisure maps

On the 1:25 000 scale for popular tourist areas, ideal if you are undertaking fieldwork in those areas.

Overseas maps

At a variety of scales, covering countries in Africa, the Atlantic Ocean, the Caribbean, Central and South America, Europe and the Mediterranean, the Indian Ocean and the Pacific Ocean. A list of maps currently available, with prices, can be obtained from: Russell Fox, Room W103, Ordnance Survey, Romsey Road, Southampton SO16 4GU.

Historical maps and guides

A small number are currently produced by the OS for areas of great historical interest, at two scales:

- 1:625 000: for Ancient Britain and Roman Britain
- 1:2500: for Bath, Canterbury, London, York and Hadrian's Wall, at different historical periods.

Historical OS maps

Ordnance Survey maps produced over the last 150 years are invaluable for demonstrating change in your local area. Check availability with local libraries and record offices. There have been many different scales, and only those thought to be of use to primary teachers for their localities and regions are noted below.

LARGE-SCALE TOWN PLANS

These were mapped for different towns and cities mostly at 1:500 and 1:1056 scales, from the 1840s to the 1890s, showing huge amounts of detail (but covering only a tiny area). Check availability in local reference libraries.

25" maps (now 1:2500)

These were introduced in the 1850s on a county basis and by the 1890s the whole of the urban and cultivated rural areas of Britain had been covered. Some of these were hand-coloured. Lancashire and Yorkshire were anomalies in having the first sheets to be mapped in the 6" but the last on the 25" scales. Thus the first 25" maps available for those two counties are from 1888-1893. Features were shown with great accuracy and in great detail. Bench marks indicated the exact height of certain features. Between the 1890s and the 1940s all areas were completely revised once, some twice, and a few three or four times.

6" maps (now 1:10 000)

The first edition dates from about the same period as the 25" sheets, and was also produced on a county basis. The second edition was introduced between the 1890s and the First World War, and the third edition, never completed, before the war for some southern counties, and between the First and Second World wars for others. left out were Lincolnshire, the East and North Ridings of Yorkshire, Hereford, Cardigan, Pembroke and Radnor. This series is a valuable complement to the 25" and can be found in local libraries and record offices. It is strongly recommended you make photocopies for your local area, as for the 25" series, to compare with the present OS maps at similar scales.

One-inch (now 1:50 000)

These went through many editions before the conversion from the 1" (1:63 360 scale) to the current 1:50 000 scale. The first edition maps have been reprinted by David and Charles. The dates vary for different parts of the country:

- 1st edition (1805 to 1860s)
- 2nd edition (1860s to 1890s)
- 3rd edition (published 1903-1913)
- 4th or 'Popular' (published 1918-1926)
- 5th edition (1931-not completed. Also temporary war revisions of earlier maps)
- 6th or 'New Popular' edition (immediate post-war based on 4th and 5th editions)
- 7th series (1952-1963, with revised editions continuing until replaced between 1974 and 1976 by the 1:50 000, named the **Landranger** in 1979).

If you wish for more information on historic OS maps, including detail for your local area, check whether your local reference library has the following:

- Harley, J.B. (1964) *The Historian's Guide to Ordnance Survey Maps.* London: National Council of Social Service.
- Oliver, R. (1993) *Ordnance Survey Maps: A Concise Guide for Historians.* London: Charles Close Society.

GOAD PLANS

The Goad Plans are land-use maps on the 1:1056 scale and cover town centres. They include the names of banks, hotels, retailers, etc., at the time the survey was made. They are valuable for project work, allowing an urban survey to update the detail on the plans. An education pack is produced for primary schools (see address list below).

Atlases

Belitha Press	**Children's First Atlas**
Collins Longman	**Atlas One**
	Atlas Two
	Keystart First Atlas
	Keystart UK Atlas
	Keystart World Atlas
	Longman Book Project: Atlas of the British Isles
Folens	**Ordnance Survey World Atlas**
	Ordnance Survey UK Atlas
Ginn	**First Atlas**
Hamlyn	**Children's Atlas of the World**
	Deans Junior Picture Atlas
Kingfisher Books	**Children's World Atlas**
	First Picture Atlas
Nelson	**Nelson Atlas**
Oxford University Press	**Oxford Infant Atlas**
	Oxford First Atlas
	Oxford Rainbow Atlas
	Oxford Junior Atlas
Philip's	**Philip's Junior School Atlas**
	Philip's Wildlife Atlas
	Philip's Environment Atlas
Schofield and Sims	**A First Atlas of the World**
Usborne	**Usborne Picture Atlas**
	Usborne Children's Atlas of the World

Geographical Association publications

Address: 160 Solly Street, Sheffield S1 4BF.

Journal: *Primary Geographer* (published from 1989 to date)

Barnett, M., Kent, A. and Milton, M. (1994) *Images of Earth: A Teacher's Guide to Remote Sensing in Geography at Key Stage 2.*

Bowles, R. (1992) *Key Stages 1 and 2 Support material: Water in the Environment; Earth in the Environment; Soils, Plants and the Environment.*

Bowles, R. (1993) *Resources for Key Stages 1, 2 and 3.*

Catling, S. (1995) *Placing Places* (revised edition).

Chambers, B. *et al.* (1995) *Awareness into Action: Environmental Education in the Primary Curriculum.*

De Villiers, M. (1995) *Developments in Primary Geography: Theory and Practice.*

May, S., Richardson, P. and Banks, V. (1993) *Fieldwork in Action 1: Planning Fieldwork.*

May, S. and Cook, J. (1996) *Fieldwork in Action 2: An Enquiry Approach.*

May, S. (ed) (1996) *Fieldwork in Action 4: Primary Fieldwork Projects.*

Milner, A.M. (1996) *Geography Starts Here! Practical Approaches with Nursery and Reception Children.*

Milner, A.M. (1997) *Geography Through Play.*

Morgan, W. (1995) *Plans for Primary Geography.*

Norris Nicholson, H. (1991) *Geography and History in the National Curriculum.*

Norris Nicholson, H. (1996) *Place in Story-time: Geography through Stories at Key Stages 1 and 2.*

Richardson, P. and Walford, R. (1998) *Fieldwork in Action 5: Mapping Land Use.*

Richardson, P. and Whiting, S. (eds) (1998) *Fieldwork in Action 6: Crossing the Channel.*

Robinson, R. and Serf, J. (eds) (1997) *Global Geography: Learning through Development at Key Stage 3.* (Note: Though addressed to key stage 3, this contains many suitable ideas for key stage 2.)

Scoffham, S. (1997) *Atlas-wise: Ideas and Themes for Atlas Work.*

Scoffham, S. (ed) (1998) *Primary Sources: Research findings in primary geography.*

Sebba, J. (1991) *Planning for Pupils with Learning Difficulties.*

Sweasey, P. (1997) *Studying Contrasting UK Localities.*

Thomas, T. and May, S. (1994) *Fieldwork in Action 3: Managing Out-of-classroom Activities.*

Weldon, M. (1997) *Studying Distant Places.*

Official publications

ACCAC (1998) *An Agenda for Action: A Report to the Secretary of State.* Cardiff: ACCAC.
Curriculum and Assessment Authority for Wales (1994) *Geography in the National Curriculum in Wales: Proposals for Consultation.* Cardiff: ACAC.
Curriculum Council for Wales (CCW) (1990) *National Curriculum Geography: CCW Advisory Paper 8: Comments on the Proposals of the Secretary of State for Wales.* Cardiff: CCW

CCW (1991) *Geography in the National Curriculum (Wales).* Cardiff: CCW.

CCW (1991) *Geography in the National Curriculum: Non-statutory Guidance for Teachers.* Cardiff: CCW.

CCW (1992) *INSET Activities for National Curriculum Geography.* Cardiff: CCW.

CCW (1992) *Environmental Education: Framework for the Development of a Cross-curricular Theme, Advisory Paper 17.* Cardiff: CCW.

CCW (1993) *History and Geography: Planning the National Curriculum at KS1 and KS2.* Cardiff: CCW.

CCW (1993) *An Enquiry Approach to Learning Geography at Key Stages 2 and 3.* Cardiff: CCW.

CCW (1994) *Fieldwork in Geography: Promoting Fieldwork across Key Stages 1 to 4.* Cardiff: CCW.

Department for Education and Science/Her Majesty's Inspectorate (DES/HMI) (1986) *Geography from 5-16: Curriculum Matters 7.* London: HMSO.

DES/HMI (1989) *Aspects of Primary Education: Environmental Education from 5-16: Curriculum Matters 13.* London: HMSO.

DES/HMI (1989) *Aspects of Primary Education: The Teaching and Learning of History and Geography.* London: HMSO.

DES (1991) *Geography in the National Curriculum (England).* London: DES/HMSO.

National Curriculum Council (NCC) (1990) *Education for Economic and Industrial Understanding: Curriculum Guidance 4.* York: NCC.

NCC (1990) *Health Education: Curriculum Guidance 5.* York: NCC.

NCC (1990) *Careers Education and Guidance: Curriculum Guidance 6.* York: NCC.

NCC (1990) *Environmental Education: Curriculum Guidance 7.* York: NCC.

NCC (1990) *Education for Citizenship: Curriculum Guidance 8.* York: NCC.

NCC (1991) *Geography: Non-statutory Guidance.* York: NCC.

NCC (1993) *An Introduction to Teaching Geography at Key Stages 1 and 2.* York: NCC.

NCC (1993) *Teaching Geography at Key Stages 1 and 2: An INSET Guide.* York: NCC.

Office for Standards in Education (OFSTED) (1993) *Geography: Key Stages 1, 2 and 3: the Implementation of the Curricular Requirements of the Education Reform Act, 1992-3.* London: HMSO.

OFSTED (1995) *Geography: A Review of Inspection Findings 1993-4.* London: HMSO.

OFSTED (1996) *Subjects and Standards: Issues for School Development Arising from OFSTED Inspection Findings 1994-5, Key Stages 1 & 2.* London: HMSO.

Schools and Curriculum Assessment Authority (SCAA) (1994) *Geography in the National Curriculum: Draft Proposals.* London: SCAA.

QCA/DfEE (1998) *A scheme of work for Key Stages 1 and 2: Geography.* London: QCA/DfEE.

QCA/DfEE (1999) *The National Curriculum: Handbook for Primary Teachers in England: Key Stages 1 and 2.* London: QCA/DfEE.

QCA/DfEE (1999) Geography: *The National Curriculum for England: Key Stages 1-3.* London: QCA/DfEE.

QCA/DfEE (2000) *A scheme of work for Key Stages 1 and 2: Geography update.* London: QCA/DfEE.

SCAA (1995) *Planning the Curriculum at Key Stages 1 and 2.* London: SCAA.

SCAA (1996) *Teaching Environmental Matters Through the National Curriculum.* London: SCAA.

SCAA (1997) *Geography and the Use of Language.* London: SCAA.

SCAA (1997) *Expectations in Geography at Key Stages 1 and 2.* London: SCAA.

Textbook series

Cambridge Primary Geography, Morgan, W., Bunce, V., Brace, S., Flint, D. *et al.*
Cambridge University Press, 1996-98. (Years 3-6, with source books, photographs and teacher's notes, and access to CD-ROM.)

Discovering Our World, Elliot, G. and Martin, K.
Oxford University Press, 1986. (Four book series: years 3-6, with a teacher's guide.)

First Geography, Thomas, S.
Oxford University Press, 1992. (Three book series: years 1-2, with teacher's books.)

Folens Geography, Harrison, P., Harrison, S. *et al.*
Folens, 1993-97. (Years N-2, with big books and teacher's guides.)

Forward in Geography, Richardson, P., May, S. and Waugh, D.
Nelson, 1997. (Years 3-6, with source books and teacher's notes.)

Ginn Geography, Chambers, W., Hughes, J., Morgan, W., Pearson, M., Rodger, R. and Smith, A.
Ginn, 1991-94. (Big book and Readers for key stage 1; eight books for key stage 2, with copymasters, teacher's guides and photobooks.)

Into Geography, Harrison, P., Harrison, S. and Pearson, M.
Nelson, 1993. (Four book series: Years 3-6, with teacher's guides.)

Mapstart, Catling, S.
Collins/Longman. (Three book series plus *OS Mapstart*: Years 1-6 , with copymasters.)

Oliver & Boyd Geography, Marsden, W., Marsden, V. and Flint, D.
Longman, 1995-96. (Readers for key stage 1, four-book series for key stage 2, with photobook, copymasters and teacher's guide.)

Our World, Kilner, S. *et al.*
Heinemann, 1991-94. (Years 1-6, in boxed sets of resources with pupil books and teacher's guides.)

Oxford Primary Geography, Almond, P., Asquith, S., Starkie, H. *et al.*
Oxford University Press, 1995-96. (Four book series: Years 3-6, with teacher's guides.)

Geography Curriculum Bank Key Stage 2, Places/Themes, Asquith, S., Chambers, B. and Donert, K.
Scholastic Press, 1996. (Two books).

Starting Geography, Harrison, P. and Harrison, S.
Nelson, 1996. (Years 1-2, with big books, posters and teacher's guides.)

Sunshine Geography: Emergent Readers, Boyle, W.
Heinemann, 1991. (Years 1-2, as a set of reading books with a teacher's guide incorporating copymasters.)

Target Geography, Sauvain, P. Ward Lock Educational, 1994-95. (Ten book series: Years 1-6, with teacher's guide.)

Time and Place, Harrison, P., Harrison, S. *et al.*
Simon & Schuster Educational, 1990-93. (Years 1-6 in boxed sets, with teacher's guides.)

World Watch, Scoffham, S., Bridge, C. and Jewson, T.
Collins 1993-96. (Four book series: Years 1-6, with box of resources, pupil books, copymasters and teacher's guides.)

The Young Geographer Investigates, Jennings, T.
Oxford University Press, 1986-88. (Series of ten pupil books.)

Photo and video packs

AID AND DEVELOPMENT ORGANISATIONS: DISTANT PLACES PACKS

Addokorpe: Life in a Ghanaian Village. Worldaware, 1992.

At Home in St Lucia/Banana Landscapes. Worldaware, 1992.

Bangalore: Indian City Life. ActionAid, 1993.

Cairo: Four Children and their City. Oxfam 1995.

Chembakolli: A Village in India. ActionAid, 1991.

Change in the Swat Valley, Pakistan. ActionAid, 1993.

Fala Favela: Brazil. DEC, Birmingham/Trocaire, 1991.

Kapsokwony: Rural Kenya. ActionAid, 1992.

Nairobi: Kenyan City Life. ActionAid, 1992.

Neighbours: The Life and Times of Yesudas Kemel: Anand Gram, North India. ActionAid 1992.

Palm Grove: A Study of the Locality at Victoria Falls, Zambia. UNICEF UK, 1992.

Pampagrande: A Peruvian Village. ActionAid 1992.

Tale of Two Cities: London and Calcutta. World Wide Fund for Nature, 1992.

The Thread of the Nile: Development Issues in Egypt for History and Geography at Key Stage 2. DEC Birmingham, 1996.

Where Camels are Better than Cars: Dourentza, Mali. DEC Birmingham, 1992.

Working Together: The People of Kanjikolly, India. ActionAid, 1994.

GEOGRAPHICAL ASSOCIATION

Flatford: A contrasting UK Locality. Jackson, E. and Morgan, W., 1996.

Focus on Castries, St Lucia. Bunce, V., Foley, J., Morgan, W. and Scobie, S., 1997. (Class sets of associated materials also available.)

Kaptalamwa: A Village in Kenya. Weldon, M., 1996.

Ladakh: An Activity-based Pack Focused on the Life of a Tibetan Community. Hughes, J., Paterson, K. and Rafferty, P., 1996.

Localities in Malawi. Bowden, D. and Trill, J., 1995.

Montreuil: A European Place Study. Garman, D. (ed) 1995.

Tocuaro: A Mexican village. Bunce V., Gibbs, F., Morgan, W. and Wakefield, D. 1998.

COMMERCIAL AND OTHER ORGANISATIONS: BRITAIN AND EUROPE PACKS

Betws-y-coed: A Contrasting Locality in Wales. Wilson, P. and Ellis, J. Field Studies Council, 1995.

A Market Town: Bury St Edmunds. Bowles, R. Scholastic, 1994.

Discover Godstone. Walker, G. and Wetton, S. National Remote Sensing Centre, 1995.

Eyam: An English Village. Bowles, R. Scholastic, 1994.

France: Wasquehal, near Lille. Ginn, 1994.

Germany: Speyer on the Rhine. Ginn, 1994.

Greece: Epidavros. Folens, 1992.

Malham Tarn. Cambridge Video Production, 1994.

Plymouth: A Waterfront City. Bowles, R. Scholastic, 1994.

Sedbergh: A Rural Locality. Harrison, P. *et al.* Folens, 1995.

A Victorian Seaside Resort: Southport. Marsden, V. Chris Kington Publishing, 1996.

Useful addresses

UK MATERIALS

Maps

Experian Goad Limited, 8-12 Salisbury Square, OLD HATFIELD, Hertfordshire AL9 5BJ.

Alan Godfrey Maps, 57 Spoor Street, Dunston, GATESHEAD NE11 9BD.
(For reduced versions of early edition 25" OS maps for many British towns and cities. Some held by local booksellers.)

Latitude, PO Box 10146, London N14 4QR.

National Map Centre, 22-24 Caxton Street, LONDON SW1H 0QU.

Ordnance Survey, Romsey Road, Maybush, SOUTHAMPTON SO9 4DH.

Stanford's Map Centre, 12 Long Acre, LONDON WC2E 9LP.

Photographs

Aerofilms Limited, Gate Studios, Station Road, BOREHAMWOOD, Hertfordshire WD6 1EJ.

Pictorial Charts Educational Trust, 27 Kirchen Road, LONDON W13 0UD.

Videos

BBC Educational Publishing, PO Box 234, WETHERBY, West Yorkshire LS23 7EU.

BBC Education Information, White City, 201 Wood Lane, LONDON W12 7TS.

Channel 4, 124 Horseferry Road, LONDON, SW1P 2TX.

Granada Television, Granada TV Centre, Quay Street, MANCHESTER M60 9EA.

ITV Association, Knighton House, 56 Mortimer Street, LONDON W1N 2AN.

Environmental/outdoor/charitable organisations

Age Concern, Astral House, 1268 London Road, LONDON SW16 4ER.

Centre for Alternative Technology, Llwyngwern, MACHYNLLETH, Powys, Wales SY26 9AZ.

Conservation Trust, National Centre for Environmental Education, George Palmer Site, Northumberland Avenue, READING RG2 7PW.

Council for Environmental Education, School of Education, University of Reading, London Road, READING RG1 5AQ.

Council for the Protection of Rural England, Warwick House, 25-7 Buckingham Palace Road, LONDON SW1W 0PP.

Countryside Commission, John Dower House, Crescent Place, CHELTENHAM GL50 3RA.

English Heritage, Fortress House, 23 Saville Row, LONDON W1X 2HE.

Field Studies Council, Preston Montford, Montford Bridge, SHREWSBURY SY4 1HW.

Forestry Commission, 231 Costorphine Road, EDINBURGH EH1 7AT.

Help the Aged, Research and Education Division, St James's Walk, Clerkenwell Green, LONDON EC1R 0BE.

National Association for Environmental Education, University of Wolverhampton (formerly Polytechnic) Gonvay Road, WALSALL WS1 3BD.

National Trust, 36 Queen Anne's Gate, LONDON SW1H 9AS.

Royal Society for the Protection of Birds, The Lodge, SANDY, Bedfordshire SG19 2DL.

Tidy Britain Group, The Pier, WIGAN WN3 4EX.

Town and Country Planning Association, 17 Carlton House Terrace, LONDON SW1Y 5AS.

Overseas materials

ActionAid, Chataway House, CHARD, Somerset TA20 1FA.

Central Bureau for Educational Visits and Exchanges, Seymour Mews House, Seymour Mews, LONDON W1H 9PE.

Centre for Global Education, York University, Heslington, YORK YO1 5DD.

Centre for World Development Education, Regent's College, Inner Circle, Regent's Park, LONDON NW1 4NS.

Christian Aid, PO Box 100, 35 Lower Marsh, LONDON SE1 7RL.

Commission for Racial Equality, Elliott House, 10/12 Allington Street, LONDON SW1E 5EH.

The Commonwealth Institute, 230 Kensington High Street, LONDON W8 6NQ.

Council for Education in World Citizenship, Seymour Mews House, Seymour Mews, LONDON W1H 9PE.

Development Education Centre, Gillett Centre, 998 Bristol Road, Selly Oak, BIRMINGHAM B29 6LE.

Friends of the Earth, 56-58 Alma Street, LUTON LU1 2PH.

Information and Documentation Centre for the Geography of The Netherlands, Faculty of Geographical Sciences, University of Utrecht, Heidelberglaan 2, NL 3508 TC Utrecht, The Netherlands.

National Association of Development Education Centres, 6 Endsleigh Street, LONDON WC1H 0DX.

Oxfam, 274 Banbury Road, OXFORD OX2 7GZ.

Save the Children, Mary Datchelor House, 17 Grove Lane, Camberwell, LONDON SE5 8RD.

Survival, 310 Edgware Road, LONDON W2 1DY.

UNICEF-UK, 55 Lincoln's Inn Fields, LONDON WC2A 3NB.

United Nations Environment Programme, PO Box 30552, NAIROBI, Kenya.

Welsh Centre for International Affairs, Temple of Peace, Cathays Park, CARDIFF CF1 3AP.

Worldaware, 31-35 Kirby Street, LONDON EC1N 8TE.

World Wide Fund for Nature (UK), Panda House, Weyside Park, Catteshall Lane, GODALMING, Surrey GU7 1XR.

OTHER MATERIALS

Fieldwork equipment
(See Chapter 14).

ICT
(See Chapter 15)

Population

Office of Population Censuses and Surveys, St Catherine's House, 10 Kingsway, LONDON WC2B 6JP.

Stamps

British Philatelic Bureau, 20 Brandon Street, EDINBURGH EH3 1BR.

Stamp Bug Club, Freepost, NORTHAMPTON NN3 1BR.

Stanley Gibbons Publications Ltd, Unit 5, Parkside, Christchurch Road, RINGWOOD, Hampshire BH24 3SH. (HQ and Retail at 399 Strand, LONDON WC2R 0LX).

Youth Philately, Royal Mail International, 62 Riverside, Sir Thomas Langley Road, ROCHESTER, Kent ME2 4BH.

Bibliography

Barnett, M., Kent, A. and Milton, M. (eds) (1994) *Images of Earth: A Teacher's Guide to Remote Sensing in Geography at KS2.* Sheffield: Geographical Association.

Blades, M. and Spencer, C. (1986) 'Map use by young children', *Geography*, 71, 1, pp. 47-52.

Bowles, R. (1992) *Key Stages 1 and 2 Support material: Water in the Environment; Earth in the Environment; Soils, Plants and the Environment.* Sheffield: Geographical Association.

Bowles, R. (1993) *Resources for Key Stages 1, 2 and 3.* Sheffield: Geographical Association.

Brand, J. (1991) *The Green Umbrella.* Guildford: WWF/A. & C. Black.

Bruner, J. (1969) *The Process of Education.* London: Harvard.

Cade, A. (ed) (1991) *Policies for Environmental Education and Training: 1992 and Beyond.* Peterborough: English Nature.

Catling, S. (1978) 'Developing stages of cognitive map representation', *Teaching Geography*, 3, 3, pp. 120-123.

Catling, S. (1990) 'Beginning mapwork: ideas for developing mapwork in the reception class', *Primary Geographer*, 3, p. 6.

Catling, S. (1992) *Mapstart Books 1, 2, 3, OS* (second edition). Harlow: Collins-Longman.

Catling, S. (1995) *Primary PGCE E880 Module 7 Geography.* Milton Keynes: Open University.

Catling, S. (1995) 'Wider horizons: the children's charter', *Primary Geographer*, 20, pp. 4-7.

Catling, S. (1996) 'Technical interest in curriculum development' in Williams, M. (ed) *Understanding Geographical and Environmental Education: the role of research.* London: Cassell, pp. 93-111.

Centre for Alternative Technology (CAT) (1995) *Crazy Idealists! The CAT Story.* Machynlleth: CAT.

Chambers, B. (1996) 'Step by step', *Junior Focus*, April pp.2-4.

Channel 4 (1995) *Geography: Whose Place? Teachers' Guide.* London: Channel 4 Learning Ltd.

Cowcher, H. (1990) *Tropical Rainforest.* London: Picture Corgi.

Curriculum Council for Wales (1992) *Environmental Education; a Framework for the Development of a Cross-Curricular Theme, Advisory Paper 17.* Cardiff: CCW.

Development Education Centre (DEC) (Birmingham) (1986) *Hidden Messages – Activities for Exploring Bias.* Birmingham: DEC.

DES (1990) *Geography for Ages 5-16*. London/Cardiff: DES/WO.

Egan, K. (1990) *Romantic Understanding: The Development of Rationality and Imagination, Ages 8-15*. London: Routledge.

Fountain, S. (1995) 'Change and the future', *Education for Development: A Teacher's Resource for Global Learning*. London: Hodder & Stoughton.

Gadsden, A. (1991) *Geography and History Through Stories*. Sheffield: Geographical Association.

Geographical Association (1999) *Leading Geography: National Standards for geography leaders in primary schools*. Sheffield: Geographical Association.

Graham, L. and Lynn, S. (1989) 'Mud huts and flints: children's images of the Third World', *Education 3-13*, 17, 2, pp. 29-32.

Grimwade, K. (2000) *Geography and the New Agenda: Citizenship, PSHE and Sustainable Development in the primary curriculum*. Sheffield: Geographical Association.

Hadley, E. (1983) *Legends of the Sun and Moon*. Cambridge: Cambridge University Press.

Harrison, P. and Havard, J. (1994) *Folens Geography 1. Big Book*. Dunstable: Folens.

Hart, R. (1979) *Children's Experience of Place*. New York: Irvington Press.

Hicks, D. (1994) *Educating for the Future: A Practical Classroom Guide*. Guildford: World Wide Fund for Nature UK.

Hicks, D. and Holden, C. (1995) *Visions of the Future: Why We Need to Teach for Tomorrow*. Stoke-on-Trent: Trentham Books.

Hillman, M. (1993) *Children, Transport and the Quality of Life*. London: Policy Studies Institute.

Howson, J. (1993) *Going Green at Home and School*. Brighton: Wayland.

Kindersley, B. and Kindersley, A. (1995) *Children Just Like Me*. London: Dorling Kindersely/UNICEF.

Law, T. (1994) *Primary Children's Ideas About Economically Developing Countries*, unpublished MA thesis in Primary Education, Institute of Education, University of London.

Manley, G. (1952) *Climate and the British Isles (New Naturalist Series)*. London: Collins.

Mansfield, K. (1996) 'Progression within the rivers theme', *Primary Geographer*, 25, pp. 23-25.

Martin, E. (1995) *Teaching and Learning through the National Curriculum*. Cambridge: Chris Kington Publishing.

Martin, F. (1995) *Teaching Early Years Geography*. Cambridge: Chris Kington Publishing.

Masheder, M. (1990) *Windows to Nature*. Guildford: WWF.

Matthews, M.H. (1992) *Making Sense of Place*. Hemel Hempstead: Harvester Wheatsheaf.

May, S. (1996) *Fieldwork in Action 4: Primary Fieldwork Projects*. Sheffield: Geographical Association.

May, S. and Cook, J. (1996) *Fieldwork in Action 2: An Enquiry Approach*. Sheffield: Geographical Association.

May, S., Richardson, P. and Banks, V. (1993) *Fieldwork in Action 1: Planning Fieldwork*. Sheffield: Geographical Association.

Mayes, P. (1985) *Teaching Children Through the Environment*. London: Hodder & Stoughton.

McFarlane, C. (1992) 'Photographs: a window on the world' *Primary Geographer*, 11, pp. 4-8.

Mills, D. (ed) (1988) *Geographical Work in Primary and Middle Schools*. Sheffield: GA.

Milner, D. (1994) contribution to *A Multicultural Guide to Children's Books*, London: Books for Keeps.

Milner, A. (1996) *Geography Starts Here! Practical Approaches with Nursery and Reception Children.* Sheffield: Geographical Association.

Nicholls, J. (1993) *Earthways Earthwise: Poems on Conservation.* Oxford: Oxford University Press.

Norris Nicholson, H. (1992) *Geography and History in the National Curriculum.* Sheffield: Geographical Association.

Norris Nicholson, H. (1996) *Place in Story-time: Geography through Stories at Key Stages 1 and 2* (revised edition). Sheffield: Geographical Association.

OFSTED (1995) *Guidance on the Inspection of Nursery and Primary Schools.* London: HMSO.

Rawling, E. (1992) *Programmes of Study: Try This Approach.* Sheffield: Geographical Association.

Richardson, P. and Walford, R. (1998) *Fieldwork in Action 5: Mapping Land Use.* Sheffield: Geographical Association.

Richardson, P. and Whiting, S. (eds) (1998) *Fieldwork in Action 6: Crossing the Channel.* Sheffield: Geographical Association.

Sack, R. (1997) *Homo Geographicus.* Baltimore: John Hopkins University Press.

Salkey, A. (1965) *Earthquake.* Oxford: Oxford University Press.

Salkey, A. (1980) *Caribbean Folk Tales and Legends.* London: Bogle L'Ouverture.

SCAA (1996) *Nursery Education: Desirable Outcomes for Children's Learning.* London: SCAA.

Scoffham, S. (1981) *Using the School Grounds.* London: Ward Lock.

Scoffham, S. (1998) 'Young children: perceptions of the world' in David, T. (ed) *Changing Minds 1.* London: Paul Chapman.

Spencer, C. and Blades, M. (1993) 'Children's understanding of place: the world at hand', *Geography*, 78, 4, pp. 367-373.

Stoker, B. and Brawn, T. (1993) *From Giant Sweets to Sponge Floors: A Schools Ground Design Guide.* Chester: Cheshire CC.

Thomas, G. (1992) *Science in the School Grounds.* Exmouth: Southgate.

Van Matre, S. (1979) *Sunship Earth.* Martinsville IN: American Camping Association.

Walford, R. (1984) 'Geography and the future', *Geography*, 69, 3, pp. 193-208.

Weldon, M. (1997) *Studying Distant Places.* Sheffield: Geographical Association.

Weldon, M. and Richardson, R. (1995) *Planning Primary Geography for the National Curriculum KS1 and 2.* London: John Murray.

Welsh Office (WO) (1991) *Geography in the National Curriculum (Wales).* Cardiff: WO.

WO (1991) *Non Statutory Guidance for Geography.* Cardiff: WO.

WO (1995) *Geography in the National Curriculum (Wales).* Cardiff: WO.

Whitaker, P. (1997) *Primary Schools and the Future.* Milton Keynes: Open University Press.

Williams, R. (1989) *One Earth Many Worlds.* Guildford: WWF.

Geography in the primary school

Bale, J. (1987) *Geography in the Primary School.* London: Routledge & Kegan Paul.

Beddis, R. and Mares, C. (1988) *School Links International: A New Approach to Primary School Linking Around The World.* Godalming: Tidy Britain Schools Group/WWF.

Blyth, A. and Krause, J. (1995) *Primary Geography: A Developmental Approach.* London: Hodder & Stoughton.

Blyth, J. (1990) *Place and Time with Children 5 to 9.* London: Routledge & Kegan Paul.

Bowles, R. (1993) *Practical Guides: Geography.* Leamington Spa: Scholastic.

Chambers, W. and Donert, K. (1996) *Teaching Geography in Key Stage 2.* Cambridge: Chris Kington Publishing.

Fisher, S. and Hicks, D. (1985) *World Studies 8-13: A Teacher's Handbook.* Harlow: Oliver & Boyd.

Foley, M. and Janikoun, J. (1996) *The Really Practical Guide to Primary Geography* (second edition). Cheltenham: Stanley Thornes.

Hicks, D. and Steiner, M. (1989) *Making Global Connections.* Harlow: Oliver & Boyd.

Marsden, B. and Hughes, J. (eds) (1994) *Primary School Geography.* London: David Fulton.

Martin, F. (1995) *Teaching Early Years Geography.* Cambridge: Chris Kington Publishing.

Palmer, J. (1994) *Geography in the Early Years.* London: Routledge.

Sebba, J. (1994) *Geography for All.* London: David Fulton.

Weldon, M. and Richardson, R. (1995) *Planning Primary Geography for the National Curriculum KS1 and 2.* London: John Murray.

Wiegand, P. (1992) *Places in the Primary School. Knowledge and Understanding of Places at Key Stages 1 and 2.* London: Falmer.

Wiegand, P. (1993) *Children and Primary Geography.* London: Cassell.

Curriculum links

Bell, G.H. (1991) *Developing a European Dimension in Primary Schools.* London: David Fulton.

Button, J. (ed) (1989) *The Primary School in a Changing World.* London: Centre for World Development Education.

Copeland, T. (1993) *Geography and the Historic Environment.* Oxford: English Heritage.

DEC (1992) *'It's Our World Too': A Local-Global Approach to Environmental Education at Key Stages 2 and 3.* Birmingham/London: DEC (Birmingham and South Yorkshire)/UNICEF UK.

Goodall, S. (ed) (1994) *Developing Environmental Education in the Curriculum.* London: David Fulton.

Hall, G. (ed) (1992) *Themes and Dimensions of the National Curriculum.* London: Kogan Page.

Harrison, M. (ed) (1994) *Beyond the Core Curriculum: Co-ordinating the Other Foundation Subjects in Primary Schools.* Plymouth: Northcote House.

Joicy, H.B. (1986) *An Eye for the Environment.* London/Guildford: Unwin Hyman/WWF.

Kimber, D. *et al.* (1995) *Humanities in Primary Education.* London: David Fulton.

Knight, P. (1993) *Primary Geography, Primary History.* London: David Fulton.

National Curriculum Council (NCC) (1989) *A Framework for the Primary Curriculum: Curriculum Guidance 1.* York: NCC.

NCC (1989) *A Curriculum for All: Special Needs in the National Curriculum. Curriculum Guidance 2.* York: NCC.

NCC (1990) *Curriculum Guidance 3: The Whole Curriculum.* York: NCC.

Neal, P.D. and Palmer, J. (1990) *Environmental Education in the Primary School.* Oxford: Blackwell.

Pumphrey, P.D. and Verma, G. (eds) (1993) *The Foundation Subjects and Religious Education in Primary Schools.* London: Falmer Press.

Steiner, M. (1993) *Learning from experience: World Studies in the Primary Curriculum.* Stoke-on-Trent: Trentham Books/World Studies Trust.

Index